Advanced J

"Bold, monumental, brilliant, and provocative. ᴅ.ᴜ. ʏ nails how America has lost its way and offers thoughtful solutions to find our way back. A courageous and important series."
– Bob Vanourek, award-winning author and former CEO, Cordillera, Colorado

"*Winning Practices* is one of the most important books that I have ever read. It is a badly-needed articulation of the problems besetting our country and the solutions to them."
– Gary Fenchuk, award-winning developer and author of *Timeless Wisdom,* Midlothian, Virginia

"Mark delves into some of our country's biggest challenges and cuts through the politics. He takes you beyond the approaches of the right or the left and presents creative and practical winning ones."
– Stephen McConnell, president of Solano Ventures, Scottsdale, Arizona

"*Winning Practices* will never, ever leave the top of my desk; it is a comprehensive guide for life. Its insight and organization are amazing."
– Dr. Story Musgrave, surgeon, Marine veteran, NASA astronaut, Hubble Space Telescope repairman, Kissimmee, Florida

"*Toward Truth, Freedom, Fitness, and Decency* is an extraordinary study . . . as compelling a read as it is thoughtful and thought-provoking. . . . Very highly recommended for both community and academic library collections and . . . for students, political activists, and ordinary folk interested in the social, cultural, economic, and political issues that so trouble our country today."
– Susan Bethany, Midwest Book Review, Oregon, Wisconsin

"*Winning Practices* provides a road map for living a useful, happy and healthy life. I love it. It should be mandatory reading for every high school student."
– Mitch Sill, retired CEO and owner of Road Machinery & Supplies, Duluth, Minnesota

"Every chapter is worth reading and pondering."
– Richard Kaufman, chair of Amstore Corporation, Chicago, Illinois

"Mark has written clearly and truthfully, a complete Operator's Manual for Life. I will share the series with those who are dearest to me."
– Haisook Somers, mother, volunteer, and philanthropist, Montreal, Quebec

"I am profoundly impressed with the *Flourish* Series. Mark has delineated and backed up with facts and thoughtful analysis timeless truths and behaviors that will help many individuals lead more fulfilled lives. His work could not come at a better time. As fewer people learn these truths and behaviors from their families and faiths, an insightful, well-organized, secular expression of them becomes ever more important."
– John Doyle, owner of Doyle Security Systems, Rochester, New York

"I find myself staring off into space and pondering Mark's ideas. I agree with what he says, and I am pleased to find so much well-synthesized and organized thought in one treatise."
– Tom Ewert, retired federal judge, Naples, Florida

"Mark blends his considerable experience to design a plan for America to not only grow but also to flourish. His practical and commonsense plan is a must read for all thinking Americans."
– Carl Youngman, former CEO of more than twenty companies, Boston, Massachusetts

"*Winning Practices* is thought-provoking and thoroughly interesting. It examines many of our country's challenges and offers a comprehensive set of solutions. It is incredibly innovative and has stimulated many discussions among our family and friends. The books are a must-read for our country's leaders and every American who is concerned about it."
– Mark Danni, conductor, founding artistic director of Theatre Zone, and president of KareMar Productions, Naples, Florida

"Even though I have a more biblical viewpoint of the world, the teaching and wisdom of *Winning Practices* should be mandatory reading for all first-year college students."
– Kenneth Lockard, founder of numerous companies, CEO of Lockard Companies, Cedar Falls, Iowa

Winning Practices
of a Free, Fit, and Prosperous People

Published by Flourish Books
Naples, FL
flourishbooks.org

Distributed by Ingram Content Group

For ordering information or special discounts for bulk purchases, please contact Ingram Content Group LLC, One Ingram Blvd., La Vergne, TN 37086, 615.793.5000

Cover design by Night Owl Freelance
Cover art by Katiana Robles

Cataloging-in-Publication data is available.

Print ISBN: 978-0-9859504-7-7

eBook ISBN: 978-0-9859504-8-4

Audiobook ISBN: 978-0-9859504-9-1

Printed in the United States of America

5-1-19

So you and future generations may realize
your full potential and do better than we have done.

Contents

Introduction 1

Section I: How Are We Doing?

Chapter 1: Three of the Most Desirable Places to Live 9
Chapter 2: Losing Our Way 15

Section II: Winning Perspectives

Chapter 3: Winning Perspectives 49
Chapter 4: Truth 51
Chapter 5: Causality 55
Chapter 6: Scale 61
Chapter 7: Evolution 67
Chapter 8: Fitness 79
Chapter 9: Human Nature 87
Chapter 10: Culture 95
Chapter 11: Periodic Disaster 105
Chapter 12: Eco-Dependency 109
Winning Perspectives Summary 113

Section III: Winning Practices of Individuals

Chapter 13: Winning Practices 119
Chapter 14: Health 125
Chapter 15: Thought 135
Chapter 16: Integrity 145
Chapter 17: Proactivity 157
Chapter 18: Prudence 167
Chapter 19: Excellence 183
Chapter 20: Thrift and Investment 187

Section IV: Winning Practices of Groups

Chapter 21: Affiliation 201
Chapter 22: Decency 207
Chapter 23: Understanding 217
Chapter 24: Leadership 223
Chapter 25: Teamwork 235
Chapter 26: Improvement 247

Section V: Winning Practices of Families

Chapter 27: Spouse Selection 257
Chapter 28: Marriage 269
Chapter 29: Responsible Parenting 279
Chapter 30: Empowering Habit Formation 297

Section VI: Winning Practices of Education

Chapter 31: Knowledge 309
Chapter 32: Universal Education 321
Chapter 33: Parental Choice 337
Chapter 34: Results-Oriented Education 347

Section VII: Winning Practices of Enterprise

Chapter 35: Free Enterprise and Markets 359
Chapter 36: Responsible Corporate Governance 371
Chapter 37: Prudent Regulation 377
Chapter 38: Enterprise Competitiveness 387

Section VIII: Winning Practices of Government

Chapter 39: Problems with Democracy 397
Chapter 40: Government of the People 405
Chapter 41: Powers, Prohibitions, and Structure 417
Chapter 42: Freedoms, Rights, and Responsibilities 431
Chapter 43: The Rule of Law 441
Chapter 44: Inclusion and Meritocracy 453
Chapter 45: Prudent Taxation 467

Chapter 46: Financial Strength 473
Chapter 47: Savings Accounts and Social Safety Nets 491
Chapter 48: Consumer-Driven Healthcare 505
Chapter 49: Assimilation 515
Chapter 50: Peace Through Fitness 525
Chapter 51: Sustainability 539
Chapter 52: Toward Truth, Freedom, Fitness, and Decency 549

Postscript 562
Acknowledgments 563

Appendix A: Alternative Types of Investments 565
Appendix B: Special Sources 569
Appendix C: Drawing from the Right and the Left 571
Appendix D: Flourish, Perspectives, Practices, and Concepts 573

Endnotes 578
Index 611
About the Author 624

List of Figures

Figure 1: Comparison of Singapore, Switzerland, and the United States. . 12
Figure 2: Median Household Income Adjusted for Inflation 16
Figure 3: U.S. Federal Spending as a Percent of GDP from 1800–2017 . . 20
Figure 4: Presidential Constitutional Failings 24
Figure 5: Supreme Court Constitutional Failings 27

Figure 6: Small and Large Masses 63
Figure 7: Small and Large Distances 64
Figure 8: Evolution of the Universe and Life Timeline 65
Figure 9: Comparison of the U.S. and Islamic Populations Over Time. . . 82
Figure 10: Environments 102

Figure 11: Operating Systems 102
Figure 12: Conflicts with Greater than 250,000 Causalities 107
Figure 13: Important Mentors 143
Figure 14: Symmetry 168
Figure 15: Positive Asymmetry 170

Figure 16: Negative Asymmetry 170
Figure 17: Positive Nonlinearity 171
Figure 18: Negative Nonlinearity. 172
Figure 19: Judicious Risk-Taking 180
Figure 20: Present Value Formulas 191

Figure 21: Present Value Annuity Formulas 192
Figure 22: How Children Succeed 353
Figure 23: U.S. Public Debt as a Percent of GDP 1967–2017 483
Figure 24: Cost of Health Insurance Relative to Income 2000–2017 . . . 506
Figure 25: Seven Drivers of the Escalation of Healthcare Costs 506
Figure 26: Winning Perspectives and Practices 552

Introduction

Good intentions, idyllic wishes, and flawed policies do not improve people's lives.

Like so many other Americans, I am a product of people who came to this country in search of a better life. Three of my grandparents were of Anglo-Saxon descent, and one was of German descent. My Anglo-Saxon ancestors came to America in the 17th and 18th centuries; my German ancestors arrived in the 19th century. And like so many other Americans, life improved for each generation of my ancestors throughout our country's history. Sadly, this has not been the case for the current generation, as our nation no longer exhibits the vitality and promise that it did in prior decades.

Many American children live with one parent, grow up in poverty, and receive a poor education. Many families cannot access or afford proper healthcare. When adjusted for inflation, most American incomes stagnated for 28 years. Our country has unprecedented levels of debt. Unknown numbers of criminals, terrorists, and unvaccinated people enter the country illegally each year. Immigrant assimilation is no longer a priority, and a common language and culture no longer unify us. Inequality increases, as social mobility declines. Identity politics and polarizing policies, news, and speech divide us. Dysfunctional federal and state governments fail us.

If these challenges were not enough, we degrade our ecosystems and spew billions of tons of climate-altering carbon dioxide into the atmosphere each year. Radical Islam and terrorists threaten us. China and Russia expand their geographic influence and footprint. The maniacal, repressive regimes of Iran and North Korea oppress their people and threaten us. Why are our challenges mounting, and why are we no longer ascending?

In 1978, at age 19, I participated in an economic development field study of Guatemala, Costa Rica, Honduras, and Columbia. In Columbia, we visited a family that was living in a one-room home which had a dirt floor and was fly-infested. The parents and seven children slept on mats. A year later, I participated in an agricultural field study of Western Europe, Eastern Europe, and the former Soviet Union. The contrasts between life in Upstate New York and many of these countries shocked me and made me ponder why some populations prosper while others merely subsist.

International economic and cultural differences were not the only ones that I experienced during my college years. I ran into our country's great cultural divide. Raised in rural America, I was given a strong Protestant faith and many accompanying perspectives and practices. In college, I found that most professors had little use for them.

After completing my undergraduate education in 1980, I again traveled behind the Iron Curtain to Poland where I taught English composition to scientists. I chose Poland because of the great political and economic unrest in the country and its many cultural contrasts to the United States. Poland was ethnically and religiously homogenous, Communist, and poor. Men and women with full-time jobs had to queue up for 15 to 20 hours a week just to purchase their food and household supplies. They lived in small apartments and remained poor no matter how hard they worked. The Polish government prohibited travel to Western countries and censored their communications, news, books, and periodicals.

Two years before my arrival, Karol Wojtyła, the charismatic cardinal from Kraków, became Pope John Paul II. His election gave the Poles tremendous confidence. While I was there, most Poles went on strike and gathered in the churches to protest their lack of freedom, living standards, and the Soviet occupation. All my students were members of Solidarity, the first independent labor union in a Soviet-bloc country. President Reagan and Prime Minister Thatcher supported the Poles' strikes and protests. Lech Wałesa, the leader of Solidarity, Pope John Paul II, and Cardinal Wyszyński, the Roman Catholic Primate of Poland, orchestrated the movement.

Cosmos and *Dragons of Eden* by Carl Sagan were two of the several books I had brought with me. They described the evolution of the universe and human intelligence. I reflected on these books, my previous three years of reading and traveling, and all that I had learned at Purdue. The better acquainted I became with the scientific explanations of the universe and life, the more I realized that my childhood faith rested on incredulous, unsubstantiated stories that conveniently dismissed scientific perspectives which better explained the origin of the universe and life. Awestruck with the cosmos and science, and skeptical of my religious tenets, I came to favor scientific thought over my faith-based beliefs and begrudgingly underwent the religious-to-secular transformation that millions of other people have undergone.

By age 26, I had traveled to 45 states and 26 countries. I had lived in two states and two countries and completed my B.S., M.S., and the courses for a Ph.D. I had read some 200 of the world's most thought-provoking books. I had confronted our cultural divide, embraced evidence-based knowledge, and detected the primary question that would preoccupy me for years.

Through my exposure to various cultures and thoughts, I encountered many conflicting perspectives and practices. As someone who is inquisitive, contemplative, and who values intellectual consistency, these conflicts did not sit well with me. They forced me to evaluate many of my childhood paradigms and grapple with many questions, such as:

How did the universe and life arise?

What are the implications of the narratives of science?

What is universal to human life and what is unique to a group, locale, or country?

Why did our country's founders distrust concentrations of power?

What fueled the extraordinary rise of the English Commonwealth countries, the United States, Western Europe, Japan, South Korea, Taiwan, Hong Kong, and Singapore?

What enables large middle classes to flourish?

How do we prevent recessions, depressions, and inflation?

When are conservative and when are liberal approaches most advantageous?

Why are the results of many public policies antithetical to their authors' intentions?

Why do people make so many decisions that inflict future suffering on themselves?

Despite my shattered paradigms and many questions, I functioned reasonably well, pursuing truth wherever it took me, being considerate of others and drawing on the habits of my youth. However, when my wife placed our son in my arms, I experienced a bit of a crisis. He came with no instruction book. What was I going to teach him? Given the perspectives and knowledge our civilization gained over the last five hundred years, what does a child need to learn? What fosters our health, effectiveness, longevity, civility, and happiness? How do we adapt our lifestyles to live responsibly and do no harm?

These questions and our faith-versus-science, right-versus-left cultural divide have haunted me for years because they separate our families, communities, and citizens. They diminish our effectiveness, social cohesiveness, and children's futures. Having spent time on both sides of these divides and having friends who are conservative, liberal, of faith, or without faith, I have felt and been saddened by the distrust and animosity the groups have for one another.

The great irony of the divide is that each side has things the other lacks. Conservatives and people of faith maintain an empowering culture and understand that doing the right thing yields positive effects. Liberals and people of science build an empowering knowledge base and recognize that life is what we make of it.

For many years, I pondered these questions, the divides, and the insights and positions of faith communities, scientists, conservatives, and progressives. I raised my family, built three businesses, and sat on numerous local, state, and national boards. I read hundreds of books, traveled to many more states and countries, attended educational programs, and ran for Congress.

Eventually, I realized that most of us lack the interest and maturity to comprehend the evolution of the universe and life and their implications while we are in high school. And unless we study the physical and biological sciences in college, we generally never fully grasp them. This is unfortunate because if we take the time to understand these perspectives and integrate them into our thinking, we can improve our effectiveness and lives immeasurably.

This book is about the perspectives and practices that enable a population to flourish. Section I examines how Americans, Singaporeans, and the Swiss are doing, and why Americans no longer ascend. Section II discusses nine perspectives that come from an understanding of the evolution of the universe and life—Truth, Causality, Scale, Evolution, Fitness, Human Nature, Culture, Periodic Disaster, and Eco-Dependency. Sections III-VIII introduce Winning Practices of Individuals, Groups, Families, Education, Enterprise, and Government.

After years of assaults on culture and major institutions, our country is at a critical crossroads. In more credibly explaining our context, origin, and nature, scientists undermined the Judeo-Christian worldview and many of its tenets. In changing how we elect U.S. Senators in 1913 and reinterpreting the "General Welfare" clause of the Constitution in the 1930s, progressives broke crucial restraints on government. Reacting to their historical mistreatment, separation, and ongoing discrimination, many African Americans embrace an oppressor-oppressed, anti-Caucasian counterculture, and lacking English proficiency and legal status, many Hispanics do not assimilate.

Without unifying leadership and culture, we fight among ourselves, lurch left, lurch right, and stagnate. A right-leaning coalition values the Constitution, rule of law, limited federal government, a strong defense, free enterprise, legal immigration, intact families, charter schools, work, and economic ascendance. A left-leaning coalition values unions, public education and healthcare, improved opportunities for women and minorities, the redistribution of wealth, larger government and more regulation, the legal and illegal admission of people into the country, the environment, and the advancement of social justice. The prevalence of Winning Perspectives and Practices decreases in our population, and the prevalence of losing perspectives and practices increases.

The path forward is unclear to many people. Ignorance, opposing ideologies, and vested interests hinder us. Our past success, accumulated wealth, and tremendous capacity to borrow enable us to ignore our problems and to be foolish for a long time.

The Winning Perspectives and Practices presented in this book are a synthesis of many of the world's most empowering perspectives and practices. They serve everyone's interests in the long term. Health, prosperity, diminished heartache, great accomplishment, and a full life await those who understand, employ, and improve them.

Section I

How Are We Doing?

Chapter 1

Three of the Most Desirable Places to Live

We have so much to learn from others.

Singapore, Switzerland, and the United States

Of all the countries I have visited and studied, Singapore and Switzerland are two of the most desirable places to live in the world. Each has a strong national identity, a democratic government, little corruption, a strong rule of law, and affordable, high-quality healthcare. The countries also have excellent education systems and large proportions of their populations flourish.

Like the U.S., Singapore and Switzerland have multiple ethnic groups with different histories, cultures, and religions. The Asian city-state of Singapore is comprised primarily of Chinese, Malay, and Indians who speak English, Mandarin, Malay, or Tamil. Its principal religions include Buddhism, Islam, Hinduism, and Christianity. The small European country of Switzerland is comprised of people with German, French, Italian, and Romansh heritages who speak their own language and historically are Roman Catholic or Protestant.

Ethnic, cultural, and religious differences were a problem in Singapore and Switzerland for years. Territorial and religious wars plagued the German, French, Italian, and Romansh areas of Switzerland in the 16th, 17th, and 18th centuries. Racial riots were common in Singapore in the 1960s when the Chinese dominated the Malays and Indians. Today, however, the Singaporeans and Swiss make social cohesiveness a national priority and enjoy enviable cultural harmony.

The populations of Singapore, Switzerland, and the U.S. are only 6, 8, and 320 million.[1] While the smaller populations of Singapore and Switzerland offer some social cohesiveness advantages, they are not the primary causes of their success. Most other small countries do not flourish like Singapore and Switzerland. Rather, their success is a function of their leadership, cultures, and prevalence of Winning Practices within their populations.

In 1940, Lee Kuan Yew was one of the top students in Singapore. After the Japanese occupation of Singapore, he studied law at Cambridge, and then returned to Singapore in the late 1950s. Singapore was poorer than Haiti at this time.[2] Drugs, gambling, and prostitution were widespread, and the annual per-capita income was less than $425.[3] Malaysia, concerned about the large Chinese population and racial riots, abandoned Singapore in 1965. Yew and his supporters took control of Singapore, implementing a strong rule of law, imprisoning political opposition, and cleaning up the mess. He became the first Prime Minister of Singapore and is considered the founder of the Republic of Singapore. Life steadily improved under Lee Kuan Yew and ever since. Today, Singaporeans have a thriving democracy, reside in one of the greenest and most livable cities, and have the 7th highest per-capita income in the world.[4]

Switzerland, another of the most desirable places to live in the world, has a much longer history as a nation than Singapore. It developed from the bottom up rather than the top down. Switzerland is interesting for many reasons, including its limited federal government, Executive Council, national referendums, and universal, affordable, high-quality healthcare. Figure 1 compares life in Singapore, Switzerland, and the United States. While we can learn much from many countries, Singapore and Switzerland provide some of the most important lessons.

Crime, Corruption, and Poverty

The information in Figure 1 indicates that crime, corruption, and poverty are much more serious problems in the U.S. than in Singapore or Switzerland. Homicide rates in Singapore, Switzerland, and the U.S. are 0.3, 0.5, and 5.4 and incarceration rates are 201, 81, and 655 per 100,000 people per year.[5] This means you are 12 times more likely to be murdered and 5 times more likely to be incarcerated in the U.S. than in Singapore and Switzerland. And if you live in one of the major U.S. cities, you are 100 times more likely to be murdered and 50 times more likely to be incarcerated. The Singaporean and Swiss rules of law protect people, deter crime, keep more families intact, and create environments for people to flourish better than the U.S. rule of law.

How about corruption—the abuse of public power for private gain? According to Transparency International, a highly respected international anti-corruption organization that uses expert reviews and opinion surveys to assess corruption, Singapore, Switzerland, and the U.S. ranked 6th, 3rd, and 16th among the countries in the world in 2017.[6] New Zealand, perceived to have the least corruption, ranked 1st, and Somalia, thought to have the most corruption, ranked 180th.[7]

Anecdotally, many people over 50 years old who lived in small communities recognize a general decline in honesty over the last 50 years in the United States. Few, if any of us, needed lockers in school to keep our belongings safe, and many of our parents did not lock their homes or cars. Life is much more pleasant when those around us are trustworthy and we do not fear them.

Child poverty is a larger problem in the U.S. than in Switzerland and most likely than in Singapore. While the poverty rates are unmeasured or unpublished in Singapore, you just do not see signs of much poverty anywhere in the country. The child poverty rates are 9 and 23 percent in Switzerland and the U.S.[8]

Figure 1: Comparison of Singapore, Switzerland, and the United States

		Singapore	Switzerland	United States
Crime[9]	Homicides / 100,000	0.3	0.5	5.4
Least Corruption[10]	Country Rank	6th	3rd	16th
Child Poverty[11]	<50% of MHI	Unknown	9%	23%
Obesity[12]	Portion of the Population	6%	20%	36%
Healthcare Expenditures[13]	% of GDP	5%	12%	17%
Life Expectancy[14]	Years	85	83	80
Per Capita Income[15]	Purchasing Power Parity	$93,900	$61,400	$59,500
National Savings[16]	% of GDP	47%	33%	18%
Public Debt[17]	% of GDP	No External	43%	115%
CO2 Emissions[18]	Metric Tons	10	4	17

Health and Longevity

If we are not doing so well compared to the Singaporeans and Swiss regarding crime, corruption, and child poverty, how are we doing regarding health and lifespans? Obesity, a primary cause of diabetes, heart disease, cancer, and large medical bills, occurs at a frequency of 6, 20, and 36 percent in Singapore, Switzerland, and the U.S. While Switzerland has some problems with obesity, the U.S. has a serious problem. What is most disheartening about the U.S. obesity rate is that we have known about the harmful nature of American diets and sedentary lifestyles for 40 years, and yet obesity rates and the incidence of related diseases keep increasing. How can we flourish when over one-third of our population is obese?

In Singapore and Switzerland, 100 percent of the population is covered by health insurance. In the U.S., after the *Affordable Care Act,* 92 percent of the population has health insurance.[19] Health expenditures as a percent of Gross Domestic Product (GDP) in Singapore, Switzerland, and the U.S. are 5, 12, and 17 percent.[20] Healthcare in Singapore and Switzerland is consumer-driven, of high quality, and a much better value. Life expectancies in Singapore, Switzerland, and the U.S. are 85, 83, and 80 years.[21] We spend one half to three times more on healthcare per person and have a shorter life expectancy.

Income and Financial Security

Per capita incomes adjusted for purchasing power in Singapore, Switzerland, and the U.S. are $93,900, $61,400, and $59,500.[22] Singaporean living standards are remarkable given the country has no natural resources, has little developable real estate, and did not have its own drinking water until recently. Gross National Savings rates in Singapore and Switzerland are 47 and 33 percent, substantially greater than the 18 percent U.S. rate.[23]

Home ownership rates are 91 percent in Singapore, 44 percent in Switzerland, and 65 percent in the U.S.[24] Singaporean home ownership is the second highest in the world, largely because of the people's strong work ethic and high savings rates. The government does subsidize home ownership for 20 percent of the lowest income citizens. Generally, when people purchase homes, they feel more financially secure, build equity as they age, and develop greater pride in their neighborhoods and country.

Singapore and Switzerland have more responsible governments than the U.S. Their low debt levels and little external debt are evidence of this.[25] Unlike the U.S., Singapore and Switzerland maintain balanced government budgets, and their citizens form the capital that their economies require.

Carbon Emissions

The U.S. pours far more climate-altering greenhouse gases per person into the atmosphere than Singapore and Switzerland. Americans emit an estimated 17 tons of CO_2 per person per year, while the Singaporeans and Swiss emit only 10 and 4 tons.[26]

Throughout most of the 20th century, America was the land of opportunity and possibility. Most people throughout the world wanted to emulate our ways and live in or visit our country. And while we have much for which to be thankful and are doing better than people in most countries, most people I meet around the world no longer hold America in as high a regard. Benchmarking life in our country against life in other countries reveals why this might be the case, teaches us what is possible, and indicates where we can find better approaches. Studying history and consulting older, accomplished souls suggests where we have gone wrong.

Chapter 2

Losing Our Way

We thought we were different . . . more able, prosperous, and blessed. And we were more of these things, as we were more honest, hardworking, and responsible, as we took marriage, parenting, and education more seriously, and as we were more community- and country-minded.

One of the most telling indications that our country is slipping is the relative change in American and Chinese living standards between 1960 and 2017. In 1960, American living standards were 120 times greater than Chinese living standards. In 2017, they were 7 times higher.[27]

Chinese living standards have improved steadily while our living standards have stagnated. Figure 2 shows real and hypothetical growing U.S. household incomes between 1988 and 2016; the upper line signifies hypothetical growth and the lower line illustrates actual growth. Adjusted for inflation, our real-median income has been flat for a generation. If our incomes had grown at an inflation-adjusted 3 percent, which is more of a historical norm, median household income would be $121,500 rather than $59,000. Not having our act together has cost all of us dearly.

Amazingly, the Chinese economy has become almost as large as the U.S. economy. If the two economies continue to grow at their recent 21st century rates, the Chinese economy will be twice as large as ours in 12 years and four times larger in 24 years.

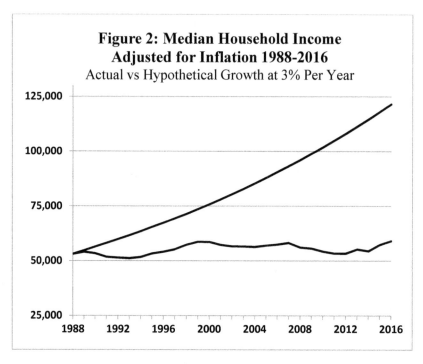

Figure 2: Median Household Income
Adjusted for Inflation 1988-2016
Actual vs Hypothetical Growth at 3% Per Year

Federal Reserve Bank of St. Louis, Economic Research Division
https://fred.stlouisfed.org/series/mehoinusa672n

Rising living standards in China are a great thing, but the combination of Chinese ascendancy and American decline is not good for Western values and populations. The Chinese have their own values and interests, many of which compete with ours. As China rises and the United States declines, China will reshape the international order to reflect its values and interests. China will encourage one-party rule around the world rather than constitutional republics and the rule of law. It will promote state prerogatives over individual freedoms. It will seize control of the South Pacific shipping lanes and make the terms of trade more favorable for China and less favorable to other countries. China's currency, the renminbi, will replace the dollar as the reserve currency, decreasing American living standards an additional 10 to 20 percent.

Rising Chinese and stagnant American living standards are not our only challenges. Radical Islam and Islamic population growth are also serious problems. While our leaders hesitate to acknowledge it, the Western and Islamic cultures collide. Where we value democratic and secular government, individual rights, and male and female parity, most Islamic leaders value authoritarian and religious rule, religious orthodoxy, and male dominance.

While we may find it incomprehensible that large numbers of Muslims hate us, the fact is that many do. Our promiscuous lifestyles, dysfunctional families, alcohol and drug abuse, and high crime rates are unappealing to them. Our freedoms, gender equality, and tolerance undermine their patterns of life. Our priorities, power, and actions thwart their leaders' aspirations.

To these serious challenges, I add seven more: (1) a failure to develop and educate many children, (2) a failure to integrate many African Americans, Hispanics, and Muslims in our country, (3) our government's dysfunction and propensity to live beyond its means, (4) our emissions of large quantities of greenhouse gases, (5) the degradation of ecosystems and ground water, (6) the eradication of many species, and (7) the tendency for Winning Practices to decrease in prevalence and losing practices to increase within our population.

Inclusion Failures

Our ancestors provided us with a stunning start. Their pragmatism, ideals, and newly minted government, courage, hard work, sacrifice, and perseverance are legendary. The problem with our start was that our ancestors took our country from the Native Americans and enslaved Africans. The institution of slavery and the eradication of most Native Americans were travesties. While we have acknowledged the horrific treatment of Native Americans and ended slavery, we have yet to integrate many Native and African Americans into our communities.

Our destruction of the Native American culture was genocide and a lost opportunity. Had we treated Native Americans more honorably and shared more of the continent with them, we might have acquired their reverence for the environment. We might emit less carbon and fewer pollutants, be healthier, and have a brighter future.

Our inclusion failures were not only at the start. They have occurred in every decade since our country's founding. Segregation, discrimenation, and education dysfunction have created animosity between white and black people and depravity within minority communities. They have created unsafe neighborhoods, broken families, poorly parented children, and widespread alcohol and drug addiction.

Majorities discriminate against minorities throughout the world, as people ally with those who are similar to dominate those unlike themselves. This behavior is instinctual. "Birds of a feather flock together" and "There is strength in numbers" are descriptive adages of this tendency. But while this instinct served hunter-gatherers well, it serves us poorly. A people comprised of different races, ethnicities, and creeds must overcome discriminatory behavior with education, training, and legal recourse.

The lack of a clean start and our integration failures divide us. They diminish minority actualization and contribution and increase our social welfare burdens. They decrease our living standards, the prevalence of Winning Practices within our culture, and our ability to overcome challenges.

Change in the Election of U.S. Senators

The powers delegated by the proposed Constitution to the federal government are few and defined. Those which are to remain in the State governments are numerous and indefinite.[28]

—James Madison

Our founders limited the scope of the federal government in the Constitution, and they enforced this restriction with the way Senators were elected. We broke this enforcement mechanism when we passed the 17th Amendment in 1913. Before the amendment, state legislatures chose the U.S. Senators. After it, the people of each state elected the Senators. State legislator–selected Senators limited federal power; citizen-selected ones expand it.

As Figure 3 illustrates, our federal government's expenditures as a percent of GNP were less than 4 percent for the first 125 years of our nation's history except for a 10-year period around the Civil War. After the passage of the 17th Amendment, federal expenditures grew more than nine-fold from 2.5 to 21 percent of GNP. Add state and local expenditures to this, and government spending comprises 35 percent of GNP.

Since 1913, our federal government has expanded its powers significantly and become a wasteful, inefficient, and corrupt colossus, regulating every aspect of our life, burdening us, and stifling the economy. The stories of the state governments are more mixed. States such as New York, Illinois, and California have created larger governments, stifling their residents' living standards; states like Florida, Indiana, South Carolina, and Texas have maintained smaller governments, furthering increases in their residents' incomes.

Ending the state legislature check on the federal government was one of our greatest mistakes, as now special interests buy our elected representatives with campaign contributions, and our elected representatives buy our votes with legislative and spending favors. Too much government burdens a country, just as too much overhead and debt burdens families and companies. You only need to compare the great gains that populations make throughout the world when their government spending is in the 5 to 15 percent of GNP range to the small increases that occur when this ratio exceeds 20 percent. The histories of Canada, the United States, Western Europe, and Japan all demonstrate this reality.

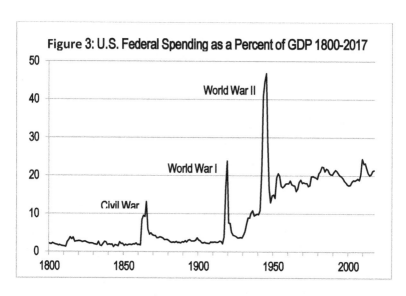

Figure 3: U.S. Federal Spending as a Percent of GDP 1800-2017

Government Spending, Download Spending Data, Multiyear Download of US Spending 1792-2017
https://www.usgovernmentspending.com/download_multi_year_1792_2017USb_17s2li001mcn_F0f

Presidential Constitutional Failings

World history is one long chronology of governments abusing their citizens. Only with the signing of the Magna Carta by King John in 1215, the signing of the Petition of Right by King Charles I in 1628, and the passage of the Bill of Rights in 1689 did English-speaking people obtain some freedom from the oppressive rule of their leaders. Only with the adoption of the Articles of Confederation in 1781, the Constitution of the United States of America in 1788, and the first ten amendments known as the Bill of Rights in 1791 did our ancestors free us of this yoke.

The Constitution and Bill of Rights of the United States are two of the most important documents ever written. Hundreds of millions of Americans as well as other people around the world have had much better lives because of them. If you have not read these documents, I highly recommend that you do so. They are ingenious, understandable, and only about five oversized pages of text.

From 1777 to 1900, Americans appreciated their Constitution—its separation of power and checks on power and specified institutions, procedures, and requirements. Most of the government leaders took their oaths of office seriously, preserving and defending the Constitution. Unfortunately, this changed with the election of Theodore Roosevelt and has continued largely unabated ever since.

Whether or not we liked Presidents Theodore Roosevelt, Wilson, Franklin Roosevelt, Truman, Johnson, Nixon, Bush 41, Clinton, Bush 43, and Obama and their policies, their flagrant failures to defend the Constitution and abuses of power should trouble us. Their failure to uphold and defend the document that defines the separations of power, checks on power, governing processes, and our rights as citizens jeopardizes our freedoms. Their misuse of the government to reward supporters and punish opponents delegitimizes the government and polarizes us. Brion McClanahan explains many presidential failings and abuses of power in his book *9 Presidents Who Screwed Up America*. Figure 4 lists several of these presidential failings and abuses of power.

Starting with Theodore Roosevelt and contrary to the separation of the legislative, executive, and judicial functions in the Constitution, numerous presidents have used the executive office, presidential favors, and executive orders to push legislative agendas. Some examples of this include: Teddy Roosevelt's Square Deal, seizure of 230 million acres of land, and 1,081 executive orders; Woodrow Wilson's New Freedom legislation and 1,803 executive orders; and Franklin Roosevelt's New Deal and 3,734 executive orders, one of which confiscated much of the gold in the country. Lyndon Johnson's Great Society legislation and 325 executive orders as well as George W. Bush's 291 executive orders, many of which ignored fundamental American rights, are other examples of serious presidential violations of the Constitution.[29]

Several presidents also supported the federal government's assumption of powers that "the people" and the Constitution never granted. Franklin Roosevelt pushed through Food Stamps, Welfare, and Social Security; Lyndon Johnson involved the federal government in education, healthcare, the arts, and public broadcasting; and Barack Obama tried to put the federal government in control of our healthcare.

Some presidents have created executive agencies with the ability to create, enforce, and adjudicate regulations. Woodrow Wilson did this with the Federal Trade Commission, and Richard Nixon with the Occupational Safety and Health Administration and the Environmental Protection Agency.

Some presidents have treated various groups more favorably or unfavorably than other ones. Woodrow Wilson exempted agricultural organizations and labor unions from the Clayton Antitrust Act of 1914, and Barack Obama's Internal Revenue Agency discriminated against conservative nonprofits.

Barack Obama made appointments to oversee the executive departments, the National Labor Relations Board, and federal courts without congressional consent. He also weaponized federal agencies against his political opposition, prohibited the enforcement of drug laws, restricted the 287(g) program that enables police officers to apprehend illegal immigrants who are stopped for other crimes, ignored the illicit activities of sanctuary cities, and eliminated federal funding to find visitors who overstay their visas.[30]

The Constitution of the United States of America gives Congress the power to declare war and the President the authority to make treaties. Theodore Roosevelt used the military in the Panama Revolution without a declaration of war from Congress. Woodrow Wilson used the military in several Latin American countries and Russia. Lyndon Johnson did this in Vietnam, Ronald Reagan in Grenada, and Barack Obama in Libya and Syria. Harry Truman used the U.S. military as an agent of the United Nations, and Bill Clinton used it 40 times around the world.[31] Historian Brion McClanahan writes:

The slew of executive legislative initiatives since the 1930s has forced Americans to believe that American government is executive government, regardless of political party. We feel confident in our guy in office and think little of the potential ramifications should our guy be out of office and the other guy take his place. Republicans who insist on impeaching Obama for his unconstitutional acts are the same who defended George W. Bush and his unconstitutional acts, and vice versa. Inconsistency and excessive partisanship—something George Washington warned against in his Farewell Address—have inflicted terrible damage on the American experiment in republican self-government.[32]

While we need to deal with crises quickly, end discrimination, look out for the poor, assist some seniors, preserve habitats, curb pollution, and defend ourselves, we also need to adhere to our Constitution if we are to preserve our freedom and prosper. I describe approaches consistent with the Constitution to achieve all these things in Section VIII.

People wonder why our federal government is so expensive, intrusive in our lives, partisan, and dysfunctional. While there are many reasons, certainly our failure to hold our presidents accountable to the Constitution is a primary one. The repeated presidential violations of the Constitution, and the failures of Congress to impeach the presidents, the Courts to find the violations unconstitutional, and the press to expose the violations do not bode well for our country. Congress, the Judiciary, the free press, and public opinion are the only mechanisms to check unlawful presidential behavior.

Figure 4: Presidential Constitutional Failings

T. Roosevelt   The Pure Food and Drug and the Meat Inspection Acts of 1906
Proclamations to Seize 230 Million Acres of Land
The Use of the Military in the Panama Revolution

Wilson   The Federal Reserve Act of 1913
Clayton Antitrust Act and Federal Trade Commission Acts of 1914
The Federal Loan Administration of 1916
Selective Service Act of 1917 and The Sedition Act of 1918
Use of the Military in Several Countries

F. Roosevelt   Agricultural Adjustment and National Industrial Recovery Acts of 1933
Executive Order Confiscating Gold in 1933
The National Housing Act of 1934
The Labor Relations Board Act of 1935
Banking Act and Social Security Acts of 1935

Truman   The Seizure of Numerous Private Businesses
The Continuation of Price Controls after the War
The Appropriation of Large Sums for the Marshall Plan and Cold War
The Use of the United States Military as an Agent of the United Nations

Johnson   Clean Air and Endangered Species Preservation Acts of 1963 and 1966
Economic Opportunity and Food Stamp Acts of 1964
The Elementary and Secondary Education Act of 1965
The Social Security Amendment of 1965 Adding Medicare and Medicaid
The Housing and Urban Development Act of 1965
Water Quality Act and Solid Waste Disposal Acts of 1965
The National Foundation of the Arts and Humanities Act of 1965
The Public Broadcasting Act of 1967 and The Bilingual Education Act of 1968
Vietnam War without a Congressional Declaration of War

Nixon   The National Environmental Policy Act of 1969 and The Clean Air Act of 1970
Department of Interior's Creation of 642 National Parks
The Occupational Safety and Health Act of 1970

G. W. Bush   USA Patriot and No Child Left Behind Acts of 2001
Invasion of Iraq without a Congressional Declaration of War
The Medicare Act of 2003

Obama   Made Federal Agency and Court Appointments without Congressional Consent
The Appropriation of the Money of GM and Chrysler Creditors
Granted Work Waivers to Welfare Recipients
The Patient Protection and Affordable Care Act of 2010
Illegal Use of the Government Agencies to Affect Election Outcomes
Failure to Enforce Drug, Immigration, and Naturalization Laws

Whether we are aware of it or not, our freedom, living standards, and well-being depend upon our leaders' and citizens' respect for and adherence to the Constitution and rule of law. When government leaders violate these rules, we must impeach them and not re-elect them. When journalists ignore leaders' unconstitutional and unlawful actions, we must boycott their organizations. If we impeached a couple of presidents, did not re-elect more of our leaders, and ended our patronage of the most irresponsible news organizations, we would curtail these undesirable behaviors. As founding father James Madison wrote:

There are more instances of the abridgment of the freedom of the people by gradual and silent encroachments of those in power than by violent and sudden usurpations.[33]

Supreme Court Constitutional Failings

Supreme Court constitutional failings refer to the periodic failure of the U.S. Supreme Court to nullify legislation and executive actions that violate the Constitution. They result from the appointment of justices who are more interested in advancing political agendas than upholding the Constitution. They enable the Executive Branch, Congress, and the federal government to usurp many state powers and the Executive Branch to assume judicial and legislative powers.

James Madison, as the primary author of the Constitution, also was very clear on the limited, specified powers of the federal government and the intended interpretation of the "general welfare" clause:

With respect to the words "General Welfare," I have always regarded them as qualified by the detail of powers connected with them. To take them in a literal and unlimited sense would be a metamorphosis of the Constitution into a character which there is a host of proofs was not contemplated by its creators.[34]

Who would have foreseen that a few well-placed progressives could transform our federal government with a reinterpretation of two words, "general welfare"? It took over 140 years, a national crisis, an activist president, and a cohort of liberal judges, but this constitutional decoupling finally happened during the Franklin Roosevelt presidency. Like water breaching a dike, the powers of the federal government have grown unceasingly once the general welfare clause was reinterpreted.

Now, our Congress favors some groups over others, has regulatory agencies fill in the details of its poorly written laws, and legislates, taxes, and spends unconstitutionally. It and our Executive Branch have assumed many state powers, regularly redistribute wealth, use racial preferences, and interfere with private contracts. Figure 5 summarizes some of these Supreme Court constitutional failings.

Abiding by the Constitution and our laws is in everyone's long-term interests. If something needs doing that the Constitution does not allow, state legislatures and federal government representatives can amend the Constitution and change the laws. Only the states and representatives of the people are authorized under the Constitution to expand the power of the federal government. Individual presidents and five of nine Supreme Court Justices should not be doing this.

Special Interests

With the state legislature check on the federal government eliminated in 1913 and other constitutional checks destroyed by the Supreme Court in the 1930s and 1940s, federal expenditures grew and grew. And as the federal government grew, the number of special interests protective of its expenditures also grew. To understand why this is, consider a government's importance to the social safety net recipients and government employees, unions, and contractors before they exist and after they emerge and start to grow. Before these government activities exist, there are no constituents. Once in place, they expand and garner more constituents each year.

Figure 5: Supreme Court Constitutional Failings

Home Building & Loan Association v. Blaisdell (1934) enabled governments to interfere with contracts between private parties.[35]

Helvering v. Davis (1937) allowed the government to enact the Social Security program, spend for the "general welfare," and redistribute wealth. It gave Congress a free hand to legislate without judicial review.[36]

United States v. Carolene Products Company (1938) enabled federal and state governments to pass legislation that devalued property without any obligation to compensate the property owners. The case allowed the government to infringe upon citizen's economic liberties without judicial review.[37]

Wickard v. Filburn (1942) extended the federal regulatory authority to nearly every productive economic activity, including activities that are neither interstate nor commerce. It ended the principle that the federal government only has the powers expressly granted to it in the Constitution.[38]

Chevron U.S.A., Inc. v. Natural Resources Defense Council (1984) gave the departments and agencies of the Executive Branch the power to interpret the law.[39]

Bennis v. Michigan (1996) gave the government the authority to seize the property of innocent people without judicial hearings.[40]

Whitman v. American Trucking Associations, Inc. (2001) enabled Congress to pass poorly defined laws and let unelected regulatory agencies fill in the details.[41]

Grutter v. Bollinger (2003) gave institutions the right to use racial preferences in their admittance procedures.[42]

Kelo v. City of New London (2005) gave governments the right to use eminent domain to seize private property for economic development.[43]

Crony capitalism is a form of special-interest government that occurs when business leaders promise to employ and handsomely compensate government officials later and/or make large contributions to candidates who will do favors for them once in office. The favors take the form of permitting market concentrations, supporting legislation that is advantageous to the contributors, and/or awarding government contracts and grants to their businesses. While some of these favors accommodate everyone, most of them benefit the contributors at the expense of taxpayers and consumers.

Crony unionization is another form of special interest government that occurs when union leaders make large campaign contributions to candidates to incentivize them to pass legislation, which enables unions to extract more from taxpayers and employers. While this exchange seems harmless, these favors decrease the competitiveness of enterprises and increase the cost of public and private products and services.

When people allow their central government to become large, special interests form and the government responds more to the special interests than to citizens. Special interests buy elected officials, and elected officials use the credit and revenues of the government to buy people's votes. These exchanges diminish our living standards and future.

Less Faith-Community Relevance

As science has exposed more of the cause-and-effect relationships of the universe, life, and related processes, it inadvertently has decreased the credibility of religions. Religious teachings, rewards, and penalties—like an eternal afterlife in heaven or hell—lost sway over progressives first, moderates second, and conservatives third. When religious institutions lose progressives, they become less adaptive. They lose the ability to keep their perspectives, practices, heroes, and art forms relevant to new generations. Also missing is the opportunity to teach large portions of the population to act in an honest, responsible, civil, and considerate manner.

We see the decline of faith communities in the change in Christian church attendance in the last 50 years. Over 60 percent of the U.S. population regularly attended services in 1960, while that number dropped to less than 20 percent in 2005.[44] The reduced influence of a dominant institution on 40 percent of the U.S. population coincides with the decline of honesty and civility in our culture and politics.

Less Integrity, Responsibility, and Civility

As faith communities emphasizing responsible conduct and service lose relevance, we would expect people to exhibit less of these characteristics, especially if other institutions do not teach and positively reinforce those behaviors. And this is what has happened. Spouses have become less committed to each other. Parents have become less courteous to principals, teachers, and coaches. Children have become less respectful of parents, teachers, and police. Employers and employees have become less conscientious about their responsibilities to one another, and many people have become less community-minded.

Consider that 25 percent of our population, ages 18 and older, now engage regularly in heavy drinking.[45] Roughly 15 percent of Americans ages 12 and older use illicit drugs each year and almost 50 percent use them sometime in their lifetimes.[46] Over 40 percent of Americans ages 18 to 59 had a sexually transmitted disease (STD) in the last 5 years.[47] 66 percent of all traffic fatalities are caused by aggressive driving.[48] The U.S. ranks 16th on the World Corruption Perception Index.[49] Our country also ranks 47th among 120 countries in incidents of crime. Azerbaijan, India, Iraq, Israel, the Palestine Territory, Russia, and Turkey all report lower incidents of crime than the U.S.[50] The prevalence of heavy drinking, illicit drug use, STDs, preventable traffic fatalities, corruption, and crime are not characteristics of an ascending population.

Promiscuity and the Decline of Marriage

Before the 1950s, most men and women married at a relatively young age, remained married for life, and provided a stable home environment for their children. Since then, marriage rates have fallen by two-thirds, and separation and divorce rates have increased threefold.[51] Incidents of promiscuity, cohabitation, and divorce have increased dramatically with the declining influence of religion, the development of highly reliable forms of birth control, the changing roles of women, and the implementation of generous welfare programs. Now, half of all marriages fail, and more than half of all children spend time in a single-parent household or nontraditional family.[52]

These new patterns of life have a greater impact on non-college graduates than on those who finish college. Robert Putnam, professor of public policy at Harvard University, writes:

> In the college-educated, upper third of American society, a "neo-traditional" marriage pattern has emerged. It mirrors the 1950s family in many respects, except that both partners now typically work outside of the home, they delay marriage and childbearing until their careers are under way, and they divide domestic duties more evenly.

> In the high-school-educated, lower third of the population, by contrast, a new, more kaleidoscopic pattern began to emerge in which childbearing became increasingly disconnected from marriage, and sexual partnerships became less durable.[53]

The adverse effects of these new patterns of life on the economically-challenged lower third of our population should concern all of us, as we cannot flourish for long as a people when one-third of our children grow up in dysfunctional families, neighborhoods, and schools.

Poorly Parented Children

While some parents who maintain healthy lifelong marriages do a poor job of parenting children, and some parents who separate and/or have multiple mates do a good job, generally the former group of parents does better for their children. Parents of traditional families have greater commitments to each other and their children. They provide them with more parental time, resources, and stability; a healthier balance of nurture, discipline, and expectation; and greater educational and mentoring opportunities.

Professor Putnam indicates that 6 percent of American children lived in nontraditional families in the 1960s, but today, more than 50 percent do so. Children with parents in the lowest educational quartile are roughly two times more likely to live with one parent during their childhood than those with parents in the highest quartile.[54] And again while some nontraditional parents do a fantastic job of raising their children, the research indicates that most do not do well. Professor Putnam writes:

> Children in divorced or remarried families face distinctive challenges, partly because their families' limited resources must be spread across more than one household, and partly because their parents' lingering grievances, and physical and emotional distance from one another, hamper effective communication and coordination. Multi-partner fertility is associated with less parental involvement, less extended kin involvement, and more friction, jealousy, and competition, especially when there are children from different partnerships living in the same household.[55]

Unionization and Liberalization of Education

In the 1960s, the Democratic Party and union leaders saw an opportunity to increase their membership and influence by unionizing the public sector. Undoubtedly, public employee compensation was low in some places, and some school boards and superintendents were undesirable employers. Yet, some 50 years later, it is painfully clear that the ill effects of this change outweigh the benefits.

Primary and secondary education have become costly and less effective throughout the country. Proportionally fewer children are proficient in math, reading, and writing, acquire empowering habits, become well-equipped to parent children, have productive careers, and become responsible citizens. Public schools no longer group students by their abilities. They are hesitant to discipline children and uphold basic behavioral and academic standards. Many no longer give children credit for doing homework, and some even forbid teachers from assigning it. Many public schools offer students multiple opportunities to retake the tests, sabotaging the chance to instill the habit of preparation in students.

Union work rules, seniority-based compensation, and tenure politicize education and hinder the employment of the ablest administrators and teachers. They cause the staff to support the candidates for public office who support the unions, increasing the number who register as Democrats and donate to the Democratic Party while decreasing the number who belong and give to the competing parties. Union work rules, seniority-based compensation, and tenure prevent administrators from adjusting teachers' compensation in accordance with their performance. They also make it difficult for administrators to terminate poor-performing teachers, create unaffordable pension liabilities, and fill the education system with people who look unfavorably on many of the Winning Practices that enable us to flourish.

Liberalized schools "dumb down" curriculum, inflate grades, and advance students who fail to master the material. They promote cultural relativism, nonjudgmentalism, and multiculturalism, concepts that I discuss later in this chapter. Most schools no longer teach children about the advantages of limited federal government, free enterprise, and free markets. Not having a *healthy mix* of conservatives, moderates, and progressives teaching children in public schools leads to poorer educational, social, and economic outcomes.

Schools affect our lives tremendously—directly and indirectly. They affect our individual and collective fitness. We devote 13 to 17 years of our lives to them. It is in everyone's best interest to correct these deficiencies and have our schools perform at a high level.

Social Justice Missteps

Given the genocide, slavery, discrimination, segregation, and limitations on women in our history, many of our greatest heroes were advocates of social justice. People like Horace Mann, Frederick Douglass, Harriet Beecher Stowe, Booker T. Washington, Elizabeth Cady Stanton, Susan B. Anthony, John Steinbeck, Jackie Robinson, Martin Luther King, Jr., and Betty Friedan worked tirelessly to break social barriers and improve the lives of women and minorities. These heroes and good-hearted souls all rejected hatred, retribution, and violence in their push for change. Their pursuit of social justice was clearly advantageous and good for the victims of injustice and the larger population.

And herein lies an important distinction. The pursuit of social justice is advantageous and laudable when it makes us more conscious of injustice, breaks senseless barriers, advances opportunity, and improves our attitudes, norms, and laws. It is beneficial and admirable when it empowers individuals, increases personal responsibility, advances education and work opportunities, and furthers civility, social cohesion, and prosperity. On the other hand, the pursuit of social justice is ignoble and counterproductive when it employs deception, lawlessness, and violence; favors some people over others; undermines personal responsibility; seeks equal outcomes; and furthers animosity and dependence.

Safe neighborhoods, school choice, remedial educational opportunities, laws against discrimination, and work opportunities are advantageous to the victims of social injustice and the larger population. Tolerance of crime and discrimination; *free* housing, food, and education; acceptance of illegal immigration; lower university admission standards; excusing disruptive behavior; irresponsible borrowing, taxing, and spending; and permissive monetary policy are disadvantageous to victims and the larger population.

While politicians have always fanned the flames of social justice concerns to garner political support, we avoided supporting the counterproductive approaches until the presidencies of Franklin Roosevelt, Truman, Johnson, Nixon, and Obama. We avoided disadvantageous responses for over 140 years; as our regard for the Constitution waned, however, opportunistic leaders employed irresponsible approaches, sowing the seeds of discord, polarization, and decline.

Cultural Relativism, Nonjudgmentalism, and Multiculturalism

Cultural relativism is the belief that truth exists in relation to culture, society, and historical context. Nonjudgmentalism is the idea that we should not judge others because they are a product of their culture and context. Multiculturalism is the idea that all cultures are equally meritorious. These concepts have appeal because there is an element of truth to them, they further tolerance, and they make people feel good about their beliefs. The problems with these concepts are that they are not entirely true, some perspectives and practices further some people's well-being better than others, and we must be able to judge the desirability of various perspectives and practices.

Cultural relativism, nonjudgmentalism, and multiculturalism discourage the discrimination between winning and losing practices and hinder our fitness because our views and behaviors are valid whether they harm or advance our and others' well-being. Yale professor and *New York Times* columnist David Brooks writes of this cultural challenge in his column "The Cost of Relativism":

> We now have multiple generations of people caught in recurring feedback loops of economic stress and family breakdown. . . . It's not only money and better policy that are missing in these circles; it's norms. . . . These norms weren't destroyed because of people with bad values. They were destroyed by a plague of nonjudgmentalism, which refused to assert that one way of behaving was better than another.[56]

Although various forms of relativism have threatened societies for a couple of thousand years, accepting all opinions as equally valuable did not become prevalent in the U.S. until the liberalization of education. Now, extreme tolerance and the idea that all cultures are equally desirable make diversity more important than social cohesion and supplant our founders' objective of *E Pluribus Unum,* or "From many, one," that served us so well for almost two centuries. They undermine both the idea that American culture has something important to offer immigrants and the practice of immigrants learning English, assimilating, and becoming American. Rather than pushing cultural relativism, nonjudgementalism, and multiculturalism on our children, we should teach them to be able to tell the difference between winning and losing practices and to adopt Winning Practices as they find them.

Declining Discipline, Poor Habits, and Less Learning

Greater affluence, the unionization and liberalization of education, and the adoption of cultural relativism, multiculturalism, and nonjudgementalism have caused parents and teachers to be permissive and less concerned about the habits that children develop. The days of showing respect to one's elders, controlling emotional outbursts, and immediately responding to the directives of authorities are passing. Minimal absenteeism, completing one's assignments on time, and doing well on a test the first time are no longer common expectations of parents and teachers.

We have left the era of discipline, the formation of constructive habits, and serious learning and have entered the age of hyped self-esteem, uncontrolled emotional outbursts, and children doing what they want. And while many children of college-educated parents learn self-control, self-discipline, and to defer gratification, many children of non-college-educated parents do not learn these empowering habits as much in school. Coming from less-stable homes, having less-involved parents with more limited means, often attending inferior schools, and being denied the opportunity to learn empowering habits, these children confront a lifetime of struggle and disappointment rather than steady progress.

Oligopoly and Monopoly

When competition, free enterprise, free markets, and prudent regulation prevail, buyers and sellers have choices, reputations matter, and people tend to do the right things. When power concentrates and governments serve special interests, people and enterprises become less responsible and more predatory. When three or fewer sellers have most of the customers, sellers over-charge, are unresponsive, and innovate less. Similarly, when three or fewer buyers make most of the purchases, buyers underpay and dictate the transactional terms.

Over the years, we have seen monopolies and oligopolies with the railroads, energy providers, auto manufacturers, telephone companies, airlines, healthcare providers, cable companies, and numerous other industries. Each time three or fewer companies dominate a market, the suppliers and customers of these firms suffer.

Free enterprise and free markets fail us when governments permit a few buyers or sellers to dominate a market, externalities exist, and when human emotions cause extreme overselling. In such situations, prudent actions by governments and central banks reduce market concentrations, mitigate the adverse effects, and restore the orderly function of enterprises and markets.

Offshoring

In the last 50 years, several companies found it advantageous to move their operations first to Japan, Hong Kong, Singapore, South Korea, and Taiwan and then to China, Malaysia, and Vietnam. And rather than looking introspectively for the causes of the exodus, our leaders attributed the movement to low-cost foreign labor.

While the low-cost labor in Asia has been a factor, there are numerous other causes of offshoring, such as: high U.S. corporate tax rates, onerous government regulations, high levels of litigation, costly and uncooperative unions, and unaffordable health insurance. A 10 to 15 percent higher corporate tax rate provides a serious incentive to locate elsewhere. Tens of thousands of pages of federal, state, and local government regulations, some of the most onerous in the world, significantly increase the cost of doing business in the U.S. Lots of lucrative litigation increases legal and insurance costs for companies in our country. Private sector unions with near monopolies on labor in some industries, and public-sector unions with absolute monopolies, suppress productivity and both directly and indirectly increase business costs in our country. Healthcare, something many businesses provide, costs at least 50 percent more in the U.S. than in most other countries.[57]

While politicians and journalists blame the loss of American jobs, technology, and enterprise on inexpensive foreign labor, the truth is that our leaders' poor policy choices are the primary causes. The unfriendly tax, regulatory, litigation, labor, and healthcare policies of the U.S. coupled with the friendlier policies of other countries incentivize companies to flee our shores.

Entitlement

The rapidly growing living standards of the 1940s and 50s made most Americans feel fortunate. Social Security, unemployment insurance, and generous pension plans provided a sense of financial security. This sense of prosperity and the green light for federal social programs from the Supreme Court enabled our representatives to pass a Disability Insurance program in the 1950s and food stamp, Medicare, Medicaid, and welfare programs in the 1960s. America was so awesome that every citizen should live well.

Supporters of these programs wanted to help people, but they also wanted to increase their political power and win elections. They branded their opposition as heartless, removed the social stigma associated with public support, worked hard to sign people up for these programs, and won the day. The level of government that could best address poverty was not a consideration. The realities that most of these programs had not been piloted, cost billions of dollars, and tended to incentivize complacency were nonissues.

Before long, the days of believing that "we must earn our own way" gave way to "I deserve a good life," and then to "I have a right to a good life." Lee Kuan Yew, the founding father and prime minister of Singapore from 1965 to 1990, understood the importance of avoiding entitlements and all their adverse effects. In just three decades, his leadership moved Singapore from Third World to First World. It transformed a poor, decrepit, crime-ridden city into a modern, affluent, orderly city-state that is perhaps the most livable city on Earth. Leaders and scholars from all over the world consider Lee Kuan Yew to have been one of the greatest leaders of the 20th century, and his example and approaches underlie many of China's recent advances. Commenting on the Western approach to poverty, he stated:

American and European governments believed that they could always afford to support the poor and the needy: widows, orphans, the old and homeless, disadvantaged minorities, unwed mothers. Their sociologists expounded the theory that hardship and failure were due not to the individual person's character, but to flaws in the economic system. So, charity became "entitlement," and the stigma of living on charity disappeared. Unfortunately, welfare costs grew faster than the government's ability to raise taxes to pay for it. The political cost of tax increases is high.

Governments took the easy way out by borrowing to give higher benefits to the current generation of voters and passing the costs on to the future generations who were not yet voters.[58]

Entitlements and the political power associated with them are ruinous. They drive ever more spending, debt, wealth redistribution, and taxation, negatively affecting the people of every welfare state. They destroy people's incentives to learn, work, and save. They precipitate a loss of competitiveness and a gradual decline in living standards. Lest you think that I am heartless and do not recognize that many people need a little help, bear with me. I explore what Lee Kuan Yew did to limit the need for entitlements and numerous Winning Practices to create a thriving population in Section VIII.

Consumerism and Debt

The rapidly growing standards of living of the 1940s and 1950s and the cradle-to-grave social safety net of the 1960s caused Americans to save less for the future, spend more freely, and borrow more. The days of waiting until we had the money to purchase something and saving for hardships and retirement ended for large portions of the population.

Americans had for decades used credit to finance their homes; in the 1970s, however, we started to purchase our cars with credit and to acquire credit cards. In the 1980s, we supplemented our lifestyles with credit cards, financing the purchase of our back-to-school clothes, birthday gifts, holiday gifts, televisions, and furniture. In the 1990s, we started borrowing to purchase houses that had twice the square footage of our parents' homes.

Throughout the 1980s, 1990s, and the first seven years of the 2000s, progressives pushed hard for low-income ownership of homes. They pressed banks to lower their lending standards and compelled Freddie Mac and Fannie Mae, federally sponsored institutions, to support more low-income home ownership. People could purchase houses with no money down; even those who had a negative net worth and just enough income to make the payments on 30-year mortgages qualified for mortgages.

In the 1980s and 1990s, more Americans started to finance their college educations. Well-intended lawmakers facilitated this practice with the federally sponsored Sallie Mae institution. This program eliminated previously required qualifications for loans and offered students lenient repayment terms. Today, seven of ten college students leave school with tens of thousands of dollars owed in student loans, and the federally sponsored system is almost insolvent.

What is the net effect of all this consumerism and debt? In 1964, the total U.S. public and private debt was $1 trillion and 60 million people were employed. In 2015, this debt was $62 trillion and 158 million people were employed.[59] This works out to $17,600 of debt per employed person in 1964 and $402,100 of debt per employed person in 2015. If we include the unfunded and underfunded commitments that federal, state, and local governments have made regarding public pensions, Social Security, Medicaid, Medicare, disability, and healthcare, the picture is far worse.

When we consume mindlessly, save little, and borrow large sums, we live today at the expense of tomorrow. We have less investment income and pay more interest. Our government receives less tax revenue and pays more interest. We as a country invest less in infrastructure, research, and development; our productivity stagnates; and our competitiveness and living standards decline.

Easy Money

Easy money occurs when a country's central bank (1) decreases the amount of reserves that commercial and retail banks must hold for each dollar they lend, (2) pays artificially low rates of interest to commercial and retail banks, or (3) buys its government's debt. Easy money causes enterprises and consumers to borrow and spend more and the prices of goods, services, and assets to increase.

The easy money policies of the late 1990s and early 2000s set up the Great Recession of 2007 to 2009. Our central bank implemented easy money policies to avoid Y2K problems and to stabilize the economy after the September 11 attacks. Afterward, it continued easy money policies to keep the good times rolling. Governments, enterprises, and consumers kept borrowing and spending. The demand for assets, goods, services, and debt, however, cannot increase at increasing rates forever. Eventually, purchases slow. When this occurs, as it did in 2008, prices and collateral values decrease. Like a receding tide exposes the beach, falling prices and collateral values expose excessive amounts of debt and financial vulnerability that oftentimes causes investors to panic.

Bear Stearns, Countrywide Financial, Fannie Mae, Freddie Mac, Goldman Sachs, Lehman Brothers, Merrill Lynch, and many others of the country's largest financial institutions had irresponsible levels of debt. To stem the ensuing panic and restore order, the central bank implemented more aggressive easy money policies in 2008 and for the subsequent seven years. While an aggressive easy money policy is an appropriate response to a financial crisis, it was not appropriate to use so much in both the years preceding and following the crisis. In addition, it was not prudent for the central bank to purchase approximately $2 trillion of U.S. debt between 2008 and 2014, essentially creating money out of thin air and keeping interest rates for commercial and retail banks under one-quarter percent through 2015.[60]

While easy money tempers economic contractions, it also distorts market prices, decreases capital formation, and creates speculative bubbles. It steals purchasing power from savers and gives it to borrowers. It encourages governments, enterprises, and consumers to borrow and spend recklessly. Easy money is like heroin: once central banks start using it, they cannot stop without causing a lot of pain and suffering.

Hubris and Nation Building

Hubris affects those who become intoxicated with success. It often manifests itself in the children of successful generations who live large, have a false sense of reality, and do not develop the necessary discipline, knowledge, work ethic, and judgment to be successful. The change in the election of U.S. Senators, constitutional decoupling, promiscuity, the liberalism of education, relativism, multiculturalism, nonjudgmentalism, entitlement, consumerism, excessive debt, and easy money are manifestations of hubris. And to this list, we should add nation building.

Having had tremendous success in helping Germany and Japan rebuild after WWII and South Korea after the Korean War, George W. Bush, Dick Cheney, Donald Rumsfeld, and others believed that we could depose any government and build a better one at will. What these leaders failed to recognize was that the Germans, Japanese, and South Koreans had more to do with their success after WWII and the Korean War than we did. The Germans, Japanese, and South Koreans already had a high prevalence of Winning Perspectives and Practices within their cultures.

Attempts to nation build in Afghanistan and Iraq were doomed from the beginning. The Afghans and Iraqis have values that are incompatible with ours, and they have a much lower prevalence of winning practices within their populations. The cost of the misguided attempts to nation build in Afghanistan and Iraq has been staggering in terms of treasure, life, and reputation.

Immigration Failures

We have many immigration failures. Porous borders allow criminals, terrorists, and people who carry life-threatening diseases to enter the United States. Millions of illegal immigrants depress entry-level wages and make it harder for our citizens to find good-paying jobs. Many illegal immigrants do not know our language, do not share our values, have no prospects for employment, and/or will depend on public resources for the rest of their lives. Desirable immigrant applicants with needed work skills wait while illegal immigration divides our population and paralyzes our government. Large immigrant concentrations in Southern California, South Florida, Chicago, and Houston overwhelm the schools, health services, police forces, courts, jails, and social services in those areas.

Five percent of the U.S. population was foreign-born in 1965 compared to 14 percent, or approximately 45 million people, in 2015.[61] In 1965, our families were more intact, our communities were safer, and our population was fitter. Real wages were increasing faster, proportionally fewer people were unemployed, and proportionally fewer people depended on the government. For the most part, we all spoke one language, our people were more unified, and we were less indebted.

Distorted News and Political Polarization

One of the great unifying forces in our country was the existence of three or four national news outlets and two or three newspapers in most communities. The few national and local television, radio, and newspaper organizations incentivized their operators to appeal to all Americans and uphold national, community, and journalism standards.

With the advent of cable television, the Internet, and social media, the few national news organizations fragmented into numerous ones, and the local newspapers lost large portions of their advertising revenue. The fragmented news organizations received revenue and audiences as they targeted their programming, appealed to our emotions, and selectively reported and sensationalized the news. Local news organizations consolidated and adopted many of the same tactics or went under. While more choice and customized services generally are desirable, this has not been the case with the news media. We now live in a world where most people only receive news that aligns with their worldviews.

Living in a country comprised of people of multiple races, religions, and ethnicities who live, attend school, and work in different communities, where half the population depends on social programs and the other half funds them, separates us. A federal legislature, where half of the elected officials plus one enacts controversial laws and the other half opposes them, also divides us.

People favor the protection of the unborn or a woman's right to choose. They support the rule of law and legal immigration or porous borders and sanctuary cities. They prefer less government, free market solutions, and lower taxes, or more regulation, higher taxes, and more social programs. They want, or do not want, the government to force the reduction of greenhouse gas emissions.

News organizations that do not factually present the news and continually reinforce the divisions make it difficult for many people to talk to each other. American social cohesion is as low now as at any time in our history except for a few years during the Revolutionary, Civil, and Vietnam wars. People assume positions that are common in their social circles. Fact-based, rational discussions are difficult. Common sense is rare. The practice of piloting policies and projects on a small scale and thoroughly examining their effects before their implementation on a large scale seldom occurs.

Separation from Nature

For some one hundred years, most Americans have lived apart from nature and had only a cursory exposure to science. While we might visit a park or camp a few times a year, most of us occupy environments of wood, steel, concrete, glass, lawns, and pavement. Few of us have experience with large populations of plants and animals, savannas, woodlands, jungles, deserts, frozen tundra, and oceans. Few of us sense our dependence upon our planet—its rhythms, climate, atmosphere, fresh water, soils, ecosystems, plants, and animals. Few of us appreciate the cycle of life—the coevolution of predators and prey and the importance of fitness.

We must compete, win, and have offspring. If we do not do these things, we perish. We are vulnerable as individuals and much stronger as members of a family, community, and country. Affluence and technology give a license to be foolish for a while, but our well-being depends on the alignment of our actions with nature. Our separation from nature is so unfortunate because there is so much wisdom within it.

Losing Our Way

Inclusion Failures
Change in the Election of U.S. Senators
Presidential Constitutional Failings
Supreme Court Constitutional Failings

Special Interests
Less Faith-Community Relevance
Less Integrity, Responsibility, and Civility
Promiscuity and the Decline of Marriage

Poorly Parented Children
Unionization and Liberalization of Education
Social Justice Missteps

Cultural Relativism, Nonjudgmentalism, and Multiculturalism
Declining Discipline, Poor Habits, and Less Learning
Oligopoly and Monopoly
Offshoring

Entitlement
Consumerism and Debt
Easy Money
Hubris and Nation Building

Immigration Failures
Distorted News and Political Polarization
Separation from Nature

Section II: Winning Perspectives

Winning Perspectives

Truth
Causality
Scale
Evolution
Fitness

Human Nature
Culture
Periodic Disaster
Eco-Dependency

Winning Practices

Health
Thought
Integrity
Proactivity
Prudence
Excellence
Thrift and Investment

Affiliation
Decency
Understanding
Leadership
Teamwork
Improvement

Spouse Selection
Marriage
Responsible Parenting
Empowering Habit Formation

Knowledge
Universal Education
Parental Choice
Results-Oriented Education

Free Enterprise and Markets
Responsible Corporate Governance
Prudent Regulation
Enterprise Competitiveness

Government of the People
Powers, Prohibitions, and Structure
Freedoms, Rights, and Responsibilities
The Rule of Law
Inclusion and Meritocracy
Prudent Taxation
Financial Strength
Savings Accounts, Social Safety Nets
Consumer-Driven Healthcare
Assimilation
Peace Through Fitness
Sustainability

Chapter 3

Winning Perspectives

Winning Perspectives come to us from an understanding of the evolution of the universe, life, and culture. They help us identify Winning Practices from a murky sea of possibilities.

Narratives are not true just because someone told us about them, approaches do not work just because they sound good, and the most successful people do not peddle inaccurate stories and faulty methods. They do not advocate something without having evidence of its truth or effectiveness. The most successful people work hard to understand the world as it is and ground their thought, decisions, actions, and speech in reality. They continuously learn—in school, at work, and in their communities, and from reading, traveling, and mentors. They test their hypotheses, pilot new approaches, and gather evidence.

Jack Welch, a former chairman and CEO of General Electric, whose leadership increased the market value of General Electric 40 times in just 20 years, attributes much of his and GE's success to his mother's relentless insistence that he face reality.[62] He writes:

The insights she drilled into me never faded. She always insisted on facing the facts of a situation. One of her favorite expressions was "Don't kid yourself. That's the way it is." [63]

Working on a farm, attending excellent schools and universities, reading hundreds of books, cultivating thousands of acres, raising millions of animals, conducting hundreds of experiments, operating several businesses, leading numerous professional and community organizations, being involved in local government, running for Congress, traveling throughout the U.S. and the world, and investing substantial sums of money, activities I have spent a lot of time doing, have brought tremendous perspective and made me unusually realistic.

Like Jack Welch and his mother, I cannot emphasize enough the importance of facing facts, what works, and reality. Fashion, idle wishes, and political correctness do not improve our effectiveness, as fashions are fleeting, idle wishes are fantasies, and political correctness is a compendium of others' political agendas. Reality is as it is and not as we wish it to be.

The study of the universe, life, and culture brings tremendous perspective. It expands our physical and time horizons and enables us to understand and glimpse otherwise inaccessible natural processes. Visiting and studying other countries and cultures jars us, frees us from groupthink, exposes us to foreign practices, makes us more insightful about our and others' practices, and gives ideas about how we can improve.

Although modernity and technology remove us from nature, we are several billion-year products of it and completely dependent upon it. We must not take our evolutionary individual, familial, and superorganism nature; ecosystems; and natural processes for granted. We must be realistic, practical, and judicious. We must work with the world, natural processes, and others as we find them. Winning Perspectives help us do this.

From such study and travel, I found the perspectives of Truth, Causality, Scale, Evolution, Fitness, Human Nature, Culture, Periodic Disaster, and Eco-Dependency to be especially helpful. So helpful, in fact, that I call them Winning Perspectives and devote the next nine chapters of the book to them.

Winning Perspectives are accurate perceptions of reality and the conditions of existence that further our effectiveness. They provide direction and help us identify Winning Practices that enable us to flourish.

Chapter 4

Truth

The truth is incontrovertible. Malice may attack it, ignorance may deride it, but in the end, there it is.[64]

—*Winston Churchill*

The first of the nine Winning Perspectives is truth. I define truth as accurate approximations of reality, natural processes, and events. While truth is understandable in concept, it is elusive in practice.

Things just are not always what they seem. For proof of this, simply step outside and gaze as far as your surroundings permit. It is no surprise that for thousands of years our ancestors thought the Earth was flat, as this is the way it appears when we are standing on it. But this is not the truth, as images of Earth from space show us. Limited perspective, the invisibility of many cause-and-effect relationships, self-interest bias, spin, and groupthink all distort our perceptions.

As with the flatness of Earth, generally we do not perceive truth until we see something from several vantage points. Children and professional magicians see magic differently. Children see the illusion. Magicians see the illusion, artistry, and deception. Children and magicians see the same performance, but magicians see it with experience, from more vantage points, and with more accuracy.

Our perceptions of our world take place on a very limited scale—a few years, one-hundredth of an inch, a few miles, and only as they directly affect us. Without science and technology, much is invisible to us. With science and technology, we see galaxies, solar systems, microscopic life, molecules, atoms, and interactions on large and small scales. I discuss science and the scientific method in Chapter 31.

Grasping truth is difficult because our ego and self-interest color our perceptions. Generally, we want to dominate more than we want to be accurate, and we see events as it is in our interest to see them. If we espouse a position, we are more often defending it than learning from others. If we collide with a car at a four-way stop, most of us will tend to blame the other driver. If one of our children is hurt in a fight, most of us will fault the other child unless our child has a history of fighting.

People also do not communicate truthfully. We want to avoid conflict and punishment, and we want others to applaud us. So we often create narratives that mask our interests and tell others what we want them to hear or what we think they want to hear. Children create stories for their parents, politicians for their constituents, and subordinates for their superiors, and vice versa. Unless we have a strong truth-telling ethic, we shade the truth rather than tell it.

Evolution has wired us to absorb others' thinking. This tendency served us well as hunter-gathers for millions of years but less well in the modern world. Absorbing others' thinking facilitates social cohesion but hinders our ability to make a complex civilization work. It ignores facts and is easy. As inventor extraordinaire Thomas Edison wrote:

> If we bother with facts at all, we hunt like bird dogs after the facts that bolster up what we already think—and ignore all the others! We want only the facts that justify our acts—the facts that fit in conveniently with [our] wishful-thinking and justify our preconceived prejudices! [65]

We also "see things not as they are but as we are," as the maxim goes. Whether we are Republicans, Democrats, Caucasians, Hispanics, African Americans, Jews, Christians, or Muslims, we do this. The views of those with whom we associate take root in us. If we learned at a young age that Native Americans were heathen murderers in the 18th century, we would hide from them and probably shoot those who strayed onto our property. We would completely miss that the Native Americans loved their children, enjoyed their families and communities, and just wanted to retain their lives and lands. Carl Sagan wrote:

The truth may be puzzling. It may take some work to grapple with. It may be counterintuitive. It may contradict deeply held prejudices. It may not be consonant with what we desperately want to be true. But our preferences do not determine what's true.[66]

Our views always become like those with whom we spend the most time. If our social circle is primarily comprised of Conservatives, we will see the government as inefficient, wasteful, and restrictive. If it is mainly composed of Liberals, we will see the government as a helpful tool to eliminate prejudice and inequality. We recognize groupthink as outsiders of groups but not as insiders.

Our tendency to absorb others' thinking is greatest when we are children and our minds are open to the views of our parents, older siblings, teachers, and coaches. It is also strong in our teens when an intense desire to "fit in" opens our minds to our peers. Then, sometime in our mid-twenties when our routines, peers, and groups stabilize, our malleable minds harden, and we develop a tendency to register information that reinforces our views and ignore information that challenges them. Others' views affect us on a much more limited basis, as mature brains do not easily substitute new neuron patterns for older ones.

While science provides the best method to discern truth, sometimes the truth eludes scientists. Newton's laws of motion exemplify this and underscore the importance of avoiding certitude. Every observation and experiment confirmed Newton's laws of motion for two hundred years, but then Einstein realized that they only approximate reality at familiar scales, and they are incorrect at large and small scales. Carl Sagan wrote:

Humans may crave absolute certainty; they may aspire to it; they may pretend, as partisans of certain religions do, to have attained it. But the history of science—by far the most successful claim to knowledge accessible to humans—teaches that the most we can hope for is successive improvement in our understanding.[67]

Because so much works against our perception of truth and truth underlies our effectiveness, we must appreciate those who express it. Leaders, authorities, famous people, and those engaged in science, research, and teaching have a special responsibility to communicate truthfully as their example impacts so many. Imagine the harm done if doctors told their patients that smoking poses no risk or teachers told their less diligent students that they were stupid.

Truth hides from us, and human nature distorts it. We must always be aware of selectively reported facts. Our initial perceptions are only a start in our quest for truth. We must ponder our perceptions, read, travel, verify what others tell us, solicit different views, conduct experiments, and gather evidence. Varied perspectives and increasing amounts of evidence improve our perceptions, making us more intelligent and our solutions iteratively more effective.

Truth – *accurate approximations of reality, natural processes, and events.*

Chapter 5

Causality

Behind every event is one or more causes.

We have poorly understood the cause-and-effect nature of the universe for most of history because most causes are invisible to us. For thousands of years, we thought capricious acts of gods, God, evil spirits, and witches caused diseases, pestilence, and famine. Not until Robert Hooke and others had the benefit of the microscope, did we learn that bacteria and viruses cause diseases. Not until we understood the gestation cycles of insects, did we discover the cause of pestilence. Only when we learned about the effects that massive volcanic eruptions had on global temperatures did we recognize that they were major causes of famine.

Without telescopes, microscopes, and other sensory aids, most of the universe and natural processes are imperceptible to us. Cosmic structure and distances, the fusion of atoms, DNA's orchestration of life, and cell division are undetectable. Without sensory aids, the knowledge of stars, general relativity, and the multibillion-year sequence of events that shaped the universe would be out of our reach. Without the fossil record, careful observation, and imagination, we could not grasp the evolution of life and the cumulative effects of innumerable small changes that occur over the span of generations.

Thousands of scientists have spent hundreds of years exposing the 13.7-billion-year sequence of causes and effects that shaped the universe and life. Although scientists have numerous details still to work out, they have deciphered a great deal.

Understanding that there are one or more causes for every event is a giant step forward. Ceasing to attribute events to gods, God, evil spirits, witches, and bad luck—and knowing the real causes of these occurrences—improves our quality of life immensely.

I learned quickly on the farm and in business that understanding the cause or causes of problems is crucial. When we do not address the causes of problems, they remain. Alleviating the symptoms of problems makes us feel better, but it does not eliminate the difficulty.

Consider the challenge of providing clean drinking water to a community where the only adequate source of water is a lake high in phosphates and nitrates. A municipality has two common choices: (1) require landowners to put in vegetation buffers and retention ponds around the lake to manage runoff from their properties, or (2) treat the water to reduce the phosphates and nitrates to acceptable levels. The first approach has a high initial cost, eliminates the contamination, and forever solves the problem. The second approach has a low initial cost, high ongoing costs, and does not eliminate the problem. Which is the better solution? The answer to this question depends on the severity of the adverse effects and the costs and benefits of the alternative approaches over time. While it is not always possible or practical to eliminate the cause(s) of a problem, understanding the cause(s) gives us this possibility and usually suggests numerous other ways to address the situation.

Fallacy, Correlation, Necessity, and Sufficiency

When thinking about causes and their effects, understanding the concepts of fallacy, correlation, necessity, and sufficiency is helpful.

*A **Fallacy** is the incorrect attribution of cause to effect.*

"You will catch a cold if you go outside with wet hair" is a fallacy. It is a fallacy because viruses cause colds, not wet hair. "Government may lower the cost of healthcare by setting the prices for it" is a fallacy, as price fixing does nothing to lower the costs of providing healthcare. Price fixing merely decreases the number of providers and increases the time people wait for the services offered by lower-cost and/or poorer-quality providers. Fallacies are more common than we realize. They occur when people are ignorant and unaccountable, and superstition prevails.

*A **Correlation** is the simultaneous occurrence of two events.*

Correlation does not imply causation. It implies coincidence. Correlations may be random, causal, or joint products of some event. One of the most common fallacies is to believe a correlation between two events implies a causal relationship. Seeing if one occurrence always precedes another suggests that the first occurrence might cause the second one and assures that the second one does not cause the first one.

Consider a hypothetical health study that finds a correlation between eating organic foods and a lower incidence of colds. Does the correlation mean that eating organic foods lowers the incident of colds? No, the correlation does not tell us this. The association of eating organic foods and fewer colds only indicates that the two events are coincident. The correlation could result from the phenomenon that people who eat organic foods have fewer children, and therefore, have less exposure to cold viruses. In this case, eating organic foods would coincide with having fewer colds, but it would not lower incidences of colds since exposure to the viruses that children carry causes colds.

Logicians and scientists distinguish the causes or conditions related to an event as contributory, necessary, or sufficient.

*A **Contributory Condition** is a circumstance that plays a role in producing an effect.*

*A **Necessary Condition** is a circumstance that must be present to produce an effect.*

***Sufficient Conditions** are the complete set of circumstances that must be present to produce an effect.*

Regular exercise is a contributory condition of good health. It furthers good health but does not assure it. Some people have good health with or without it. Regular training is a necessary condition of winning a marathon. Entrants do not win marathons without it, but it alone does not assure victory. Running full speed into a concrete wall is a sufficient condition to harm oneself. The act alone guarantees harm. The causality perspective teaches us that events are not arbitrary. When conditions are sufficient for an event to occur, it will.

Of these three types of conditions, sufficiency is the most interesting. Sufficiency refers to the set of conditions that produce an effect. Knowing the set is powerful. The conditions for sufficiency, like most cause-and-effect relationships, are usually difficult to determine, but we may discover them with careful observation and experimentation. Science excels in determining the sufficient conditions for events.

The Inanimate and Animate Worlds

Until rather recently, we did not know about these conditions, processes, and events. We thought the heavens, Earth, and life were the handiwork of gods or God. The processes occurred on such a small scale, so far away, and/or so long ago that we did not perceive them. Knowing the sufficient conditions of effects and events is ever more helpful.

As things happen at the atomic and cellular levels given the right conditions, so they occur at the organism and superorganism levels. The only difference between events at the organism and human levels is that higher animals inject some unpredictability into events. Higher animals overrule their instincts and make choices. For example, when someone is mean to us, we can reciprocate meanness, flee, or respond in a completely counterintuitive way with kindness. Our relative strength affects others' treatment of us and our responses. Responding with kindness is not an instinctive response but a choice. Sufficient conditions for an event at the atomic and cellular levels are much more straightforward than those at the human level.

"We reap what we sow"—a reality that we receive in accordance to what we do—is a causality that generally holds. Others compensate us as we work. Others assist us as we assist them, and others harm us as we harm them. While we may not always receive our due in the short term, we frequently do in the long term.

The invisible nature of causal relationships blinds us to the effects of many of our actions. Parents, teachers, mentors, and experts expose the long-term effects of our actions and help us act more prudently. The obvious positive impact of counsel by wise, caring authorities is among the most important information we ever receive. All children in the past and today benefit by heeding early in their life, and considering later in their life, the counsel of the elders in their families and great teachers in their communities.

Our world is comprehensible. The cause-and-effect relationships are predictable at the atomic and cellular levels and largely predictable at the human level. Our beliefs, prayers, and preferences do not alter these causal relationships. They may affect our behavior and people's responses to ours, but they do not change causal relationships. As historians, philosophers, and authors Will and Ariel Durant wrote in their eleven-volume *The Story of Civilization:*

In the end, nothing is lost. Every event, for good or evil, has effects forever.[68]

Causality – *the reality that every effect has one or more causes.*

Chapter 6

Scale

Fleeting specs of dust are we—transient and minute relative to the age and scope of the universe.

Our understanding of the universe, the composition of matter, and time has expanded so much over the last 500 years. Five hundred years ago, we understood masses as small as a mosquito (10^{-6} kilograms) and as large as an ocean-going ship (10^5 kilograms). Today, we understand masses as small as an electron (10^{-32} kilograms) and as large as a galaxy (10^{42} kilograms).

Just a few centuries ago, we understood distances as small as the thickness of a human hair, about 10^{-4} meters, and distances as great as a 30-day horseback ride, about 10^6 meters. Today, we understand distances as small as one Planck length, about 10^{-35} meters, and as large as our universe, about 10^{27} meters.

Five hundred years ago, we had a sense of 100 human generations or 2,000 years. Today we think in terms of millions of human generations and billions of years. Figure 6: Small and Large Masses, Figure 7: Small and Large Distances, and Figure 8: Evolution of the Universe and Life Timeline delineate the scale of our current perspectives.

As our understanding of the scale of distance, mass, and time expands, so does our understanding of our place in the universe. Five hundred years ago, we thought Earth was flat and God created everything for our benefit. We thought we had dominion over the planet and other lifeforms. Now, we understand that we live in one of the billions of galaxies, orbit around one of the billion stars in our galaxy, and live on one of the billions of potentially hospitable planets in the universe. We realize that all earthly lifeforms descend from a common lifeform, we are the products of over three billion years of natural selection, and we may become a dead leaf on the evolutionary tree, or a branch to hundreds, thousands, or even millions of generations of life.

Our views of the universe and life have changed so much in the last 20 generations. Now the universe seems endlessly divisible and expansive, and life incredibly complex. The universe and life are wondrous and dazzling! As naturalist and Pulitzer Prize winning author Annie Dillard writes:

> After the one extravagant gesture of creation in the first place, the universe has continued to deal exclusively in extra- vagances, flinging intricacies and colossi down eons of emptiness, heaping profusions on profligacies with ever-fresh vigor. The whole show has been on fire from the word go. I come down to the water to cool my eyes. But everywhere I look I see fire; that which isn't flint is tinder, and the whole world sparks and flames.[69]

Scale – *understanding that the magnitudes of distance, mass, and time in the universe are very different from those we experience every day, and realistically grasping our place in the universe.*

Figure 6: Small and Large Masses

	English Description	Metric Name	Number	Scientific Notation
Electron	0.9 thousandth trillionth trillionths		0.000,000,000,000,000,000,000,000,0009	0.9×10^{-27}
Hydrogen Atom	1.7 trillionth trillionths	1.7 yoctograms	0.000,000,000,000,000,000,000,0017	1.7×10^{-24}
Small Protein	55.0 billionth trillionths	55.0 zeptograms	0.000,000,000,000,000,000,055	55.0×10^{-21}
Human Sperm Cell	22.0 trillionths	22.0 picogram	0.000,000,000,022	22.0×10^{-12}
Average Human Cell	1.0 billionths	1.0 nanograms	0.000,000,001	1.0×10^{-9}
Human Ovum	3.6 millionths	3.6 micrograms	0.000,0036	3.6×10^{-6}
Mosquito	2.5 thousandths	2.5 milligrams	0.025	2.5×10^{-3}
Blue Whale	200.0 million	200.0 megagrams	200,000,000	200.0×10^{6}
Human Population	400.0 trillion	400.0 teragrams	400,000,000,000	400.0×10^{12}
Moon	73.0 trillion trillion	73.0 yottagrams	73,000,000,000,000,000,000,000,000	73×10^{24}
Earth	6.0 trillion quadrillion	1.7 yoctograms	6,000,000,000,000,000,000,000,000,000	6.0×10^{27}
Sun	2.0 billion trillion trillion	55.0 zeptograms	2,000,000,000,000,000,000,000,000,000,000,000	2.0×10^{33}
Milky Way Black Hole	8.0 trillion trillion quadrillion quadrillion		8,000,000,000,000,000,000,000,000,000,000,000,000,000	8.0×10^{39}
Milky Way Galaxy	1.2 billion trillion trillion trillion			1.2×10^{45}
Universe	2.0 trillion trillion trillion trillion trillion quadrillion			2.0×10^{63}

Orders of Magnitude, Wikipedia, http://en.wikipedia.org/wiki/Orders_of_magnitude_(mass)

Figure 7: Small and Large Distances

	English Description	Metric Name	Number	Scientific Notation
	Meters		Meters	
Planck Length	0.16 trillionth, trillionth, trillionth		0.000,000,000,000,000,000,000,000,000,000,000,016	1.6×10^{-35}
Electron Diameter	5.6 millionth billionths	5.6 femtometers	0.000,000,000,000,0056	5.6×10^{-15}
Hydrogen Diameter	5.0 trillionths	5.0 picometers	0.000,000,000,005	5.0×10^{-12}
Smallest Transistor Gate	2.5 billionths	2.5 nanometers	0.000,000,0025	2.5×10^{-9}
Red Blood Cell Diameter	7.0 millionths	7.0 micrometers	0.000,007	7.0×10^{-6}
Human Hair Diameter	0.1 thousandths	0.1 millimeters	0.000,1	0.1×10^{-3}
Moon Diameter	3.5 million	3.5 megameters	3,500,000	3.5×10^{6}
Earth Diameter	12.8 million	12.8 megameters	12,8000,000	12.8×10^{9}
Sun Diameter	1.4 billion	1.4 gigameters	1,400,000,000	1.4×10^{9}
Earth to the Sun	150.0 billion	150.0 gigameters	150,000,000,000	150.0×10^{9}
Sun to Pluto	5.9 trillion	5.9 terameters	5,900,000,000,000	5.9×10^{12}
One Light Year	9.5 quadrillion	9.5 petameters	9,500,000,000,000,000	9.5×10^{15}

Orders of Magnitude, Wikipedia, http://en.wikipedia.org/wiki/Orders_of_magnitude_(length)

Figure 8: Evolution of the Universe and Life Timeline

	Millennia Ago	Generations (25 Years)	Years Ago
The Big Bang	13,700,000		13,700,000,000
Nucleosynthesis	13,700,000		13,700,000,000
Star Formation	13,200,000		13,200,000,000
Milky Way Galaxy Formation	8,800,000		8,800,000,000
Solar System Formation	4,600,000		4,600,000,000
Simple Cells	3,600,000		3,600,000,000
Photosynthesis	3,000,000		3,000,000,000
Complex Cells	2,000,000		2,000,000,000
Sexual Reproduction	1,200,000		1,200,000,000
Multicellular Life	1,000,000		1,000,000,000
Fish	500,000		500,000,000
Land Plants	475,000		475,000,000
Insects	400,000		400,000,000
Amphibians	360,000		360,000,000
Reptiles	300,000		300,000,000
Mammals	200,000		200,000,000
Birds	150,000		150,000,000
Primates	75,000	3,000,000	75,000,000
Hominini	7,000	280,000	7,000,000
Homo Erectus	1,800	72,000	1,800,000
Homo Sapiens	200	8,000	200,000
Mitochondrial Eve	150	6,000	150,000
Y-Chromosomal Adam	140	5,600	140,000
Human Migration to South Asia	50	2,000	50,000
Human Migration to Europe	40	1,600	40,000
Domestication of the Wolf/Dog	15	600	15,000
Beginning of Agriculture	10	400	10,000
Beginning of the Calendar	2	80	2,000
Beginning of the United States	0	9	233

Chronology of the Universe, Wikipedia, http://en.wikipedia.org/wiki/Chronology_of_the_universe

Timeline of the Evolutionary History of Life, Wikipedia,
http://en.wikipedia.org/wiki/Timeline_of_the_evolutionary_history_of_life

Timeline of Human Evolution, Wikipedia,
http://en.wikipedia.org/wiki/Timeline_of_human_evolution

Chapter 7

Evolution

*What elegant simplicity—particles, cooling, a few natural processes,
self-assembly, variation, competition, the continuation of what works,
and the discontinuation of what does not work over and over again.*

The Evolution of the Universe

In the fractions of a second after the start of the universe some 13.7 billion years ago, elementary subatomic particles formed. As the universe cooled, the slower motion and greater density of these particles allowed the formation of the nuclei of simple atoms, like hydrogen, helium, and deuterium. As the universe cooled more, the even slower motion and greater density of these particles permitted nuclei to capture free electrons and simple atoms to form. As the universe cooled even more, the slower motion and greater densities of the simple atoms allowed them to aggregate.

The aggregation of atoms generates gravity, pressure, and heat. When enough hydrogen, helium, and deuterium aggregate, temperatures reach over 25 million degrees Kelvin, simple atoms fuse, and stars ignite. Two hydrogen protons form a deuterium nucleus and eject a positron and neutrino in the process. Large stars fuse the deuterium nuclei and heavier nuclei into all the elements on the periodic table up to iron. Then, as the largest of these stars exhaust their supplies of these lighter elements, they collapse and explode, creating pressures and temperatures that fuse the heavier elements.

Some of the exploded debris assembles into molecules or collections of atoms that share electrons. One carbon and two oxygen atoms assemble into carbon dioxide. One nitrogen and three hydrogen atoms form ammonia. One oxygen and two hydrogen atoms form water. The debris made up of light elements, heavy elements, and molecules coalesce into planets, asteroids, comets, and new stars. Comets of ice bombard planets, and liquids pool and evaporate. Planetary seas and atmospheres form. With the right combination of gases, liquids, temperature, and molecules, some of the molecules assemble into nucleotides and amino acids. Scientists replicate nucleotide and amino acid self-assembly in test tubes.

A study of the evolution of the universe suggests that scientists understand much of the 13.7-billion-year sequence of events. Scientists' explanations are logically coherent and supported by the (a) astronomical observations, (b) expansion of the universe, (c) cosmic microwave background radiation, (d) the relative amounts of light and heavy elements in the universe, galaxy, solar system, and on Earth, and (e) experimental data from all branches of science on natural processes.

The Evolution of Life

Like our knowledge about the first few seconds of the universe, the origin of the first cell and life is murky. Scientists know that early Earth was a hot, radioactive, and violent place 4 billion years ago. Asteroids and comets bombarded the planet with radioactive debris and water from earlier supernova explosions.[70] Gases from the debris and evaporation formed our atmosphere; water from the comets formed oceans. Given the available molecules, the early atmosphere would have been a mix of hydrogen, nitrogen, oxygen, carbon, carbon monoxide, carbon dioxide, and hydrogen sulfide. The oceans would have been quite acidic.[71]

After Earth's crust cooled, conditions were right for the building blocks of life to self-assemble.[72] Scientists discovered that amino acids, nucleobases, phospholipids, and RNA templates naturally form when they replicate these conditions, but they have yet to resolve how the building blocks of life became DNA, proto cells, and the first cell. Life originating in space and finding its way to Earth is a possibility, but the leading theory is that life originated deep in the ocean near a hydrothermal vent, and when conditions were just right, DNA and proto cells formed.[73]

Scientists know that once cellular life started, mutations, sex, and recombination varied cellular traits. The organisms that survive and reproduce increase the frequency of their kind and their heritable traits. Drawing resources from the environment, these organisms transform the resources around them. The environment acts on life, life acts on the environment, and the interaction changes the mix of traits that enables continued success. This ever-so-slow iterative interaction creates all the terrestrial lifeforms and transforms the Earth itself in the process.

One of the first organisms, the chemoautotrophs, used carbon dioxide to oxidize inorganic materials approximately 3.5 billion years ago. A little later, prokaryotes evolved. Prokaryotes free energy from organic molecules and store it as adenosine triphosphate (ATP), a process utilized in almost all organisms today. Photosynthesizing cyanobacteria evolved 3 billion years ago. They produce oxygen, and their arrival caused oxygen levels in the atmosphere to rise. Eukaryotic cells, membrane-bound organelles with diverse functions, appeared some 1.8 billion years ago.[74]

Mutations are changes in DNA sequences. They result from sections of a chromosome duplicating and inserting into a gene, or small parts of genes duplicating, recombining, and finding their way into a gene.[75] Ultraviolet radiation causes mutations, and it was much more intense when life started 3 to 4 billion years ago than it is today.[76] Sex and recombination involve the unraveling of two parents' chromosomes and a mixed recombination of them. Sex and recombination do not alter trait frequencies within gene pools, but they do produce offspring with new combinations of chromosomes.

The evolution of life accelerated with the rise of sexual reproduction approximately 1.2 billion years ago. Sexual reproduction creates more variation among offspring than mutations alone do. The traits that aid survival are "naturally selected" in the environment and become more prevalent in the population's gene pool over time.

The progression of life on Earth is dazzling. Protozoa emerged as little as 1 billion years ago. Enough oxygen accumulated in the atmosphere to form the ozone layer, shielding Earth from much of the deadly ultraviolet radiation, and enabling life to emerge on land some 580 million years ago. The earliest fungi evolved approximately 560 million years ago, the first vertebrates 485 million years ago, the first plants on land 434 million years ago, the first insects 363 million years ago, the first amphibians 340 million years ago, and the first reptiles 305 million years ago. The first dinosaurs appeared 225 million years ago, the first flowering plants 130 million years ago, and the first ants 80 million years ago. The earliest mammals arrived 30 million years ago, apelike animals 2 million years ago, Neanderthals 350 thousand years ago, and modern humans 200 thousand years ago.[77]

At least 3.5 billion years have passed since life began. To gain a sense of a billion years, consider that 100 human generations span 2,000 years, while 50 million human generations span a billion years. From the fossil records, carbon dating, and DNA records, scientists estimate that humans evolved from a more primitive species some 400,000 years ago, or 20 thousand generations ago.[78] Four hundred thousand years represents less than one-hundredth of a percent of the 3.5-billion-year period.

Today each of us is alive because of the successful struggle of some 20 thousand generations of human ancestors, as well as the successful struggles of all the species from which humans descended. To think we are the result of 13.7 billion years of the universe's evolution and over 3.5 billion years of proto cell, cell, organism, and species struggle is mindboggling, ennobling, and humbling. Just pondering the viruses, bacteria, and natural predators that the 20 thousand generations of our human ancestors overcame makes one realize how consequential some battles are and how long their effects ripple through time.

A study of the evolution of life reveals scientists' detailed understanding of most of the 4-billion-year sequence of events. When we carefully consider scientists' narratives with an open mind, we find that their explanations are logically coherent and supported by the (a) fossil record, (b) anatomical and time-related progression of species, (c) selective breeding experiences, (d) experimental data from all branches of science on natural processes, (e) cellular commonality, and (f) progression of DNA sequences.

Competition and Comparative Advantage

Competitions drive evolution. They winnow the slackers from the enterprising, the weak from the strong, the losers from the winners. They force individuals and organizations to perform—to learn, prepare, work hard, and innovate. They cause people to give their best efforts. They determine whose progeny and genes continue; whose perspectives, practices, and priorities prevail; and which schools, universities, enterprises, governments, and countries endure.

Without competitions, people take advantage of their positions, shirk responsibility, and freeload. Religions and political parties take their members for granted. Governments abuse rather than serve their citizens. Businesses provide inferior products and services. Teachers and professors with tenure do not work as hard as those without tenure.

Though some participants in competitions lose, comparative advantage assures that there are opportunities for everyone. The comparative advantage insight originates in economics and explains the benefits of trade between countries.

Comparative Advantage is the reality that when individuals or countries specialize and trade, each doing what he, she, or it does best, each party benefits. Even when one party does everything more efficiently than the other, each party benefits from specializing, selling some output, and using the proceeds to purchase what others do best.

Comparative advantage makes competition palatable. When we lose in one arena, we can succeed in other ones. If we do not make the high school basketball team, we may make the swim or volleyball teams. Or, if we are artistic, we might sing in the chorus, play in the band, or act in a drama production. Even though some people might do all these activities better than us, they do not have time to do them all. If we search and persist, we find openings and opportunities. Competition condemns no one to ongoing failure. Only resignation—something in our control—perpetuates failure.

Because we do not have the time and energy to enter all competitions, and our opportunity to win some of them is greater than others, judicious selection of competitions improves our likelihood of success.

Competitions benefit both the winners and losers. Winners secure favorable positions and losers learn and hone their skills. When we compete for a job and do not receive it, we improve our job interviewing skills. When we compete for a position that requires training and certification, we improve from the training and certification even if we do not get the job.

We also benefit from the reality that competitions make everything which we depend upon work better. Competitions allocate positions and resources to those who most ably use them. When we award positions in a competitive manner and only retain those who perform well, the ablest people occupy the positions in our organizations. CEOs who competitively earn their positions are the ones most likely to make their organizations flourish. Teachers who competitively win their positions are the best instructors. Police officers who competitively earn their positions are the ones most able to keep our neighborhoods safe. We benefit from all these competitions in the form of better-functioning schools, enterprises, communities, and governments, even if we do not directly win any of the competitions.

Need stimulates our appetite for competition. Affluence diminishes it. When we need something, we willingly expend the energy to secure it. When we have everything we need, we conserve our energy, avoid competitions, and atrophy. When poor people do not have comfortable social safety nets, they develop their skills, look for work, and find it. A little work improves their lives much more than it improves the lives of wealthy people.

Although few of us consider it, competition supports our representative democracy and free enterprise system. We form our views from the information we receive from competing news organizations. We select our products and services from arrays of competing ones. We choose our elected officials from slates of competing candidates, and our representatives select our policies from numerous competing ones.

Without competition, leaders, political parties, journalists, and scientists do not have enough incentive to challenge one another's self-serving actions and inaction. They are less honest, do not work as hard, and do not innovate as much. Those assigning jobs give them to their friends rather than to the best applicants. Incompetent people become leaders, researchers, doctors, engineers, and teachers. Inefficiency increases, little works well, and living standards decline. While competition is hard on some individuals, history demonstrates repeatedly that its benefits outweigh all other alternatives.

And despite what some people say, competitions among countries need not result in war. Countries can compete with one another and peacefully coexist when they (a) have access to needed resources, (b) stabilize their population growth, (c) maintain physical, technological, financial, and military fitness, and (d) have healthy inter-country relationships. We need only look to the Swiss to see how this is done. In the middle of war-torn Europe, the Swiss have lived peacefully for more than 150 years, and they have done this by satisfying these conditions.

Competition is a) two or more ideas, practices, or things vying for some form of superiority, or b) two or more organisms battling for territory, resources, mates, influence, or existence.

Competitions improve the effectiveness of our organizations, enterprises, and government. They make us fitter, lower the costs of goods and services, and improve the accuracy of our views and the quality of our lives. While the best leaders, teachers, coaches, and parents may choose to shield our youngest children from competition for 4 to 5 years, they otherwise embrace it, understanding that competitions create individual, organizational, and population excellence; competitions are the most objective, fair, and effective method for allocating resources and positions; and comparative advantage assures there are opportunities for everyone.

Natural Selection and Gradualism

Before the 1800s, no one imagined that life was the handiwork of a simple natural process and billions of years. Natural selection, undetectable in one generation, becomes detectable and comprehensible over several generations. Charles Darwin, the first to recognize this process, wrote in 1859:

> Owing to this struggle, variations, however slight and from whatever cause proceeding, if they may be in any degree profitable to an individual of a species, in their infinitely complex relations to other organic beings and to their physical conditions of life, will tend to the preservation of such individuals, and will generally be inherited by the offspring. The offspring, also, will thus have a better chance of surviving, for, of the many individuals of any species which are periodically born, but a small number can survive. I have called this principle, by which each slight variation, if useful, is preserved, by the term Natural Selection, in order to mark its relation to man's power of selection.[79] . . . One general law, leading to the advancement of all organic beings—namely, multiply, vary, let the strongest live and the weakest die.[80]

Natural selection requires generations, inheritable traits, variation of the traits, and competition—conditions that are characteristic of all life. All organisms live, reproduce, and die. Their lifespans range from hours to hundreds of years, but in all cases, their lives follow this pattern. All organisms can have offspring with a different mix of inheritable characteristics. Mutations, intercourse, gene recombination, and gene flow cause these traits to vary among organisms and across generations.

The offspring of all organisms inhabit competitive environments. If territory and resources initially are ample, the organisms proliferate to the point that the territory and resources become in short supply. Once life establishes itself in an area, territories and resources take work to acquire. The offspring that are better able to fulfill their needs and reproduce in the environment continue. They are "naturally selected," and the frequency of their traits increases in the population. This ever-so-slow generational and iterative process evolves all lifeforms.

Natural Selection is a natural process that requires inheritable traits, variation of the traits, generations, and competition, where those organisms better suited for their environments place more offspring into the next generation, increasing the frequency of the genes governing the advantageous traits.

As hard as it is to believe, all organisms—bacteria, algae, fungi, worms, spiders, bananas, frogs, crocodiles, robins, monkeys, and humans—result from a long series of successive and infinitesimally small changes over large spans of time. The concept of gradualism helps us understand evolution and the process of natural selection.

Gradualism is the reality that a series of imperceptible, small changes accumulate into tremendous, unrecognizable transformations over large spans of time.

Consider the evolution of giraffes from a species similar in nature to the zebra. Some 30 to 50 million years ago, zebra-like animals were numerous on the plains of Africa. Some of these zebra-like animals had slightly longer necks and could graze on the higher vegetation. These animals could feed themselves, survive, and successfully reproduce when the vegetation closer to the ground became in short supply. As these flourishing longer-necked animals mated with one another, more of their longer-neck genes populated this gene pool. As this process occurred iteratively over hundreds of years, a reach advantage of inches became feet.

Giraffes with necks longer than modern giraffes did not do well. Their necks were too long and interfered with daily life. These giraffes did not reproduce as well as their shorter-neck counterparts. In this manner, natural selection lengthened the necks of giraffes to the point where longer necks provided an advantage in feeding, but not a disadvantage in daily living.

The ability of the longer-necked animals to survive and successfully reproduce provides an example of how a series of small changes accumulated into a large one over generations. Amazingly, each form of life has changed and adapted to its environment in a similar manner, but because the process is glacially slow, it is imperceptible to us.

The breeding of animals by humans for hundreds of years is an example of a directed selection process. We can see the handiwork of this iterative selection or "breeding" in dogs. From the Chihuahua to the Great Dane, all the breeds of dogs descend from a common gray wolf ancestor that lived some 130 thousand years ago and people's selection of offspring with various desired traits over thousands of years.[81] World-renowned Harvard biologist E. O. Wilson writes:

> The theory of population genetics, and experiments on other organisms, show that substantial changes can occur in the span of less than 100 generations, which for man reaches back to the time of the Roman Empire.[82]

The domestic turkey, with which I have years of experience, is now over two hundred generations removed from the wild turkey. By selectively breeding the white-feathered, broader-breasted, faster-growing turkeys, breeders have made commercial turkeys very different from wild turkeys in relatively few generations. The evolution of life and natural selection become clearer to us as we selectively breed plants and animals. College students can observe this process in shorter maturation species like fruit flies in biology courses in just a few weeks.

Interrelated Products of the Past

It is a mistake to think that the past is dead. Nothing that has ever happened is quite without influence at this moment. The present is merely the past rolled up and concentrated in this second of time. You, too, are your past; often your face is your autobiography; you are what you are because of what you have been; because of your heredity stretching back into forgotten generations; because of every element of environment that has affected you, every man or woman that has met you, every book that you have read, every experience that you have had; all these are accumulated in your memory, your body, your character, your soul. So, with a city, a country, and a race; it is its past, and cannot be understood without it.[83]

—Will and Ariel Durant

From every existing cell's architecture and DNA, scientists know that at least one original cell became a reproductive dividing machine. This cell and its progeny outcompeted all other cells, and since its formation, no other cell seems to have formed from scratch and parented life. All the living cells that scientists have examined appear to come from divisions of this first dominant cell. One human body alone is comprised of a few trillion cells. Imagine the cell divisions that have occurred from the original dominant cell throughout the last 3.5 billion years to form every bit of life and cell that has ever lived on Earth.

Germ cells—those in ovaries and testes—start all forms of life and make the interrelatedness of life possible. They are immortal. They do not age. Under the right conditions and with access to the necessary resources, they may divide ad infinitum. It is the somatic cells, the rest of the cells in our bodies, which age and die.

Thus, we share an interrelated past with all life on Earth. We share a common human ancestor with all other people and common ancestors with primates. We share common ancestors with mammals, reptiles, amphibians, insects, fish, and plants. Most amazing of all, it appears that we share basic nucleotide sequences of the first surviving cell with all terrestrial lifeforms.

The evolution of the universe and life is wondrous in every sense of the word! Science reveals how the universe and life evolve but nothing about why they evolve. Implicit in why is "intent"; scientists find no more intent in evolution than in the flow of a river.

The universe and life as we know it are the cards nature deals us. Perhaps it does not matter why. What matters is what we do with these cards—how we advantageously align with the flow; utilize our circumstances and gifts to advance our families, communities, country, and life; and bridge the 13.7-billion-year past and future.

Evolution – the gradual change of the universe, life, organization, government, culture, or something else over time. In the case of the evolution of life, it involves variation, inheritable traits, generations, comparative advantage, competition, and natural selection, where organisms better suited for their environments place more offspring into the next generation, increasing the frequency of the genes governing the most advantageous traits.

Chapter 8

Fitness

To be or not to be?
—William Shakespeare

Shakespeare's character Hamlet, contemplating existence, poses the question of all questions. While humans sometimes ponder this conundrum, most forms of life just want "to be" by nature. The instinct "to be" is the natural impulse of life that supports the existence of organisms, families, communities, enterprises, countries, and cultures. If this were not the case, these lifeforms and organizations of life would "not be" because being is difficult.

Meritocracy

We always have needed territory, water, food, and shelter to survive. Our continuation depends on these things. For most of us, however, our ancestors secured our territory, and now we only need to purchase or rent a small slice of it, contribute to its defense, earn our livelihoods, buy our resources, and pay our taxes to exist. The defense of territory and procurement of resources for many in the West have become so easy that we forget that we require them. We forget that organisms and groups must win a long series of minor and major competitions for them, and that we only flourish as we prevent others from taking our territory and resources. We hold our ground, or we perish. This has been the reality for billions of years, and it will not change in our lifetimes.

As much as some of us would like to live apart from nature, remove ourselves from competition, and avoid the work of being fit, such thinking is fanciful and foolish. Individuals and organizations wither without competition and the winnowing of the fit from the unfit. One world order, a socialist state, monopolies, quotas, price controls, and socialism are futile pursuits. They are corrupting, debilitating, temporary, and contrary to evolution, and they eventually give way to competitive and meritocratic arrangements.

Meritocracy assigns the fittest, or the ablest and most qualified people, to the available roles and positions within a group regardless of age, gender, religion, race, or ethnicity.

I only introduce meritocracy here and note that it is an essential part of fitness in this chapter. A more detailed discussion of it appears in Chapter 44.

Procreation

Besides assigning roles and positions meritoriously, fitness requires procreation. It requires organisms to place as many or more offspring into the next generation as their competitors. Most forms of life are programmed to do this. It is in their DNA and they cannot do otherwise. Humans have choice, and today many couples choose to have fewer children and fewer domestic demands. Those begetting fewer children want compelling careers and express concern about the finite carrying capacity of Earth. Those having several children play out the program that nature gives us.

Unfortunately, there is a downside to having fewer children that most people do not consider. Having fewer than 2.1 children per family on average erodes the vitality of a population and culture. The numbers shrink. Its ability to defend itself, its culture, its winning perspectives and practices, and its influence all decline, while the ability of other populations to do these things grows.

Procreation is the tendency for people to mate and parent children. Family sizes of 2.1 children per female maintain a population, and larger ones increase it.

We may think we would be happier without children, choose our career over having children, and think that having children harms the environment, but we need to replace and increase our numbers to maintain our relevance. We do not need to out-procreate every competitor, but we do need to remain competitive over time. Our personal desires and concern for Earth's ecology do not change our need for demographic and cultural fitness.

Countries may augment their numbers with immigrants, but immigrants who do not assimilate create minority subcultures and crippling division. They decrease the prevalence of a highly successful population's Winning Perspectives and Practices and its fitness. The U.S., France, Germany, Greece, the United Kingdom, and Sweden currently have these problems.

So how do we maintain relevance but not overpopulate the world? And, how can we enjoy a high quality of life without degrading the environment? The solution lies in working with other countries to reduce population growth, just as we work with them to reduce nuclear weapons; more specifically, we succeed by utilizing the Winning Practices described in this book.

Generally, we do not see the Islamic cultures as being particularly successful, but they are highly successful. Like medieval Christianity, most expressions of Islam are extremely Darwinian. They encourage their practitioners to have large families. We can see this from Islamic teachings and by examining the growth of Islamic populations over time. Islamic numbers have grown from 0 to 1.8 billion people and one-quarter of the world's population in just 1,400 years. No other religious group has achieved such growth so quickly.

Figure 9 compares the U.S., Islamic, and world populations over time. At current growth rates, Islamic numbers will grow to 5.9 billion people and almost half of the world's population in 100 years. Without immigrants, the U.S. shrinks.[84] With immigrants, our population grows from 325 to 650 million or about 5 percent of the world's population.

	2015 Population in Millions	Percent of World Population	Percent Annual Growth Rate	Years to Double	Population After 100 Years in Millions	Percent of World Population
Figure 9: Comparison of the U.S. and Islamic Populations Over Time						
U.S. Population	325	5	0.7	99	650	5
Islamic Population	1,800	25	1.2	58	5,930	45
World Population	7,300	100	0.6	63	13,300	100

https://en.wikipedia.org/wiki/List_of_countries_by_population_growth_rate
http://www.pewresearch.org/fact-tank/2017/04/06/why-muslims-are-the-worlds-fastest-growing-religious-group/
https://www.nationmaster.com/country-info/stats/People/Population-in-2015

The unstated and underlying aim of most expressions of Islam is population growth. Most adherents are taught to maintain their faith and distinctive dress, disperse throughout the world, have large families, convert other people to their faith, and gradually change the ethnic mix, culture, and laws of a country. The Islamic threat to the non-Islamic world is not terrorism, but demographic and cultural in nature.

From an evolutionary perspective, Jewish populations have the meritocracy aspect of fitness right, and Islamic populations have the procreation aspect of it right. Most developed Western populations have both wrong; more recently, China has both right.

Procreation and immigration are part of life, and what the Islamic populations are doing is nothing new. They are just doing it more successfully now than other populations. In the 17th and 18th centuries, the English and Spanish populations were very Darwinian. They seeded new lands with their people and cultures and nearly annihilated the indigenous people of North America, Central America, South America, Australia, and New Zealand. Their Darwinian actions in the 18th century set up our dominance in the 19th and 20th centuries. UCLA professor of geography and Pulitzer Prize winning author Jared Diamond indicates that such ruthless dominance has been the norm for thousands of years:

Twelve thousand years ago, everybody on Earth was a hunter-gatherer; now almost all of us are farmers or else are fed by farmers. The spread of farming from those few sites of origin usually did not occur as a result of the hunter-gatherers elsewhere adopting farming; hunter-gatherers tend to be conservative. . . . Instead, farming spread mainly through farmers outbreeding hunters, developing more potent technology, and then killing the hunters or driving them off all lands suitable for agriculture.[85]

Those who think that we have evolved beyond this Darwinian behavior are sadly mistaken. Such behavior has been the way of all life for millions of years. Our DNA carries instructions for domination, and whenever territory and resources are scarce, ruthlessness and self-righteous justifications for it emerge. Thus, we can no more unilaterally decrease our procreative, political, economic, or military power than our nuclear power. Just as we only decrease our nuclear arsenal as our competitor, Russia, decreases its arsenal, so we can only decrease our procreation as China, India, Brazil, and the Islamic countries decrease their procreation.

A study of evolution, the universe, and life also suggests that one day we will face competition from extraterrestrial life. This is not certain but it is likely. The redundancy observed throughout the universe, the predisposition of the universe and life to self-assemble, and the existence of billions of potentially habitable planets all suggest that the universe probably is teeming with life. This insight raises a question that I oftentimes posed to my management teams over the years: Are we fit enough to withstand the competition from unknown as well as known sources?

Fitter organisms must have the offspring, and the offspring must realize as much of their potential as possible for a population to succeed over time. Ironically, as Western countries grow more complex, those who are the least fit for modern life have many children and those who are most fit have few children.

Although our ancestors did not understand evolution, they worked out many advantageous practices to raise fit and well-adjusted children. The practices of postponing sex until marriage, marrying young, having larger families, and cherishing lifelong marriages gave us large numbers of well-adjusted, able children.

Contrast these past practices to the current practices of "hooking up," separating, single-parenting, and having small families, and one quickly gains a sense of our procreative and child- development failures. Where past generations focused more on the next generation, we focus more on ourselves. Birth control, abortion-on-demand, recreational sex, career-centric fathers and mothers, weak marriage commitments, STDs, and infertility all diminish our population's long-term health, development, and viability.

Our current practice of channeling one-third of our public resources to less fit and productive people is also counterproductive. Such misguided policies increase poverty and human suffering over time. Channeling more of these resources into research and development, general fitness, and the colonization of space would enhance our fitness and benefit future generations more. In later chapters, I discuss superior, less costly ways to empower people and reduce poverty.

To be clear, I am not suggesting that we should control people's procreation, but I am suggesting that our culture and policies should encourage fit, married people to have children and discourage unmarried people from having them. Although this approach might seem old-fashioned, it aligns with the practices of the most successful cultures. Moreover, it diminishes human suffering and improves a people's health and fitness over time.

Consider the effects of the following six realities, first individually and then collectively. While each reality should concern us, the six realities together are tantamount to cultural suicide and the surrender of all we hold dear. They are a disaster for our great-grandchildren and should cause us to change our ways.

1. At current growth rates, the number of Muslims in the world will increase by several billion in the next one hundred years.

2. Most Muslims have perspectives and practices that are antithetical to traditional Western ones.

3. As extremist members of these groups attack us, rather than decisively retaliating against the governments who fund them and the mullahs who instruct them, we only pursue those committing the violent acts. Rather than prohibiting the entry of the zealous mullahs and Muslims into our country, we invite them and financially support many of them. Rather than acting to expeditiously end the conflicts and discourage future attacks, our actions oftentimes prolong the conflicts, maim our youth, and drain our treasury.

4. We have children at rates that do not sustain our population and culture.

5. Many of the people who have children are the people least able to raise them.

6. Though our numbers decrease, and Muslim numbers rapidly increase, we expend massive amounts of resources to advance democracy throughout the world.

We do not foresee the cumulative and long-term effects of our policies, programs, and practices. If we did, we would change them.

The Underlying Aim of Life

Thomas Jefferson wrote in the Declaration of Independence:

We hold these truths to be self-evident, that all [people] are created equal, that they are endowed by their creator with certain unalienable rights, that among these are life, liberty, and the pursuit of happiness.[86]

Somehow, many people have interpreted this declaration of people's equality before the law and basic rights to primarily be about the pursuit of happiness. This is unfortunate, as those who pursue happiness seldom find it. In my experience, the happiest people are those who pursue fitness, or in other words, people who maintain their health, treat others well, apply themselves in school, make their marriage work, parent children well, earn their livelihood, contribute to their communities, and mentor their grandchildren.

Happiness is not the aim of life. Fitness is the aim of life. Fitness brings happiness and is its own reward. Fitness brings us health, competence, and affiliation with able people. It brings us the esteem of others, desirable mates, and longevity. It brings us offspring and the continuation of our culture and institutions.

Evolution delineates our end and circumscribes our means. It gives us some latitude to be foolish in the short term but not the long term. It reveals that fitness is our end, and unilaterally shrinking our population assures irrelevance and extinction. The sooner we make fitness our individual, familial, and collective goal, the sooner we will rediscover our way, enjoy greater success, and find greater happiness.

Fitness – the ability of organisms to flourish, procure needed resources, and reproduce relative to other organisms. Fitness is the underlying aim of life and its own reward.

Chapter 9

Human Nature

We avoid pain and pursue pleasure. We compete for resources, mates, and influence. We pursue our self-interest and children's interests first, our affiliated interests second, and others' interests third. These inclinations work on us 24 hours a day, 7 days a week.

Scientists have persuasively demonstrated that genes direct the development of our bodies and our inclinations. Genes nudge us to engage in numerous behaviors that aid survival and perpetuate our DNA. If this were not the case, we would exit the evolutionary stage.

The consistency with which our genes drive our inclinations results in common tendencies that we call human nature. Naturalist Charles Darwin and psychologist Abraham Maslow did an excellent job characterizing human nature and identifying a hierarchy of human needs. My thoughts build on their insights.

Individual Nature

Seeking pleasure and avoiding pain are fundamental to our well-being. They are life-preserving inclinations. We eat food and drink water because they sustain us, alleviate pain, and bring pleasure. We procure clothing, shelter, and security because they protect us, comfort us, and relieve pain. These tendencies are self-evident. We would not live long without them.

Other tendencies are psychological, less obvious, and often culturally shaped. We work to earn money to purchase the things that bring us pleasure. We work to obtain social acceptance and the esteem of others. We tell the truth to gain our parents' approval and avoid their anger. In these instances, the pleasure sought and the pain avoided are not physical but psychological. They are shaped by our genes, families, cultures, and environments.

We have strong inclinations to understand the world, develop, and actualize. We devote large portions of our time and resources to learning and developing skills. We attend school for 13 or more years and spend weeks, months, and years learning our jobs. We also want to play on the stage. If we have musical ability, we make beautiful music. If we have artistic talent, we create beautiful art. If we have athletic ability, we compete in athletic competitions. If we have leadership ability, we lead. We develop and deploy the predilections that we inherit and that others encourage.

We are self-centered creatures, especially when we are young. Life is about us. When we are parents, life is largely about our children and us. When we are grandparents, life is about our children, grandchildren, and us. We focus on ourselves and our progeny much more than on others. Self-centered tendencies diminish as we age and as our parents, schools, workplaces, and culture teach us to care about others.

Because we evolved primarily at a time when there was more benefit to short-term rather than long-term thinking, we are short-term oriented. We respond to short-term rewards more than long-term ones. Our short-term tendencies are most apparent in impatient infants and young children. Without strong cultural conditioning to learn to defer gratification, these inclinations do not end in childhood.

Adults who do not learn to defer gratification continue to live impulsively, purchasing things with credit rather than with cash and lowering their living standards 10 to 20 percent.

Our short-term orientation comes not only from a natural impatience but also from a tendency to overweigh what is freshest in our minds. Recent memories dominate longer-term ones. After a series of misfortunes, we become pessimistic. After a run of good fortune, we become overconfident. We want to invest in the assets that did well last year, even though they cost more, and avoid assets that declined in value and are more likely to appreciate.

Our short-term tendencies make many of the activities that lead to success in modern life—like studiousness, frugality, perseverance, and accomplishment—difficult for us. They make rising after several defeats and exercising good judgment after several successes challenging.

Most of us also prefer smaller definite rewards to larger uncertain ones. Our aversion to losses makes entrepreneurship and investing unappealing to most people, and it is a primary reason entrepreneurs and investors must have substantial opportunities to profit. Without substantial opportunities to profit, people are too risk-averse to start businesses, save, invest, and undertake many of the other activities that improve our lives.

We also have a strong desire to create homes and reside in aesthetically pleasing places. Homes are comfortable refuges, opportunities to actualize, and statements of social status. We spend many resources and much discretionary time procuring and shaping our homes.

Familial Nature

Along with our individual nature, we have a strong familial one. We want to love, be loved, procreate, and see our children and grandchildren flourish. We fall in love, mate, have children, and spend 20 to 30 years raising our children. Then, we help our children raise their children for 20 to 30 years. If this were not the case, our species would not do well. Familial tendencies are so strong that they dominate adult motivation.

Social Nature

Along with our individual and familial natures, we have a social nature. At some point in our past, our ancestors found living in groups beyond the family advantageous. In groups, they could better defend themselves. They could more easily build homes, grow food, kill five-ton mastodons, and clothe themselves. E. O. Wilson observes:

> The only other mammalian carnivores that take outsized prey are lions, hyenas, wolves, and African wild dogs. Each of these species has an exceptionally advanced social life, prominently featuring the pursuit of prey in coordinated packs. . . . Primitive [humans] are ecological analogs of lions, wolves, and hyenas. . . . And they resemble four-footed carnivores more than other primates by habitually slaughtering surplus prey, storing food, feeding solid food to their young, dividing labor, practicing cannibalism, and interacting aggressively with competing species. Bones and stone tools dug from ancient campsites in Africa, Europe, and Asia indicate that this way of life persisted for a million years or longer and was abandoned in most societies only during the last few thousands of years.[87]

Scientists consider animals that ally with others to be "super-organisms." Superorganism affiliation conveys fitness—the strength found in numbers, economies of scale, and opportunities to specialize, trade, and synergize.

*A **Superorganism** is a subpopulation of a species bound together genetically, biologically, and sometimes culturally that functions and competes as a unit.*

Ants form colonies; bees, hives; wolves, packs; lions, prides; gorillas, troops; and humans—families, clans, tribes, cities, states, and countries. Humans belong to numerous superorganisms simultaneously and form clubs, associations, enterprises, universities, international alliances, and countless other organizations.

Eons of natural selection have honed our social and superorganism nature. We are fitter allying with others—specializing, trading, and affecting the agendas of groups. Thus, we want to be accepted and appreciated by those in groups. We want to fit in, adhere to the group's norms, complete group assignments, and improve our standing within groups.

We also have a very strong natural tendency to absorb the thinking of our groups and disregard information that challenges it. This inclination furthers affiliation and our opportunity to reap its benefits. It increases our ability to work with others and strengthens groups. And most of the time, we are not even aware of this tendency. It eludes us when we are inside groups and frustrates us when we are outside of groups.

Once we understand our superorganism and social nature and its importance, we realize that (a) the individual is not preeminent, (b) we have individual, familial, and social natures, (c) we must balance the requisites of these natures, and (d) sometimes we must sacrifice our desires and selves for a larger group.

Environmental Alignment

Our genes did an excellent job of driving our behaviors when we were hunter-gathers living in hunter-gather environments; as E. O. Wilson notes:

The selection pressures of hunter-gatherer existence persisted for over 99 percent of human evolution.[88]

But this is no longer the case. Most humans no longer live in small, mobile groups or tribes comprised of individuals who spend most of their time defending themselves and securing scarce nutrients on African savannas. As our environment has become significantly different from that of hunter-gatherers, we have had to consciously direct more of our behaviors and override some of our genetic inclinations. Natural selection takes generations to shape our genetic inclinations. When our environment changes a lot in just a few generations, as has been the case in the last 150 years, the ability for leaders, parents, and teachers to enculturate us with different tendencies has become extremely important.

Tobacco, alcohol, drugs, caffeine, sweets, fats, salt, and pornography were not readily available throughout our evolutionary history. Thus, natural selection has not populated the gene pool with genomes that incline us to avoid these things, and thus these pleasure-titillating substances and activities pose serious challenges to us. Once they pleasure our brains, we want more of them even though they may be harmful to us. If we are fortunate, our parents, teachers, coaches, and mentors teach us to avoid many destructive behaviors and substances. If we are not so fortunate, we must develop an aversion to them ourselves.

We also want to create laws, policies, institutions, and environments to mitigate these challenges as much as possible because it is tough for people to counter these tendencies on their own. Getting people to avoid highly addictive substances and activities that can cause cravings 24 hours a day, 7 days a week takes concerted effort.

If we want to improve our families and institutions, we must utilize practices developed with an understanding of human nature. Ignorance of human nature coupled with the attempt to improve the world has serious unintended consequences. David Brooks writes:

I believe we inherit a great river of knowledge, a flow of patterns coming from many sources. The information that comes from deep in the evolutionary past we call genetics. The information passed along from hundreds of years ago we call culture. The information passed along from decades ago we call family, and the information offered months ago we call education. But it is all information that flows through us. The brain is adapted to the river of knowledge and exists only as a creature in that river. Our thoughts are profoundly molded by this long historic flow, and none of us exists, self-made, in isolation from it.[89]

The genius of prudently regulated free enterprise and free markets is that when they are tempered by common ethics, sound laws, and an effective justice system, they work with human nature, encouraging people to pursue their self-interest in ways that benefit the larger superorganism. Entrepreneurs and employees who work hard to prosper improve the affordability and desirability of products and services.

Unlike free enterprise, socialism does not harness people's self-interest, and socialistic, non-meritocratic groups eventually lose to freer, meritocratic ones. People's rewards must vary with the risks they take and their quantity and quality of work. People cannot be demeaned and ostracized for working hard, taking risks, and doing well as they frequently are in socialistic arrangements.

Free enterprise sometimes offends our sense of fairness but improves our living standards. Socialism mollifies our sense of fairness but diminishes our living standards. In Chapters 36, 37, and 45, I describe stakeholder inclusion and Goldilocks minimum wage arrangements that make free enterprise fairer, align with human nature, and enhance living standards.

Human nature is one of the cards that nature deals us. It is not something that we can change in our lifetimes. Winning Practices harness human nature and stream positive effects. Losing practices ignore human nature and stream unintended consequences. Understanding human nature and aligning our policies, organizations, and practices with it improve our fitness and well-being dramatically.

Human Nature – a collection of universal individual, familial, and social tendencies that include: (a) avoiding pain and pursuing pleasure, (b) seeking water, food, clothing, shelter, security, and others' esteem, (c) understanding the world, developing, and actualizing, (d) seeking money, power, and influence, (e) loving, being loved, and procreating, (f) doing the best by one's children, (g) having a short-term orientation, (h) having an aversion to losses, (i) securing aesthetically pleasing environments, (j) affiliating with others in mutually beneficial ways, (k) absorbing others' thinking, and (l) pursuing one's interests first, the interests of those with whom we affiliate second, and the interests of others last.

Chapter 10

Culture

While many things are necessary to flourish, the overarching one is culture, one of the most potent and poorly understood forces on the planet. Like the air we breathe, its effects remain unnoticed until it fails.

"Culture" means different things to different people. In the broadest sense, culture encompasses the norms—perspectives, practices, and prohibitions—and the history, art, laws, institutions, technologies, and special occasions that a group of people shares. At the core of culture—and what I focus on—are the perspectives, practices, and prohibitions common within a group.

Culture is the shared beliefs and practices that guide people's discretionary behavior.

Culture can be thought of as human software, a secondary operating system that is layered onto our instinctual one. Culture affects our attitudes, actions, and interactions with others; our ability to lead, be led, and function in groups; and every level of human organization—the individual, family, group, education, enterprise, and government.

Cultural norms form around people's history, ethnicity, gender, age, relatedness, education, profession, living standard, and political and religious affiliations. They help us with our roles as citizens, men, women, children, students, spouses, parents, grandparents, employees, and members of religious and political communities. Cultural norms assist us with the universal challenges of the division of territory and resources, people's admittance into groups, the assessment of their standing, and the removal of people from groups.[90]

Why does culture work? Culture works because we find strength, instruction, opportunities for specialization, exchange, synergy, and economies in groups and because we have evolved to affiliate with groups to realize these benefits. Being alone is painful, so we naturally seek others' companionship, acceptance, and esteem. We feel pride when we please those in our social circles and shame when we disappoint them. We want to be good and loyal members of our groups as opposed to bad and disloyal ones.[91]

Consequently, we are tribal. We divide into "we(s)" and "they(s)" with our families, schools, companies, communities, and country being our modern-day tribes. We are comfortable with our "we(s)" and uncomfortable with many "they(s)." We like those who are similar to us and are suspicious of those who are unfamiliar. We help those in our groups and tend to avoid, discriminate against, and sometimes even demonize outsiders.

What our groups deem acceptable and unacceptable circumscribes much of our behavior. It affects what we do, what we do not do, and what we become over time. If our group believes we can accomplish anything with education and hard work, we oftentimes do. On the other hand, if our group thinks we are victims, and education and work are of little consequence, we tend to accomplish less.

Transmission of culture happens whether we are aware of it or not. Families, schools, workplaces, religious institutions, news organizations, prominent figures, and more recently, producers of television, movies, and social media are the primary transmitters of culture. They pass their perspectives, practices, and prohibitions to us, and they reinforce the transmissions by whom and what they recognize and shun.

Divisions and mergers of groups occur periodically. Historically, tribes divided when leaders and viable portions of the group had irreconcilable differences and went their separate ways. Tribes merged when they became vulnerable, and the men of one tribe killed the men of another one and integrated the women into their tribe. Deteriorating leadership, culture, and group cohesiveness are primary causes of divisions and mergers.[92] Network effects and economies of scale cause groups to merge more than divide.

Divisions and mergers of companies, schools, and communities adhere to a legal process and proceed civilly, while divisions and mergers of countries may be civil or violent. The former Soviet Union provides an example of a violent merger of disparate peoples and a relatively civil separation of them decades later. The reunification of East and West Germany in the 1990s exemplifies a civil merger.

Cultural Relativism

Cultural relativism, a concept found in Anthropology and Sociology and widely accepted in academic institutions today, is a world view that has weakened American culture, fueled polarization, and slowed our progress.

Cultural Relativism is the idea that no one has a basis to judge the perspectives and practices of people of other cultures, and that no culture is better than another.

Cultural relativism makes people feel good but is not true and causes people to suspend critical judgments. Some cultures benefit their members more than others as we see by comparing the quality of life in North and South Korea, Haiti and Switzerland, and Singapore and Afghanistan. Viewing all cultures as equally desirable is like viewing all children's work as equally meritorious.

Not making distinctions between sloppy and well-organized, factually correct and incorrect, and dysfunctional and functional work negatively affects learning. And, not making distinctions between the advantageous and disadvantageous perspectives, practices, and prohibitions adversely affects people's acquisition of beneficial practices. Cultural relativism does not allow us to prescribe personal, social, or economic improvements. To be effective, successful, and persist through time, we must make such qualitative distinctions among perspectives, practices, and prohibitions and teach our children to make them as well.

So how do we further cultural harmony and still make qualitative distinctions? We let others—those who mean us no harm and do not infringe on our freedoms—be; then critically examine ours and others' perspectives, practices, and prohibitions; reject and stigmatize the undesirable ones; and test, support, and adopt the advantageous ones. And to be clear, we do these things with the perspectives, practices, and prohibitions of cultures—not with the goodhearted, law-abiding people of the cultures.

The Path of Fitness

Some cultures benefit their members more than others. This is obvious in the extreme. Being born in South Korea, Switzerland, or Singapore is far more advantageous than being born in North Korea, Haiti, or Afghanistan. Typically, however, a culture's comparative desirability is more difficult to determine. We must compare the trending fitness of populations or examine whether the underlying population moves along the Path of Fitness.

The Path of Fitness is a cultural trajectory or collection of perspectives, practices, and prohibitions that provides a large and increasing portion of a population (a) protection from predatory people, groups, and countries, (b) clean water and healthy diets, (c) adequate clothing and necessities, (d) individual, marital, and family rights, (e) quality healthcare, (f) desirable education, occupation, and residency opportunities, (g) sustainable lifestyles, and (h) three-generation life expectancy.

Effective cultures steadily improve people's well-being and fitness. They align individual purpose with the public interest. The most effective cultures in the age of science, technology, and large populations are the ones with a Judeo, Protestant, or Confucius basis or those found in Northern Europe, Canada, Australia, New Zealand, the United States, Singapore, Hong Kong, Taiwan, Japan, South Korea, Israel, and China.[93] But even these cultures do not remain effective forever. Too often, success leads to arrogance, and arrogance leads to poor judgment, loss of discipline and drive, and entitlement mentalities.

From the formation of the United States through the 1960s, Americans moved steadily along the Path of Fitness. Women had fewer options than men and some minorities did not benefit as much as those in the majority, but for the most part, large and increasing portions of the population enjoyed a steadily improving quality of life.

Since the 1960s, many women, African Americans, and Hispanics have enjoyed more opportunities and improved their lives. But these gains have come at the expense of high standards within our institutions, family solidarity, and the well-being of many children. Zealotry, ignorance, political opportunism, and flawed polices have created many win-lose arrangements and halted American movement along the Path of Fitness. This is not to say that the progress of women, African Americans, and Hispanics needs to slow, only that we need to find ways for it to coincide with impartial laws and policies, meritocracy and high standards, family solidarity, and child well-being.

Operating System I

I devote several chapters in this book to the discussion of evolution, fitness, and human nature because few people realize how much our past affects our present. From 200 thousand to 7 million years ago, or about 97 percent of human history, our ancestors lived as nomadic hunter-gatherers in ethnically pure, subtropical communities. Generally, they lived in groups of less than 150 people, traveled limited distances on foot, were untouched by technology, and traded little.

Life was a struggle. Most people lived on the edge, trying to eliminate their competitors before their competitors eliminated them. Common fictions unified their thinking and orchestrated their activity. Like most social animals, our ancestors lived in hierarchies. The strong dominated the weak. The strongest males with the most formidable networks ruled, impregnated multiple females, and passed on more of their tendencies to subsequent generations.

Obtaining enough of the right nutrients required tremendous work, especially during the dry seasons and before hominoid mastery of fire some 800 thousand years ago. Food shortages were common, and people ate until they were full when food was available. People's jealousies tempered the hierarchies, ensuring that most people received food and furthering a sense of fairness. The interplay of our ancestors' genes and environments over several million years formed our cerebral hardware and primary operating system.

Operating System II

The challenge with Operating System I is that most of us no longer occupy the savannas of Africa, operate entirely in hierarchies, or live with our extended families in groups of 150 or less. Most of us do not want only the stronger males to rule or men to impregnate multiple females. We are not nomadic generalists. Territory, property, free enterprise, specialization, free markets, and trade raise our living standards, and there is no longer an advantage in excluding those of different religions, races, and ethnicities from our companies, communities, and country. We require a more sophisticated operating system than the one with which we are born.

Nature accommodates our need for a more sophisticated operating system. The brains of modern sapiens are an evolutionary synthesis of a reptilian core, a mammalian overlay, and a cerebral cortex. They feature neural networks of over 100 billion nerve cells, each having some 10 thousand connections. When we perform an activity, groups of neurons fire, and "neurons that fire together wire together."[94] When we do an activity enough times, the firing patterns harden. We no longer need to consciously think about what we are doing. Our brains automate our performance of the activity. Once this happens, we play out most of our days on autopilot, selecting and then playing one learned routine after another.

For people to flourish in the modern world, their neural networks must house several critical perspectives, practices, and prohibitions, like the perspectives of causality, evolution, fitness, and eco-dependency that I discuss in this section, and the practices of integrity, proactivity, thrift, marriage, education, representative democracy, the rule of law, and inclusion that I write about later in this book. Some practices conflict with our instinctive operating system, such as deferred gratification associated with frugality, monogamy associated with marriage, the need to avoid conflicts of interests in representative democracy, and the inclusion of those unlike us in our groups.

The challenges of nature's solution and modern life are that the most advantageous collection of perspectives, practices, and prohibitions is poorly understood, changing, and political in nature, and its transmission depends on the quality of our parents, schools, and communities. History suggests that we can override many conflicts between our instincts and secondary operating system with groupthink, social stigmas, belief in an omniscient and omnipresent God, the rule of law, training, and self-discipline. But the need for us to continuously override some of our instincts is difficult. Wise leaders minimize this need, as in their preference for free enterprise over communism, but our complete elimination of conflicts between our instincts and Operating System II is impossible given our ideals and the scale, complexity, and multicultural nature of modern life. Figure 10 describes our primary and more recent environments, and Figure 11 compares Operating Systems I and II.

With greater understanding of our past, instinctual operating system, our brain's function, and the role of culture in layering on a secondary operating system, we can see that how we spend our time, and the perspectives, practices, and the prohibitions that parents, teachers, coaches, mentors, and peers instill in us dramatically impact our development, fitness, effectiveness, and well-being. While we need a habitable planet, territory, resources, a family, a home, work, and friends to flourish, we also need a collection of Winning Practices. Evolution and our genes give us an instinctual set of routines, and our culture layers on another collection of them.

Figure 10: Environments

Environment I	Environment II
7 million to 200,000 Years Ago	200,000 Years Ago to Present
97% of Our History	3% of Our History
Small Groups of 150 or Less	Large Groups of Millions
Mono-Racial and Ethnic	Multi-Racial and Ethnic
Climates Without Winter	Climates with Winters
Scarcity	Abundance
Nomadic	Rooted
Local in Scope	Global in Scope
Static	Rapidly Changing

Figure 11: Operating Systems

System I	System II
Hardware, Instinctual	Software, Learned
Acts on Us 24/7	Varies with Cultures
Default System for Subsistence	Determines Effectiveness
Hierarchical	Hierarchical and Democratic
The Rule of One	The Rule of Law
Patronage System	Lawfulness
Communal	Private Property
Economic Equality	Economic Inequality
Polygamous	Monogamous
Discriminatory	Inclusive
Mythical, Emotional	Factual, Emotional
Groupthink	Rational, Groupthink
Immediate	Immediate and Deferred
Reactive	Reactive and Proactive
Generalists	Specialists
Win-Lose	Win-Win
Eat Until Full	Maintain a Healthy Weight

As the echo of our Judeo-Christian heritage fades and the hard work of previous generations spoils us, our incomes stagnate, debt explodes, and fitness wanes. China ascends, the world's population grows unsustainably, atmospheric carbon dioxide levels rise, and critical natural habitats degrade. By not addressing these problems and not transferring Winning Practices to large portions of our population, we place the next generation in a weaker position than the previous one for the first time in our nation's history.

Sections I and II provide the heartbreaking evidence that substantiates this view, while Sections III to VIII of this book provide a collection of practices that move populations along the Path of Fitness and enable us to flourish.

Culture – the shared perspectives, practices, and prohibitions that parents, teachers, and others transmit to us, which affect our discretionary behavior, and the people and achievements that we celebrate to reinforce the transmission.

Chapter 11

Periodic Disaster

Life is not for the faint of heart. The universe and planet are violent and perilous places.

The Earth's fossil record indicates that more than half of all living species became extinct during five catastrophic periods, occurring approximately 70, 200, 250, 380, and 450 million years ago.[95] Mass extinctions occur infrequently, but when they do, they dramatically change the mix of life on Earth. Scientists are not sure of the causes of these mass extinctions, but they hypothesize that supernova explosions, solar eruptions, asteroid impacts, planetary polarization changes, volcanic eruptions, and platonic shifts sometimes alter climate and sea levels enough to cause them. These five catastrophic extinctions warn us that conditions can change adversely on Earth.

Along with dramatic climate changes, diseases and famines have periodically devastated populations throughout history. Virulent viruses and bacteria reduced some European populations by more than 50 percent in the 7th and 14th centuries.[96] Famines accelerated the decline of the Egyptian, Roman, Mayan, and Byzantine empires.[97]

Historians estimate that famines reduced the populations by more than one million people in the following locations: Central America (800–1000), France (1693–94), Iran (1870–71), Ireland (1845–49), Indonesia (1944–45), Cambodia (1975–79), and the Congo (1998–2004). In the last one hundred years, millions of people died due to famine in the former Soviet Union during 1916–17, 1932–33, 1941–44, and in 1947. China lost 45 million people during the 1810, 1811, 1846, and 1849 famines, 60 million people during the 1850–73 famine, another 25 million people during the 1907–11 famine, and millions more during the 1928–30, 1936, and 1959–61 famines. India lost millions of people during nine major famines between 1700–1950.[98]

War also reduced populations throughout history. Figure 12 lists the major conflicts with more than 250 thousand casualties. The figure suggests that the world is seldom free of war and should give pause to those who maintain that we have evolved to the point where we no longer need a strong defense.

The planetary record and history indicate that life must overcome many hardships. They suggest that we would be wise to prepare for epidemics, famines, wars, and challenging times; to learn to deflect asteroids from Earth; and to develop technology to colonize space. Carl Sagan wrote:

> Since, in the long run, every planetary society will be endangered by impacts from space, every surviving civilization is obliged to become spacefaring—not because of exploratory or romantic zeal, but for the most practical reason imaginable: staying alive.[99]

We live in a rough neighborhood. The universe is a dangerous place. We are on our own. Our continuation depends on numbers, fitness, preparation, healthy planetary habitats, and our eventual dispersion throughout our galaxy.

Periodic Disaster – *events reminding us that our universe and planet are dangerous places. Earthquakes, typhoons, tsunamis, tornados, wildfires, floods, famines, disease, and war regularly erode our populations. Quasars, supernovas, solar eruptions, asteroid impacts, planetary polarization changes, volcanic eruptions, and major platonic shifts periodically trigger significant climate and sea level changes that devastate or even eliminate many forms of life.*

Figure 12: Conflicts with Greater than 250,000 Casualties

Second Punic War	218–201 BC
Gallic Wars	58–0 BC
Three Kingdoms War	184–280
A Lushan Rebellion	755–763
Crusades	1095–1291
Mongol Conquests	1206–1324
Conquests of Timur	1370–1405
Conquest of Mehmed II the Conqueror	1451–1481
Conquests of the Americas	1492–1691
French Wars of Religion	1562–1598
Japanese Invasions of Korea	1592–1598
Qing Conquest of Ming Dynasty	1616–1662
Thirty Years War	1618–1648
Wars of the Three Kingdoms	1639–1651
Great Northern War	1700–1721
War of the Spanish Succession	1701–1714
Seven Years War	1756–1763
Napoleonic Wars	1803–1815
Shaku's Conquests	1816–1828
Taiping Rebellion	1850–1864
American Civil War	1861–1865
Dugan Revolt	1862–1877
Mexican Revolution	1910–1920
World War I	1914–1918
Russian Civil War and Foreign Intervention	1917–1922
Chinese Civil War	1927–1949
Spanish Civil War	1936–1939
Second Sino-Japanese	1937–1945
World War II	1939–1945
First Indochina War	1946–1954
Korean War	1950–1953
Algerian War of Independence	1954–1962
Vietnam War/Second Indochina War	1955–1975
Biafra War	1967–1970
Bangladesh Liberation War	1971
Ethiopian Civil War	1974–1991
Soviet War in Afghanistan	1979–1989
Iran-Iraq War/First Persian Gulf War	1980–1988
Somali Civil War	1986–Present
Civil War of Afghanistan	1989–1992
Second Burundian Civil War	1993–2005
War on Terror	2001–Present
Syrian Civil War	2011–Present

https://en.wikipedia.org/wiki/List_of_wars_by_death_toll

Chapter 12

Eco-Dependency

Our prowess and procreation serve us well until we deplete needed resources or irrevocably harm our planetary ecosystems.

We and all life need natural habitats. Natural habitats do many things for us, and they do them better and at a lower cost than our best engineers. They provide fresh oxygenated air to breathe, clean water to drink, and fertile soil to grow food.

Wetlands and floodplains filter water and reduce flooding. Topsoil, earthworms, and bacteria provide us with a medium to grow food and a means to decompose waste. Farmlands, grasslands, and forests filter water and convert carbon dioxide to oxygen. They provide us with animal feed, food, wood pulp, and timber. Mangroves, coral reefs, oyster reefs, and seagrass beds filter water and protect coastlines. They provide us with fish and seafood. Eco-dependency is the reality that we depend on natural habitats for clean air and water, food, and a hospitable climate.

Rachel Carson made many people aware of our negative impacts on natural habitats with her publication of *Silent Spring* in 1962. Scientists have inventoried these impacts since, and large portions of our population have learned about their findings. We discovered that we drained and developed millions of acres of wetlands and floodplains; contaminated our groundwater, streams, rivers, and lakes with fertilizers, petroleum products, sewage, road salt, pesticides, herbicides, hormones, and other harmful substances; destroyed thousands of miles of mangroves, coral reefs, and oyster reefs; and dumped millions of tons of trash into the seas.

We learned of the disastrous effects of clearing millions of acres of forests and grasslands, rising carbon dioxide levels in our atmosphere, and contaminating our atmosphere with carbon monoxide, nitrous oxide, sulfur dioxide, lead, and other harmful molecules. We also discovered that our government scuttled ships with radioactive reactors and that it stores approximately 81 thousand metric tons of radioactive waste which must remain sealed for tens of thousands of years.[100]

Each year we destroy a few hundred of the estimated two million species, even though we depend on so many species and habitats directly and indirectly. Species destruction is irreversible, and it negatively affects critical ecosystems, which in turn affect Earth's climate. E. O. Wilson writes:

> The worst thing that can happen during the [near term] is not energy depletion, economic collapse, limited nuclear war, or conquest by a totalitarian government. As terrible as these disasters would be for us, they can be repaired within a few generations. The one process ongoing in the [near term] that will take millions of years to correct is the loss of genetic and species diversity by the destruction of natural habitats. This is the folly that our descendants are least likely to forgive us.[101]

We cannot and should not attempt to preserve every species at all costs. Our resources are finite, and the extinction of an unfit species is a natural part of evolution. We can reduce our environmental footprint, however, to protect as many species as practically possible and save the species that are critical to our ecosystems.

Asteroid impacts, polarization changes, volcanic eruptions, and other extra-terrestrial shocks can dramatically change Earth's climate; now it seems that humans can as well. Scientists persuasively demonstrate that carbon dioxide (CO_2), methane (CH_4), nitrous oxide (N_2O), and other greenhouse gases trap solar energy in the atmosphere and increase planetary temperatures. They estimate that post-industrial human activity adds 30 billion metric tons of CO_2 to the atmosphere each year.[102] It is in our best interests to reduce our greenhouse gas emissions.

Although the specific predictions of temperature, rainfall, and sea level changes associated with various human activities and the best ways to mitigate our negative impacts are controversial, most well-informed people agree that we are seriously harming the flora, fauna, and natural habitats on which we depend. We must mitigate our negative impacts on the environment as much as practically possible, and we must slow the world's population growth.

Undoubtedly, enough of a change in the concentration of CO_2 and other greenhouse gases in the atmosphere will change Earth's temperatures and climate. Common sense alone suggests that photosynthesis—CO_2 depletion—must balance with respiration and fossil fuel use—CO_2 emission—in the long term for the climate to remain stable. Our tremendous emission of greenhouse gases and deforestation of thousands of acres every year are unsustainable and climate-altering.

Greenhouse gas emissions and deforestation represent externalities that governments must incentivize us to curb. What are externalities?

Externalities *are situations where one agent's activities harm or benefit another agent who did not choose to be harmed or receive the benefit. CO_2 emissions and deforestation are examples of externalities. The public, rather than the carbon users and landholders, bear most of the undesirable ancillary effects of these activities in the form of sickness, disease, shortened lifespans, and climate change.*

One of the best ways to address undesirable externalities is for governments to tax them and thus incentivize individuals, enterprises, and other organizations to reduce their harmful activities. If the government taxed CO_2 emissions, emitters would raise the prices of their products to recoup the tax in the short term and develop more carbon-neutral forms of energy in the long term. In response to the higher prices, customers of large CO_2 emitters would purchase fewer of their products and decrease CO_2 emissions in the short term.

Taxing externalities is one of the best ways to curtail them because a tax does not narrowly address the problem, enlarge the government bureaucracy, or micromanage their reduction. Taxing externalities penalizes the undesirable activity; in doing so, it incentivizes everyone to find ways to curtail the undesirable activity.

Finally, we must protect our ecosystems all over the planet. We may procure our oxygen, water, and nutrients locally, but ecosystems on the other side of Earth affect us. We must clean up our activities at home as other countries must clean up their activities. Heavy CO_2 emission in North America and Asia, deforestation in South America, and desertification in North Africa affect everyone.

Our lives and future depend on our ecosystems. We must take commonsense steps to stop harming them. Human activity is sufficient now to irreparably turn our beautiful life-giving planet into a desolate one. Carl Sagan writes:

> A tiny blue dot set in a sunbeam. Here it is. That's where we live. That's home. We humans are one species, and this is our world. It is our responsibility to cherish it. Of all the worlds in our solar system, the only one so far as we know, graced by life.[103]

Eco-Dependency – *the reality that Earth's ecosystems sustain us and we must minimize our impact on them, protect other species as much as possible, use sustainable agricultural practices that protect groundwater and preserve topsoil, stop the destruction of savannahs and forests, and help plants and animals repair the damaged ecosystems. Eco-Dependency compels us to develop environmentally friendly alternatives to harmful biological, chemical, and nuclear agents; responsibly dispose of the existing ones; recycle our waste; maintain friendly carbon-dioxide-to-oxygen ratios; use carbon-neutral forms of energy; and work with other countries to reduce the world's population growth.*

Winning Perspectives Summary

The Winning Perspectives indicate that we are perceptive, thinking beings who must both proactively and prudently look out for ourselves.

Truth is accurate approximations of reality, natural processes, and events. Like an accurate roadmap, truth enables us to grasp reality, trust one another, and work together. Our initial perceptions are only a start in our quest for truth. We must ponder our perceptions, read, travel, verify what others tell us, solicit different views, conduct experiments, and gather evidence. Increasing amounts of evidence improves our perceptions, makes us more intelligent, and makes our solutions iteratively more effective.

Causality is the reality that one or more causes underlie every event and that there exists a set of conditions or recipe for everything that happens. Knowing the set of conditions to produce an effect is powerful. The invisible and delayed nature of many causal relationships blinds us to the effects of many of our actions. Mentors, experts, science, and experience expose the effects of our actions and help us act more prudently.

Scale reveals the enormity of the universe and the minuteness of its building blocks. It provides us with a realistic view of the universe, its workings, and our place in it. We learn that we live in one of the billions of galaxies, orbit around one of the one billion stars in our galaxy and live on one of the billions of potentially hospitable planets in the universe. We realize that all of Earth's lifeforms descend from a common lifeform, we are the products of over three billion years of natural selection, and we may become a fallen leaf from the evolutionary tree, or a branch to hundreds, thousands, or even millions of forthcoming generations of life.

Evolution is the ultimate creation and improvement story. It involves particles, natural processes, self-assembly, variation, inheritable traits, generations, comparative advantage, competition, and natural selection. The universe starts, cools, and self-assembles to form the atoms, molecules, planets, stars, and galaxies. Organisms that are better suited for their environments place more offspring into the next generation, increasing the frequency of the genes governing the most advantageous traits. Evolution reveals that fitness is our end, fitness enables us to persist through time, and competitions and comparative advantage play important roles in our lives. Competitions drive evolution. They winnow the disadvantageous from the advantageous, decide who wins, and allocate positions and resources to those who most ably use them. Comparative advantage assures that there exists a role for everyone in a community.

Fitness is the ability of organisms to flourish, procure needed resources, and reproduce relative to other organisms. It requires competence, meritocracy, and procreation. Fitness furthers health, performance, and affiliation. It brings the esteem of others, desirable mates, offspring, and lifelong well-being. It enables our families, institutions, communities, country, and culture to persist through time. Fitness is the aim of life, and happiness is a by-product of it. Happiness eludes us as we pursue it and comes to us as we are fit.

Human Nature is a collection of universal individual, familial, and social tendencies that include: (a) avoiding pain and pursuing pleasure, (b) seeking water, food, clothing, shelter, security, and others' esteem, (c) understanding the world, developing, and actualizing, (d) seeking money, power, and influence, (e) loving, being loved, and procreating, (f) doing our best by our children, (g) having a short-term orientation, (h) having an aversion to losses, (i) securing aesthetically pleasing environments, (j) affiliating with others in mutually beneficial ways, (k) absorbing others' thinking, and (l) pursuing one's interests first, the interests of those with whom we affiliate second, and the interests of others last.

Culture is the perspectives, practices, and prohibitions that parents, teachers, and others transmit to us, as well as history, art, laws, institutions, technologies, special occasions, heroes, and achievements that people celebrate to reinforce the transmission. Culture is human software, a secondary operating system that is layered onto our instinctual one that affects our attitudes, interactions with others, and actions, as well as our ability to lead, be led, and function in groups. Culture affects every level of human organization—the individual, family, group, education, enterprise, and government. We can do everything correctly as individuals but have a miserable life if our culture perpetuates dysfunction at the other levels. Transmission of culture happens whether we are aware or unaware of it. Families, schools, workplaces, religious institutions, news organizations, prominent figures, and more recently, producers of television, movies, and social media are primary transmitters of culture.

Periodic Disaster is the reality that our universe and planet are dangerous places and that our continuation depends on our ability to survive catastrophes, diseases, famines, and wars. Earthquakes, typhoons, tsunamis, tornados, wildfires, floods, famines, disease, and war regularly erode our populations. Quasars, supernovas, solar eruptions, asteroid impacts, planetary polarization changes, volcanic eruptions, and major platonic shifts may trigger significant climate and sea level changes that eliminate many forms of life. Our continuation depends on numbers, fitness, preparation, healthy planetary habitats, and our eventual dispersion throughout our galaxy.

Eco-Dependency is the reality that (a) Earth's ecosystems sustain us, (b) we must minimize our impact on them, (c) protect other species as much as possible, (d) use sustainable agricultural practices that protect groundwater and preserve topsoil, (e) stop the destruction of savannas and forests, (f) help plants and animals repair the damaged ecosystems, (g) develop environmentally friendly alternatives to harmful biological, chemical, and nuclear agents, and responsibly dispose of the existing ones, (h) recycle our waste, (i) maintain friendly carbon-dioxide-to-oxygen ratios, (j) use carbon-neutral forms of energy, and (k) work with other countries to reduce the world's population growth.

Winning Perspectives provide accurate and important depictions of reality. They provide insight and direction. They help us to avoid being foolish and balance our preoccupation with the past, the present, and the future. Winning Perspectives help us identify Winning Practices from a murky sea of thousands of possibilities. They have helped me immensely throughout my life, and I am confident that they will help you.

Winning Perspectives – *accurate perceptions of reality and conditions of existence. Substantial evidence exists for them. They further our effectiveness and help us identify Winning Practices.*

Section III: Winning Practices of Individuals

Winning Perspectives

Truth
Causality
Scale
Evolution
Fitness

Human Nature
Culture
Periodic Disaster
Eco-Dependency

Winning Practices

Knowledge
Health
Thought
Integrity
Proactivity
Prudence
Excellence
Thrift and Investment

Universal Education
Parental Choice
Results-Oriented Education

Free Enterprise and Markets
Responsible Corporate Governance
Prudent Regulation
Enterprise Competitiveness

Affiliation
Decency
Understanding
Leadership
Teamwork
Improvement

Government of the People
Powers, Prohibitions, and Structure
Freedoms, Rights, and Responsibilities
The Rule of Law
Inclusion and Meritocracy
Prudent Taxation

Spouse Selection
Marriage
Responsible Parenting
Empowering Habit Formation

Financial Strength
Savings Accounts, Social Safety Nets
Consumer-Driven Healthcare
Assimilation
Peace Through Fitness
Sustainability

Chapter 13

Winning Practices

Because we find strength, economies, efficiencies, and synergy in working together, we depend on multiple levels of human organization. We can do everything correctly as individuals but still have a difficult life if our culture fails us at the other levels.

Human life is complex. We are born into families, develop into individuals, and form families of our own. A lot must go right for us to flourish. We need advantageous genes, able parents, excellent schools, profitable employment, good governments, and empowering cultural norms. We attend school, obtain work, affiliate with many groups, and reside in a country. An individual, familial, and social tri-nature permeates our lives.

When thinking about the practices necessary for fitness and well-being, I have the benefit of the Winning Perspectives. They helped me understand our individual, familial, and social tri-nature and recognize the importance of several levels of human organization: individual, family, group, education, enterprise, government, and culture.

Individual Level

Organizationally, the individual level of human life is particularly important as we are individuals first, and the effectiveness of the other levels depends on the fitness of the individuals who constitute them. Millions of years of natural selection hardwired us with Operating System I, a collection of tendencies that act on us unconsciously 24 hours a day, 7 days a week. These tendencies incline us to pursue our individual and family interests first, the interests of those with whom we affiliate second, and others' interests third. The failure to recognize and harness our self-interest is a primary cause of our goals and policies not producing the desired or expected results.

Group Level

Modern humans belong to numerous groups or communities, which are generally educational, recreational, professional, religious, or political in nature. These communities enhance our fitness and well-being. We learn, play, earn our livelihoods, provide and receive services, socialize, and further common objectives in communities. We specialize, enjoy economies of scale, exchange goods and services, realize synergies in them, develop leadership and team skills, and aid those in need in our communities.

Family Level

Our parents shape us before we shape ourselves. They pass half their genes to us and teach us innumerable perspectives, practices, and prohibitions. They influence who we become and what we do more than anyone except for ourselves. They do things for us that no other level of human organization does.

Human maturation is a tremendous amount of work that takes a long time. Good parents provide love, perspective, instruction, discipline, resources, and opportunities to their children for years. They love them unconditionally; help them develop self-control, consideration for others, an ability to defer gratification, and perseverance; and teach them to be open to new perspectives and experiences. School teachers and other mentors help parents with their children's development, but there is no substitute for engaged parents and grandparents.

Education Level

Education provides the knowledge and skills that we need to navigate the world, earn a livelihood, successfully raise a family, and contribute to the larger community. It gives us access to the immense reservoir of the perspectives and information accumulated overtime.

Education supplements our primary operating system with a secondary one. It is more important today than ever before because life is so complex. Food, materials, homes, appliances, cars, communication, and medicine are so much more technical than they were just one hundred years ago. Larger communities and populations, science, technology, microprocessors, the Internet, and artificial intelligence increase the complexity of our environment, work, products, and lives immensely.

Schools are our primary agents of education, enabling children to play, learn, and interact with others. Effective schools teach children basic reading, writing, speaking, and math skills; as well as the scientific method and science's findings regarding the evolution of the universe, Earth, and life. They teach us career and life skills as well as about our multicultural heritage and history. Effective schools familiarize children with our knowledge base, provide them with helpful role models and mentors, and help them form enabling habits.

Children enjoy a smorgasbord of activities in good schools. They experience different types of art and music. They learn how to speak foreign languages, be physically fit, and win and lose gracefully. They learn about free enterprise, free markets, good government, the real world, and what works.

Enterprise Level

Efficient, competitive, and stakeholder-oriented enterprises create affordable products and services. They enable us to earn our livelihoods, support our families, and contribute to our communities. Such enterprises supply affordable, high-quality housing and related services and allow one-in-four-hundred people to provide our population with inexpensive, high-quality food products. They indirectly fund our defense, education, healthcare, research, government, social safety net, and retirement, and make unprecedented amounts of free time possible.

These enterprises provide safe and desirable work environments. They compensate their employees well, offer superior benefits, and provide opportunities to advance. Some enterprises provide our computers, communication devices, and Internet access. Many eliminate repetitive, menial jobs. Most enterprises steadily improve our productivity and raise our living standards. Some enterprises export products and services, decreasing the relative cost of imports.

Government Level

Government is one of the most consequential levels of human organization. Its effect on its citizens can range from extremely positive to extremely negative. When governments are well-conceived and their leaders honest and competent, they liberate and empower their citizens. When governments are dictatorial and their leaders corrupt and incompetent, they harm their populations, sometimes for generations.

Unfortunately, far more examples of corrupt and incompetent governments exist throughout history than honorable and competent ones. One only needs to study the last four thousand years of history or to learn about Chad, Nigeria, Somalia, Sudan, Zimbabwe, Afghanistan, Syria, Yemen, North Korea, Laos, and Haiti today to recognize the preciousness of competent and well-functioning governments. The governments of Norway, New Zealand, Singapore, and Switzerland do an excellent job for their citizens.

Winning Practices

If we study science, we learn that scientists have formulated few laws, and they do not view any of the laws as absolutes. Cause-and-effect relationships only qualify as laws when substantial empirical evidence supports them, no contradictory evidence disputes them, and the relationships they describe hold throughout the universe. When new observations contradict established laws, scientists reformulate the laws.

Similarly, few practices qualify as Winning Practices, and we should not view the ones that do as absolutes. Viewing a practice as a convention or one of many possibilities is superior to seeing it as "the right way" to do something. This may not be apparent when we are young and have not traveled much, but it becomes apparent as we gain experience. There are many ways to do something, and our approaches are merely a subset of a larger set of possibilities. They may or may not be the best ones. Thus, we should only prefer a practice until we find a better one.

This view of our approaches is superior to simply seeing them as the right ways to do things because it conveys temporariness and openness to change and facilitates improvement. Just as avoiding certitude in science facilitates the development of more accurate theories and laws, avoiding certainty in our daily lives facilitates our adaptation and fitness.

Another challenge with practices is that people evaluate the relative desirability of them differently. Most people care more about a practice's short-term effects on themselves or their group. Few consider the effects they have on others, on the environment, and in the long term. For example, some people might see not working overtime as a best practice for them. They may have all the money they need, so being home to parent their children may more effectively utilize their time. From the standpoint of their employers and colleagues, however, their decision to not work overtime is not a best practice. Rather, the best practice when considering the interests of their family, employer, and colleagues may be to only work overtime when it is critical to the business.

We may consider buying a new car, taking good care of it, and keeping it for several years to be a best practice. It eliminates the risk of acquiring an unreliable used car, and it costs less than the habit of buying a new car and selling it every couple of years. This practice may not be best when we have limited credit and need to borrow money to purchase the car, however, as the debt may negatively affect us more during an economic downturn than the cost of an occasional problem with a quality used car.

To counter these limitations when evaluating various practices, I developed the concept of a Winning Practice. Winning Practices take more time to identify and develop but generate fewer negative effects. Winning Practices consider an approach's effects in five ways: (1) on the individual, (2) on the group, (3) on the environment, (4) in the short term, and (5) in the long term.

Collegial improvement is a sub-practice of Improvement, one of the Winning Practices that I discuss in the *Flourish* series. Collegial improvement comes from my observation that conservatives, moderates, and progressives all add value to the improvement process. Progressives identify potentially advantageous changes and push for their implementation. Conservatives defend the status quo and identify the adverse effects of changes. Moderates, at their best, pilot the proposed changes, examine the effects, mitigate the negative impacts, and support the changes that *prove* advantageous. Collegial improvement is a Winning Practice because we obtain fairer, more effective, and more widely supported outcomes for individuals, the larger group, and the environment in the short and long term when we use it to create policies, laws, and institutions.

Page 117 summarizes the 37 overarching Winning Practices discussed in this book. The Winning Practices in bold are discussed in the next section. The prevalence and quality of the execution of these practices and numerous other related ones in a population determine whether its people flourish, decline, or merely subsist. We align our lives with Winning Practices, or we forgo their positive effects. We convey Winning Practices to our citizens and children, or we lose the benefits they bring to our organizations, government, and lives.

Winning Practices – approaches that yield predominately positive effects to individuals, the larger group, and/or the environment in the short and long term.

Chapter 14

Health

Good health does not just happen—it requires work on our part.

Generally, we take our health for granted until disease strikes or we become elderly. We work, play, and socialize with little thought about it. We eat indiscriminately and exercise little. Only as we cross the 50- and 60-age thresholds do we realize that what we did in the first half of our lives affects the second half. Only then do we start to learn strategies to postpone and hopefully avoid diabetes, heart disease, arthritis, dementia, and cancer.

The Winning Practices discussed in this chapter help keep our bodies and minds in good working order and extend the time that we enjoy good health or our healthspans. Well-maintained bodies and minds, like well-maintained machines, function better and last longer. Children are so fortunate when they learn these health-promoting habits.

Hygiene

Hygiene affects our health and relationships with others. If we do not keep our bodies, clothes, and environment clean, we become hosts to harmful viruses, bacteria, and fungi. While there is nothing difficult or complicated about good hygiene in an era of plenty, we still must learn the practices.

Hygiene involves washing daily brushing and flossing after meals, and keeping our hands clean. It requires us to keep our dishes, utensils, and kitchen surfaces clean and periodically launder our clothes, nightwear, and bed sheets. It involves properly disposing of our waste and trash and keeping rodents and insects away from our living environments. Clean bodies, clothes, and environments minimize the spread of harmful viruses, bacteria, and fungi as well as the risk of them entering our bodies if our hands touch contaminated surfaces and then our eyes, mouth, or open wounds.

Nutrition

Along with hygiene, nutrition has a tremendous impact on our health. Proper nutrition enables the optimal development of our body and mind. It yields a favorable weight; creates an attractive, productive, and long-lasting body; and fuels an alert, intelligent, and well-functioning mind. Eating well also strengthens our immune system, reducing incidences of sickness and disease.

When food is unprocessed, scarce, and difficult to acquire, which has been the case for most of human history, obtaining enough nutrients is a challenge. But when food is processed, abundant, and inexpensive, limiting nutrient intake becomes the challenge.

Given our population's current 36 percent obesity rate and its negative impact on American lives, we must teach children to eat a balanced diet and limit their food intake. Our eating patterns, like so many other things, become habit. Once we learn to eat limited quantities of healthy, nutritious foods, we develop a natural adversity to unhealthy foods and overeating. Teaching children to: (a) eat lots of vegetables, fruits, nuts, and fish from clean waters, (b) eat small amounts of meat from animals on vegetarian diets, (c) avoid sugary, salty, and fatty foods, snacks, and drinks, and (d) limit their alcohol consumption is what develops important heuristics in their minds that serve them well throughout their entire lives.

Periodic Fasting

Scientists have known for years that continuous calorie restriction increases animal and human healthspans by as much as 30 to 40 percent, but they did not know why. Now, they know that continuous calorie restriction and periodic fasting have similar effects on our bodies. Nick Lane, a London-based biochemist, writes:

By lowering free radical leak [in mitochondria], bolstering mitochondrial membranes against damage, and bolstering the number of mitochondria, calorie restriction effectively "resets" the clock of life back to "youth." In so doing, it switches off hundreds of inflammatory genes, returning genes to their youthful chemical environment, while fortifying cells against programmed cell death. The combination suppresses both cancer and degenerative diseases and slows the rate of aging.[104]

These findings are stunning. Our health is ultimately a function of the health of the trillions of cells that make up our bodies. Calorie restriction and fasting extend our lives by improving the health of each of our cells. It does this by lowering insulin and an insulated-related hormone glucagon, shifting our bodies from growth to repair mode, and improving the function of mitochondria in each of our cells.[105] And, it appears that we can postpone and/or avoid diabetes, heart disease, arthritis, dementia, cancer, and numerous other diseases simply by periodically restricting our caloric intake and maintaining proper body weight.

I find that the most practical approach to realize these benefits is the 5:2 diet. Developed by Dr. Michael Mosley of the United Kingdom, the 5:2 diet consists of reducing one's caloric intake by two-thirds for two nonconsecutive days each week and eating normally the rest of the time. Fast days involve small morning and evening meals of 250 to 300 calories each. Besides postponing and avoiding many diseases, periodic fasting reduces belly fat, improves blood sugar, reduces inflammation, increases the production of the proteins that protect brain cells, enhances the body's ability to repair DNA, and improves our bodies' ability to handle future assaults.[106]

Sleep

Sleep plays an important role in our development, immune system function, mental acumen, outlook, and avoidance of accidents. The practice of going to bed and rising at a similar time each day, sleeping for around 8 hours, and obtaining about 2½ hours of deep sleep and 1½ hours of rapid eye movement (REM) sleep yields numerous benefits.[107]

Although we can get by on less than 8 hours of sleep a day, we ask for trouble when we habitually get too little sleep. Deep sleep and REM sleep strengthen our immune system, improve our memory and mood, and enhance the quality of our work and play. Sleep deprivation impairs our judgment, coordination, immune system, and outlook in ways that increase the incidences of bad decisions, accidents, diseases, and depression.

The practice of going to bed around 10:00 at night and rising around 6:00 in the morning served previous generations well. It coincides with darkness and the time when most people sleep. It furthers sound sleep, health, and well-being; generally, we accomplish more when we work and socialize when others do the same.

Exercise

Exercise is also critical to our health. Our bodies are comprised of trillions of cells that require a steady supply of water, nutrients, and oxygen, as well as the continuous removal of carbon dioxide and other waste products. Daily exercise elevates our heart rate and facilitates the delivery of nutrients and oxygen and the removal of waste from each cell. It strengthens our skeletal, muscular, pulmonary, and cardiovascular systems, dissipates stress-related hormones, and facilitates sound sleep.

People were much more physically active before modern conveniences. Today, sedentary lifestyles and high caloric intake make our health extremely dependent on regular exercise. While the amount of needed exercise varies with our caloric intake and activity, 20 to 30 minutes of vigorous exercise everyday benefits us tremendously.[108]

Avoiding Harm

Good health also depends on learning about the things that can harm us in our environments and taking steps to protect ourselves from them. Injuries happen in seconds, yet healing takes days, weeks, or months. Some injuries last a lifetime or are lethal. Avoiding injury requires awareness, caution, heeding others' warnings, and good judgment.

Keeping current on vaccines and flu shots and treating infections with antibacterial solutions promote good health. Frequently washing our hands, not drinking out of the same containers as others, and avoiding sexual relations outside marriage help keep harmful viruses and bacteria away. Minimizing exposure to the sun and using sunscreen protect our DNA from cancerous mutations. Using car seats, seatbelts, and bicycle helmets reduce the adverse effects of accidents.

Noncontact sports are as much fun as contact sports—with the bonus that they reduce the risk of injuries. Obtaining instruction from qualified people regarding the safe operation of power tools and equipment and reading instructions on prescriptions and chemical containers also reduce the likelihood of injuries. Not operating power equipment or driving while using cell phones or under the influence of alcohol and drugs protect us and others from harm.

Medical and Dental Care

Regular medical and dentalcare facilitate good health. Pregnant mothers learn about prenatal care. Parents learn to care for infants and young children. Children receive critical immunizations. Periodic dental cleanings and exams prevent tooth decay and the need for fillings, root canals, and tooth extractions. Timely attention to broken bones, wounds, infections, and illness, along with regular physical examinations, prevent common assaults from becoming life-threatening ones. Early detection of diabetes, heart disease, cancer, and numerous other diseases leads to positive outcomes.

Healthcare becomes accessible and affordable to people when governments (a) incentivize people to purchase catastrophic health insurance and save money to purchase routine care, (b) limit the market shares of health providers, pharmaceuticals, and insurers, and (c) prevent attorneys from extracting large amounts from the healthcare system. We cannot flourish as a people when a large portion of our population lacks access to good healthcare. I describe Winning Practices that make medical and dental care universally accessible and affordable in Chapter 48.

DNA Fidelity

Science continuously provides us with new perspectives that can help us as a people. One of the more important ones involves the relationship between the age of parents and the number of mutations in their children's DNA. The human body almost defies comprehension. Each of its trillions of cells carries the instructions for the entire body's development. The instructions come in the form of a strand of deoxyribonucleic acid (DNA) that is comprised of some three billion pairs of nucleotides. Each of our trillions of cells arises from the division of the first cell created by the union of an egg and a sperm, and each cell's DNA is a subsequent copy of this first cell's DNA. Thus, we each depend upon the integrity of our DNA in our first cell and the integrity of the DNA copying process. Nick Lane, University College London biochemist and best-selling author of *Life Ascending*, writes:

> Each letter is copied with a precision bordering on the miraculous, recreating the order of the original with an error rate of about one letter in 1,000 million. Even in DNA, though, errors build up, if only because the genome is so very big. Such errors are called point mutations, in which one letter is substituted for another by mistake. Each time a human cell divides you'd expect to see about three mutations per set of chromosomes. And the more times that cell divides, the more such mutations accumulate, ultimately contributing to diseases like cancer. Mutations also cross generations.

If a fertilized egg develops as a female embryo, it takes about
30 rounds of cell division to form a new egg cell;
and each round adds a few more mutations. Men are even
worse: 100 rounds of cell division are needed to make sperm,
with each round linked inexorably to more mutations. Because
sperm production goes on throughout life, round after round of
cell division, the older the man, the worse it gets. . . . But even
an average child of youthful parents has around 200 new
mutations compared with his or her parents.

Natural selection, by casting away all but the least of these
monsters, is actually a force for stability. DNA morphs and
twists, selection straightens. Any positive changes are retained,
while more serious errors or alterations miscarry, literally.
Other mutations, less serious, may be associated with disease
later in life.[109]

This perspective has tremendous implications. It suggests that if we
want to live long, healthy lives, we must take care of our DNA. We must
vaccinate ourselves against harmful viruses that mutate DNA. We must
avoid hazardous chemicals and radiation from the sun, CAT scans, x-
rays, and other radiation-emitting electronic equipment that mutates
DNA as much as possible. And, we must protect babies and young
children from the causes of DNA mutations.

This perspective also suggests that we should conceive children
when we are in our 20s and early 30s. Even though this may
inconvenience us, we must do this for our children and grandchildren.
Postponing children until middle age condemns some children to
developmental problems early in life and cancers later in life. We should
not be corrupting our children's DNA, weakening our gene pool and
population, and making life more difficult for future generations.

Reflection

Reflection positively affects our health and lives. It improves our awareness, mood, and outlook. It involves the daily or weekly practice of reading or listening to inspirational and timeless thoughts, being thankful for our blessings, reviewing our activities and interactions with people, and aligning our actions with our priorities.

Regular exposure to empowering insights and practices nourishes and inspires us. It replaces debilitating perspectives and practices with winning ones. Stephen Covey, best-selling author of *7 Habits of Highly Effective People,* wrote:

If you organize your family life to spend even ten or fifteen minutes a morning reading something that connects you with these timeless principles, it's almost guaranteed that you will make better choices during the day—in the family, on the job, in every dimension of life. Your thoughts will be higher. Your interactions will be more satisfying. You will have a greater perspective. You will increase that space between what happens to you and your response to it. You will be more connected to what really matters most.[110]

Reflection provides a regular opportunity to adjust our habits, speech, and actions to improve our relationships and effectiveness. We become aware of our insensitivity to others and our neglect of the people most important to us. We focus on what matters, overcome natural tendencies to procrastinate and blame others, and appreciate others more.

Reflecting on our blessings is also extremely beneficial. We can see our lives positively when we reflect on the positives more than the negatives. Philosopher and Roman emperor, Marcus Aurelius, wrote:

When you arise in the morning, think of what a precious privilege it is to be alive—to breathe, to think, to enjoy, to love.[111]

Part of good health is paying attention to our bodies—being aware of psychological or physical pain, understanding its causes, and adjusting our behaviors. Awareness and early intervention prevent small problems from becoming large ones. Periodic quiet time and reflection relax us, improve our awareness, and facilitate this adjustment process.

Prayer, a form of meditation, can be extremely beneficial, but I have found no evidence that we receive external guidance from it. As Dewey Bunnell wrote in the lyrics of America's Tin Man, "Oz didn't give anything to the Tin Man that he didn't already have." [112] So it is with prayer. Prayerful insights come from within us.

Prayer and meditation calm our minds and bring order to them. They favorably alter our brain's chemistry. We may access stored insights, make better sense of our circumstances, and assemble more effective responses. We may program our minds and positively affect our mood, outlook, reactions, and actions. Done collectively, prayer and meditation strengthen relationships and communities.

Purpose and Social Interaction

Purpose and social interaction play important roles in our health. After we establish ourselves, raise our children, and secure our retirement, having a purpose and being around people improve our health.

Purpose keeps us thinking and active. It causes us to awaken from a night's sleep, engage with the world, and be active. Having people around us dissipates loneliness, satisfies basic human needs, and provides a reason for being. We need to connect with others and require their love, caring, friendship, and esteem. And once we leave childhood, we only receive these things as we give them. If we do not love others, care about them, and initiate friendships, people do not return love, caring, and friendship.

Without purpose and social interaction, we frequently lie in bed, sit around, overeat, and watch television too much. Little by little, we atrophy and become despondent. We compromise our immune systems and open ourselves up to disease. Purpose and social interaction keep us connected and contributing to the larger community. They incline us to belong, do, care, feel good about ourselves, and live more fully.

Balance

Balance furthers health. It is a simple concept but difficult to realize, in part because it involves a healthy mix of sleep, time with people, activity, and renewal. As the Delphi Oracle suggested, "Nothing in excess." We must do many things correctly to realize balance.

Living purposefully, maintaining healthy lifestyles, caring about others, listening, and seeking to understand others are all important aspects of balance. Preparing for school, work, and upcoming activities, working, playing, and relaxing before bed further balance. And at least one day a week, refreshing our outlook, reflecting on our lives, and taking extra time to enjoy our families and friends keep us mindful of our priorities and purpose.

When our lives are in balance, we make better choices and meet our challenges head-on. Generally, we have healthier relationships with our spouses, parents, children, friends, and associates. Living a balanced life increases the likelihood that our family will remain intact, our children will do well, and our work and careers will be on track.

On the other hand, when our lives are out of balance, we react. We tend to obsess about our relationships and responsibilities, eat compulsively, become overweight, and sleep poorly. Gambling, pornography, and drugs become more appealing. We often overspend, borrow too much, let bills pile up, or skip school, work, and medical checkups. When our lives are out of balance, we are more likely to feel stressed, become sick or depressed, and have accidents.

Health – *maintaining our minds and bodies by utilizing the practices of hygiene, nutrition, periodic fasting, sleep, exercise, avoiding harm, medical and dental care, DNA fidelity, reflection, purpose, social interaction, and balance. Disease and atrophy are antitheses of health.*

Chapter 15

Thought

Human creation first occurs in the mind, where thought transforms information into originality and the seemingly impossible into the possible.

Because all lifeforms have evolved incrementally from previous ones, our brains are a composite of the central nervous systems of innumerable species and have been developing for over a billion years. They are a synthesis of a rudimentary nervous system, a reactive reptilian vertebrate core, nurturing mammalian overlays, and intelligent primate lobes.

The brains weighs about three pounds and comprises a neural network of some 100 billion neurons.[113] The cerebral cortex, the site of self-control, imagination, abstract thought, and reasoning, is its dominant feature. Our brain represents roughly 2 percent of our body weight yet consumes over 20 percent of the total oxygen and glucose that our body utilizes.[114] Our brain's neural network is incomprehensible, and consciousness is miraculous. Director of the Neurosciences Institute and Nobel Laureate, Gerald Edelman, along with neuroscientist Giulio Tononi, wrote:

> The most recently evolved outer corrugated mantle of the human brain, cerebral cortex, contains about 30 billion neurons and 1 million billion connections, or synapses. If we counted one synapse per second, we would not finish counting for 32 million years.

> If we considered the number of possible neural circuits, we would be dealing with hyper-astronomical numbers: 10 followed by at least a million zeroes. There are 10 followed by 79 zeroes, give or take a few, of particles in the known universe.[115]

Consciousness and thought are relatively new attributes on the evolutionary stage. They enable rapid adaptation and culturally coordinated super-organisms. They are our most potent attributes and greatest competitive advantages. Appropriately utilized, thought furthers our fitness and well-being as much as any other Winning Practice.

Assimilation

Our brains unconsciously filter and assimilate prodigious amounts of information. When young, we effortlessly soak up everything around us. As we age, we absorb information at gradually declining rates.

The breadth, depth, and accuracy of the information that we assimilate affect the quality of our thoughts. Thoughts built on erroneous information yield fewer positive effects than those built on accurate information. Unlearning or dislodging incorrect information is more difficult than learning new information.

We want to assimilate accurate information, attend quality schools, learn from the most knowledgeable books and instructors, and obtain news from the most objective sources. We want to be skeptical of information from unqualified sources, particularly when inaccuracy furthers their self-interest. Parents and teachers who expose us to information that accurately reflects a broad swath of reality do us a great service.

Objective and accurate information is hard to come by. Most religious, political, and media groups play to people's emotions and do not provide such information. Though not perfect, reputable scientific institutions and news organizations deliver the most accurate information.

Thoughts precede speech and action. Generally, positive and accurate thoughts precipitate speech and action that yield more beneficial effects than dark and inaccurate thoughts. As Marcus Aurelius wrote over two thousand years ago:

The happiness of your life depends upon the quality of your thoughts.[116]

Visualization

Critical to the successful resolution of a challenge is visualization. With enough experience, our brains develop spectacular reservoirs of knowledge. When we confront a difficulty, we search our memories for relevant information. Like computers recalling and assembling the pixels of an image, our minds recall memories and assemble a helpful collection of visuals.

Visuals are packages of information assembled into images. Visualization requires imagination, the interim steps, and the end results. By visualizing a project's players, components, completed form, and benefits, we conceive its creation and create desire for it. As we dwell on these images and their benefits, we can develop the resolve to overcome opposition and impediments. British philosopher and author James Allen wrote:

> The greatest achievement was at first and for a time a dream. The oak sleeps in the acorn; the bird waits in the egg; and in the highest vision of the soul a waking angel stirs. Dreams are the seedlings of realities.[117]

Creativity

To many, creativity is a mysterious gift that a few lucky people possess. The truth is that we all have creative ability. Once we understand evolution, we realize that nature creates the incredible tapestry of life without conscious or intelligent direction. Its only tools are infinitesimally small changes, natural selection, iterations, and time. Human creativity and nature's creativity are quite similar.

As we think, we recall, disassemble, and assemble our memories in new and different ways. Like nature, our creativity is a trial-and-error process. We conceive an array of potential solutions and consider their relative effort, cost, and effectiveness one by one in our minds. Eventually, we discern and refine a solution. Thomas Edison's creation of the electric light bulb occurred in just this manner. It involved trying alternative filament materials and configurations hundreds of times until he found the most functional one.

Nature's creativity takes centuries and millennia, whereas human creativity takes minutes, hours, and days. Human creativity is faster because much of it occurs in our minds rather than in the real world. Creativity is within everyone's reach. We simply must experiment and work at something for days, weeks, or years to find better solutions.

Need is the mother of creativity. We generally do not create something until we need it. Creativity is work, and we avoid work until need motivates us. For example, Europeans and Americans in the early 1800s found traversing the ocean in sailboats slow, difficult, and unreliable. Richard Wright sought a faster, more reliable way to cross the ocean. Building on John Fitch's and Robert Fulton's steam-powered riverboats, he built the first ocean-going steam ship in 1813.

Experience and practice facilitate incremental creativity and hinder radical creativity. While experience and practice help people make improvements and find solutions more quickly in a field, they also harden the landscape in our minds. More radical leaps and improvements come from youth, interaction with others, the cross-pollination of disciplines, and fresh eyes.

After creating something or developing a solution, effective people share their creations with other interested parties, elicit feedback from them, and reshape their creations to mitigate unforeseen and undesirable outcomes and improve the acceptance of their creations.

Reverse Engineering

When we confront a problem and visualize a solution, reverse engineering is our best approach to work out the necessary steps to find the solution. If we start with current circumstances and try to engineer our way forward, we will find that there are an infinite number of paths ahead. If we start with the visualized end state and engineer our way backward, the paths are finite. For example, if we start with an early cell phone, we might say to ourselves, "This device could be better; let's improve it." In this situation, we confront an infinite number of paths forward.

Alternatively, if we imagine a phone with a colored touch screen, one that plays music and runs a myriad of small computer programs, then improving an early cell phone is easier. We know the new phone must be big enough for people's fingers to work the screen and small enough to carry conveniently. The new phone needs a color touch screen and a microchip processor. It requires a rechargeable battery, speakers, a wireless antenna, and a port connection for charging. Once we inventory the components, sourcing them and placing them within the phone become the challenges.

Research

Sometimes the end states we envision could be better. We just do not have enough information to imagine a highly desirable end state or know enough to reverse engineer an envisioned end state. In both cases, research enables us to augment our knowledge and improve the quality of our product. Research takes time and resources.

The challenge with research is that we do not know what we do not know, and we do not know if the time and resources devoted to research will bear a solution. The best ways we can resolve this dilemma are to recognize that (a) millions of creative, hardworking people confronted similar challenges, and (b) there is value in doing a little more research than others.

Unless we are doing cutting-edge work, the knowledge that we lack usually is only a library visit, Internet connection, or phone call away. Library and Internet searches, along with consulting vendors, peers, and experts are some of the best ways to surface helpful information. Networking, traveling, reading, and "being in motion" help immensely. These activities generate new approaches, stimulate creativity, and reduce the rigidity of our paradigms.

Choice and Alignment

> The space inside of us between stimulus and response is the space of our freedom to choose. . . . It is what makes us human, and not stimulus-response animals.[118]
>
> —Stephen Covey

Our ability to think is very liberating. Unlike most lifeforms, humans are not captive to evolutionary stimulus-response sequences. From our memory database, we may create an array of options and choose the one that generates the largest stream of positive effects. We may sift through our experiences, run mental experiments, and select more effective responses. We may even defer our responses, sleep on a problem, and wake with better approaches.

Unlike most animals, we direct our thoughts and actions. We can ponder whether we have been merely reacting; thoughtfully align our words and actions with our values and priorities; and utilize winning or losing practices. If the past did not go well, we can reflect on it. We can formulate different future words and actions. We may contemplate others' challenges and interests, forgive their transgressions, dissipate anger, create positive thoughts, and improve our interpersonal relationships. If we lied to others or hurt others, we may apologize to them, tell the truth, and avoid unwelcome exchanges in the future.

Focus

Focus, along with choice and alignment, facilitates effectiveness. Focus involves determining the things we can and cannot affect, and then directing our thoughts toward the things we can affect. Focus enhances our efficiency and effectiveness, and it also reduces lethargy and despondency, as we direct our thoughts to our priorities and away from senseless worry.

There are around 16 wakeful hours in a day, and a focused person will make so much better use of them than an unfocused one. Focus causes us to prioritize, plan, prepare, concentrate, and complete our projects. It enables us to finish our work in less time, effectively carry out our responsibilities, and have more time and resources to enjoy life.

If we live near one of Earth's major faults and constantly fear earthquakes, we preoccupy our minds with a danger we cannot influence. If we realize that worrying has no effect on the likelihood of earthquakes and is a misuse of our time, however, we may consider the risk, attempt to mitigate it, and then gracefully accept the remaining risk or move.

Rehearsal

Mental rehearsal enables us to practice our speech and actions before we speak and act. It allows us to conserve energy and resources, better prepare for challenges and future events, and improve our relationships and effectiveness. A leader, carpenter, or any worker who visualizes each day's work ahead of time is more likely to arrive with the needed tools and supplies, make fewer missteps, and waste less time.

Mental rehearsal also imprints routines into our unconscious and allows us to perform activities without conscious effort. Actors, musicians, athletes, and those who perform at the highest levels frequently visualize their performances. Mental rehearsal is not as powerful as actual rehearsal, but it is a useful supplement and oftentimes the only form of rehearsal available. Extemporaneous performances seldom approach the quality of well-rehearsed ones.

Mentors

Being close to outstanding individuals who excel in their fields accelerates our progress. As I reflect on the last five decades of my life, I cannot overstate the importance of mentors. My mother taught me things like being honest, considerate, and helpful. My father taught me things like taking responsibility, making tough decisions, having high standards, not abusing power, and doing well by stakeholders. My grandparents taught me the importance of good habits, hard work, and community mindfulness. A few teachers, professors, and coaches stretched me with rigorous demands. Several elderly friends provided helpful counsel. All this instruction has helped me immensely throughout my life.

Figure 13 and Appendix B provide the names of some one hundred mentors who have influenced me. Though few of us will ever know all our mentors personally, they materialize in our lives through books and other media. Having been where we are going, mentors usually know the way. They exemplify critical behaviors, share valuable insights, help us form empowering habits, and provide inspiration. Mentors affect our thoughts and actions in the present and future. Frank Herbert, journalist, writer, and a novelist best known for the *Dune* science fiction book series, wrote:

> The mind can go either direction under stress—toward positive or toward negative: on or off. Think of it as a spectrum whose extremes are unconsciousness at the negative end and hyperconsciousness at the positive end. The way the mind will lean under stress is strongly influenced by training.[119]

The way our minds learn under stress is influenced by the thoughts and behaviors our mentors instill in us. Finding good mentors, recalling and appreciating them, and later in life, being a good mentor are important to people's growth and development.

Figure 13: Important Mentors

Craig Benjamin, Cynthia Stokes Brown, David Christian, Albert Einstein, Robert Hazen, Isaac Newton, Carl Sagan	Universe and Science
Charles Darwin, Richard Dawkins, Christian de Duve, Robert Hazen, Nick Lane	Origin of Life and Evolution
Dale Carnegie, William Golding, Yuval Noah Harari, Frank Herbert, Leo Tolstoy, E.O Wilson, Robert Wright	Human Nature
James Allen, Gerald Edelman, Plato, Socrates	Human Mind, Thought
Rachel Carson, The Nature Conservancy, Mark Tercek, E.O. Wilson	Environment
Janice Bitz, Linda and Richard Eyre, Jesus, Martin Luther King, Jr., Martin Luther, Moses	Moral Development
Ariel and Will Durant, James Michener, Steven Pinker	History
Metta Bitz, Dale Carnegie, Kenneth Cooper, Steven Covey, Ray Dalio, Charles Duhigg, Chaim Potok	Individual Well-being
Steven Covey, Milton Friedman, John Gray, Erica Komisar, John Locke, M. Scott Peck, Robert Putnam, E.F. Schumacher, Paul Tough	Family, Child Development, and Education
Robert Bitz, Jim Collins, James Gwartney, Dwight Lee, David Ricardo, Paul Samuelson, Adam Smith, Richard Stroup, Nassim Taleb, Jack Welch	Economics and Business
Ken Blanchard, Max Depree, Mariah Gandhi, Pope John Paul II, Spencer Johnson, Nelson Mandela, Ronald Reagan, George Washington, Jack Welch	Leadership
John Bogle, Warren Buffett, George Clason, Al and Ruth Dettbarn, William Thorndike, Jr.	Frugalness and Investing

Benjamin Franklin, Milton Friedman, Alexander Hamilton, John Jay, Thomas Jefferson, Charles Krauthammer, Robert Levy, James Madison, Brion McClanahan, William Mellor, Robert Morris, David Moss, George Orwell, Cleon Skousen, Lee Kuan Yew	Government
Alexis De Tocqueville, Max Dimont, Niall Ferguson, Philip Gooden, Lawrence Harrison, Frank Herbert, Arthur Herman, Verne Freeman, Geert Hofstede, Gert Jan Hofstede, Michael Minkov, Samuel Huntington, Max Weber	Culture

Thought is one of the most potent Winning Practices. It precedes all human creation. It helps us find solutions to our most pressing challenges. It is hard work, and consumes time and energy, but it is less work, less costly, and less time-consuming than real-world trial and error. As James Allen and Stephen Covey wrote:

> You are today where your thoughts have brought you; you will be tomorrow where your thoughts take you.[120]

> Sow a thought, reap an action; sow an action, reap a habit; sow a habit, reap a character; sow a character, reap a destiny.[121]

Thought – *the practice of utilizing our minds to filter, assimilate, and organize prodigious amounts of information. Thought involves assimilation, visualization, creativity, reverse engineering, research, choice, alignment, focus, rehearsal, and mentors. Thought enables us to respond constructively to stimuli and imagine new states. It requires insignificant amounts of energy, time, and resources relative to real-world experimentation, and it exponentially increases our effectiveness. Vegetation and reactiveness are the antitheses of thought.*

Chapter 16

Integrity

Our parents, teachers, and community give us our initial sense of integrity, but we may shape it in adolescence and later in life.

Integrity involves aligning our thoughts, speech, and actions with our priorities and what is true. It implies honesty, honorableness, and reliability and facilitates human function and interaction. Dishonesty, corruption, and unreliability are antitheses of integrity. When exposed, they destroy people's trust in us and impede their interaction. Our level of integrity affects our fitness and how our life goes for us.

Truthfulness

Truthfulness is essential to integrity. Saying what we mean and doing what we say enable us to interact with others and benefit from the interaction. If we are honest and open with our parents, we benefit from their wisdom and experience. If we are truthful and diligent in school, we learn skills needed to succeed in life. On the other hand, if we lie about our eligibility for a team, we jeopardize the teams' standing and our place on it. Everything works better when people are truthful and poorly when they lie.

We are short-sighted and our desire for others' approval is strong, and so lying may cause others to look favorably on us for a while. Thus, most children experiment with lying and become skilled at it unless their parents and others penalize them for it. Thomas Jefferson expressed the ease with which we fall into a habit of lying as follows:

It is of great importance to set a resolution, not to be shaken, never to tell an untruth. There is no vice so mean, so pitiful, so contemptible; and he who permits himself to tell a lie once, finds it much easier to do it a second and third time, till at length it becomes habitual; he tells lies without attending to it, and truths without the world's believing him. This falsehood of the tongue leads to that of the heart, and in time depraves all its good dispositions.[122]

We must model truthfulness and develop it in children because they mimic our behavior and because truthfulness affects our fitness and well-being. Rewarding honesty and penalizing lying more than other misconducts incentives children to tell the truth.

Authenticity is another aspect of truthfulness involving being and becoming our natural selves. We come into the world with varying gifts of stature, strength, beauty, empathy, intelligence, leadership, voice, and athleticism. Authenticity requires us to detect, develop, and utilize these gifts. As Albert Einstein indicated, some of the most satisfying experiences are bound up with the development of our own feeling, thinking, acting, and unique gifts.[123]

Authenticity is also about accurately representing ourselves and aligning our speech and actions with our being. We cannot be a doctor without completing medical school or advocate monogamy and have extra-marital affairs. To be authentic, we must continuously evaluate our words and actions to ensure that they accurately represent us.

Honorableness

When we are honorable, we act in ways that benefit the larger community. We respect others, their property, and the environment and act lawfully and ethically. We do not cheat and are good sports. We treat others who mean us no harm as we want them to treat us. We do not speak disparagingly of others. We fulfill our responsibilities and pay our taxes. We do not act in ways that would sadden us to see reported in a newspaper. Honorableness rejects self-indulgence elevating our conduct.

Disparaging others is one of the most common forms of dishonorable behavior. Speaking poorly of others reflects badly on us, as those who hear our comments realize that we may make similar remarks about them. The triple filter—*Is it true? Is it kind? Is it necessary?*—checks counterproductive speech.[124]

Earnestness, another aspect of honorableness, involves having a genuine concern for others. Earnestness is easier for us when we recognize that we need others and develop an interest in others. Thankfully, my parents, grandparents, and faith communities taught me throughout my childhood about the importance of other people and the larger community. Perhaps the most memorable instruction about this came from my great-aunt, Nellie Bitz, as I left for college:

Give your best to the others, and they will give their best to you.[125]

Reliability

Reliability, a third aspect of integrity, is about keeping our commitments. When we tell people that we will do something, we must do it. Being reliable brings opportunities, and everything works better when we do what we say.

If our parents, teachers, and coaches help us learn self-control and to defer gratification, we find it easier to learn to live with integrity. Mastering basic discipline-related behaviors makes mastering more advanced ones easier. People who are reliable do not weigh the pros and cons of keeping commitments. Instead, they just fulfil their promises and go through life in this manner.

One-on-one contact and community increase our empathy for others, make our reputations important, and cause us to be more honest, reliable, and decent. We cannot control others' behavior, but we can control ours. We may align our speech and conduct; marry a person who is truthful, honorable, and reliable; and teach these behaviors to our children. We may exhibit these behaviors and expect others to do so.

Priorities

Priorities further integrity as they focus our thoughts and actions on the people who matter most to us and the thoughts and actions that yield more meaningful outcomes. Having priorities helps us do the most advantageous activities in the most beneficial order. Some priorities are universal, some specific to groups, and some specific to us. Children are universal priorities for parents as are grandchildren for grandparents. The scientific method is a priority specific to scientists.

Our predilections, experiences, and interests affect our priorities. Intelligent people tend to make reading and learning priorities, athletic people make physical fitness and sports priorities, those living in the country make rural issues priorities, and those who grow up in cities make urban issues priorities.

Certain priorities, like health, family, school, and work, have positive effects on us in the short and long term. If we are fortunate, our parents instill these priorities within us, and we can wait until we have sufficient maturity to reshape the priorities. If our parents do not instill these priorities in us, we must learn from able people and shape our priorities at a much earlier age.

Most of us operate with the priorities our parents teach us until our peers and other influences in our lives challenge these priorities. When this occurs, we become aware of our priorities and question them. Some time in our late 20s and early 30s, we tend to settle on our priorities and become more set in our ways. Priority selection requires us to ask ourselves several questions. Whom do I value most? What approaches, activities, and things do I value? Is my allocation of time consistent with whom and what I value?

To answer these questions, we must understand the priorities that have been instilled in us and learn about alternative ones. A solid understanding of the evolution of the universe, life, and our culture, as well as a good sense of other cultures, facilitates this process. Reading, traveling, and living in other countries increases our awareness of our priorities and exposes us to alternatives.

While living in Poland I learned as much about my culture, country, and people as I did about the Polish ones. Just as we lack depth perception if we have only one eye, so we lack awareness of our priorities and perspective without multiple vantage points.

Our geography, history, and culture affect our priorities. For example, historically, populations from lower latitudes sheltered and fed themselves more easily than other groups. They lived in larger groups and had more centralized governments. Generations of Roman and Chinese rule reinforced these circumstances. Consequently, those from lower latitudes came to value authority, obedience, leisure, and the present.[126]

In the higher latitudes of the Germanic tribes, food was scarcer and the winters severe. People lived in smaller, more geographically dispersed groups under decentralized governments. Their survival depended on forethought, proactivity, and cooperation. These circumstances caused people from the northern latitudes to value democracy, cooperation, planning, deferring gratification, work, and the future more than those from lower latitudes.[127]

We do not want to choose too many priorities to avoid reducing the potency of each one. A few people, a few approaches, and a few activities should commonly comprise our priorities. In my case, my health, family, close friends, colleagues, work, community, and country are foremost priorities, while the Winning Perspectives and Practices in this book comprise many of the others.

Quiet time brings our most important priorities into focus. Author, producer, director, and actor Christopher Reeve suggested that we have better judgment and make superior choices when we escape from the noise and many demands on us and are still:

I think we all have a little voice inside us that will guide us. It may be God, I don't know. But I think that if we shut out all the noise and clutter from our lives and listen to that voice, it will tell us the right thing to do.[128]

While I agree with Christopher Reeve on the value of the voice within us, we must be careful with it. This voice sometimes inclines us to make bad choices. In fact, it is not really one voice but a cacophony of genetic, cultural, and self-interest-related voices.

How might genetic predispositions influence this voice? First, we know that affiliation conveys fitness. People who affiliate with a family, clan, tribe, kingdom, and/or country place more offspring into the next generation than loners do. Second, we know that groups welcome empathetic people more readily than callous people into their fold. Empathetic people sense others' pain, do not want to hurt others, and feel badly when they do. Empathy is an attribute associated with successful affiliation. Like most human attributes, people's level of empathy varies among individuals. We are predisposed with some level of empathy, and therefore, have a voice that advocates for decency.

A second voice within us is a product of our culture. It is the sense of right and wrong that parents and other authorities convey to children. The specifics and intensity of this voice vary greatly among people. Consequently, the voice within us is neither singular nor completely benign. The voice within us depends on what gave the preceding generations a survival advantage and what our parents and other authority figures teach us.

Consider John, a married man who develops a crush on Mary, a woman who is not his spouse. His genetic predisposition and the voice associated with it says, "Go for it," but John does not begin an affair with Mary because another stronger voice within him says, "Not so fast." John's parents and other respected mentors served as effective role models. They taught him that crushes pass and the well-being of his spouse and children depend on his fidelity. John stays focused on his spouse and avoids an extramarital entanglement.

What do you think John would have more likely done if his mother had divorced three times and most of the adults that he knew growing up were divorcees? What do you think he would have done if he had been taught to just follow his heart and that divorce is normal?

In quiet, we must sense and may pare our list of potential priorities to a few major ones. Before we make something a priority, however, we must test it. Just because we value something, and a voice inside us urges us toward it, does not mean it conveys streams of positive effects. Drug addicts value their suppliers and drugs, but their suppliers and drugs are not good for them. If we care about outcomes, we will select priorities that stream positive effects. The Effects Test helps us do this.

The Effects Test examines whether a perspective, priority, or practice yields predominately positive effects for individuals, families, groups, education, enterprises, governments, and/or the environment in the short and long term.

Thus, we must use a two-step approach to select our priorities. Potential priorities arise during times of stillness and quiet, and then we determine their desirability by examining their effects on ourselves and others in the short and long term. Priority awareness and selection mean little until we commit to a set of priorities and act on them. Often, serious differences exist between what we think are our priorities and how we allocate our time. If our families, friends, and community are truly priorities, then we allocate time for them and put our priorities on our calendars. As Stephen Covey wrote:

> You have to decide what your highest priorities are and have the courage—pleasantly, smilingly, non-apologetically—to say "no" to other things. And the way you do that is by having a bigger "yes" burning inside. The enemy of the "best" is often the "good."[129]

The key is not to prioritize what's on your schedule, but to schedule your priorities.[130]

After defining and scheduling our priorities, it is advantageous to regularly review them. Life places many demands on us; before we know it, our priorities sometimes slip away. Prioritization requires periodic review and scheduling. Aligning our speech and actions with our priorities is powerful. It impacts our relationships, accomplishments, and character, and even our destinies over time. Stephen Covey wrote:

> How different our lives are when we really know what is deeply important to us, and keeping that picture in mind, we manage ourselves each day to be and to do what really matters most.[131]

Health, family, friends, work, community, and country are critical priorities for nearly everybody because they are integral to being human. Good health enables us to be vital and effective, while poor health sidelines us. Family and friends are those whom we count on for help and we most readily assist. Work brings us the means to live, and we spend a large portion of our wakeful hours working. A well-functioning community and country protects us from the predatory behavior of others. They contain the people with whom we have the most in common and the institutions on which we depend most.

One of the more instructive and memorable stories about ordering our lives is the story of "The Jar and the Rocks." Its original author is unknown, and I have altered the story slightly to underscore the importance of priorities.

> A professor stood before his philosophy class, picked up a jar, and proceeded to fill it with rocks. He asked the students if the jar was full. The students indicated the jar was full.
>
> Then the professor picked up a box of pebbles and poured them into the jar. He shook the jar lightly. The pebbles rolled into the open areas between the rocks. He asked the students again if the jar was full. The students again indicated the jar was full.

Next, the professor picked up a box of sand and poured it into the jar. He shook the jar, and the sand filled in the gaps between the pebbles. He asked once more if the jar was full. The students replied "yes."

Then the professor filled two glasses of water and poured the water into the jar. The students laughed.

"Now," said the professor as the laughter subsided, "this jar represents your life. The rocks are the important things—your health, family, and friends. From the beginning to the end of your life, this is what will always matter the most to you. The pebbles are the other things that matter, like your education, work, country, and culture. If everything else was lost and only the rocks and the pebbles remained, you would still have a full life.

The sand is everything else—the small stuff. It is the prestige and material things that add to our lives but are not important and we do not need. If you put the sand into the jar first," he continued, "there is no room for the rocks or pebbles. So it is with your life. If you spend all your time and energy on the small stuff, you will not have room for the things that matter the most and are important to you.

Pay attention to the things that are critical to you and your loved ones' long-term fitness and well-being. Take time to get medical checkups, a good night's sleep, and exercise. Spend time with your spouse, children, parents, grandparents, and friends. Apply yourself in school, do your best at work, and serve your community and country. Understand what is best about your culture and teach it to your children.

Know who and what matters over time. Prioritize and schedule time for these people and activities first. Take care of the rocks and the pebbles—the things that really matter first. The rest is just sand."

One of the students raised her hand and inquired what the water represented.

The professor smiled and said, "I'm glad you asked. The water represents the serendipity of life or unexpected pleasant surprises that come our way when we get the rocks and pebbles right, when we treat others as we want them to treat us, and when we regularly give our best effort. As the water fills the jar, so serendipity and the streams of positive effects that accompany Winning Perspectives and Practices fill our lives."

Teaching priorities to our children positively affects their well-being and happiness, and it does not prevent them from one day reshaping them. Not teaching our children priorities is like turning them loose in a jungle and hoping that they safely find their way.

As many children no longer learn about integrity from their parents or from faith communities, placing greater emphasis on it in our schools and detention centers would improve our communities and country. Just as parents can help children direct their thoughts, speech, and actions in a positive manner and form good habits, so teachers and detention center personnel can do this with their populations.

We have little control over many of our circumstances. We can choose our thoughts, speech, and actions, however, as well as our friends and pastimes. We decide whether to indulge in immediate pleasures or defer for better future circumstances, quit or complete our tasks, and interact respectfully or disrespectfully with others. We choose to be truthful or deceitful, reliable or unreliable, honorable or dishonorable.

In short, we determine the level of integrity with which we live and the practices that we utilize. We affect much of what happens to us. When we live with integrity, everything works better. We experience less conflict and frustration, and we are individually and collectively fitter, more effective, and happier.

Integrity – *truthfulness, honorableness, reliability, and internalized hierarchical rankings of the relative importance of various people, practices, and activities. More specifically, integrity involves (a) saying what we mean and doing what we say, (b) acting in an ethical and lawful manner, (c) avoiding conflicts of interest, (d) having others' best interests at heart, (e) doing what is right regardless of what others do, (f) acting in a manner worthy of others' esteem, and (g) fulfilling our responsibilities. Dishonesty, corruption, and unreliability are antithetical to integrity.*

Chapter 17

Proactivity

Anticipatory, thoughtful, responsible, and constructive speech and actions yield streams of positive effects.

None of us chose our start—our time, place, genes, parents, or schools. If we are fortunate to have two responsible, loving, and able parents, then we are better for it. If not, then we have some ground to make up. Although much of life is not fair, we do reap as we sow amid its unfairness. Once we leave school, we choose how we act, treat others, and spend our time. Rather than feeling sorry for ourselves and losing more ground, we are better off making the best of our circumstances. The following excerpt from *The Well Kept Secret* by author and *New York Times* writer, David Brooks, speaks to this point:

> For about the past hour it had been dawning on me that lying beneath the hurt that I felt over his horrible semester may have been the life-long hurt I had felt from Mom and Dad. Glimpses kept coming to me that perhaps my confusion about school was only a symptom of the betrayal that I had been feeling all my life from parents who either didn't love me or didn't know how to show it in a way that I could recognize.
>
> Given the crappy hand I had been dealt so far in life, whose responsibility is it to fix the problem? None of Boy's ancestors had had it easy, but all of them responded the same way. They each understood that whatever our starting point, we can and must reinvent ourselves as soon as we are mentally strong enough to stand up to the weaker parts of our personalities. Instead of harboring resentment against my parents forever, I imagined for a minute that the approach that would actually

build me up and allow me to break free of my past would be to forgive them and make a new promise to myself, a promise that I would not pass such uncaring tendencies on to the next generation. Instead, I could watch over my children and protect them like the best mothers in all the ages. Did I have the power inside me to reinvent myself, to rise-up above my past, and force a strong and happy future onto myself and the family I would one day have?[132]

No matter our start, proactivity is a ticket to a better life. Proactivity—anticipatory, thoughtful, responsible, constructive speech and action—makes all the difference. We live in a cause-and-effect world. Being responsible, speaking and acting positively, developing good habits, learning and preparing, detecting our purpose, working hard, and serving others causes others to return the same and more to us.

Purpose

Proactivity is easier when we detect our purpose in life. Most people naturally develop a purpose over time but knowing how to go about it helps. Our genes and environments individualize us. Early recognition of the things we do well causes us to develop them and create comparative advantages. When we learn easily, we develop our minds and intellectual interests. When we have high emotional intelligence, we develop social skills and interests. When we have athletic ability, we develop physically and play sports. Small advantages when we are young become large advantages over time.

Detecting our purpose involves identifying the convergence of what we like to do, what we do well relative to others, and what others value. The next step after identifying something that we enjoy doing and do well relative to others is to consider how we might contribute to our family, community, and country—entities that sustain our well-being and that we want to support and strengthen.

Oftentimes, what we like to do aligns with what we do well and what others value because we receive recognition for these activities. Sometimes our desires do not align with our predilections and what others value. In these instances, our path forward is more difficult. If we do what we do poorly, disregard others' preferences, or ignore our preferences, positive results materialize more slowly. In these instances, two insights help us. First, our affection for something grows as we give ourselves to it. Second, when we do something unenjoyable to us that others value, often we do not have to do it for long. We do it for some of the day or for a few years, make the best of our situation, and do what we like after work or later in life.

When we do find the convergence of what we like to do, what we do well, and what others value, dreams form in our minds. And while dreams are precious, they sometimes need shaping. Well-founded dreams fuel our rise better than quixotic ones. Consultation with accomplished mentors helps us distinguish between the two types of dreams. If our mentors affirm the plausibility of our desires, we move forward. If not, we want to consider more realistic variations of our dreams.

Fears surface along the way. This is natural and sometimes helpful, as fears cause us to prepare and proceed carefully. Pondered and bridled, fears prepare us for setbacks and help us to achieve better outcomes. Obstacles are part of life, but they need not mean failure. We only fail when we give up. The best baseball players strike out, pop out, and are thrown out twice as often as they get on base. The best basketball players miss more than half their shots. Swinging the bat and shooting the basketball yield continuing setbacks, but they also yield singles, doubles, triples, home runs, baskets, and game-winning runs and points.

Responsibility

Responsibility recognizes our ability to author our lives and involves a commitment to be accountable for our actions. It helps us realize that our affiliation with others carries obligations as well as benefits, and it requires the steady fulfillment of these commitments. Responsible people make the best of the cards they are dealt. They do not blame others for their position and for what happens to them.

In a developed country, most of us take for granted our security, abundant fresh water and food, extensive wardrobes, spacious homes, free education, quality healthcare, comfortable cars, innumerable opportunities, and free time. Yet all of this does not just magically materialize. Rather, it results from the responsible actions of millions of people throughout the last 300 years.

For at least five out of every seven days, most of us must go to work, arrive on time, complete our assigned duties, and follow the rules. For at least 180 days a year, every student must go to school, arrive on time, pay attention in class, do their assigned work, learn the material, and follow the school rules. And every month or year, we must pay our rent, mortgage, bills, and our local, state, and federal taxes.

To enjoy a good life, we must act in our interests and on behalf of others' interests. We must follow the laws, find out who are the best candidates for elective office, and vote. We must say what we mean, do what we say, and fulfill our responsibilities. If we need to learn, we must take steps to acquire that knowledge. If we need income, we must work. If we have children, we must nurture and guide them for years. And if we are to enjoy a good life, our neighbors, colleagues, and fellow citizens also must do these things.

Constructive Speech and Action

Constructive speech and action are important aspects of proactivity. To understand their importance, consider how we communicate and act when we feel pressured and tired, and we speak from the reptilian portions of our brains. We freely express irritation and pummel others' feelings. We do not take the time to understand others, empathize with others, or imagine how to make a situation better. We do not check our negativity; rather, we escalate conflicts, damage relationships, and make many situations worse.

On the other hand, when we pause and take time to understand others and their circumstances before speaking and acting, we anticipate the effects of our words and actions. We choose our responses carefully and creatively improve situations. We replace reactive speech and actions with something more constructive, avoiding the negative effects of the former and reaping the positive ones of the latter. We dissipate conflict and strengthen relationships.

Preparation

Preparation involves envisioning upcoming events, anticipating future needs, and doing what we can ahead of time to make the events go smoothly. Preparation increases our productivity and is especially important for leaders, as their lack of preparation adversely affects large numbers of people.

Homework prepares us for exams, and exams prepare us for life. Homework magnifies the value of classroom instruction and facilitates the learning process. Thinking about our objectives each day, week, month, and year helps us better allocate our time and sequence our activities. Thinking through the tools, materials, and supplies needed for the next day's work and arriving with them enable us to accomplish more. Preparing agendas for meetings makes our meetings more productive.

Work

Living requires work. We cannot satisfy our needs or realize success without it. If we work hard in school, we develop the habits, skills, and histories desirable to employers. If we work hard at work, we develop competencies, receive greater remuneration, and realize more opportunities. Winning Practices of Individuals and Groups mentioned here and discussed in more detail in Chapters 14 through 26 further work.

Health permits us to have good attendance and arrive at work rested and ready to go. It enhances our energy, alertness, and congeniality. It increases our output, improves our quality of work, and decreases the frequency of accidents.

Integrity affects the degree to which people trust us, how they treat us, and how openly they communicate with us. Under-promising and over-delivering allow us to exceed others' expectations and delight them with our work. Employees who exceed their employers' expectations flourish, as do companies that exceed customers' expectations.

Thought enables us to imagine new states and improve our organizations, processes, and products. It helps us use fewer resources, identify opportunities, and improve our processes and products more quickly. Copywriter and author, Joseph Sugarman, wrote:

> Each problem has hidden in it an opportunity so powerful that it literally dwarfs the problem. The greatest success stories [are] created by people who recognize a problem and turn it into an opportunity.[133]

Excellence, or doing things well, improves outcomes, particularly when they involve numerous steps and components. A lack of excellence, or shiftlessness and sloppiness, endangers people and wastes time and resources. The effects of excellence or the lack of it ripple well beyond the object and present. The loss of the mission, resources, and life caused by the Space Shuttle Challenger's O-ring specifications underscore the importance of excellence in specification and production.

Thrift furthers work. It lowers costs and creates surpluses. Thrifty team members create capital to fuel improvements in facilities, processes, products, employment, and investor returns. The positive effects of thrift ripple through organizations for years.

Affiliation connects us with our colleagues. It involves being present, punctual, presentable, congenial, and accountable. Attendance and punctuality increase our productivity more than most people realize. Those who have good attendance, start and finish on time, and commence and end breaks on time accomplish so much more than people who are frequently absent and late.

Leadership sets the mission, standards, and objectives of organizations. Those who exhibit leadership assign work, monitor its progress, conduct evaluations, and influence people's compensation. They decide who joins and leaves our workplace.

Teamwork significantly influences our individual and company's successes. We accomplish so much more in groups than we can alone. There is strength in numbers and opportunities for economies of scale, to specialize, and realize synergies. The more team members trust one another and work together, the better the individual members and organizations do.

Because we spend so much time working and readily adapting our lifestyles, enjoying our work is more important than earning large amounts of money. Most people work some 50 thousand hours in their homes and 100 thousand hours in their workplaces over the course of 50 years. Why be miserable for large portions of our life when we can adjust our lifestyles, do what we like, and be happy? As the adage goes, "Choose a job you love, and you will never have to work a day in your life." And as Donovan Leitch's lyrics of "Brother Sun, Sister Moon" go:

If [we] want [our] dreams to be, build them slowly and surely.
Small beginnings, greater ends, heartfelt work grows purely.[134]

Fitness-Related Service

A desire for service springs from rootedness. When we are rooted in a family, organization, community, and country, we grow to love them. Members of our groups look out for us and we look out for them. Their efforts make huge differences in our lives. Albert Einstein wrote:

> A hundred times every day I remind myself that my inner and outer life are based on the labors of other [people], living and dead, and that I must exert myself to give in the same measure as I have received and am still receiving.[135]

Fitness-Related Service is the idea that it is advantageous to help those in the groups on which we depend before we help those in other groups.

Our resources are limited, and many people within our communities and country need assistance. Moreover, we can influence others more throughout the world if our families, schools, communities, and governments function well. Switzerland and Singapore, each with populations of just a few million, affect billions of people around the world. Their disproportionate influence does not come from foreign aid but from others' desire to replicate their quality of life.

Those who so readily help foreigners follow their heart more than their head. They do not understand evolution and believe that people can learn to put the interests of the international community ahead of their country's interests. They forget that all life is programmed to secure territory, obtain resources, and proliferate. They do not understand that people are primarily loyal to their local tribes, and this loyalty asserts itself in difficult times. They fail to realize that foreign assistance too often enriches corrupt leaders, enables poor people to multiply their numbers and misery, and strengthens future rivals. And they do not grasp that they are free to hold their views because more realistic people shield them from harm. Foreign assistance is only advantageous as we direct it to our closest allies.

Singapore and Switzerland further fitness-related service and social cohesion among their people by requiring young adults to complete two years of military or civil service. These programs have important benefits. They further the maturation and employability of males, and in Switzerland's case, all the males and the females who volunteer for service. They give critical help to those in need, improve their country's defense, deter foreign aggression, and expose young people to the rewarding nature of service.

Fitness-related service fills our lives with purpose and assists others. If we withdraw to our sofas, vegetate with electronic devices, and contribute little to others, our lives are empty. Idleness, pleasure, and entertainment do not fulfill us. World-renowned author Leo Tolstoy wrote in *Anna Karenina*:

> [They] soon felt that the realization of [their] desires gave [them] only one grain of the mountain of happiness [they] had expected. It showed [them] the mistake [people] make in picturing to themselves happiness as the realization of their desires.[136]

Proactive people do whatever is necessary to move forward. They take responsibility, learn, and form good habits. They anticipate, pause, think, and creatively respond. They prioritize, plan, practice, and enlist the support of others. They do repetitive and menial work, persevere, and serve others. They multiply opportunities as they seize them.[137]

The differences between proactive students and reactive ones determine who goes to trade schools or college, and who has excellent employment opportunities or has the less desirable, low-paying jobs. Proactive students attend classes, take thorough notes, rewrite their notes, do their assigned reading and homework, complete their assigned papers and projects, and prepare for tests. They seek extra help when they do not understand something and find out the correct answers to the mistakes made on their homework, projects, and tests.

As we do our homework, study, and complete our chores, we receive good grades and our parents give us more freedom. As we show up for work and do our best, our employers compensate us, give us raises, and consider us for promotions. As we assist people in our community, others assist us. As we apply for a credit card, pay all our charges each month, and pay at least 20 percent of the value of a house up front, we qualify for mortgages at more favorable rates and minimize the interest we pay in our lifetimes.

Proactive people do not blame others for their situation and problems. They reject excuses, procrastination, feel-good rationalizations, and resignation. They do not burden others but find opportunity in everyday life. When proactive people harm others, they provide restitution. Proactive people treat others who do not mean them harm as they want others to treat them. They earn people's trust and respect and avoid verbal, physical, and litigious entanglements.

Proactive people give freely to their workplaces, communities, and country. As a past employer of hundreds of people and friend to numerous business leaders, I know firsthand that companies want to employ proactive people and that proactivity is one of the best predictors of their future performance.

Proactivity – *(a) anticipatory, thoughtful, constructive speech and action, (b) assuming responsibility for our speech, actions, and lives, (c) developing empowering habits, (d) having purpose, (e) being prepared, (f) working hard, and (g) providing fitness-related service. Reactivity, irresponsibility, sloth, and freeloading are antithetical to proactivity.*

Chapter 18

Prudence

We are a product of our past and thousands of hour-by-hour, day-by-day choices.

As the Winning Perspectives suggest, nature places us in a universe governed by unseen natural processes in a community on a habitable planet in competition with other lifeforms and communities. Our continuation depends on understanding our context and making prudent choices. As products of evolution and our parents, schools, and environment, we author our lives within the confines of this preparation and our available opportunities.

Nassim Nicholas Taleb, options trader, student of history, philosophy, and mathematics, and renowned author of *The Black Swan* and *Antifragile*, has devoted his life to studying decision-making, or in other words, making prudent choices. He is the source for many of the thoughts in this chapter.

Fitness, Courage, Knowledge, and Discipline

Prudence involves making choices that yield predominately positive effects on our planet, larger community, family, and ourselves. Fitness, courage, knowledge, and discipline—attributes I discuss in Chapters 8, 24, 30, and 31—facilitate prudence. Rather than repeat the discussions in this chapter, I will simply note that these attributes improve our decision-making and instead focus on antifragility, prohibitions, optionality, judicious risk-taking, practical experience, consulting accomplished people, and being slow to make important decisions.

Symmetry and Nonlinearity

Most people simplistically think that events generate positive or negative outcomes. Unknowingly, people usually imagine symmetric, linear effects. They do not realize that the effects of events are more nuanced—symmetric, asymmetric, linear, nonlinear, accelerating, or decelerating.

Symmetric events produce effects with a similar upside and downside. If we work 40 hours a week and are paid an hourly wage, the effect of working one more or one fewer hour increases or decreases our week's pay by the hourly rate. Figure 14 illustrates event x with symmetrically positive and negative effects f(x).

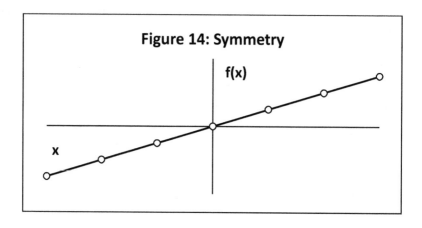

Figure 14: Symmetry

Symmetry is a description of events having similar upside and downside.[138]

In the natural world, people reap what they sow symmetrically. If we secure food, water, and shelter, we live a few more days. If we fail to do this, we become hungry and die in a few days. If we do something of value for others, they appreciate it and reward us. If we work hard to become the most qualified applicant, we receive the position. If we are unqualified, we do not receive it. If we do a good day's work, we are paid. If we do not work, we are not paid. If we ably fulfill our responsibilities, we advance. If we shirk responsibilities or abuse our position, we lose our job. If we risk our capital and time to start a business, operate it successfully, and others buy our product, we profit. If we have no capital or are unwilling to risk it, we do not profit. Life works best when people benefit as their actions help others and themselves, and they lose when their actions harm others and themselves.

Two of the most unethical behaviors in modern life are stealing others' upside and transferring our downside to them without their permission. Corporate executives who pay themselves large bonuses when their companies lose money steal their stakeholders' upside. Professionals who err frequently and keep their licenses harm more clients. Attorneys who profit handsomely from others' errors raise insurance premiums and steal others' upside. Majorities that discriminate against minorities steal their upside. When our government borrows large sums and we degrade critical habitats, we steal our children's and grandchildren's upside.

Mortgage originators who sell the debt of underqualified borrowers transfer their downside to others without their permission. Executives and directors who sell their company's equity because they know it will decrease in value transfer their downside to others. Able-bodied people who take advantage of a generous social safety net and do not actively look for work or accept available work transfer their downside to others. Like heaters without thermostats, people who do not experience the positive and negative effects of their actions do not do the right thing.

When relationships exhibit positive asymmetry, they have limited downside and have unlimited upside. The balance in a savings account has a positive asymmetry over time. The balance steadily increases and has no downside. Figure 15 illustrates positive asymmetry.

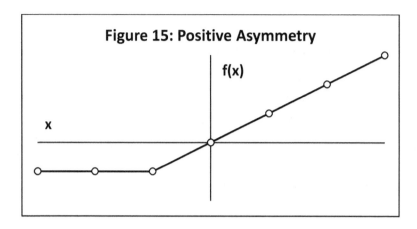

Positive Asymmetry is a description of events with limited downside and unlimited upside.[139]

On the other hand, relationships with limited upside and unlimited downside exhibit negative asymmetry. The value of money kept at home when there is inflation has a negative asymmetry. Inflation erodes the value of the money by a similar amount every day or about 2 to 4 percent a year in many countries. Figure 16 illustrates negative asymmetry.

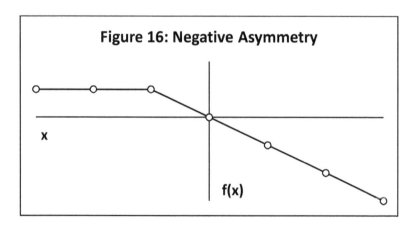

Negative Asymmetry is a description of events having limited upside and unlimited downside.

Asymmetric relationships can be nonlinear as well as linear. Relationships with positive nonlinearity have limited downside and unlimited upside that accelerate over time. Amazon's stock price exhibited positive nonlinearity during the 2015 to 2018 period, increasing by $500 the first two years and $800 the second two years. Figure 17 illustrates positive nonlinearity.

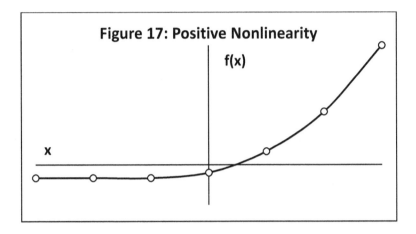

Positive Nonlinearity is a description of events having limited downside and unlimited upside that accelerate or snowball.[140]

Relationships with negative nonlinearity have limited upside and unlimited downside that accelerates. The losses of companies two to three years before they go bankrupt are usually negatively nonlinear as the companies' revenues decline and their mounting principal and interest payments consume more of their cash flow. Figure 18 illustrates negative nonlinearity.

When we are among a group of disciplined, successful people who want to create something with large network effects, outcomes can be positive, then very positive, and then incredibly positive. When we are among a group of unruly, troubled people seeking to avenge smoldering grievances, outcomes are likely to be negative, then very negative, and then incredibly negative.

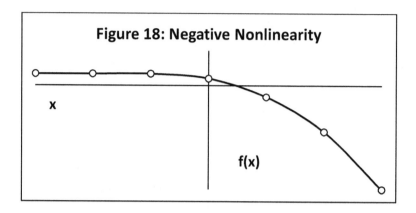

Figure 18: Negative Nonlinearity

Negative Nonlinearity is a description of events having limited upside and unlimited downside that accelerate or snowball.

Nonlinear-related events and their effects are oftentimes hidden. Large changes in conditions affect these nonlinear-related events and their effects more than they affect linearly-related ones. Surpluses, shortages, and bottlenecks produce nonlinear effects. Each situation becomes costlier as its magnitude increases. Government deficits increase nonlinearly for each 1 percent decrease in GNP, and even more nonlinearly when governments have excess debt.

The reality that some events produce positive and negative nonlinear effects makes it in our interests to identify and address the most consequential ones. When thinking about this, I identified seven of the most important events. Surprisingly, we only fully control the last one. If the first six events occur in our lives, we have won the lottery.

(1) Living in a country able to defend itself;

(2) Having a constitutionally and institutionally limited government with an impartial and uniform rule of law;

(3) Having DNA fidelity, good health, and able parents;

(4) Living in a safe neighborhood and having honest, quality peers;

(5) Attending excellent schools and having apprenticeship opportunities;

(6) Having a free enterprise, market-based economy; and

(7) Making prudent choices and being proactive.

Although we only control the last one of these seven important life occurrences, the Winning Practices and sub-practices in this book help us realize all of them. If we all learn these practices and teach them to our children, more of us will enjoy all seven of these occurrences.

Antifragility

Modern life is comprised of large numbers of people, institutions, and complex systems, which have innumerable interdependencies. Consequently, actions of these people, institutions, and systems generate incalculable secondary effects; sometimes, they cascade streams of harmful effects—or, as Nassim Taleb puts it, they create a "Black Swan."

*A **Black Swan** is an event that produces streams of harmful outcomes.*[141]

Some Black Swans, like the giant asteroid impact on Earth that created the moon, occur once; other Black Swans, like massive earthquakes, reoccur. Furthermore, just because something has not occurred does not mean that it will not occur. Taleb speaks of the "Turkey Problem," which likens our complacency toward the future with that of turkeys who believe that the next day always will be like the previous one . . . only to learn just before Thanksgiving that this is not always the case.[142]

Fearful of Black Swans, many people try to predict them. They attempt to calculate their likelihood by conveniently and incorrectly assuming Black Swans occur with some known distribution. This practice is a waste of time and misleading, as the distributions of rare events usually are not normal, asymptotical, or otherwise. They are unknown. If we have concern about the future, a better approach is to assess the fragility of our institutions and systems and work to make them more robust or antifragile. What do I mean by fragility, robustness, and antifragility?

Fragility *is the tendency for something to be* <u>*harmed or weakened*</u> *by stress, disorder, or volatility.* [143]

Robustness *is the tendency for something to be* <u>*indifferent*</u> *to stress, disorder, or volatility.* [144]

Antifragility *is the tendency for something to* <u>*benefit from or be strengthened*</u> *by stress, disorder, or volatility.* [145]

Fragility likes calm, order, and stability. Robustness is unaffected by stress, disorder, and volatility. It lies between antifragility and fragility. Antifragility thrives on stress, disorder, and volatility. It protects us against Black Swan events and is the antidote to fragility.

Shocks, which gradually increase in intensity, strengthen life, organizations, and systems. Shocks that are too intense cause serious destruction. Continuous streams of small shocks and variability make systems antifragile, whereas the absence of stress and suppressed volatility make them fragile. Not foreseeing Black Swans is normal, but not seeing fragility and making our organizations, systems, and selves fragile is irresponsible.

The ability to recognize fragility, avoid Black Swans, and make our lives more antifragile furthers our well-being. Concentrations of power, scale, complexity, opacity, ill-conceived regulations, debt, and entitlement cause fragility. Why is this? Because when we try to control life too much, organisms fight back, and when life is too comfortable, it atrophies.

People who acquire power want more of it. Powerful people and organizations usually have the drive and means to accumulate more power and make large entities larger and more influential . . . at least for a while. Complex and secretive operations increase in complexity and opacity, and individuals wielding power often become arrogant, corrupt, and entitled. A shift can occur, and they lose the drive, discipline, and the stakeholder orientation that enabled their success. Their exercise of power gradually becomes oppressive, unmanageable, and exposed, and they become soft. At some point, something triggers a Black Swan, and the order breaks. The Assyrian, Ottoman, Roman, and British Empires all provide examples of how power, scale, and complexity grew, became fragile, and finally broke.

Decentralized, smaller organizations and countries disciplined by competition avoid fragility and this fate. Switzerland, a federation of seven small Cantons, is antifragile. The Swiss do not allow federal power to aggregate, the country is small, and the culture discourages softness and entitlement.

Ill-conceived regulations that reside on bookshelves and in physical and digital files micromanage people's lives and stifle human activity. They are another source of fragility. Studies, reviews, approvals, licenses, permits, and other forms of regulatory compliance take time and increase costs. They cause many conscientious people and their capital to flee to less-regulated locales and other people to cheat. Education, optionality, and a few well-conceived regulations are antifragile alternatives to ill-conceived regulations. They are easy to remember, waste little time, and do not cost much. Education causes people to want to do the right thing of their own volition.

Debt increases fragility. Debt is the exchange of money today for the payment of principal and interest tomorrow. People who borrow lots of money, like the turkey, think tomorrow will always be like today. They do not realize that one day their situation may change. Their lender may see that the likelihood of them repaying the money is low, call their loans, and demand repayment. The more we borrow, the more difficulty we have covering our expenses and obligations when interest rates increase, our income declines, and/or our expenses rise.

When parents, employers, governments, and others take care of able-bodied adults, they shield them from stress and the need to work. The coddled, able-bodied adults learn less, accomplish less, and atrophy. They and their communities become fragile. On the other hand, when able-bodied adults work, they learn, develop skills, and contribute to their communities. Need and regular small doses of stress reduce fragility.

Individuals are also more fragile than groups. Accidents, disease, failures, and disasters harm individuals and take many lives, but these disasters also cause others to make different choices and strengthen the gene pool in the process. When we honor heroes, we compensate people for taking risks and making sacrifices, and we incentivize others to take risks and make sacrifices as well. Explorers, entrepreneurs, soldiers, and emergency responders take risks to benefit our communities every day.

People who do not have skin in the game or some personal interest in an outcome, also make our institutions and organizations fragile. Employees, whose unions ensure their pay and tenure, underperform compared to those whose employment and compensation depend on their performance. The leaders of Bank of America, Bear Stearns, Countrywide, Fannie Mae, Freddie Mac, Lehman Brothers, and Merrill Lynch had lots of upside, little downside, and an inadequate amount of skin in the game in 2007, otherwise they would not have allowed their organizations to become so fragile.

Currently, our order is very fragile, we are unaware of our fragility, and we are susceptible to Black Swans. Our rapid political, social, and economic development; people's natural aversion to uncertainty, pain, and losses; our attraction to stability, comfort, and power; and our tremendous technological prowess drive this fragility. Our self-interest, groupthink, short-term biases, and detachment from nature make us naïve about our fragility. Ever-increasing amounts of uncurated, sensationalized information distort our view of reality. The decline of the

Judeo-Christian unifying culture; neighborhood, family, and education dysfunction; obesity; drug and alcohol addiction; federal deficits, debt, and political corruption; illegal immigration and related lawlessness; human degradation of natural habitats; weapons of mass destruction; and cyber dependence make us fragile.

The short-term gratification gained from spending money produces the debt crises of tomorrow. The relief from the unnecessary use of antibiotics creates superbugs. The suppression of small forest fires fuels out-of-control infernos. Today's desire for larger empires and mergers bring the shareholder losses and divestitures of tomorrow. The good intentions of the public housing and low-income subsidies produce unsafe, dysfunctional neighborhoods. The government deficit spending and central bank interest rate suppression of yesterday create the speculative bubbles, bankruptcies, and unemployment of tomorrow.

Black Swans hurt a lot. It is in our interest to avoid them. Decentralization, competition, redundancy, and simplicity deliver small doses of stress, make life more understandable and manageable, and keep us more humble, honest, focused, and disciplined. Transparency keeps us informed and reduces the unforeseen. Skin in the game, or reaping the upside and downside of our actions, makes us more responsible. Savings and optionality provide us with resources and alternatives. Time and large shocks test for fragility, trigger Black Swans, and wash fragility away. Species, institutions, systems, and practices that have survived many large shocks and that persist through time deserve our respect.

Prohibitions

Many of the greatest leaders in history recognized thousands of years ago that some human behaviors predictably and invariably stream negative effects. Rather than explain to people why these behaviors are to be avoided and leave curtailing them to people's discretion, leaders unequivocally forbade them. The number of forbidden behaviors was small because there are few actions that cascade negative effects, and a few prohibitions are more enforceable and memorable than many. What might such a list look like today?

> Do not harm or kill others except in self-defense
>   and the defense of your country.
>
> Do not lie or cheat.
>
> Do not covet or steal what belongs to others.
>
> Do not falsely accuse others.
>
> Do not freeload.
>
> Do not commit adultery.
>
> Do not neglect your children.

Today, people do not accept prohibitions blindly. So why do we want to adhere to them? Because they prevent negative things from happening to us and others. Harming a member of our community hurts us and invites retaliation. Lying gives others a distorted view of reality and eventually destroys the trust they have for us. Coveting what others possess preoccupies and prevents us from proactively living our own lives. Stealing takes what belongs to others, destroys people's confidence in one another, and invites punishment and/or retaliation. Falsely accusing others hurts them in the short term and harms us in the long term, as they know the accusations are false, and fight back to clear their names. Freeloading is a form of parasitic behavior that harms others and makes us fragile. Adultery destroys any faith our spouse has for us, strains the marital relationship, and frequently results in divorce, something which negatively affects all members of a family. Neglecting children sets back their development and disadvantages them for life.

Optionality and Judicious Risk-Taking

Optionality is the practice of making decisions sequentially through time rather than all at once. It recognizes the dynamic effects of actions and that we will know more in the future. Act, learn, choose. Act, learn, choose. Act, learn, choose, *breakthrough;* and so our lives progress as we practice optionality.

Optionality is selecting the most advantageous alternative at hand, seeing what comes of it, and repeating this process.[146]

Nature uses optionality. Change occurs, and selection follows. Human trial-and-error replicates this natural process. Only with human trial-and-error do we learn what does not work and narrow the possibilities of what might work. We also do not wait a generation to make our selection and try again.

Judicious risk-taking is a form of optionality, which involves doing our best to avoid activities with ruinous or lethal outcomes; this is what Nassim Taleb calls the "Barbell Strategy."[147] Except for purposely sacrificing our well-being for the larger group, prudence and judicial risk-taking involve avoiding actions that have some likelihood—maybe greater than 1 in 100,000—of ruining us. Education provides opportunities and optionality, but it also can blind us to optionality if we miss opportunities when we become too confident and rigid in our knowledge.

The idea of the Barbell Strategy or what I call "Judicious Risk-Taking" is that we do what is necessary to secure the well-being of our family and selves first—things that conservatives naturally do—and then we take some risks to improve and profit—things that liberals inherently do. We do well in school but supplement our formal education with outside reading, activities, work, and travel experiences. We find steady employment and engage in entrepreneurial activity after work. We invest some of our wealth in safe, low-return government and corporate bonds, and we put the rest of it in higher-return, more volatile real estate and equity investments.

Figure 19 illustrates Judicious Risk-Taking. The lighter line shows the absence of downside and limited upside of the low-risk activity, and the darker line shows the limited downside and positive nonlinear upside of the high-risk activity.

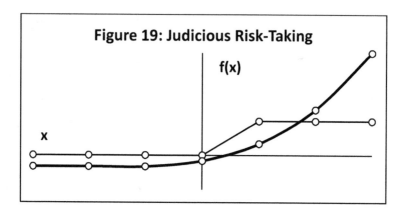

Figure 19: Judicious Risk-Taking

Judicious Risk-Taking *is acting in a manner that avoids doing things with ruinous or deadly outcomes, doing what is necessary to secure our well-being, and then taking some risks to improve and profit.*

Practical Experience

Along with antifragility, optionality, and judicious risk-taking, we must struggle with what is before us and reflect on the effects of alternative courses before making choices. There is no substitute for doing things in life. We can have someone teach us to swim, ride a bike, fly a plane, speak publicly, or run a business in a classroom, but until we do these things in the real world, we are unable to do or teach them proficiently. Classroom teaching does not convey many real-life nuances or develop the neurological pathways, heuristics, and judgment.

Humans have the natural ability to sense and do many things, like communicate, eat, speak, and walk without classroom instruction. Humans are born with instinctual responses to stimuli and to mimic others' behaviors. We pick up so much from just observing and imitating those around us.

Of the two types of learning (1) mimicking and apprenticing (observe, try, do), and (2) formal classroom instruction (sit, listen, read, and remember), I believe we underemphasize the importance of the former and overemphasize the latter in the modern world. Beyond instruction in basic reading, writing, arithmetic, science, and history, the best learning occurs when we observe, imitate, and apprentice under practitioners or when teachers with practitioner experience instruct us.

More theories and innovations are created from practice and practitioners tinkering than by formal research. Einstein's development of the Theory of Relativity and the related practical insights and innovations are two of the most famous exceptions of this rule.[148]

Accomplished Souls and Collective Wisdom

One of the challenges of modern life and rapid technological change is that people are more technologically savvy when they are younger. This reversal in the relationship of age and knowledge gives us the illusion that we know more than our elders. This is unfortunate because while we are technologically more knowledgeable than our elders, we know a lot less about life.

Whenever possible, we want to befriend and consult accomplished souls or elder mentors, especially when we are young. Their experience and counsel give us additional things to consider, help us avoid mistakes, and may help connect us to other uniquely knowledgeable people. Our life cycles and roles have not changed much in thousands of generations. We still move through the infant-child-young adult-spouse-parent-grandparent life cycle and apprentice-teacher-elder learning cycle. We still have individual, familial, and community natures and roles. People acquire much experience, knowledge, and wisdom about their context and life by moving through these cycles and fulfilling these roles as they age. While we need not follow the counsel of our elders mindlessly, we are foolish not to consider it. Our parents, grandparents, and accomplished souls have wisdom that we lack, and they usually will have our best interests at heart.

We also enhance our ability to make good choices when we consult several accomplished souls simultaneously at a meeting or on conference calls. People feed off one another in groups, offering ideas that they would not surface on their own. Twenty neural networks with a total of two trillion neurons are many times more experienced, knowledgeable, connected, and creative than one neural network with 100 billion neurons. Well-moderated, focused, and knowledgeable groups bring a tremendous amount of wisdom and knowhow to any situation. We cannot really comprehend this power until we experience it a few times. The leaders of every country, state, business, and organization should convene groups to discuss their most consequential challenges and actions.

Being Slow to Make Important Decisions

Along with doing and consulting accomplished people, being slow to make important decisions enhances the quality of those decisions tremendously. We store vast amounts of information in our minds and then unconsciously and consciously shape the information into effective responses. Recalling the information, considering innumerable permutations, and assessing them takes time. I have found superior approaches awaiting the next morning when I struggle with decisions and wait to respond to them. Taking some time to make important decisions and consulting with one or more accomplished people enable us to make much better decisions.

Prudence – making choices that yield predominately positive effects on our planet, larger community, and ourselves. It requires fitness, courage, knowledge, and discipline; people to reap what they sow; antifragility; avoiding certain behaviors; optionality; judicious risk-taking; practical experience; consulting accomplished people; and being slow to make important decisions.

Chapter 19

Excellence

Universally, people cherish excellence.

Excellence is the quality of being outstanding in form or function. It is the product of unusual vision, skill, commitment, and hard work. Universally, people notice and cherish excellence. We love excellent teachers. They care about us and our progress, and they present the material clearly. They expect our best, and we gladly give it to them. We love to watch the best teams compete. The coaches are knowledgeable, organized, and disciplined, and the players are skilled, hardworking, and team-oriented. We love excellent music, art, and architecture. Their originality, beauty, and perfection inspire us. We cherish Beethoven's Fifth Sympathy, Michelangelo's David, da Vinci's Mona Lisa, and the breathtaking and inspiring cathedrals of Cologne and Notre Dame.

We appreciate excellent companies. Their leaders and teams have integrity, are hardworking, and rise above their peers. Their work environments, products, and services are highly desirable. Their leaders expect people's best and their employees deliver it. The work is safe, team members are well-compensated, and companies are profitable.

We like to live in excellent communities and countries, like the communities of Aspen, Jackson Hole, and Naples, and the countries of New Zealand and Switzerland. Children attend excellent schools, adults have well-paying employment opportunities, and most everyone has a high quality of life. We feel safe and enjoy the cleanliness, charm, and beauty of these communities and countries.

Extra Thought, Focus, Effort, and Time

Excellence involves making the ordinary extraordinary. It requires extra thought, focus, effort, and time. We must imagine, concentrate, and work at something for a long time for it to become excellent. Businessman Ronnie Oldham wrote:

Excellence is the result of caring more than others think is wise, risking more than others think is safe, dreaming more than others think is practical, and expecting more than others think is possible.[149]

Near-Perfect Practice and Perseverance

Near-perfect practice and perseverance further excellence. The performances of accomplished musicians and athletes seem effortless, but behind their performances are years of near-perfect practice. Near-perfect practices create neurological pathways that yield excellent performances; sloppy practices create pathways that yield suboptimal performances. Undoing the flawed pathways and replacing them with near-perfect ones is much more difficult than forming ones of excellence from the start. We do our children a great service when we provide them with accomplished teachers and encourage them to practice with precision.

"Anything worth doing is worth doing well." Doing things correctly the first time spares us from having to do them over again, and near-perfect practice produces excellence over time. Michelangelo apprenticed for years and worked continuously for two years on his sculpture of David. St. Peter's Basilica took more than 100 years to build. Vince Lombardi, the legendary Green Bay Packers coach, said:

> We are going to relentlessly chase perfection, because in the process we will catch excellence.[150]

High Standards and Attention to Detail

We realize excellence by improving the appearance, function, and/or durability of something. Just as advantageous genes become more common in a population over time, the excellence of yesterday sometimes becomes the commonplace of today. The world does not stand still. If we are not improving, others are surpassing us.

All the details of something need to be done well for it to be excellent. The standards for excellence are high and encompassing. If we paint a house and ignore the peeling trim, our work is not excellent. If a plot of a story is clever but our writing is organized poorly and riddled with grammatical errors, then our work is not excellent. Excellence requires us to pay attention to the details and eliminate defects.

Facilitators and Impediments

Everyone loves excellence, but few want to bear its rigors. CEOs shield themselves from competition and the rigor of excellence by putting their friends on their boards, and they shield their enterprises with patents, branding, and market concentration. Workers evade the rigors of excellence and competition by organizing and implementing protective work rules. Elected officials avoid them by gerrymandering districts, and special-interest groups exchange campaign contributions for advantageous laws, regulations, and tariffs or restrictions on imports.

Many parents allow their children to avoid the rigors of excellence by permitting them to spend lots of time watching television, playing video games, interacting on social media, and partying. Children need time to play and interact socially, but they also need to learn to work, be responsible, engage in real life activities, and experience the satisfaction that comes from excellence. Children benefit tremendously from learning to do their schoolwork and chores well, to play musical instruments proficiently, or to excel in a sport. Engaging in real activeities, developing the Habits of Individual and Group Effectiveness, and learning to win and lose gracefully prepares children for life.

Leaders, parents, and teachers set our standards, and we achieve excellence as a people when they set the standards high. Leaders, parents, and teachers advantage children, students, and team members when expect them to do their best and disadvantage them when they indulge them too much. If we do not learn to compete and pursue excellence from our parents, teachers, and coaches, we want to learn to compete and excel from other mentors or by immersing ourselves in competitive environments. Otherwise, we coast through life, never engaging, realizing our potential, or creating much music.

Competition and certain forms of organization incentivize people to do their best and advance excellence. People, schools, businesses, and governments all focus, work harder, and function at higher levels in competitive environments. Outside directors improve the decision-making of corporate boards. Governments and businesses function better when right-to-work laws prevent unions from curtailing meritocracy and performance incentives in organizations. Elected officials better represent their constituents when they do not have incumbent advantages. Children develop critical education and work ethics when teachers expect them to do homework and parents expect them to do chores. Children learn more when schools homogenously group them and create some educational competition.

The pursuit of excellence yields many benefits. It brings a vast array of highly functional, aesthetically pleasing orders, products, and services. Excellence also causes people to beat a path to the door of those who create it and reduces incidents of discrimination. People do not care about the age, gender, race, ethnicity, religious preference, or appearance of the authors of excellence.

Excellence – the quality of being outstanding in form, function, or durability. Excellence requires extra thought, focus, effort, and time; high standards; attention to detail; continuous improvement; and perseverance. Competition and great parents, leaders, teachers, coaches, and mentors facilitate excellence, and an absence of competition and the overindulgence of people impedes it. Inferiority, deficiency, and mediocrity are antithetical to excellence.

Chapter 20

Thrift and Investment

One dollar invested weekly, earning 10 percent a year, becomes more than $76,000 in 50 years and over $11 million 100 years later!

Do I really need to buy this item? Would foregoing it now and investing the money put me in a better position in the future? These questions capture the essence of thrift and investment behaviors that create wealth. Conscientious thrift and investment can make us financially secure in just a few years. They create reserves for unexpected challenges, provide sources of future income, fund financial legacies, reduce our environmental footprint, and form the capital necessary to fuel our living standards.

The Norwegians, Singaporeans, and Swiss know that wealth and financial security are within everyone's reach. They have acted thriftily and invested wisely for generations. Their thrift and investment enable them to avoid much heartache and bring them a high quality of life.

Consider that $20 invested weekly in a portfolio of 20 diversified stocks, earning 10 percent a year, becomes $197,900 in 30 years and $4,161,200 in 60 years. The difference between someone who saves and invests $20 a week versus someone who pays $20 a week of interest over 60 years is over $8 million. Every able-bodied person in our country can be wealthy and enjoy peace of mind in a few years by saving and investing a few dollars each week.

Minimizing Expenditures

Minimizing our expenditures is the essence of thrift. It requires us to discriminate between what we need and desire, distinctions that become clearer if we consider our purchases for a few days and utilize a budget to restrain our spending. My family's failure to do this well became apparent when we emptied our home after 24 years of residency. We had purchased and given each other many unneeded things. We had made too many weekend trips to the mall and done too much mindless shopping. If our family had been thriftier, we would have wasted less, invested more, and be leaving a larger financial legacy.

Minimizing expenditures also requires us to limit our overhead. By overhead, I mean the things that we do not readily consume. Our homes, cars, and household appliances comprise overhead in our personal lives. The grounds, offices, things, and people not involved directly in the creation of products and services comprise overhead at our workplaces. Our federal, state, and local governments, the entities that govern our lives, also are overhead to us all.

Most people have little overhead after leaving school, finding their first jobs, and buying their first homes. New businesses and governments have little overhead. But as people, businesses, and governments age, generally they add overhead.

While some overhead is necessary, too much diminishes our surplus to invest and burdens us. Large houses, luxury cars, and impressive offices are expensive to build, own, and maintain. Similarly, large governments are costly. Our federal government costs hundreds of billions of dollars to operate, spends trillions of dollars on poorly conceived military operations and social programs, and forces us to spend billions of dollars complying with endless regulations. Large governments suppress people's productivity, freedom, and living standards.

Minimizing debt is another important aspect of thrift and investment as debt used to purchase things that we consume must be repaid with interest. When we borrow, buy something, and consume it, we live today at the expense of tomorrow. The only time that debt is advantageous in our personal lives is to obtain an education and purchase a home. Education and homes have long lives. The former enhances our earning power for decades and the latter is often worth as much as we pay for it when we no longer need it.

Similarly, the use of debt in business and government is only advantageous when leaders use it to make investments that return more over time than the cost and interest associated with financing the investments. Business leaders who borrow for everyday expenses and overhead live today at the expense of tomorrow. Government borrowing is only advantageous for infrastructure, spending during financial crises, and defense. When governments use debt to pay for ongoing operations, non-essential wars, and social programs, they steal from and diminish future generations.

Minimizing resource use, overhead, and debt require planning, budgets, savvy procurement, continuous improvements, and incentives that reward these efforts. This requires leaders to make hard choices and use private and public resources frugally. Competition forces businesses to do these things, but governments must be constitutionally limited and people taught to defer gratification, be frugal, and invest their surplus to make wise decisions on an ongoing basis.

Automated Investment

When we are young, we have more strength, energy, drive, and time to multiply our money than when we are older. If we consume less when we are most vital and invest some of our earnings, we create additional sources of income as we age and have brighter futures.

To further thrift and investment, we can automate our investment. This is easy and only involves having our employer deduct some of our earnings from our paychecks and deposit this money into our investment account. Deducting and investing just $10 to $20 a week for 25 to 50 years creates significant wealth. When automating our investing in this manner, we put some earnings out of reach and do not need to save and invest the money each week. Automated investment assures follow-through. We determine what we need to live on, set up the automated deduction and investment, and limit our spending accordingly.

Financial Tools

Familiarity with some basic financial tools facilitates our ability to create wealth. The Rule of 69, present value, future value, present value of an annuity, and future value of an annuity are tools that every person should learn. Detailed instruction can be found on the Internet and in financial textbooks, but is beyond the scope of this book. While financial calculators and spreadsheets make the calculations easy, I include these tools in this chapter to familiarize readers with them. The more people understand these tools and save, the less they need to depend on politicians and governments for their financial security.

The Rule of 69 indicates that investments double in value every 69 divided by r years, where r is the Rate of Return that the investment earns.

This formula works because 0.69 is the natural log of 2, and if we divide the growth rate of something by the natural log of 2, we find the frequency with which it doubles. For example, if something grows 8 percent a year, then it doubles every 0.69/0.08, or 8.6 years. When calculators are unavailable, we may use 72 rather than 69 to figure approximations in our heads. We use 72 rather than 69 because 1, 2, 3, 4, 6, 8, 9, 12, and 36 all divide into 72 evenly. In this case, if investment grows at 8 percent a year, we can estimate that it doubles approximately every 72/8 or 9 years.

In finance, we learn that a dollar received in the future is worth less than a dollar received today because we may invest our dollar today and increase its value over time. The dollar and its earnings will be worth more than one dollar in the future. The formula to calculate the difference between a dollar's present and future values and other present value formulas are shown in Figures 20 and 21. The figures also show the effects of various rates of growth on the value of invested surpluses over time and the real costs of borrowing money. We can see the advantages of being frugal, avoiding the use of credit, creating surpluses, and investing the surpluses in a manner that multiplies them over time.

Figure 20: Present Value Formulas

Present Value of Future Amount

$$PV = FV / (1+r)^n$$

Future Value of a Current Amount

$$FV = PV \times (1+r)^n$$

Where "PV" is the Present Value of a Future Amount, "FV" is the future amount, "n" represents the Number of Periods into the future, and "r" is the Risk-Free Interest Rate or Treasury Bill Yield over "n" periods.

These formulas are used to calculate the present and future values of any amount. Using the formula, the present value of $10,000 in 20 years when the 20-year Treasury bill yield is 5 percent is $PV = \$10,000 / (1+0.05)^{20}$ or $3,800.

Using the formula, the future value of $10,000 in 20 years, and the 20-year Treasury bill yield is 5 percent, then $FV = \$10,000 \times (1+0.05)^{20}$ or $26,500.

Figure 21: Present Value Annuity Formulas

The Present Value of an Annuity

PVA = Pmt [1-(1+i)$^{-n}$] / i

The Future Value of an Annuity

FVA = Pmt [(1+i)^{n}-1] / i

Where "PVA" is the Present Value of an Annuity or series of principal and interest payments. "Pmt" is the amount of the Payments, "n" represents the Number of Periods into the future to value the annuity, and "i" is the Interest Rate for a period.

These formulas are used to calculate the present value of an annuity or a stream of future payments. Using this formula, the present value of 30 years of monthly mortgage payments of $1,000, given an annual interest rate of 7 percent, is:

$$PVA = \$1,000 * [1-(1+0.07/12)^{-30*12}] / (0.07 / 12)$$
$$= \$1,000 * [1-(1.005833)^{-360}] / 0.005833$$
$$= \$150,300$$

If we want to know the future value of saving $20 a week for 50 years, given an average annual return of 8 percent on the invested savings, then:

$$FVA = \$20 * [(1+0.08/52)^{50*52} -1] / (0.08/52)$$
$$= \$20 * [(1.001538)^{2600} -1] / (0.001538)$$
$$= \$694,600$$

Investments

Most people only need to know about six types of basic investments:

(1) Certificates of Deposit (CDs)and Money Market Funds,

(2) Debt Instruments or Notes and Bonds,

(3) Real Estate,

(4) Common Stocks or Equities,

(5) Preferred Stock, and

(6) Exchange-Traded Funds (ETFs).

Each of these investments has advantages and disadvantages. Each of them may be helpful at some point in our lives. More detailed explanations of them appear in Appendix A.

Investing requires the assessment of the risks and rewards of alternative investments over time. The risks include the magnitude of fluctuations of investment value and the possibility of not receiving the investment's earnings and investment itself sometime in the future. The potential rewards are the investment's earnings and appreciation of the investment.

Two common distinctions made when investing are: (1) putting money into investments that fluctuate little in value over time, like money market funds, CDs, debt instruments with short-term maturities, and ETFs of these underlying assets when the funds will be needed in the next seven years, and (2) putting money into more volatile investments that earn higher returns over time like long-term bonds, preferred stocks, equities, and ETFs of these underlying assets when the money will not be needed for at least seven years.

Having spent years studying Warren Buffett, considered by many to be the greatest investor of all time, let me share a few of his timeless investment insights:

- Successful investing does not require tremendous intelligence, but it does require research, method, emotional control, and patience.[151]

- The regular purchase and retention of low-cost exchange traded funds yield better investment returns than those of 90 percent of investors.[152]

- When an investment declines in value, it must increase by 2 times the percentage of the decline to return to the former level. If it decreases by 10 percent in value, it must increase by 20 percent to return to its former level. Consequently, we want to invest in assets that are more likely to increase 100 percent than decline 30 percent in value.[153]

- The most common cause of low prices is investor pessimism, and the most common cause of high prices is investor optimism. We want to buy equities when investors are most pessimistic and sell them when they are most optimistic. Contrary to what we emotionally sense, investing when people are most afraid to invest is much less risky than when they are excited about investing.[154]

- We should only buy investments that we fully understand. Such a discipline causes us to pass up some great investments, but it also causes us to avoid numerous disastrous ones and increases our returns over time.[155]

- Leverage or buying stocks on margin amplifies risks, returns, and losses. Most investors do better without leverage.[156]

Advantageously Buying and Selling Assets

Buying low and selling high seem like simple things, but they are quite difficult for most of us. Human emotions betray us at market highs and lows. We buy when prices have appreciated, and most people are buying; and we sell when prices have declined, and most people are selling. We only overcome these natural tendencies with method and self-control.

Most investors, particularly young and inexperienced ones, find it advantageous to invest their accumulated surpluses every week. If they invest in a few high-quality equity ETFs and hold on to them, they will do better than most investors and are pretty much guaranteed long-term success. Although the business and long-term debt cycles do not affect this method of steady investing, it is helpful if investors are aware of them and their influence on asset prices.

Business Cycles are cyclical fluctuations in the gross national product (GNP) or the value of all the goods and services produced in our country in one year. These cycles are caused by (1) the growth of demand for goods and services exceeding the growth of their supply, and (2) the growth of the supply of goods and services exceeding the growth of demand for them. Business cycles typically last 3 to 5 years.

Central banks attempt to moderate these cycles by increasing and decreasing short-term interest rates. They lower short-term interest rates to spur demand for goods and services and raise rates to curtail it. The business cycle provides opportunities to make additional investments when prices are low.

The other cycle, the long-term debt cycle, usually only occurs once or twice in our lifetimes.

Long-Term Debt Cycles are more pronounced cyclical fluctuations in GNP than business cycles, which arise from the growth of debt exceeding the growth of income and then the growth of income exceeding the growth of debt. These cycles cause asset prices to rise and fall as the borrowers' and lenders' appetite for debt moves from one extreme to the other. Long-term debt cycles usually occur over three generations.

Knowledge of these two cycles and experience suggest that asset prices modestly move above and below their long-term trends every 3 to 5 years and substantially above and below them every 50 to 80 years.

Minimizing Taxes

Minimizing the taxes on our investment proceeds is critical to successful investing. Typically, governments tax interest, dividends, and the appreciation of assets. The appreciation of assets held less than one year is taxed at higher rates than the appreciation of assets held for more than one year. Buying and holding common stock, mutual funds, and ETFs of well-managed, financially strong, growing, and profitable companies with competitive advantages for several years minimizes the taxes paid on these investments.

The Keys to Wealth are (a) working, (b) consuming less than we earn, and (c) prudently investing the difference.

In 1960, American living standards were over 120 times greater than Chinese living standards. In 2017, just 57 years later, they were only 7 times greater.[157] Throughout these 57 years, the Chinese consumed only 50 percent of what they earned and invested the rest, while Americans consumed more than they earned and borrowed the difference. Americans must rediscover the Winning Practice of Thrift and Investment or continue to experience a relative decline in living standards relative to the Chinese and numerous other populations.

Wealth accumulation may seem formidable, but it is like anything else. Most of us can learn to invest successfully with a good mentor and a little practice. Many of the most successful investors have no formal training. They simply utilize the Winning Practices in this chapter; minimize their expenditures, overhead, and debt; and automate their investing in 4 to 5 ETFs. Having substantial sums of money in our checking and investment accounts and not owing money also reduces our stress levels, creates tremendous peace of mind, and multiplies our individual and collective fitness, opportunities, and well-being.

Wealth is a great blessing when we honorably earn and prudently invest our money. It provides us with comfortable lifestyles, steady income, and the opportunity to be charitable. It provides enterprises with capital and governments with tax revenues. Honorably accumulated wealth requires deferred gratification, frugality, proactivity, hard work, risk-taking, and investment—characteristics that further our individual and collective fitness and well-being. Those who honorably accumulate wealth do the rest of us a great service, and we should celebrate and not denigrate them.

Thrift and Investment – (a) minimizing expenditures, (b) creating a surplus, (c) obtaining some basic financial knowledge, (d) letting others temporarily use our surplus in return for interest, dividends, and/or asset appreciation, (e) automating this process, (f) advantageously buying and selling assets, and (g) minimizing taxes. Extravagance and indebtedness are antithetical to thrift and investment.

Section IV: Winning Practices of Groups

Winning Perspectives

Truth
Causality
Scale
Evolution
Fitness

Human Nature
Culture
Periodic Disaster
Eco-Dependency

Winning Practices

Knowledge

Health
Thought
Integrity
Proactivity
Prudence
Excellence
Thrift and Investment

Universal Education
Parental Choice
Results-Oriented Education

Free Enterprise and Markets
Responsible Corporate Governance
Prudent Regulation
Enterprise Competitiveness

Affiliation
Decency
Understanding
Leadership
Teamwork
Improvement

Government of the People
Powers, Prohibitions, and Structure
Freedoms, Rights, and Responsibilities
The Rule of Law
Inclusion and Meritocracy
Prudent Taxation

Spouse Selection
Marriage
Responsible Parenting
Empowering Habit Formation

Financial Strength
Savings Accounts, Social Safety Nets
Consumer-Driven Healthcare
Assimilation
Peace Through Fitness
Sustainability

Chapter 21

Affiliation

Satisfying the expectations and norms of groups brings acceptance.

History indicates that we have aggregated into larger and larger groups over time. Families assemble into clans, clans into tribes, tribes into city-states, city-states into states, and states into nations. Each of these larger aggregations spurred our development of communication, government, and culture and enhanced our ability to protect ourselves, procure food, control territory and resources, specialize, and synergize.

Aggregation works because our biology makes loneliness, disapproval, and ridicule painful; it makes companionship, acceptance, and the esteem of others pleasurable. When communities become too large, however, people's affinity for others, willingness to make sacrifices for others, and concern about their reputations lessen, weakening the bonds of affiliation.

Accountability

Aggregation improves our lives until anonymity and opaqueness make it difficult for us to hold the leaders and members of our groups accountable. Members see less of what goes on in large organizations. Leaders love power, and everyone enjoys free lunches. Leaders want to provide advantages to their relatives, friends, and selves. Members want to obtain the benefits of affiliation without bearing the costs. If opportunities exist for leaders and members to do these things, then many will.

If we want the benefits associated with groups, then we must fulfill our obligations to them or be removed from them. If we want a school to provide us with an education and diploma, we must complete the requirements for them. If we want a company to provide us with a livelihood, then we must finish the assigned work. Similarly, we must pay taxes to have secure neighborhoods, good roads, excellent schools, and a social safety net. Failing to meet our obligations to our groups shortchanges them and jeopardizes our standing in them.

Groups only perform optimally when leaders enforce sensible norms, leaders and members conscientiously follow them, and the members are competent and engage with each other. Leaders must steer the boat, orchestrate member activity, and remove the poor performers. Members must do what is asked of them, work together, and pull hard on the oars.

Attendance

Attendance is an important aspect of affiliation. When we are absent from any of our groups, we shortchange them and ourselves. We do not fulfill our responsibilities nor receive all the benefits of membership. When children do not go to school, they do not acquire the perspectives, habits, and skills that enable them to earn their livelihoods, become good parents, and contribute to their communities. When adults do not go to work, they create extra work for their colleagues and do not earn their livelihoods.

The difference between the contributions made and benefits received by those with good and poor attendance is much greater than most realize. Consider students who miss a day of school every 2 weeks over their 13 years. They lose about 18 days of a total of 180 days a year, 10 percent of their class time, or 1.3 years of school. It is hard for students to master the material and excel when they miss so much instruction.

Similarly, consider employees who miss 1 day of work every 2 weeks throughout a 50-year career. They lose some 25 days, or 5 weeks of work a year, and 1,250 days, or 5 years of work, over the 50 years. They earn 10 percent less—which if saved and invested could accumulate to more than $2 million over the 50 years. Absenteeism negatively affects employee compensation, shareholder returns, a company's competitiveness, and government tax receipts.

Punctuality

Punctuality dramatically improves our productivity and effectiveness. Tardiness reduces them and is inconsiderate of others. If 10 people attend a meeting, the meeting does not start until everyone arrives, and the last person is 10 minutes late, then the last person wastes 1½ cumulative hours of others' time.

We can deal with unexpected delays and avoid being late by planning to arrive at events early. A five-minute cushion generally works when our travel time to an event is less than 15 minutes, whereas larger buffers are necessary as our travel times increase.

Appearance and Congeniality

Affiliation requires us to appear like others in a group. People who do not know us initially form their opinions about us from our appearance. Whether stated or unstated, members of groups more readily accept new people when they dress like the members of the group. We want to be individuals, but we also want to be accepted in our groups. To do this, we must temper our individuality and comply with the norms for appearance of groups.

Congeniality also facilitates affiliation. We naturally enjoy being with those who pleasantly express themselves, listen to us, and generally affirm our views. People who smile, laugh, and feel good make us do the same. People who complain, confront, and criticize make us uneasy and bring out similar tendencies in others. Congeniality is especially important during introductory periods when we are outsiders of groups. Only familiarity, good performance, and time cause others to see us as insiders.

While too much congeniality masks our individuality, perspectives, and feelings, generally it is advantageous to be more congenial than contrary. Good relations with others require us to be more focused on others than ourselves. People want airtime, attention, and affirmation. Good manners, similarity in appearance, consideration for others, and congeniality further affiliations.

Independent Thought

Because affiliation has benefited us so much for millions of years, we unconsciously absorb others' thinking. This is a double-edged sword, though. It is advantageous when it aligns with Winning Perspectives and Practices, and it is disadvantageous when it conflicts with them. Personally, I consciously try to maintain a healthy skepticism of others' perspectives and practices and subject them to the Effects Test to determine whether a perspective, priority, or practice yields predominately positive effects for individuals, families, groups, education, enterprise, government, and/or the environment in the short and long term as discussed in Chapter 16.

If our peers in high school and college encourage promiscuity and we are not sure about where we stand, the Effects Test enables us to assess the desirability of this practice. One-hundred percent alignment with most groups is not necessary to be a member in good standing of a group in our county. In my experience, we only need to align our speech and action about three-quarters of the time to be in good standing and enjoy the benefits of affiliation.

Friendship

Friendships are one of our greatest joys in life. They warm our hearts and energize us. Friendships require effort, though. They convey perspective, companionship, and opportunity but require commitment, time, and work. We gain from being affiliated with our friends and they benefit from their interactions with us. In this case, the cliché you learned in elementary school is correct: "To have a friend, you must be a friend."

Friendships form most easily when two people have things in common. They may be of the same gender, race, or ethnicity. They may be about the same age, go to the same school, work for the same company, or live in the same community. They may have the same faith, values, and objectives or share similar experiences. The more two people have in common, the more likely they are to become friends, benefit from interaction, and have an enduring relationship.

If we are active, we can become friends with many people. Yet we want to choose our friends carefully, as meaningful friendships require significant effort and time. Directing our attention to compatible, interesting people of good character is advantageous, as we are always becoming a little more like the four to five people with whom we spend the most time, and things go better for us when we associate with high-integrity, able people. George Washington counseled:

> Be courteous to all, but intimate with few, and let those few be well tried before you give them your confidence. True friendship is a plant of slow growth and must undergo and withstand the shocks of adversity before it is entitled to appellation.[158]

We should also realize that friendships with colleagues oftentimes have competitive and political aspects to them. For us to flourish and maintain these friendships, we must avoid politics, follow the rules, and compete honorably because people only accept losing to their colleagues when they play fairly.

We want to be open to new friendships and retain the friendships of people who have stood by us in the past. Friends who stand by us in both good and bad times are precious. They only come along a few times in our lives. It is foolish to take these friendships for granted.

We cannot force others to accept or like us, but we can do much to cultivate our affiliations. We can be accountable, present, punctual, presentable, congenial, and still think for ourselves. We may align our lives with the Winning Perspectives and Practices and reap their positive effects, and we may exhibit a sincere interest in others.

Affiliation – *(a) connecting to groups, (b) complying with their norms, (c) fulfilling our obligations to them, (d) receiving benefits from them, (e) being accountable, present, punctual, presentable, and congenial, and (f) making friends. Independent thought enables us to contribute to our affiliated groups and prevents group interests and thought from overwhelming us. Alienation is the antithesis of affiliation.*

Chapter 22

Decency

Our happiness and effectiveness depend on the quality of our relationships with others. When others mean us no harm, we treat them as we would like them to treat us.

Once humans found greater survival advantage in larger groups, civility, decency, and trust became important attributes. People could not specialize, trade, and realize synergies without some goodwill. Religions evolved to further civility and trust among larger groups. The Judeo-Christian-Islamic concept of an omniscient, omnipotent, omnipresent God who punishes bad and rewards good behavior has done much to promote these attributes *within* populations.

In a more evidenced-based world, many people reject this depiction of God, or at least do not take it seriously. But how do we incentivize people to be decent and do the right thing without God watching our behavior? Does the reality that our actions precipitate compensatory effects that aggregate into a self-created heaven or hell do it? We live in a cause-and-effect world. We reap largely as we sow, not always nor necessarily in the short term but generally in the long term. Is this sufficient to motivate people to do the right thing?

We are all connected. Our hearts sense this and our DNA substantiates it. The well-being of our families, institutions, country, ecosystems, and other lifeforms depend on one another. Thus, our actions and means matter. Decent actions further these connections and relationships. They cause others to reciprocate decency, and in doing so, enable a civil, sustainable world.

Genes, emotion, parental investment, and shared dependency and experiences cause family members to bond and be good to one another. And although the causal links are not fully understood, we seem to care for family members in proportion to the genes we share with them. Typically, we care most about our parents, siblings, and children who share approximately 50 percent of our genes, next most about our grandparents and grandchildren who share 25 percent of our genes, and next most about our first cousins who share roughly 12.5 percent of our genes.

Abundance and Decency vs. Scarcity and Ruthlessness

Humans have numerous strategies for living. Ruthlessness and decency, two opposite approaches, bound the alternatives. With the ruthless approach, people treat those within their community well but take advantage of those outside their community. With the decent approach, people treat those both inside and outside their communities well. The two strategies originate from two very different environments.

The ruthless strategy originated from nomadic, resource-scarce environments; the decent strategy originated from agrarian, resource-rich environments. Ruthlessness serves populations well when resources are scarce, and people do not have permanent addresses. Decency serves populations well when people have home addresses and resources are plentiful. Ruthlessness permits the fit to take what they need. Decency facilitates specialization, trade, synergy, economies of scale, and higher living standards. And if we can secure enough territory and resources to flourish, decency is much more advantageous than ruthlessness.

Ally Acquisition

When we enter the world, only our grandparents and parents have our full interests at heart. And to some extent, we compete with everyone else for status, position, power, and resources. As children, we compete with our siblings for our parents' attention. In school, we compete with our peers for status, position, and good grades. As young adults, we compete for boyfriends or girlfriends, university acceptances, and jobs. As adults, we compete for positions and mates, and as citizens of countries, we compete with citizens of other countries for territory, resources, and markets.

Obtaining allies is easier for some people than others. Extroverted people have high emotional intelligence and acquire allies naturally. They love to be with others, and others love to be with them. Generally, they emphasize cordiality and relationships more than candor and efficiency. On the other hand, introverted people generally place greater emphasis on candor, productivity, and efficiency than cordiality and relationships.

People exhibit these tendencies because both are advantageous to populations. Those with a stronger people orientation become the facilitators of relationships and work, while those with a stronger task orientation become the engineers, tradespeople, and great solitary achievers. Regardless whether we have a stronger people or task orientation, developing healthy relationships with others and acquiring allies are important activities. We are interdependent creatures and must interact with numerous people regularly.

Our allies can be casual or serious, where casual means having a friendly relationship and the alliance requires little work, and serious means the alliance requires significant work by both parties. The acquisition of casual and serious allies enables us to capitalize on shared intelligence, comparative advantages, specialization, and win-win arrangements.

We have little control over many things, but we can choose our allies. Choosing them as carefully as we choose our spouses is advantageous. The more we ally with able, responsible, and helpful parties, the more we flourish. Promises are less important than deeds when weighing prospects. Just as our integrity, accomplishment, and reputation affect who wants to ally with us, so these characteristics should affect with whom we ally.

Best-selling author and speaker Dale Carnegie spent his life writing and speaking about human relationships and acquiring allies. His counsel is straightforward, simple, and powerful. I find that a periodic review of it enhances my relationships with others.

Actions speak louder than words, and a smile says, "I like you. You make me happy. I am glad to see you."[159]

A person's name to that person is the sweetest and most important sound in any language.[160]

You can make more friends in two months by becoming interested in other people than you can in two years by trying to get other people interested in you.[161]

The difference between appreciation and flattery? . . . One is sincere and the other insincere. . . . One is unselfish, the other selfish. One is universally admired, the other universally condemned.[162]

When dealing with people, remember you are not dealing with creatures of logic, but with creatures bristling with prejudice and motivated by pride and vanity.[163]

Criticism is dangerous, because it wounds a person's precious pride, hurts his [or her] sense of importance, and arouses resentment.[164]

You can't win an argument. You can't because if you lose it, you lose it; and if you win it, you lose it.[165]

Be wiser than other people if you can; but do not tell them so.[166]

Let's never try to get even with our enemies, because if we do, we will hurt ourselves far more than we hurt them.[167]

When we hate our enemies, we are giving them power over us: power over our sleep, our appetites, our blood pressure, our health, and our happiness.[168]

Respectfulness

Valuing and respecting other people, their property, and our laws, regulations, authorities, and the environment makes our lives better. Although everyone is not always honorable, giving them the benefit of the doubt, being respectful, and carefully choosing our battles minimizes the number of people who will harm us.

Respect requires courteous and considerate speech. Rather than just reacting to comments, questions, and criticism, being respectful to others involves pausing and formulating tactful and helpful responses. Not taking offense, letting things go, and using self-deprecating humor help us avoid conflict and develop friendships. Respect also requires us to withhold many criticisms. If we must be critical, cloaking criticism with consideration and sharing it privately improve its reception. Abraham Lincoln wrote:

I am very little inclined on any occasion to say anything unless I hope to produce some good by it.[169]

There is a place for anger in the world, or it would not be a common human emotion. Controlled anger yields better outcomes than uncontrolled anger, though. Controlled, respectful anger signals to others that their conduct upsets us. Uncontrolled anger begets retaliatory ire, triggers defensiveness, and escalates conflict. Marcus Aurelius observed:

How much more grievous are the consequences of anger than the causes of it.[170]

Consideration and Appreciation

Life is so much better when we have healthy relationships with our families, friends, and colleagues. Our hearts warm. We smile, laugh, and play more. We are less vulnerable, alone, and defensive. We offer and receive information, advice, and assistance more readily. We feel good about life and accomplish more.

Being considerate and appreciative of others is an important component of decency. Life is hard, oftentimes much harder for others than for us. Everyone fights many battles. Being considerate and appreciative of others causes them to be considerate and appreciative of us. Taking the time to listen, understand others' perspectives, affirm their feelings, and extend kindness conveys to others their importance.

Consideration and appreciation also convey caring. The mother who sacrifices what she would like to do to help us, the teacher or coach who takes extra time with us, and the colleague who helps us with our assignment make real differences in our lives. And when others do things for us, we want to do things for them.

Because we have reptilian drives and reactions, especially when tired, we are fortunate when our parents and mentors teach us to check these reactions, be considerate and appreciative of others, and invest in long-term relationships. As parents teach children to say "please" when making a request and "thank you" upon receiving a consideration, they teach their children to be considerate and facilitate healthy relationships with others.

Consideration and appreciation are investments in those around us. They may not bring immediate rewards, but they do affect the way others view us the depth of our relationships, and who we become. Harvard professor Clay Christensen suggests that the way we measure success is unconsciously given to us by our culture, and that if we reflect more on how we measure success, we would be less self-centered and short-term oriented. We would be more considerate and appreciative of others, and we would invest more in our families and long-term relationships.[171]

The Modified Golden Rule

The Modified Golden Rule is a variation of the Golden Rule—do unto others, as you would have them do unto you. I like it better than the Golden Rule because the Golden Rule instructs us to treat everyone well, including those who mean us harm. My reading of history suggests that playing nice with those who mean us harm is a losing practice. "Turning the other cheek" to the Nazis, Russian KGB, and jihadists allows monsters to develop. The Modified Golden Rule does not direct us to treat these bad actors as we wish to be treated. It exempts them from this standard and enables us to defend ourselves, punish, and incarcerate those who mean us harm.

The Modified Golden Rule includes (a) do to others as we would have them do to us when they mean us no harm, and let others' inconsequential transgressions go, (b) defend ourselves and seek retribution under the law when others materially harm us, and (c) offer others restitution and seek their forgiveness when we harm them.

The Modified Golden Rule requires practicing humility; considering others' circumstances, needs, and desires; and making accommodations for others. The Modified Golden Rule furthers trust, understanding, synergy, and effectiveness. It encourages reciprocal considerations. It obliges us to notify others of fraud and trespass if we observe it.

The Modified Golden Rule rejects "the-ends-justify-the-means" approach that too often sanctions lying, character assassination, stealing, lawlessness, takeovers, torture, murder, terrorism, and genocide. The Modified Golden Rule creates a world in which we want to live. It furthers trust, mutuality, and civility while minimizing destructive behaviors. We do reap what we sow in the long term, and people do radiate what they receive.

Apology and Forgiveness

An apology occurs when a trespasser expresses regret to a harmed person for a transgression. Forgiveness occurs when the harmed person lets go of any resentment for the trespasser. Apologies and forgiveness dissipate animosity, facilitate goodwill, and heal relationships.

While trespassers should always apologize, the intention of the trespass affects whether people should forgive trespassers. When the harm is unintentional and of little consequence, forgiveness dissipates ill-will and furthers future interaction. Most people feel badly about their trespasses, and our best course is to put them at ease about them. When the harm is unintentional and significant, trespassers should apologize and provide restitution. Responsible people make others whole when they harm them. Once we are made whole, our forgiveness of trespassers restores the relationship.

When trespassers intentionally harm us, we do not want a future relationship with them, and we have no responsibility to foster these connections. If the harm is of little consequence and the trespasser does not apologize, ignoring and avoiding him or her is the best course. While we need not openly forgive such trespassers, we may want to forgive them privately to dissipate our angst and move on. If significant harm is done, we should seek restitution under the law, as this compensates us for the harm and discourages the trespasser from harming others.

We are responsible for the harm we do to others but not for the harm done by our ancestors to others. People are responsible for only what they do. Anybody who thinks people are responsible for their ancestors' actions abandons a workable order and seeks to advance a political agenda. Martin Luther King, Jr., wrote:

Forgiveness does not mean ignoring what has been done or putting a false label on an evil act. It means, rather, that the evil act no longer remains as a barrier to the relationship. Forgiveness is a catalyst creating the atmosphere necessary for a fresh start and a new beginning.[172]

Apology and forgiveness dissipate tension, foster positive relations with others, and incline others to reciprocate these behaviors. They end destructive cycles of conflict and violence, and they help us coexist peacefully.

Expenditure of Time, Energy, and/or Resources

Respectfulness, consideration, and appreciation are common among acquaintances. Yet these expressions only mean as much as they require of us, and we often do not know if they are heartfelt, rote, or deceptive. Only the expenditure of time, energy, and/or resources on behalf of others without expectations of reciprocity signifies genuine caring.

If we think about those who care most about us, we think of our parents, grandparents, spouses, and close friends. We think of our better teachers, coaches, and mentors. We register caring by the others' efforts on our behalf, and others register our caring by our efforts on their behalf.

———————————

Decency is our best approach with others who mean us no harm when territory and resources are abundant. Operating lawfully, purchasing what we desire, and creating win-win arrangements create friends and yield superior outcomes. Decency works because people generally treat us as we treat them. Decency transforms competitors into allies and reduces people's desire to harm us. We only depart from decency as others violate our freedoms, rights, property, laws, and selves.

Decency – our preferred approach with others, as it inclines others to be good to us and transforms potential competitors into allies. Decency involves (a) respectfulness, consideration, and appreciation, (b) treating others who mean us no harm as we want them to treat us, (c) appreciation, apology, and forgiveness, and (d) expenditures of time, energy, and resources on others' behalf. Ruthlessness and callousness are antithetical to decency.

Chapter 23

Understanding

We must walk a mile in others' moccasins to understand them.

—Cherokee Proverb

The practice of understanding is the key to developing strong, lasting relationships with our families, friends, and colleagues. Understanding allows us to learn the perspectives, needs, and preferences of others. It allows us to resolve misunderstandings and conflicts, coordinate our activities, and bond with them. It enriches our lives and makes our challenges more surmountable. A lack of understanding fuels estrangement, alienation, and ineffectiveness.

Humility

Humility starts with recognition of the preciousness, interconnectedness, and transience of human life, and our relative unimportance and contingency. Each of us is unique, has descended from 99 percent of the same ancestors, and only lives for a handful of the 12 thousand generations of human life. Humility causes us to listen to others and learn from them, furthering trust and our ability to work with others.

We like those who are attentive and considerate and dislike those who are arrogant, rude, and dismissive. So it is with others. They like us when we are attentive and considerate and dislike us when we are self-centered and inconsiderate. We learn humility as we experience setbacks and others' arrogance and observe others' successes.

Trust

When two people trust one another, they share information, attach greater credibility to it, and more willingly act on it. When people distrust one another, they avoid each other. Stephen Covey wrote:

Trust is the glue of life. It's the most essential ingredient in effective communication. It's the foundational principle that holds all relationships. . . . When the trust account is high, communication is easy, instant, and effective.[173]

For trust to develop between two people, they must have good experiences with each other and sense integrity in one another. In *The 7 Habits of Highly Effective People,* Stephen Covey suggests that deposits and withdrawals of goodwill in people's emotional bank accounts affect the level of trust between them.

*The **Emotional Bank Account** is the reservoir of positive or negative feelings that people have with one another, which increases each time we are honest, reliable, and considerate to others and decreases when we are dishonest, unreliable, or inconsiderate. When our account balances are high with others, they trust and work with us. When our balances are low or negative, they distrust and avoid us.[174]*

Developing large balances of goodwill in people's emotional bank accounts requires us to restrain our criticism. Whether we realize it or not, we verbally assault people when we criticize without invitation. If people invite criticism or we wish to be helpful, we need to have high emotional account balances of goodwill and cloak our criticism with consideration for others to appreciate our thoughts.

Listening

We know listening furthers understanding, yet often we do not listen well. Most of us are so anxious to express ourselves that we interrupt others frequently and hardly register what they say. We formulate our thoughts while they speak, interrupt them, and barrel ahead with our opinions. This is not listening. It does not give others the opportunity to develop their thoughts and prevents us from perceiving their nonverbal cues and the context of their words.

I will never forget the lunch my wife and I had with one of our sons after he transferred to a very competitive college and then broke up with his girlfriend. He said he was fine, but his nonverbal cues and tone suggested to my wife that he was not okay. I wanted him to be happy with his decision to transfer and only heard his words. If my wife had not perceived his inner turmoil and had me follow up with him, what turned out to be a relatively easy intervention, might have been a difficult one.

Active listening, or listening with full concentration and all our senses, requires deliberate intent until it becomes habit. It demands that we check our tendency to interrupt; register others' facial expressions, body language, and tone; and focus on what they say. Active listening, like most human behaviors, can become a habit if we work at it and repeatedly do it.

Clarification

Asking clarifying questions helps us when people hold back or generalize. When we need to ask a personal clarifying question, we need to be careful. People oftentimes fear that we will judge them or tell them what to do. We cannot be too direct or press too hard. Asking open-ended questions and letting people talk provides the opportunity for them to surface their thoughts and feelings. A high level of trust and an unhurried, attentive, and caring approach causes people to communicate more freely. It signals that we are going to listen and not judge them or tell them what to do.

Following the lunch with our son, my wife thought we needed clarification. She suggested that I meet with him again and give him more time to express himself. I feared my wife might be right; after sleeping on it, I met with our son the next day. I indicated to him that his mom and I had some concerns. I listened, asked a clarifying question, and listened some more. Eventually, the dam burst and our son's concerns spilled out.

People also make many generalizations during conversation, some of which create misunderstandings. Generalizations usually expedite communication but sometimes can hinder it with the omission of important details. When missing information does not matter, receivers interpret the messages as the senders intend. When the omitted details matter, however, receivers may incompletely or inaccurately perceive the message. Effective communication requires us to clarify what is unclear or restate something that is said in a slightly different manner to confirm its accuracy.

Shared Experience

Our context and experiences shape us. They affect our perceptions, attitudes, and actions. Learning about others' context and experiences helps us understand others, find common ground, develop relationships, and create win-wins.

Nothing advances understanding better than spending time with others and seeing firsthand where they live, work, and play. People's perspectives, practices, and priorities make more sense as we learn their histories and circumstances. Understanding children's withdrawals in classrooms is easier upon meeting their parents and visiting their homes. Understanding people's distrust of the police makes more sense after visiting regions and countries where majorities and authorities abuse minorities.

Shared experiences eliminate misperceptions, erode prejudices, and improve relationships. They generally advance understanding, but they often do not eliminate differences, align interests, or make things harmonious. Sometimes, people respectfully agree to disagree.

Understanding is powerful. Our perceptions and relationships improve as we exhibit humility, establish trust, actively listen, ask clarifying questions, and learn about others' context and experiences. Little is more damaging to relationships than wallowing in our misconceptions and not registering critical information. My variation of the "Captain and Lighthouse" story, whose author is unknown, illustrates this point.

> One night, the captain of a large ocean liner was standing on deck when he heard on his radio a voice advising him to turn south. Not to be inconvenienced, he radioed back, "I am the captain of a five-hundred-ton freighter. I will not change course. You change course." Whereupon the voice on the radio replied, "I am the operator of a lighthouse, and you are about to run ashore."

Effective people always have their ear to the ground. They listen to others and clarify uncertain, confusing, and conflicting information. They absorb, assess, and process the new information, and alter their speech and actions accordingly.

Understanding – *accurate perceptions of others and the world, facilitated by humility, trust, listening, clarification, and shared experiences. Ignorance and misunderstanding are antithetical to understanding.*

Chapter 24

Leadership

Lead with integrity, courage, competence, and caring, and people's best efforts follow.

The leaders with whom we align impact our lives greatly. Their importance becomes apparent once we experience both well-led and poorly led teams. On well-led teams, members engage, work well together, and flourish. The teams win frequently and accomplish much. On poorly led teams, members find fault, form factions, and struggle. The teams frequently lose and accomplish little. Able leaders have integrity, employ Winning Practices, and serve their stakeholders. Leaders affect the performance of our teams, enterprises, institutions, and country more than anything else.

Although most people have some ability to lead, the genes of a small percentage of a population equip them to be highly effective leaders. Usually, these individuals have superior cognitive, organizational, and communicative abilities. They want to be out in front, believe they can do a better job, step forward as opportunities arise, assume numerous leadership roles throughout their lives, and generally achieve superior results. They see solutions to challenges before others, inspire people, and become agents of change. They are visionary, pragmatic, decent, and effective. Poor leadership and disorganization frustrate them.

Good Decisions

Leaders must make many good decisions for their organizations to do well. While well-stated intentions are more desirable than poorly stated ones, the results of leaders' decisions are what matters. As business consultant and *Good to Great* author, Jim Collins, wrote:

Bad decisions made with good intentions are still bad decisions.[175]

The best leaders carefully ponder the effects of various courses of action before selecting them. This seems easy, but it is not because anticipating the effects of many actions is difficult. While experience and research help leaders anticipate the effects, they still must act in the face of much uncertainty.

Effective leaders understand that there is an optimal time to make decisions. Decisions made too soon reduce the time for critical information to surface, while decisions made too late slow organizational progress and result in lost opportunities. The ideal time to make decisions is the moment before waiting any longer diminishes opportunity.

The best leaders do not make themselves the center of all decision-making. They empower team members to make the decisions in their areas. Managers, supervisors, and team leaders know their team members and circumstances better than remote leaders and must take responsibility for them.

Along with thinking through the effects of potential decisions, the best leaders obtain the thoughts of their stakeholders before they take decisive action. They are always listening, floating trial balloons, and pondering others' perspectives to improve their decisions.

Mission, Vision, and Strategy

Some leaders start organizations and others assume the leadership of existing ones. When leaders establish organizations, they shape their missions. When they succeed other leaders, they continue missions. Involving members in the creation of the mission of new organizations increases the members' ownership of it.

Mission statements express the purpose of organizations. They should be easy-to-remember, one-or-two-sentence statements, and displayed so that everyone in the organization regularly sees them. The mission statement for one of my companies was "Provide the finest turkey products available."

Visions, unlike missions, change over time. They are distinct to leaders and time. Visions are descriptions of what people want an organization to be at a specific future date. Leaders must have a good understanding of their organization—its mission, history, stakeholders, capabilities, personnel, and competition—to create superior visions. They must understand the organization's competitive environment, comparative advantages, products, and services. Creating effective visions is critical to the success of organizations. Good leaders do a considerable amount of homework and carefully ponder visions before creating them. As Stephen Covey wrote:

If the ladder is not leaning against the right wall, every step we take just gets us to the wrong place faster.[176]

Strategies enable organizations to compete and advance their mission effectively. They involve determining (a) what to do, (b) who to serve, (c) how to do it better than others, (d) how to finance it, (e) who to involve, (f) where to do it, (g) what to source, and (h) how to market, sell, and distribute the products and services.

One of our family business strategies consisted of (a) producing the finest turkey products, (b) for upscale, growing supermarket chains with 10 to 200 stores, (c) using turkeys fed a vegetarian diet and grown without antibiotics, using only natural ingredients, and continuously layering on other differentiators, (d) financing our operations with 60 percent internally generated earnings and 40 percent debt, (e) employing people living in nearby rural areas, (f) operating in Central New York, (g) sourcing equipment, supplies, and ingredients from all over the U.S., (h) using our labels, store ads, and word-of-mouth to publicize our products, and (i) delivering the products with our own trucks, LTL carriers, and a network of distributors.

A couple of these strategies brought enormous benefits to our company. The strategy to sell our limited supply of products to upscale, growing supermarket chains having 10 to 200 stores was one of them. This approach prevented one or two large customers from dictating terms to us and enabled the company to grow steadily as our customers' businesses grew. A second critical strategy was to layer differentiating attributes onto our products every few years to have ongoing advantages over our competitors and eliminate the need to adjust our prices with the supply and demand of other turkey products. This approach also brought us a premium for a product that covered the additional costs associated with operating in a high-tax state like New York. The two strategies affected the customers our salespeople called on, how we responded to larger supermarket requests for our products, and our research and development.

Structure and Stakeholder Inclusion

Effective leaders create intelligible structures and involve their stakeholders. The legal framework, departments, positions, and rules of an organization comprise its structure. Lean, simple, and flat structures further stakeholders' interests and work better than complex, multilayered ones.

The people impacted by organizations have a stake in them. Prudent leaders involve and elicit feedback from these stakeholders. In the case of a school, the stakeholders are the students, parents, taxpayers, boards of education, administration, faculty, staff, vendors, area residents, local businesses, and the environment. In the case of an enterprise, the stakeholders are the shareholders, directors, management, team members, customers, vendors, area residents, and the environment. Although the environment is not a being, the actions of organizations impact the collection of living organisms that comprise it.

As leaders develop ideas, they will find it advantageous to share them with their stakeholders, solicit feedback, mitigate legitimate concerns, and improve their thoughts. While an organization's team members primarily affect its success, other groups also influence it. As leaders share information with these stakeholders, involve them, and elicit their input, they make better decisions, and the stakeholders feel better about the organization. Stakeholder involvement requires ongoing small investments of time but returns significant benefits.

Goals, Budgets, and Plans

Leaders and team members need to understand where they are going and how they are going to get there. Once leaders create missions, visions, strategies, and structure they can develop goals and plans. The best way to do this is to envision an end state and work backward. I discussed this process of reverse engineering in Chapter 15. Completing work under budget, to specification, and on time determines organizational success. Organizations and people without goals, budgets, and plans are like voyagers without destinations, means, and compasses.

Setting goals defines expected outcomes with measurable quantity, quality, and time components. If a group wants to bike from New York to San Francisco in one month for less than $15,000, the creation of interim goals and daily budgets increase the likelihood of success. The simplest way to do this is to divide the distance by 30 days, plan daily stopping points 100 miles apart, and think about how much money will be needed each day. If the group covers too little ground or spends too much one day, then they must travel farther or spend less another day.

Some leaders keep their goals, budgets, and plans to themselves and task the members each day. While this approach may be the best one in rapidly changing, high-stress environments or with immature team members, it undermines people's autonomy and ability. In most cases, team members work harder and achieve more when they participate in the planning process and goal setting, have some independence, and are kept abreast of the progress being made toward the goals.

Accountability and Assignments

Organizational fitness and success require boards of directors of private and public organizations to employ able leaders, use incentives to align leaders' interests with the organization's mission, measure the leaders' performance, and only retain those who deliver results. Similarly, leaders of the organizations must fill other positions inside the company with able people, use incentives to align team members' interests with the organization's goals, measure team members' performance, and only retain the most proficient team members.

While dispersing and checking power protects us from tyrants, dispersing too much power reduces the effectiveness and accountability of leaders in private organizations. The solution to this dilemma is to have federal and state governments protect the stakeholders of private organizations. In this manner, organizations can give their leaders the power to affect their success—to hire, discipline, fire, and compensate employees—and team members do not need unions as they and other stakeholders are protected from abusive leaders by government agencies. Boards with directors appointed by outsiders do a better job of checking leaders' power and holding them accountable than those selected by the leaders of the organization.

The assignment of a competent, high-performing person in each position also has a tremendous impact on an organization. Each team member affects the cost and quality of products and services. As leaders assign work to people appropriately, they efficiently and effectively complete it. When leaders assign work to people inappropriately, they jeopardize the team members and the organization. One person's negligence in an airplane part's manufacture endangers the safe operation of the plane and the lives of hundreds of people.

Leaders assign people to positions more optimally when they are aware of the requirements of each job and people's experience, intelligence, and interpersonal and technical skills. Although some people may have the technical skills for a position, assigning them roles that require a lot of interaction with others can yield poor outcomes.

Incentives and Evaluations

Knowledgeable leaders understand that people accomplish more when organizations establish incentives for the completion of work in accordance with the goals. Incentives commonly take the form of opportunities for bonuses and equity in the organization. Properly structured incentives encourage people to achieve the goals and minimize the need for leaders to manage people. As Jack Welch, one of the greatest CEOs of all time, observed:

Vision is an essential element of the leader's job. No vision is worth the paper it's printed on unless it is communicated constantly and reinforced with rewards. Only then will it leap off the page—and come to life.[177]

Getting every employee's mind into the game is a huge part of what a CEO's job is all about. Taking everyone's best ideas and transferring them to others is the secret. There's nothing more important.[178]

Incentives work best when they vary with the desired results. If a company wants to increase its sales 10 percent this year and sales associates sold 100 thousand units last year, the company might incentivize them with a $500 bonus for each 1 percent increase in unit sales and an extra $2,500 for a 10 percent sales increase. In this manner, the company encourages the sales associates to sell as much as possible and gives them extra incentive to reach the 10 percent level.

If sales associates have the authority to discount prices, however, organizations do not want to incentivize incremental sales because this causes the associates to lower prices to achieve their goals rather than work hard to sell more product at higher prices. When sales associates can lower prices or offer discounts, prudent companies reward increases in gross margin dollars—the difference between the sales and the cost of goods. Entrepreneur and founder of Singularity, Peter Diamandis, said it simply:

You get what you incentivize.[179]

Because humans evolved in a time when long-term thinking had minimum value, people respond better to short-term rather than long-term incentives. In many circumstances, I find that semi-annual goals, incentives, and evaluations work best. Setting goals and incentives and reviewing them too frequently wastes valuable time and doing so too infrequently reduces the effectiveness of the incentives.

Good boards of directors and leaders address poor performers. They learn the causes of poor performance and deal with them. Sometimes they help people with a challenge outside of work, reassign team members, or provide additional guidance or training. And other times, they discipline bad behavior or remove people from the organization.

Evaluations require objective and candid feedback. They affirm and document superior, acceptable, and unacceptable effort, work, and results. They recognize achievement and note areas for improvement. Jack Welch wrote:

You have got to be rigorous in your appraisal system. The biggest cowards are managers who don't let people know where they stand.[180]

Effective evaluations require honesty and encouragement. Unless people are in way over their heads, they respond to specific, intelligible feedback and support. Just as parents encourage and correct their children as they develop, so leaders must encourage and guide their team members.

Winning Practices of Individuals and Groups

The best leaders move others in quiet, understated ways. They learn the Winning Perspectives summarized in Chapters 4 through 12. They master and use the Practices of Individual Effectiveness—Health, Thought, Integrity, Proactivity, Prudence, Excellence, and Thrift and Investment—discussed in Chapters 14 through 20, and they master and use the Practices of Group Effectiveness—Affiliation, Decency, Understanding, Leadership, Teamwork, and Improvement—described in Chapters 21 through 26.

One of these practices, decency, warrants special mention. Leaders have tremendous power over people, and the better ones treat people well. Our genes predispose us to affiliate with organizations, absorb their orthodoxy, and respond to leaders. We naturally trust leaders. The better leaders responsibly use this trust to further the success of their groups. Respecting and caring about people are the right and advantageous things to do. When leaders do these things, people give their best to leaders and organizations. As Stephen Covey wrote:

You can buy a person's hand, but you can't buy his heart. His heart is where his enthusiasm, his loyalty is. You can buy his back, but you can't buy his brain. That's where his creativity is, his ingenuity, his resourcefulness.[181]

The best leaders have both people and task orientations. They have integrity and care about their team members. They shape missions, visions, and plans; assign people work, hold people accountable, and make good decisions; and set goals, incentivize team members, and evaluate their progress. The best leaders respect, involve, and appreciate stakeholders. They have an array of abilities and iron will. They venture into the unknown, shape cultures, create structure, develop strategies, and execute plans. Paraphrasing Irish playwright George Bernard Shaw:

> Some [people] see things as they are and say, "Why."
> [Leaders] dream things that never were and say, "Why not."[182]

When leaders must discipline or remove someone from a group, the best leaders do this with caring. Life does not equip some people as well as others. Sometimes people just mess up. Effective leaders want people to learn and recover from their errors. How long they allow people to feel the sting of their mistakes depends on people's conscientiousness and frequency of errors.

Realism, Courage, Passion, and Perseverance

The best leaders are realistic. They are aware that the effectiveness of their visions, plans, and goals depends on an accurate understanding of their circumstances. They know how things work and the likely outcomes of various courses. They allocate significant amounts of time and resources to assimilate needed information and work hard to understand their customers, team members, organization, communities, and environments.

The path forward is uncertain, yet the best leaders steadily advance their organizations. They are courageous and cautious, exploring, piloting, and mitigating the risks of their initiatives. Challenges worry them like everyone else, but they develop large amounts of self-confidence and act despite their fears. Their intelligence, past successes, methods, and resolve enable them to instill confidence in others.

Effective leaders, passionate about their missions, visions, plans, and goals, inspire their colleagues. People are emotional, and they respond as leaders make them feel good about the objectives and express optimism.

Leadership requires perseverance. As our organizations become larger, technologies become more complex, and regulatory hurdles greater, some projects need years to complete. Tackling these projects is not for the faint of heart. Thomas Edison, one of America's greatest businessmen and inventors, wrote:

> Many of life's failures are people who did not realize how close they were to success when they gave up.[183]

Culture of Success

Culture is human software or mental programming that orchestrates group activity. Leaders advance cultures by what they do, advocate, tolerate, praise, and celebrate and by whom they hire and fire. The best leaders advance cultures of truth, freedom, fitness, and decency. They exhibit and teach Winning Perspectives and Practices and expect their colleagues to do likewise. The best leaders create environments that empower people and help them succeed.

Leaders may direct their colleagues' day-to-day activities, or they may empower, train, and monitor them. While directing their associates may yield the best short-term results, empowering, training, and monitoring them usually brings better long-term results. People want to own their work and shine. When leaders enable their colleagues to develop competencies and assume responsibility for their work, their colleagues think more, work harder, and feel better about their jobs.

Leaders who create strong cultures delegate responsibility and encourage two-way communication. They set goals with their teams, reward their accomplishments, and appreciate their work. Colleagues identify with the enterprise and its goals, freely discuss challenges, and tend to seize more opportunities. Because team members want to carry out their responsibilities, organizational success occurs whether the leaders are present or absent.

Cultures of success encourage people to respect, understand, and appreciate one another, as well as to do their jobs and work together responsibly. They further individual and organizational performance and move groups along the Path of Fitness. Cultures of success are the most distinguishing characteristic of great organizations and teams.

Few of us recognize the importance of effective leaders and all that leadership involves. Decent, organization-minded, honest, and effective leaders advance our teams, enterprises, organizations, and country more than anyone or anything else. Self-serving, corrupt, mediocre, and incompetent leaders harm our institutions and us. When assessing leaders, the difficulty of their past challenges, their former colleagues' experiences, and their past results are the best indicators of their future performance.

Leadership – *the orchestration of the activities of a group, involving (a) good decisions, (b) mission, vision, and strategy, (c) structure and stakeholder involvement, (d) goals, budgets, and plans, (e) accountability and assignments, (f) incentives and evaluations, (g) mastery of the Winning Practices of Individuals and Groups, (h) realism, courage, passion, and perseverance, and (i) cultures of success. Disarray and ineffectiveness are antithetical to leadership.*

Chapter 25

Teamwork

In groups, we satisfy our need for affiliation, affirmation, and actualization. We improve our fitness, enhance our well-being, and accomplish unimaginable things.

Teamwork offers a solution to many of life's challenges. On teams, we ably defend ourselves; secure water, food, and resources; and raise and educate our children. We earn our livelihoods and produce products and services. We build roads, bridges, cars, ships, airplanes, large buildings, and cities, and conduct research and explore space.

Teams form when someone sees a challenge that affects several people, and they mobilize family, friends, colleagues, and/or other interested parties to address the challenge. Human nature is such that we feel an obligation to help those in our immediate communities when they ask us.

Teamwork is a product of millennia of natural selection. It requires effective and engaged leaders and team members. Able leaders articulate a mission, a vision, and goals, build an effective culture, and orchestrate member activity. The members of teams receive direction from their leaders and work together.

Winning Practices of Individuals and Groups

People who regularly utilize the Winning Practices of Individuals and Groups discussed in Chapters 14 through 26 make the best team players. Usually, these people are healthy and fit, exhibit self-control, and readily defer gratification. They have integrity, prioritize their actions, are proactive and prudent, exhibit excellence, and are thrifty. People who learn the Winning Practices of Individuals and Groups do well in school and in life. They exhibit decency and understanding, do not need to be the center of attention, know how to work with others, and want to improve their lives and the lives of others.

Leader Selection and Retention

Leaders play extraordinary roles in our lives. We choose our leaders, and then, our leaders affect much of what happens to us. People are not telepathic. They require leaders to bring people together and define common objectives, coordinate groups' activities, and oversee the addition and removal of members to and from the groups. Leaders, more than anyone else other than ourselves, determine whether we win or lose. While I discuss leadership more thoroughly in the previous chapter, I also address the importance of leaders to teams in this chapter.

One simply needs to ponder the impact that George Washington, Thomas Jefferson, and Abraham Lincoln had on millions of Americans; the effects of Lee Kuan on Singaporeans; the effects of Henry Ford, Walt Disney, Tom Watson, Sam Walton, Warren Buffett, Jack Welch, John Bogle, Bill Gates, Steve Jobs, Ray Dalio, and Jeff Bezos on the stakeholders of their companies; and the influence of Vince Lombardi, Bear Bryant, John Wooden, Don Shula, Tom Landry, Phil Jackson, Bill Parcells, and Mike Krzyzewski on their teams and players. Great leaders alter outcomes by one hundred-, one thousand-, and ten thousand-fold.

Decent, organization-minded, honest, and effective leaders advance their organizations and the well-being of their stakeholders. They imagine what is possible, build trust, say what they mean, do what they say, and obtain results. They share information, elicit feedback, and make adjustments. They correct what is amiss.

In contrast, selfish, dishonest, ineffective leaders advance their personal agendas and care little about their stakeholders. They deceive and harm organizations and people, are secretive, care little about others, and let problems grow. They kick down, suck up, deceive, blame, and take credit for others' successes.

The behaviors that leaders exhibit ripple through their organizations and affect who joins and remains. Honest, caring, and competent leaders enrich people's lives and attract honest, caring, and competent team members. Disingenuous, callous, and incompetent leaders make people miserable and attract people like themselves.

Selecting our leaders carefully and conditioning their tenure upon their ongoing truthfulness, honorableness, competence, and performance are essential to the fitness and well-being of our organizations, communities, and country. How do we identify honest, caring, and competent leaders? We examine their records and interview those who employed them, worked with them, and reported to them. We probe, listen, and substantiate.

Member Selection and Retention

The members of a group are critical to its performance as well. Groups want members who possess complementary and necessary skills and who are team-centered. Jim Collins, in *Good to Great,* uses a metaphor of "getting the right people on the bus" for member selection. In his "First Who . . . Then What" chapter, he observes that we want members who optimize group performance and make the experience of being together enjoyable.

> For no matter what we achieve, if we don't spend the vast majority of our time with people we love and respect, we cannot possibly have a great life. But if we spend the vast majority of our time with people we love and respect—people we really enjoy being on the bus with and who will never disappoint us—then we will almost certainly have a great life, no matter where the bus goes. The people we interviewed from the good-to-great companies clearly loved what they did, largely because they loved who they did it with.[184]

Leaders and team members who become aware of the strengths and weaknesses of their members have the best opportunity to optimize team performance. They must provide the opportunity for the other team members to communicate and display their unique talents, perspectives, and knowledge. When one or a few members dominate a team, these groups underutilize their reticent members' strengths. American businessman and writer Max DePree wrote:

We need to give each other the space to grow, to be ourselves, to exercise our diversity. We need to give each other space so that we may both give and receive such beautiful things as ideas, openness, dignity, joy, healing, and inclusion.[185]

To build effective teams, leaders and team members must humbly recognize that each person is one of several on the team and that the team needs everyone's contributions. They must listen to each other, interact respectfully, and appreciate everyone's unique talents, perspectives, and knowledge. The best leaders and team members facilitate this awareness and interaction.

Beneficial Diversity

Beneficial diversity improves the effectiveness of groups. It increases the opportunities for cooperation, specialization, exchange, and synergy. People are far more alike than different but do have varying mixes of physical stature, strength, coordination, and beauty; the ability to sing, act, empathize, and emotionally connect; and the ability to observe detail, learn, associate, visualize, and think logically. People accumulate varying mixes of cultural perspectives, practices, and taboos. Small differing abilities early in life become significant ones over time because we tend to develop these early comparative advantages and characteristics that others recognize.

Not all diversity is desirable, though. "Different" may be beautiful, and it may be ugly. Some characteristics, perspectives, and behaviors are undesirable. Opening groups and teams up to everyone in the name of diversity can harm our teams and groups. We want people with varying abilities, perspectives, and practices, not unethical, unlawful, and/or destructive people in our groups. Terrorists, traitors, murderers, drug dealers, and freeloaders are examples of undesirable types of diversity.

Just as natural selection winnows harmful, unfit organisms and destructive mutations from populations, so we must winnow harmful perspectives, practices, and people from our teams, organizations, communities, and country. This is a challenge for caring people. Understanding comparative advantage and the reality that some people fit better in some groups than others helps us up to a point. There are a few people, however, who should not be in any of our groups. What do we do with these people? There is no simple answer to this challenge, but the first step is to fashion an order that minimizes the number of these people. And my complete solution, one that has taken me half a lifetime to conceive, is captured by the Winning Practices assembled in this book.

As natural selection advances fitness in nature, we must advance fitness in our groups, organizations, and country. Including everyone is foolish. We simply should not include terrorists, traitors, criminals, and able-bodied freeloaders. This is a losing approach to life that guarantees our demise. In a competitive world, teams, organizations, and countries that keep their groups populated with able team players dominate those with counterproductive ones.

In sports, for example, successful basketball coaches distinguish between beneficial and harmful diversity. Differences in player height, quickness, and shooting range are desirable, whereas differences in team-mindedness, work ethics, conditioning, and commitment to excellence are undesirable. Good basketball coaches seek the former diversity and reject the latter.

Equal Opportunity and Meritocracy

The continuation of life depends on fitness and so do our teams, organizations, and country. Equal opportunity, meritocracy, and performance-based rewards further fitness better than other organizational approaches. When everyone can compete for positions, and we award them meritocratically, then the most qualified people fill them. When groups fill positions and compensate people meritocratically, their members and group perform at a high level.

Equal opportunity involves an absence of favoritism and unlawful discrimination. Essentially, the same rules apply to everyone; if leaders are doing their jobs, everyone has similar opportunities. Gender, race, ethnicity, and religion do not affect the application of the rules or people's opportunities. Favoritism, discrimination, and non-meritorious assignments and compensation are taboo.

Except for paying people between the ages of 21 and 65 a basic minimum wage, it is advantageous to compensate people in accordance with their experience, skillsets, and performance. Few people would have good attendance and perform well if poor attendees and performers were paid as much. Few people would become doctors if orderlies with 4-year-post-secondary education were paid as much as doctors with 11 years of education and training.

One reason our country is in relative decline is that critical portions of our workforce no longer operate meritocratically. Most public-sector organizations fill positions more by connections, politics, and seniority than merit. Public education is one example. After the initial hire, base teachers' compensation depends more on years of service than performance. Public schools pay longer-tenured, lower-performing teachers more than they pay shorter-tenured, higher-performing ones.

While most union members tell you that performance-based compensation and lack of political diversity do not affect their work, this is not true. My experience, the experience of hundreds of CEO friends, the research of most business schools, and common sense say otherwise. People work harder and more competently when organizations tie their employment and compensation to their performance. And children do better when they are taught self-control, to defer gratification, and to be conscientious, characteristics that conservatives instill in children far more than progressives. Chapters 30 and 34 discuss this in more detail.

Skin in the Game

"Skin in the Game" is the state of being vested in something and bearing the downside risks and effects associated with it as well as the upside ones. Entrepreneurs have skin in the game, often having years of their lives and most of their wealth invested in their enterprises. Professional artists and athletes have skin in the game when their future depends on the quality of their current performances. On the other hand, politicians, bureaucrats, and pundits have little skin in the game, being largely immune to the effects of the outcomes of their words, policies, and actions. Students who take classes without grades and attend schools that advance them despite their performance have no skin in the game.

Skin in the Game is being vested in something and bearing the downside and upside risks and the effects associated with it.[186]

Skin in the game causes people to be more responsible and better team members. When they have skin in the game and their conduct and performance affect their standing on the team, playing time, or share of the team's spoils, they behave better, practice more diligently, and perform at a higher level. In contrast, without skin in the game and when their conduct and performance do not affect their standing, playing time, or share of the spoils, they have much less concern about their conduct and performance.

Skin in the game converges intention and consequence, talk, and action.[187] When we are vested in something, have our well-being, reputation, or property at risk, and must bear the effects of our speech, choices, and actions, we engage, learn, and make more prudent decisions. We are acquainted with the consequences of our words and actions and maintain a consistency between our speech and behavior. Trusting the words and actions of those who have skin in the game and being skeptical of others' words and actions is prudent. Creating teams, organizations, and institutions such that every member has skin in the game makes the teams, organizations, and institutions more antifragile, fit, and functional.

Win-Win

Win-win is an arrangement that improves the position of the involved parties. I need some money; you need some work completed. I do the work; you pay me. I win; you win. We are both better off for having made the arrangement.

Win-lose is an arrangement where one person's gain is another person's loss. When used-car sales people knowingly sell defective vehicles to us, they win and we lose. We pay, and they receive, more for the car than it is worth.

When integrity is high within groups, win-win arrangements are natural and easy. People deliver what they represent, or they make it right. In small communities, our truthfulness, honorableness, and reliability convey reputations of integrity and cause people to trust, socialize, and conduct business with us.

Win-win arrangements improve the likelihood of favorable interactions. Integrity and win-win arrangements are especially important among families, teammates, businesses, and organizations as these people regularly interact with one another for years. Former Federal Reserve Chairman Alan Greenspan wrote:

> I have found no greater satisfaction than achieving success through honest dealing and strict adherence to the view that, for you to gain, those you deal with should gain as well.[188]

Cooperation, Specialization, Coordination, and Synergy

Teams provide opportunities for cooperation, specialization, coordination, and synergy. Capitalizing on these opportunities furthers our fitness and well-being and is also one of the greatest joys of life. The amount that we capitalize on these opportunities depends on the characteristics and abilities of the leaders and team members.

Crew, as much as any other sport, reveals the power of cooperation, specialization, coordination, and synergy. When a coach puts people randomly in a crew boat, the nine individuals flail and struggle to move the shell. When a coach strategically places nine people in the boat and instructs them for several months, then the rowers synchronize their movement, and the shell flies through the water.

For crew teams to perform at high levels, eight of the nine people must spend hours each week improving their conditioning. The coach must spend months observing and instructing each crew member on how to improve their conditioning and stroke. The coxswain must learn to maneuver the boat and set the rowing pace. The stroke must learn to maintain the instructed pace, and all the rowers must learn how to synchronize their motions. When everyone does these things well month after month, the shell glides almost effortlessly through the water. Cooperation, specialization, conditioning, coordination, and synergy underlie every great team's performance.

Associations

Joining with others to fulfill our needs and overcome challenges is one of the most powerful innovations of evolution. Such association is important for us to be able to overcome many individual challenges and compete with other groups. And it is especially important in the absence of well-developed institutions and governments, which was the case during the formation of our country.

Although joining with others to address our challenges is in our DNA, some populations do it better than others, and those who settled our country did this exceptionally well. The harshness of the winters and frontier had something to do with this proficiency. Only the ablest, most resourceful, and cooperative people prospered in these conditions. Inaction, sloth, isolation, and discord brought hardship and death. Proactivity, hard work, affiliation, and teamwork brought success and life. In the early 1800s, French historian and political commentator Alexis de Tocqueville observed:

Americans of all ages, all stations of life, and all types of disposition are forever forming associations. . . . In democratic countries knowledge of how to combine is the mother of all other forms of knowledge; on its progress depends that of all the others. . . . Americans combine to give [festivals], found seminaries, build churches, distribute books, and send missionaries to [far off places]. Hospitals, prisons, and schools take shape in that way. Finally, if they want to proclaim a truth or propagate some feeling by the encouragement of a great example, they form an association. In every case, at the head of any new undertaking, where in France you would find the government or in England some territorial magnate, in the United States you are sure to find an association.[189]

Informal, formal, volunteer, and nonprofit associations have enriched our lives tremendously. Early on, associations helped frontier families clear land, construct homes, build barns, form faith communities, and build churches. They enabled people to fight fires, plow roads, operate ferries, dispose of waste, shovel sidewalks, and protect neighborhoods. Even now, some 200 years later, various volunteer and nonprofit associations have provided us with emergency response assistance, hospitals, libraries, schools, and universities.

For decades, associations like 4-H, Boy Scouts, Girl Scouts, the YMCA, the Boys and Girls Clubs, and Parent-Teacher Associations have facilitated youth development. Associations such as the Free Masons, Knights of Columbus, Kiwanis, Lyons, and Rotary have enriched communities. Associations such as the United Way, Salvation Army, Catholic Charities, American Red Cross, Habitat for Humanity, Feed the Children, and numerous others have provided for those in need. Trade associations have helped professionals develop and businesses innovate. Baseball, football, basketball, soccer, music, and other associations have kept children active and busy after school.

These associations address many needs and bring numerous benefits. They help us overcome countless challenges. They reduce the need for politically oriented, inefficient government bureaucracies. Volunteers develop leadership and team skills and fulfill many social needs. Staff members earn their livelihoods, and recipients benefit from their free or lower-cost services.

I have personally benefited immensely and received much satisfaction from my affiliation with these associations. They taught me to be a more effective team member and leader and provided me with many helpful family and business insights. I had opportunities to learn and travel and made numerous friends through these organizations.

Volunteer and nonprofit associations are easy to form, operate, and disband. They are democratic. They right-size themselves, growing large enough but not too large to address the needs and challenges, and they only last if people need them. Everyone has a voice but those willing to do the work usually have a greater voice. The leadership of the associations typically rotates every one to five years. Ineffective leaders serve their terms and are gone.

Volunteer and nonprofit associations have a few extremely important advantages over for-profit organizations. First, they attract and mobilize an immense amount of talent and labor in the form of volunteers. Second, they oftentimes self-fund themselves with donations. Faith, youth, poverty, and disaster-related associations attract millions of hours of volunteer time and billions of dollars of donations every year. These associations do not always have the most motivated and able staff and volunteers, but the low cost of this labor supply and operating and investment capital make up for these shortcomings.

Two unfortunate trends in our country are the decline in our citizens' involvement in these associations and our increased dependence on local, state, and federal governments. In the last 40 years, citizen involvement in nonprofit associations has declined precipitously. Television, the Internet, and behemoth local, state, and federal governments divert our time and resources from these associations. They result in the substitution of edifying pastimes and apolitical, low-cost, effective associations for vegetative amusement and politically motivated, expensive bureaucracies.

Inactivity and cradle-to-grave safety nets are antithetical to initiative, citizen fitness, and effective solutions to community challenges. The more governments do for us, the less we do for ourselves, and the more dependent many people become on the government. Associations and electronic screens are competing keystone habits, e.g., activities and routines that affect several other activities and routines.

As the habit of vegetating in front of electric screens grows and that of addressing our challenges with associations declines, the habits of reactiveness, sloth, overeating, and indebtedness replace those of proactivity, leadership, teamwork, and financial strength. Preceding generations' tendencies to form associations and develop many related constructive habits were critical to our ascendency, fitness, and well-being.

———————————

We accomplish significantly more as we specialize and pull together on well-led teams than we do by working independently or looking to the government to address our needs. There are few greater joys in life than affiliating with a high-performing, winning team. Competent leaders and dedicated team members create beautiful music and have wonderful times doing so.

Teamwork – a group of people working together for mutually beneficial purposes. It requires (a) initiative and relationships, (b) mastery of the Winning Practices of Individuals and Groups, (c) leader selection and retention, (d) member selection and retention, (e) beneficial diversity, (f) equal opportunity and meritocracy, (g) skin in the game, (h) win-win arrangements, and (i) cooperation, specialization, coordination, and synergy. Disunity, discord, vulnerability, and ineffectiveness are antithetical to teamwork.

Chapter 26

Improvement

We improve, or we fade away.

Our learned routines are comfortable. Improvement is disruptive and hard work. We continue as we have until our dissatisfaction with the present overwhelms our unease with change or the next generation comes along. Humans do not like change, but organizations, enterprises, communities, countries, life, and the universe continue to change and evolve. No matter how knowledgeable, able, and efficient we are, we can always improve and become fitter.

Evolution and Competition

As stated in Chapter 7, evolution is the ultimate improvement process. Organisms compete, and the fittest ones place more offspring into the next generation, increasing the frequency of their advantageous traits. Competitions drive improvement and evolution. They force people to be honest, prepare, work hard, and innovate. Competitions allocate positions and resources to those who most ably use them. They winnow the disadvantageous from the advantageous.

Some people think we have evolved beyond competition and can evade it. They fancifully think students, schools, workers, unions, businesses, states, and countries need not compete. They do not understand that life is hardwired to compete, and that other people and lifeforms readily take our place when we stop competing.

Without competition, there is little creative struggle and separation of what works from what does not work. People abuse their positions and freeload. Governments, corporations, and unions treat their citizens, employees, and members poorly. Leaders, political parties, journalists, and scientists do not expose the self-serving actions, inaction, and inaccuracies of others.

An absence of competition invites corruption, exploitation, mediocrity, and subsistence. We atrophy and fossilize, or we energetically learn, develop, and flourish. We let our territory and resources limit our growth, or we secure more. We reside on our shores or venture offshore. We can remain on Earth or colonize the galaxy. Evolution is clear. We run the race, or we become extinct.

Trials and Pilots

Trials compare a current approach to a different one. If the different path yields better results than the current one, we adopt it. If it does not, we keep the existing approach. As we do this over and over, trying one modification at a time, comparing the effects of the existing and new approaches, and by adopting the ones that yield more positive effects, we steadily improve.

Iterative trials underlie the creation of all life. Iterative trials and selection yield unimaginable results over time, but the process is glacially slow. Mental and computer simulations accelerate the process, but they are only as good as the accuracy of the simulating effects. The advantages of mental and computer simulations are the decreased cost and time of the trials.

Pilots are more involved trials. They allow us to examine the effects of changes on individuals, larger groups, and ecosystems over time. They enable us to evaluate changes on a small scale before implementing them on a larger scale. They expose unforeseen effects and allow us to modify or abandon disadvantageous approaches. Pilots are portals of discovery. The more pilots we conduct, the fewer big mistakes we make. And when piloted changes are not advantageous, we learn what does not work.

People in business pilot most innovations. Resources are too scarce, mistakes too costly, and the environment too competitive to implement untested changes. If our public-sector and elected leaders were as careful and thorough when implementing changes as entrepreneurs, our schools and governments would work better and cost less.

Research and Development

Research helps us avoid repeating past failures. It permits us to start our iterative processes from advanced states. This is important in today's highly technical, rapidly changing, and globally competitive world.

While much of what we learn in school becomes obsolete, learning where to obtain information and how to evaluate sources are skills that help us our entire lives. We may find hundreds of books and thousands of pages of information on almost any topic in libraries, bookstores, and cyberspace. When confronted with a challenge, consulting a few authoritative sources on the subject is worthwhile, as usually others have found solutions to our challenges. Generally, learning from others is less expensive and takes less time than learning through trials of our own.

Research and development involve searching, reading, traveling, and interacting with others, experiencing different circumstances, and disturbing our routines and paradigms. They require us to understand our facilities, equipment, processes, colleagues, products, and organizations' challenges; identify bottlenecks and waste; gather ideas from trade publications and shows; research our competitors; visit users of our products and services; make previously unmade associations; and pilot promising ideas. In short, we must jar ourselves and see our challenges from new vantage points.

The development portion of research and development involves visualizing a better future state and then reverse engineering the steps to achieve it. Visualization and reverse engineering are forms of thought that I discussed in Chapter 15.

W. Edwards Deming, an American mathematician, physicist, and statistician, worked with Japanese industries after World War II. He was one of the first to think methodically about improvement. Although he did not use the term "Total Quality Management," he was a primary creative force of the movement. Philip Crosby, a medical doctor, corporate manager, consultant, and author, built on Deming's work. The following is my interpretation of some of their major ideas.

- Minimize the cost of inputs by utilizing one or two suppliers for each input and develop long-term relationships with suppliers.[190]

- Organize the workforce into teams to help members do a better job.[191]

- Create opportunities for team members to take pride in their work and the team's accomplishments.[192]

- Institute on-the-job training and other educational opportunities.[193]

- Clearly communicate product specifications, production and quality goals, and the progress toward these goals throughout the organization.[194]

- Create measures throughout the production process to determine where quality problems lie and evaluate the progress toward the goals.[195]

- Create incentives that correspond to the measures.[196]

- Create opportunities and incentives to encourage people in different departments to work together.[197]

- Listen carefully to customers, team leaders, and team members to identify challenges and opportunities.[198]

- Create a culture of continuous improvement by teaching, recognizing, and rewarding improvement processes and improvements.[199]

Continuous Improvement

If we are to flourish, we must continuously improve. We must be in motion, disturb our routines and paradigms, and incorporate time to work on improvements into our weekly, monthly, and annual schedules. Our competition improves, so if we are not improving, we are falling behind. No matter how good we are currently, we must learn to work and live more sustainably and become more organized, efficient, and productive.

Although some improvements require time and money upfront, many are free and have quick paybacks. The best leaders and most innovative people make lists of possible improvements, periodically evaluating the costs and benefits of the projects and prioritizing them. Russian-American novelist, philosopher, and playwright Ayn Rand wrote:

> Throughout the centuries there were [people] who took first steps down new roads armed with nothing but their own vision. Their goals differed, but they all had this in common: that the step was first, the road new, the vision unborrowed, and the response they received—hatred. The great creators—the thinkers, the artists, the scientists, the inventors—stood alone against the [people] of their time. Every great new thought was opposed. Every great invention was denounced. The first motor was considered foolish. The airplane was considered impossible. The power loom was considered vicious. Anesthesia was considered sinful. But the [people] of unborrowed vision went ahead. They fought, they suffered, and they paid. But they won. [200]

Collegial Improvement

As presented in Chapter 13, collegial improvement comes from the observation that conservatives, moderates, and progressives all add value to the improvement process. Progressives identify potentially advantageous changes and push for their implementation. Conservatives defend the status quo and identify the adverse effects of changes. Moderates, at their best, pilot the proposed changes, examine the effects, mitigate the negative ones, and support the changes that *prove* advantageous. Although most of us exhibit each of these three tendencies at various times, we exhibit one of them more than the others.

Sustainability-Related Improvement

As discussed in Chapter 12, natural habitats do many things for us, and they do them at a lower cost than our best engineers. Wetlands and floodplains filter water and reduce flooding. Topsoil, earthworms, and bacteria provide us with a medium to grow food and a means to decompose waste. Farmlands, grasslands, and forests filter water and convert carbon dioxide to oxygen. They provide us with animal feed, food, wood pulp, and timber. Mangroves, coral reefs, oyster reefs, and seagrass beds filter water and protect coastlines. They provide us with fish and seafood.

Although our lives are short, and individually our negative impacts on our natural habitats are small, collectively these impacts are large. Sustainability-related improvements reduce our negative impacts on our flora, fauna, air, fresh water, land, and seas. They protect the trees and plants. They conserve our small quantities of fresh water, limit topsoil losses, and protect other species. They deter the development of harmful biological, chemical, and nuclear agents. They dispose of the existing harmful agents, recycle waste, help maintain friendly carbon-dioxide-to-oxygen ratios, use carbon-neutral forms of energy, and reduce the world's population growth. They advance hydro, wind, and solar energy, and they cluster housing, retail outlets, and workplaces to reduce greenhouse gas emissions and other pollutants.

Many past so-called improvements solved one problem and created others. As we pilot new approaches, we must expose and mitigate unforeseen impacts. All things being equal, sustainability-related improvements—such as overhead, waste, and harmful emissions reductions—stream positive effects for years. These improvements must be the norm more than the exception. Utilizing environmentally harmful approaches when reasonably affordable, sustainable alternatives exist is indefensible.

Winning Practices

The Winning Practices in this book provide one of the finest collections of readily available, advantageous improvements. Each practice yields predominately positive effects to the individual, larger group, and the environment in the short and long term. If one or more of these practices is not part of your repertoire, their positive effects await you.

If we genuinely value our lives—and our families, associations, organizations, enterprises, and country—we evolve. We establish cultures of continuous, collegial, and sustainability-related improvement. We think, make lists, prioritize, pilot, and evaluate, and then reject, alter, or implement. We utilize Winning Practices and steadily improve.

Improvement – the continuous and collegial process of enhancing our fitness and well-being, which utilizes Winning Practices and involves competition, trials, pilots, research and development, and sustainability-related enhancements. Stagnation and decline are antithetical to improvement.

Section V: Winning Practices of Families

Winning Perspectives

Truth

Causality

Scale

Evolution

Fitness

Human Nature

Culture

Periodic Disaster

Eco-Dependency

Winning Practices

Knowledge

Health

Thought

Integrity

Proactivity

Prudence

Excellence

Thrift and Investment

Universal Education

Parental Choice

Results-Oriented Education

Free Enterprise and Markets

Responsible Corporate Governance

Prudent Regulation

Enterprise Competitiveness

Affiliation

Decency

Understanding

Leadership

Teamwork

Improvement

Government of the People

Powers, Prohibitions, and Structure

Freedoms, Rights, and Responsibilities

The Rule of Law

Inclusion and Meritocracy

Prudent Taxation

Spouse Selection

Marriage

Responsible Parenting

Empowering Habit Formation

Financial Strength

Savings Accounts, Social Safety Nets

Consumer-Driven Healthcare

Assimilation

Peace Through Fitness

Sustainability

Chapter 27

Spouse Selection

Proceed cautiously when love casts its spell, as our spouses provide half our children's genes, convey their perspectives and practices to them, and significantly impact our lives. Do this because when the intoxication of love fades and reality emerges, we want to find ourselves with as loving, able, and pleasant a partner—and parent to our children—as possible.

Natural selection has made pairing up a matter of chemistry far more than most of us realize. Visual cues incline us to investigate prospects and set off a flow of chemicals. In close proximity, we exchange pheromones that may trigger interest. Unconsciously and consciously, we gauge the desirability of prospects from visual, auditory, and olfactory data. Our comfortableness with another's race, culture, age, appearance, abilities, and personality influence with whom we fall in love, and scientists recently discovered that the degree to which our immune systems complement one another also affects with whom we fall in love.[201]

Exhilarating chemicals flow once we are smitten with love. The resulting intoxication causes those in love to obsess about one another and generally lasts a couple of years. During this period, couples initiate intercourse and/or marry. If the couples are compatible, the sex is good, conflicts are of little consequence, and pleasant feelings of emotional and physical intimacy replace those associated with the more fleeting feelings of infatuation.

Pairing up and mating are not entirely conscious processes. While natural selection has largely automated them, it has not automated harmonious, lifelong marriages. Such relationships require preparation, commitment, work, and discipline. M. Scott Peck, the psychiatrist and best-selling author of *The Road Less Traveled,* wrote:

Of all the misconceptions about love, the most powerful and pervasive is the belief that "falling in love" is love or at least one of the manifestations of love. . . . But two problems are immediately apparent. The first is that the experience of falling in love is specifically a sex-linked erotic experience. We do not fall in love with our children even though we may love them very deeply. We do not fall in love with our friends of the same sex—unless we are homosexually oriented—even though we may care for them greatly. We fall in love only when we are consciously or unconsciously sexually motivated.

The second problem is that the experience of falling in love is invariably temporary. No matter whom we fall in love with, we eventually fall out of love if the relationship continues long enough. This is not to say that we invariably cease loving the person with whom we fell in love. But it is to say that the feeling of ecstatic lovingness that characterizes the experience of falling in love always passes. The honeymoon always ends. The bloom of romance always fades.[202]

Despite Hollywood portrayals of the existence of a perfect soul mate for us, we could have a successful marriage with numerous people. Experience suggests we may fall in love with about 1 in 30 people of our preferred gender and probably only about 1 in 3 of them would be a good match for us. These numbers are estimates and not important in themselves. The important points are that there are many people with whom we may have a successful marriage and we need not despair when we lose a prospect.

How we pair up affects the division of the work associated with earning a living, creating a home, and raising children. It affects our living standards. It energizes and uplifts or aggravates and depresses us. How we pair up impacts us day in and day out for as long as we are with our spouses and often the remainder of our lives.

How we pair up and maintain our marriages also affects our children. Infants do not become well-adjusted, able adults on their own. Since the 1950s, marriage rates have fallen by two-thirds, and separation and divorce rates have increased three times.[203] Now, half of all marriages fail, and more than half of all children grow up in a single-parent household.[204] In *The Unexpected Legacy of Divorce,* divorce-authority Judith Wallerstein, psychology professor Julia Lewis, and award-winning scientist Sandra Blakeslee discuss what happens to children when divorces divide their families:

> If the truth be told, and if we can face it, the history of divorce in our society is replete with unwarranted assumptions that adults have made about children simply because such assumptions are congenial to adults' needs and wishes.

> Children in post-divorce families do not, overall, look happier, healthier, or more well-adjusted even if one or both parents are happier. National studies show that children from divorced and remarried families are more aggressive toward their parents and teachers. They experience more depression, have more learning difficulties, and suffer from more problems with peers than children from intact families.

> Children from divorced and remarried families are two to three times more likely to be referred for psychological help at school than their peers from intact families. There is earlier sexual activity, more children born out of wedlock, less marriage, and more divorce.[205]

Robert Putnam, professor of public policy at Harvard University, writes:

> Children who grow up without their biological father perform worse on standardized tests, earn lower grades, and stay in school for fewer years, regardless of race and class. They are also more likely to demonstrate behavioral problems such as shyness, aggression, and psychological problems such as

increased anxiety and depression. Children who spend part of their childhood in a single-mother home are also more likely to have sex earlier and to become young, single parents, re-creating the cycle.[206]

We know the quality and durability of our marriages affect our spouses and ourselves. If we open our eyes to the world, we learn they impact our children, their ability to parent, and subsequent generations.

Differences between Men and Women

Discussing the differences between men and women is politically incorrect and often controversial. While gender differences are generalizations, exaggerations, and sometimes fictions, some differences have evolutionary and biological bases. The evolution and mechanism for the differences are well understood. X and Y chromosomes and different estrogen and testosterone levels underlie the differences. While the perspectives and counsel that follow do not apply equally to everyone as hormone levels vary within each gender group, they do help us understand general tendencies and practices that further healthy marriages and child well-being.

In nature, most organisms do not mate for life, but a few do. Generally, the organisms that mate for life have immature offspring with lengthy developmental periods. In these species, the quality of the parenting affects the quality and fitness of the individuals who populate the next generation. Characteristic of humans and other mammals that mate for life is the reality that some differences between males and females convey an evolutionary advantage. Biologically, women can only have a few offspring. They invest an egg and years of their lives carrying, nursing, and nurturing their children, whereas men can sire thousands of children, investing only sperm. Biologically, males who impregnate numerous females and females who hold their mates close to them place more of their genes and tendencies into the next generation. Thus, most men have polygamous and most women have monogamous tendencies.

Competing male polygamous and female monogamous tendencies destabilize both arrangements and feed other behavioral differences in men and women. Although there have been many more successful polygamous populations than monogamous ones throughout history, presently monogamous populations dominate the global landscape. When male attrition is high, such as in times of war, polygamy offers a better opportunity for populations to recover. When male and female numbers are similar, and men and women have permanent addresses, monogamy provides a better opportunity for populations to grow, develop children, and civilly coexist. Not surprisingly, polygamy prevails in more resource-scarce nomadic cultures and monogamy prevails more in resource-rich agrarian cultures.

The polygamous and monogamous tendencies of men and women affect our approach to selecting a spouse. Men's polygamous tendencies make them extremely responsive to physical beauty and fertility. They want to plant their seed where it will bear fruit. Youthful feminine beauty, indicative of fertility, affects men so much that it causes them to do many shortsighted, foolish things throughout their lives. Only when parents teach their sons gentlemanly, monogamous behaviors, and as their communities stigmatize philandering ones, do males become desirable monogamous partners. Only as parents teach their sons to value women for more than their beauty and fertility, and men gain experience, do they place greater weight on the character, intelligence, ability, personality, and fidelity of women.

Women's largely monogamous tendencies make them responsive to masculine prowess, ability to provide, and fidelity. They want to develop their seed in a secure environment with ample resources. Being more long-term security-oriented about relationships than men, women seek handsome mates, but above all they want fit, able, considerate, and faithful providers. They want men who will stay by their side and help raise their children.

Men and women who understand these differences and pay attention to them have an advantage in attracting partners and enjoying lifelong marriages. Men who are fit, faithful, and appreciative and obtain good jobs attract and retain women better than other men. Women who are fit, faithful, appreciative, and able and pay attention to their appearance attract and retain men better than other women.

Vetted Love

If a couple plans to have children, there exists an optimal time to date and marry. Adolescence sets the lower age boundary for dating and the completion of college and securing work set the lower boundary for marriage. Higher frequencies of sperm and egg mutations and pregnancy complications set the upper age boundary for marriage and having children.

Starting to date around age 16 with the intent on marrying before age 28 optimizes family outcomes. It provides up to 12 years to identify a spouse, 2 years to establish a marriage, 8 to 10 years to build a career, and a minimum of 4 years to have children before infertility and sperm and egg mutation levels become concerns.[207] Couples may have children in their late thirties and beyond, but lower fertility rates, sperm and egg deterioration, and pregnancy and health-related complications are reasons to avoid this.

Because the consequences of marriage are so weighty and falling in love diminishes our judgment, people are wise to test a relationship with someone for a minimum of two years before marrying. This guideline is not absolute but provides time to become acquainted with the real person and not just a well-managed facade. Two years is long enough for us to assess the compatibility of each other's priorities, habits, and aspirations. M. Scott Peck wrote:

Sooner or later, in response to the problems of daily living, individual will re-asserts itself. He wants to have sex; she doesn't. She wants to go to the movies; he doesn't. He wants to put money in the bank; she wants a dishwasher. She wants to talk about her job; he wants to talk about his. She doesn't like his friends; he doesn't like hers. So both of them, in the privacy of their hearts, begin to come to the sickening realization that they are not one with the beloved, that the beloved has and will continue to have his or her own desires, tastes, prejudices and timing different from the other's. One by one, gradually or suddenly, the ego boundaries snap back into place; gradually or suddenly, they fall out of love. Once again, they are two separate individuals. At this point, they begin either to dissolve the ties of their relationship or to initiate the work of real loving.[208]

Besides learning about our relationship prospects over time and deciding whether to continue, vetting prospects with our families and friends is helpful. Families and friends have their own likes and dislikes, but generally, they see our prospects more objectively than we do. They have our best interests at heart and can raise concerns that we may miss.

Deferred Sex

Although large portions of recent generations think otherwise, dating does not have to include intercourse. If we think of dating as the time to evaluate potential partnerships and intercourse as the time to bond and procreate, we enjoy better marital outcomes. Some of the problems with premarital sex include: (1) it causes premature bonding with someone who may not be a good match, (2) it creates illusions of commitment and correctness that cloud people's judgment, (3) it traps people in relationships; and (4) it reduces the opportunity to find suitable enduring partners.

While the promiscuity of the small portion of our unmarried population that meticulously practices safe sex does little harm, promiscuity among large, less-disciplined portions of our population does great harm. Widespread promiscuity increases the frequency of sexually transmitted diseases, compromises immune systems, increases the incidence of cancers, diminishes reproductive health, increases infertility, increases the number of mutations in our children's DNA, raises the cost of health insurance, and increases the use of public resources. And widespread promiscuity and serial cohabitation, a more recent alternative to marriage, increase the incidences of unwanted pregnancies, abortions, divorces, single-parented children, abused children, and children growing up in poverty.

Promiscuity and serial cohabitation lead to many unwanted pregnancies. People make mistakes, contraception fails, and many pregnancies result despite people's best intentions. Little interferes with education, careers, and spouse selection more than unwanted pregnancies. Little is more unfair and unfortunate than being born without the benefit of two committed, loving, and able parents. Later-term abortions are a horrific form of birth control. While abortion may yield more positive effects than negative ones in some cases, the destruction of large numbers of fetuses devalues human life.

We should also be aware that sex is addictive. It titillates major pleasure centers in our brains. Like addictive drugs, we do not just have sex once and stop. Once we have good sex, we seek it in every intimate relationship. And then in always seeking sex, we may limit our access to many of the more fit, able, disciplined, and desirable marital prospects.

Deferring intercourse provides an opportunity to test a prospect's self-discipline and assess a match. It offers an opportunity for two people to learn to be affectionate in nonsexual ways. Deferring intercourse eliminates the risks of contracting sexually transmitted diseases and unwanted pregnancy. The best way to avoid the streams of negative effects associated with promiscuity is to refrain from compromising situations and intercourse until marriage.

Necessary Marital Attributes

Because marriage significantly shapes our families and ideally lasts a lifetime, we want to consider our marital prospects carefully. We must never marry thinking that we will change our spouse. Young adults are largely baked. They will change to a degree, but we can only count on normal lifecycle changes.

In assessing marital prospects, it is advantageous to remember that the habits and actions of prospects and their parents and grandparents reveal more about them than their words. When assessing marital prospects, I recommended the following criteria to my sons:

- Physical, mental, and emotional health,

- Freedom from debilitating addictions,

- A high level of integrity,

- Compatible perspectives, habits, priorities, and aspirations,

- A pleasant personality, work ethic, and record of achievement,

- Mastery of the Winning Practices of Individuals and Groups, and

- Family-centeredness and interest in having children.

The merit of marrying someone who is physically, mentally, and emotionally healthy, and free from debilitating addictions is self-evident, but for whatever reasons, many people ignore these criteria. I would not do this. "Until death do us part" is a very long time, and divorces harm children and emotionally and financially drain us.

Marrying a person who has integrity is critical to a successful marriage. If our spouses do not say what they mean and do what they say, we set ourselves up for a difficult time. When others deceive us, we lose respect for them and no longer trust them. Communication deteriorates and relationships end.

Marrying a person who has compatible perspectives, habits, priorities, and aspirations places the union on a common trajectory. While opposites attract and round out a union, couples do better when they are compatible in these ways. Nothing hurts marriages more than recurring conflict. Friendship, love, sex, career support, and children are common priorities, but they are not universal; today, people view them very differently. Some people want to practice a faith and expose their children to it while others do not want these things. Some people want frequent and varied sex, and other people have limited interest. Some people want to advance their careers, and others wish to place more emphasis on children. Some people are willing to relocate, but others do not want to leave their communities. Some people prefer to live in rural areas, some in the suburbs, and some in large cities.

A pleasant personality is another important characteristic in a marital prospect. We do not want to go on a several-decade voyage with someone who is miserable. While we often must make tradeoffs between personality and industriousness, knowing a person for at least a couple of years helps us determine if a prospect's mix of these characteristics is acceptable to us.

A work ethic and record of achievement are important criteria for prospects because marriage is a lot of work. Earning a living, creating a home, and raising children involve decades of hard work. Children are a 24-hour-a-day, 7-day-a-week responsibility for years. Laziness underlies so many undesirable behaviors and outcomes, some of which include lying, cheating, indebtedness, unemployment, philandering, gambling, pornography, and drug addiction. Selecting a spouse who has integrity, a strong work ethic, and record of achievement increases the likelihood of having a good standard of living, an equitable division of the work, and a more pleasant life.

The importance for a prospective spouse to have mastered the Winning Practices of Individuals and Groups is less widely understood. I discuss these practices—Health, Thought, Integrity, Proactivity, Prudence, Excellence, Thrift and Investment, Affiliation, Decency, Understanding, Leadership, Teamwork, and Improvement—in Chapters

14 to 26. These practices help people to be successful in school, work, and life. I recommended to my children and others that they find spouses who have made these practices habit. While some young people may not be able to attract someone who has made these practices habit, it is advantageous to look for these attributes in our spouses. Life goes so much better with a partner who habitually utilizes these practices.

Finally, considering a prospect's view about having children is very important because nature made children a normal part of our lives and children bring us purpose and joy. Without question, children create anxiety and work, but few parents regret having them. Children are also a prerequisite to grandchildren, cute little tikes who immeasurably enrich the later third of our lives. Agreeing before marriage whether to have children, how many children to have, and the preferred timing of having them eliminates potentially unwelcome surprises.

Family Decision-Making

When two people marry, they become a family unit. Opportunities exist for specialization, coordinated activity, and synergy. Spouses retain some individuality but typically find it advantageous to function as a team when they can work out a satisfactory decision-making arrangement.

Numerous decision-making arrangements work. One person may make the career- and financial-related decisions and the other the household-related decisions. One person may make the day-to-day decisions and the other the long-term decisions, or the decision-making may be divided and shared in other ways.

Couples may settle on various approaches through trial and error or negotiation. A trial-and-error approach takes time and may result in suppressed hard feelings. Negotiated arrangements require empathy, understanding, and constructive win-win approaches, where couples seek to satisfy as many of each other's preferences as possible. Outcomes may give husbands or wives the final say or both the final say in different areas.

Dominance is a challenge in most marriages, but particularly one when two very dominant people marry. These couples will enjoy each other's company more as they recognize and accommodate their strong inclinations to shape their environments. Dividing shared domains into less-shared subdomains in accordance with each spouse's relevant competencies diminishes conflicts. The more introverted, orderly, and frugal spouse might manage the finances and the more extroverted, gregarious spouse might handle the social calendar.

The decision-making arrangement that does not work is the naïve default approach where each spouse has equal say about everything and the couple plans to work out all the day-to-day decisions as they occur. While this approach avoids conflict initially, it sets the marriage up for years of tension and does not work in the long term. Reoccurring friction and conflict weaken marriages, whereas fairly-distributed responsibilities with minimal discord strengthen them.

With marriage carrying such weighty consequences, some forethought, discussion, and agreement on a decision-making process is prudent. When priorities and decision-making are found unresolvable before marriage, we can withdraw from relationships with few negative effects. When they align, we enter marriage more confidently.

––––––––––––

Ultimately, the success of our marriage, like the success of most partnerships, depends on the selection of our partner and preparation. The work we do up front to identify healthy, compatible, and faithful partners and taking the time to sufficiently validate our choice make a tremendous difference in our lives.

Spouse Selection – at its best, a conscious process to identify a lifelong mate that ideally starts around age 16 and concludes with marriage by age 28. It involves vetting prospects, deferring sex until marriage, utilizing some minimal criteria to screen prospects, and evolving a family decision-making process. Hooking up and promiscuity are antithetical to thoughtful spouse selection.

Chapter 28

Marriage

Effective marriages bring health, purpose, and happiness to us our entire lives and ripple positive effects to our progeny for generations.

Once we have completed our schooling and obtained full-time work, marriage is an opportunity. We have some maturity, our education, and a livelihood. Then, when we find someone we love and who loves us, who satisfies important criteria, has compatible habits, priorities, and aspirations, and who vets well, we may think about merging two lives together. Marrying before accomplishing these things compromises our education, career, and time to prepare for marriage.

Love and Accommodation

Mutual self-interest fuels our relationships, and the marital relationship is no exception. If our partner does not satisfy some of our needs for companionship, affirmation, and love and we do not satisfy some of his or her needs, then the relationship will not last. If we want children and our spouse does not or cannot have them, then we may need to rethink the relationship.

Everyone wants their spouse to be healthy, fit, respectful, attentive, and faithful, but not everyone works at being these things. When people fail to maintain a healthy weight, let their health deteriorate, are inattentive, or unfaithful, their desirability diminishes. Unfit partners jeopardize their health and burden their partners. Inattentive and unfaithful partners create relationship rifts.

Recognizing the need to be fit and desirable to our spouse, and to create an ongoing series of win-win arrangements, are keys to successful marriages. In *Men Are from Mars, Women Are from Venus*, American family therapist, lecturer, and author John Gray wrote:

If I seek to fulfill my own needs at the expense of my partner, we are sure to experience unhappiness, resentment, and conflict. The secret of forming a successful relationship is for both partners to win.[209]

Men and women generally seek somewhat different things in marriage. Women want their husbands to listen and be emotionally close to them. Women want their husbands to help provide a decent living, carry their weight in the home, and be fully engaged with the children. They want their husbands to love them and be by their sides for a lifetime. When husbands do these things, they strengthen their marriage. John Gray continues:

When a man can listen to a woman's feelings without getting angry and frustrated, he gives her a wonderful gift. He makes it safer for her to express herself. The more she is able to express herself, the more she feels heard and understood, and the more she is able to give a man the loving trust, acceptance, appreciation, admiration, approval, and encouragement that he needs.[210]

Men want their wives to respect them, listen to them, and be good mothers to their children, but as much as anything, men want their wives to be attractive and provide regular sex. This is not politically correct and does not fit the marriage ideal that many women have, but it is reality. Regular sexual arousal and intercourse help keep men monogamous. The reason for this is that near the prostate and the bladder are three small reservoirs: two seminal vesicles for semen and the ampulla for sperm. In mature healthy males, the reservoirs continuously fill. When they fill to a high enough level, men's thoughts turn to beautiful women and sex. The longer the reservoirs remain full, the more the desires grow. Women do not have this biology.

The Chinese worked out optimal frequencies for emptying these reservoirs hundreds of years ago. In the courts of the emperor, they advised men to engage in intercourse at a frequency of a man's age multiplied by 0.2 days. For a 25-year-old, this would be every 5 days; a 30-year-old, every 6 days; a 40-year-old, 8 eight days; and a 50-year-old, every 10 days, and so on.[211] Certainly, this is only a guideline; a couple's health, the quality of their relationship, and the wives' preferences affect the frequency. Nevertheless, couples who regularly empty these reserves and accommodate women's varying libidos reduce male and female tendencies to stray and strengthen marital relationships.

As husbands are more attentive, emotionally intimate, and sensitive, wives become more attentive to their appearance and receptive to lovemaking. As wives are attentive to their appearance and responsive to lovemaking, husbands become more attentive, emotionally intimate, and sensitive to their wives. Ideally, husbands advance this cycle as much as wives, but oftentimes this is not the case, as women's higher levels of estrogen and brain development incline them to be more relationally oriented than men.

Understanding the sociobiology of marriage and relational needs of men and women increases the number of successful marriages and happy, well-adjusted men, women, and children more than additional laws, regulations, political correctness, arrests, and litigation can. It decreases the numbers of women and children living in poverty; those who require government assistance; and young, highly-sexed, detached males who carouse, miss work, misuse women, and violate laws more than their married counterparts.

We have learned much about marriage, lifelong monogamy, and why marriage is fragile and difficult in recent years. While this insight challenges some of our cherished ideals, it also enhances our ability to create enduring marriages. Certainly, couples form tighter bonds and enjoy healthier, more enduring marriages when they are respectful; appreciative; and accommodative of each other; and committed to win-win arrangements, maintaining their fitness, and regular intimacy.

Family Centeredness and Specialization

When two people marry, they become a family, and both the husband and the wife must continuously consider what is best for the family. They must take care of themselves, maintain their health and weight, obtain adequate sleep, and regularly renew themselves, because sickly, weakened, and incapacitated partners weigh families down. And they must subordinate their individual interests to the family's interest.

When two people marry, opportunities for specialization and synergy exist. One may work and the other may organize the household. One may protect, set high expectations, and discipline, while the other socializes, nurtures, and comforts. One may make the day-to-day scheduling assignments, and the other may handle the household finances. As two people specialize, they more efficiently and ably earn a livelihood, maintain a home, and raise children. Germane to specialization is comparative advantage.

Comparative advantage is the reality that when individuals specialize—each doing what he or she does relatively better—and they trade or share, then all benefit. The concept of comparative advantage applies to marriages just as it does to groups and countries. Couples increase their effectiveness as they specialize in accordance with their strengths. Dividing responsibilities and work is much more productive than each person doing each task half of the time. Division of work according to relative strengths improves the quality of the work and decreases the time it takes to do it. It eliminates the conflicts associated with always having to decide how to divide the work.

Win-win arrangements also facilitate marriages and families by improving the position of each involved party. Suppose a couple does not want to interrupt their careers, wishes to have two children two years apart, and have a parent stay at home with their children the first year of their lives. Finding a win-win arrangement to accomplish this might involve each spouse sharing their objectives with their employers to determine how much family-leave each has and whether opportunities exist for working part-time or from home for a while. If, after consulting their employers, they learn that each spouse has three months of family leave and the opportunity to work an additional three months from home, the couple can satisfy their objectives by alternating their family leave and time working from home. In finding this win-win arrangement, the couple satisfies their goals, something that they could not do with a win-lose mentality or alone.

While we should always look for win-win arrangements, a problem with the above example is that often we cannot find such equitable, relatively pain-free solutions. When such arrangements are unavailable, at least one of the objectives must be dropped and usually one spouse must make a real sacrifice. While this is difficult, most sacrifices are temporary. There are unexpected opportunities in sacrifices, and the other spouse becomes obligated to make the next serious sacrifice.

Family Centeredness involves finding win-win arrangements, selecting courses that yield predominately positive effects for the family, and subordinating one's interest to the family's interests.

Commitment and Fidelity

The institution of marriage is in trouble. In the last 50 years, the number of married adults between the ages of 25 and 64 declined from 82 to 58 percent of the population.[212] Fewer people marry, and 50 percent of marriages fail.[213] The percentage of unmarried males, ages 25 to 34, increased from 17 percent to 64 percent.[214] If anyone wonders why the institution of marriage is in trouble, why we fear for our safety in many U.S. cities, and why parents no longer let their children play unsupervised outside their homes, it is because:

– Religious institutions and their teachings have little relevance with much of the population and little social stigma is associated with premarital and extramarital sex;

– Few parents teach their children about the negative effects of premarital and extramarital sex and the best ways to identify and obtain a desirable spouse;

- The television and film industries celebrate promiscuity;

- The rule of law readily accommodates divorce and entitlement programs make it easy for men to leave their families;

- Many young males do not have readily available, willing sexual outlets;

- Many poorly behaved and unemployable people enter the country illegally; and

- Guns are readily available to large numbers of troubled and/or irresponsible people.

Reining in male polygamous tendencies and merging two lives have always been challenging but are especially difficult today. Men and women routinely work and travel together. Contraception enables sex without the fear of pregnancy. Cultural icons portray extramarital sex in movies and on television. Divorces are easy and common. American scholar, award-winning author, and journalist Robert Wright wrote:

> Lasting love is something a person must decide to experience. Lifelong monogamous devotion is just not natural—not for women even, and emphatically not for men. It requires what, for lack of a better term, we can call an act of will. . . .

> This is not to say that a young man can't hope to be seized by love. . . . But whether the sheer fury of a man's feelings accurately gauges their likely endurance is another question. The ardor will surely fade, sooner or later, and the marriage will then live or die on respect, practical compatibility, simple affection, and (these days, especially) determination. With the help of these things, something worthy of the label "love" can last until death.[215]

Not only are marriages inherently fragile and less reinforced by our culture today, but they are also limiting and irritating at times. Most of us marry someone who is very different from us. The masculine bonds with the feminine, the courageous with the timid, the social with the reticent, the energetic with the lethargic, the analytical with the intuitive, the calm with the excitable, and so on. Natural selection has favored diverse pairings because they strengthen and balance the unions. They create opportunities to specialize and for synergy, but they also grate on us at times, particularly after our children leave home and before our grandchildren arrive.

We can do several things to overcome the irritations in our marriages. Intimacy and healthy sexual relations bring pleasure that compensate for some of the aggravations. Conscious effort to respect and appreciate our spouse and win-win arrangements facilitate interaction and minimize hard feelings. Avoiding personal attacks, counter attacks, and contentious subjects, especially when we are tired and stressed, keeps conflicts from escalating. Spending time with friends gives couples breaks from each other.

Additionally, the natural stimuli that bring men and women together can also pull them apart. There are plenty of times in marriage when the grass looks greener elsewhere. Pregnancies, business travel, illnesses and injuries, and women's declining midlife estrogen levels accentuate the extramarital green pastures. While women cannot prevent midlife changes, they should be aware that the loss in femininity associated with lower estrogen levels and aging cause younger, fertile women to be quite tempting to men.

So, what happens when the feelings for our spouse diminish? If our parents have had a successful, lifelong marriage and set a good example, we find it easier to maintain marital relationships. If we value our family, want to keep it intact, and remain focused on it, our marriage is more likely to last. If we remember that affairs are trouble, attractions fleeting, and divorce guarantees emotional and financial toll, we are more likely to remain faithful partners. In his book, *The 7 Habits of Highly Effective People*, Stephen Covey addresses the question of deteriorating marital love as follows:

"My wife and I just don't have the same feelings for each other we used to have. I guess I just don't love her anymore and she doesn't love me. What can I do?"

'The feeling isn't there anymore?" I asked.

"That's right," he reaffirmed. "And we have three children we're really concerned about. What do you suggest?"

"Love her," I replied.

"I told you, the feeling just isn't there anymore."

"Love her."

"You don't understand. The feeling of love just isn't there."

"Then love her. If the feeling isn't there, that's a good reason to love her."

"But how do you love when you don't love?"

"My friend, love is a verb. Love—the feeling—is a fruit of love, the verb. So, love her. Serve her. Sacrifice. Listen to her. Empathize. Appreciate. Affirm her. Are you willing to do that?"[216]

Enduring, healthy, and happy marriages require us to give our best to our spouse. Love is not just a feeling. It is action that does what is best for the other person. If we married the perfect person who met our every need, we would not be happy. Always having our way does not fulfill us. Loving others and seeing our families do well fulfill us.

Marital happiness also involves appreciating what we have rather than coveting something else. We are not aware of this when we are young, but we learn this as we age. There always will be others who are more beautiful, intelligent, talented, responsive, and fun; rather than chasing rainbows, our life goes better when we appreciate the relationships and things we have.

Having someone with whom to share our life is one of the most wonderful aspects of living. Longtime couples know how their partners will react to things before they happen. They shield their partners from things that might hurt them. They encourage and pick up their partners when they are down. As the following words eloquently express:

> Never ignore a person who loves you, cares for you, and misses you. Because one day, you might wake up from your sleep and realize that you lost the moon while counting the stars.
>
> —Author Unknown

Healthy, lifelong marriages are challenging, but they are the most rewarding of all human relationships. Everything is more fun with another person. Challenges seem smaller and are easier to overcome. Healthy, lifelong marriages bring companionship and opportunities for regular and safe intercourse, constructively channeling male and female sexual drives. They create greater numbers of well-adjusted, able children and the most precious relationships in life—husband-wife, parent-child, and grandparent-grandchild.

In the end, healthy, lifelong marriages, like so many things in life, depend on two people's commitment. Seeing our marriage as a lifelong commitment leads to a more successful marriage, as belief is one of the most powerful directors of human behavior. When we believe, we create an image that permeates our unconscious and affects our behavior 24 hours a day for our entire lives. "For better or worse, until death do us part" is a Winning Practice that furthers the fitness and well-being of our children, grandchildren, and subsequent generations.

Marriage – a lifelong commitment to another person that requires love, accommodation, commitment, and fidelity, and provides opportunities for specialization, synergy, and procreation. Healthy marriages bring tremendous benefits to our children, grandchildren, communities, and country. Promiscuity is antithetical to marriage.

Chapter 29

Responsible Parenting

If I had one wish, it would be that every child is born into a family with a wise, loving, and able mother and father. No child deserves less, and the well-being of our enterprises, organizations, country, and culture depend on this.

Human life is as much about the next generation as the current one because human populations that successfully develop the next generation overwhelm those that neglect them. And up until the 1960s, every American generation gave the next generation a leg up in life. But is this still the case? Is the increasing number of dysfunctional families, neighborhoods, schools, obese children, and our out-of-control indebtedness indicative of a generation that cares about the next generation?

While sexually mature adults can conceive children, only responsible parents equip children to do well in school, realize their full potential, earn decent livelihoods, and become good parents in turn. Only conscientious parents teach children the perspectives and practices that enable them to succeed in modern life and contribute to their communities and country.

Progeny Consciousness

Often, I meet young women who indicate that they are not planning to have children. While I understand having children is not for everyone, I wonder if many young adults making this decision recognize the lifelong rewards and joy of having children.

They understand that children are work and lifelong concerns, but do they sense the purpose, energy, and happiness that children bring? Do they realize that children bring many emotional and psychological rewards and are prerequisites to grandchildren, which is the greatest consolation of aging for most people?

Responsible parenting begins long before couples conceive. It starts with young adults maintaining their reproductive health and continues with their eventual selection of a spouse and marriage commitment. And once children are conceived, responsible parenting requires us to put our children's well-being ahead of our personal desires and careers.

Life with another person changes after our infatuation for him or her fades and the realities of earning a living, household chores, and covering expenses materialize. When two people marry young enough and before pregnancies, they have time to establish their marriage. They may test their compatibility, learn to divide the work, develop a decision-making approach, and realize marital synergies. They may establish harmonious patterns of life or surface irreconcilable discord.

As I discussed in Chapters 14 and 27, it is advantageous to have children before we are in our mid-30s. People have less trouble conceiving children and their eggs and sperm carry fewer mutations.[217] Women have fewer complications with pregnancies. Children are born healthier and fitter. If parents can remain home with children until they enter school, it is beneficial to the children. Surrogate caregivers generally do not give infants as good a start as invested mothers and fathers. They simply do not have the interest, focus, or motivation that most parents have. Once children enter school, parents have a lifetime to advance their careers.

If families are frugal and plan, indebtedness need not force young couples to delay having children. They can obtain a good education without going deeply into debt. Being frugal, saving when young, and working part-time in high school and college reduce the need to borrow money. Doing well in school brings scholarships and financial aid. Attending less costly community and four-year colleges reduces the need for loans. Support from grandparents, parents, and other family members helps young people establish themselves without indebtedness.

We only need to observe the generation of the Great Depression to see how families can accomplish this. That generation had lower living standards, smaller houses, less-expensive cars, and fewer possessions, and yet, they had a greater proportion of intact, functional families. They also had their children at younger ages, generally did not use nonfamily caregivers, and raised well-adjusted, able children.

The generation of the Great Depression demonstrated a progeny consciousness beyond their immediate family. Despite incurring tremendous Depression-related and World War II debt, they did not leave our generation with huge amounts of debt, large unfunded Social Security, Medicaid, Medicare, pension obligations, and a government that must default on its liabilities, inflate them away, or oppressively tax its citizens to fulfill the commitments.

Nurture and Discipline

Parenting is not a casual project because it involves 18 to 21 years of prenatal, infant, childhood, and adolescent nurture and guidance. Children come into the world needy, insecure, curious, and desirous. They are self-centered, frail, and emotionally volatile. They make innumerable mistakes and exhaust parents' patience. Responsible parents love their children, provide an array of stimulating experiences, and help their children form healthy habits.

Children are malleable sponges and mirrors, soaking up and reflecting the feelings, language, and behaviors around them. Their parents' degree of nurturing, guidance, and discipline—or lack thereof—affect who these children become. What we give our children, they give to others. When we love, respect, affirm, and care about children, they do the same to others. When we are indifferent, insensitive, callous, and cruel to them, they treat others in this manner. Rare is the loved child who does not love others, or the unloved child who loves others.

Unable to do many things, children need protection, assistance, and unconditional love and encouragement through thick and thin. They need mothers and fathers willing to make ongoing sacrifices for them. As John Gray wrote:

> To love someone is to acknowledge the goodness of who they are. Through loving a person, we awaken their awareness of their own innate goodness. They cannot know how worthy they are until they look into the mirror of our love and see themselves.[218]

Unconditional Love *is actively caring about others, accepting and affirming them, sharing our time and resources with them, and having their best interests at heart regardless of how they treat us.*

Children are extremely sensitive, and some criticisms and embarrassments haunt them for life. Children and adults respond far better to praise than to critiques. Positive feedback energizes us and helps us cross finish lines. Criticism discourages us. Children and adults need several encouragements to counter each criticism.

Good parents stretch children and expect their best without placing unrealistic expectations on them. My dad told my sister, brother, and I repeatedly that "There is no such word as 'can't,'" "You can accomplish anything you put your mind to," and "When the going gets tough, the tough get going." He expected our chores to be done and for each of us to do well in school. His encouragement, expectations, and counters to our natural fears, laziness, and self-pity caused us to do and want to do many things well. In trying to excel, we experienced many small wins, and eventually, larger and larger wins, steadily increasing our confidence over time. Good parents want their children "to be all they can be" but recognize that they have varying potential. Good parents do not compare their children to each other or their peers. They have a sense of their children's potential and set their expectations for them accordingly.

While most parents love their children, generally mothers love them more unconditionally than fathers. The gestation and nursing phases which mothers experience and their higher levels of estrogen provide them with an extra form of emotional bonding that fathers lack. While men exhibit these characteristics, younger, higher-testosterone men exhibit them to a lesser extent. This does not give fathers a pass on early child development, but it does suggest that mothers and fathers are predisposed differently toward it.

While most men are less equipped for early childhood development than mothers, they are better equipped to handle teenage development, as the strong maternal instincts that facilitate early child development hinder teen separation. Psychologist and sociologist Erich Fromm addresses the mother-adolescent separation challenge in the following way:

> In erotic love, two people who were separate become one. In motherly love, two people who were one become separate. The mother must not only tolerate, she must wish and support the child's separation. . . . Only the really loving woman, the woman who is happier in giving than in taking, who is firmly rooted in her own existence, can be a loving mother when the child is in the process of separation.[219]

Responsible parenting involves disciplining children as well as nurturing them. Human nature is not entirely benign. Deceit, predation, sloth, and addictions develop more easily than honesty, service, industry, and health. Discipline has fallen out of favor with our population, and a lack of it jeopardizes our children's fitness perhaps more than anything else. M. Scott Peck makes a case for discipline as follows:

> Life is difficult. This is a great truth, one of the greatest truths . . . . What makes life difficult is that the process of confronting and solving problems is a painful one. . . . When we teach ourselves and our children discipline, we are teaching them and ourselves how to suffer and also how to grow.

What are these tools, these techniques of suffering, these means of experiencing the pain of problems constructively that I call discipline? There are four: delaying gratification, acceptance of responsibility, dedication to truth, and balancing.[220]

Exposure to environments with boundaries and consequences for their violation facilitates children's development. Previous generations understood and appreciated this much more than we do. Life was very difficult for most people just a few decades ago, and difficulty magnifies the importance of discipline. When previous generations were undisciplined, their crops, livestock, and enterprises did poorly. They did not survive the winters. They lost their jobs and struggled to obtain new ones.

Parents who discipline their children empower them with self-control, the ability to defer gratification, and self-discipline. They help them form essential habits of success. Parents who do not discipline their children handicap them. Unknowingly, they make their children's lives much more difficult. Parents avoid disciplining children because they want to be "nice" and/or believe discipline harms children. The truth is that excessive discipline and permissiveness both harm children, and it is the judicious balance that enables them to focus and accomplish things and prevents their impulses from frustrating others and themselves.

Parents, teachers, leaders, and other authorities establish helpful boundaries and rules in environments of judicious discipline. They say what they mean, mean what they say, penalize people for violating rules and laws, and reward people for compliance. In such environments, people cannot avoid the penalties and receive the rewards without mastering self-control, deferred gratification, and self-discipline. Parents, teachers, and authorities teach children how to act by what they allow and forbid.

When we lack self-control, we are selfish and inconsiderate. We have difficulty forming lasting relationships and being on teams. Others avoid us and extend fewer opportunities to us. When we are unable to defer gratification, we are less productive and timely. We eat, drink, socialize, play, and avoid work, or we rush through our work and do not do it well. We do not economize or save money. Rather than fulfilling our responsibilities ahead of time and seizing opportunities, we neglect our duties and miss opportunities. When we lack self-discipline, we do not finish what we begin. We enthusiastically start things, talk a good game, do not complete our work, and frustrate many people. We settle for lower-paying, less-rewarding jobs or depend on the social safety net.

Our current politically correct approaches to child development cause many parents and teachers to struggle with children. Proponents of these methods view some of the past ones that worked well as "insensitive" or "barbaric." They advise us to ignore rather than check children's bad behavior. When they ask children to do something and the children ignore their requests, they sheepishly plead with children and move on. This type of parenting and teaching helps no one. It handicaps children, permits rude and disruptive behavior that interferes with other children's learning, makes parenting and teaching much more difficult, and causes people to avoid becoming parents and teachers.

Discipline is effective and relatively easy when done correctly but emotionally draining and ineffective when done incorrectly. Our current culture frowns on spankings; however, the judicious use of them benefits children. I support teaching young children to do as their parents ask and backing up those requests with spankings. Previous generations, many of my friends, and my wife and I raised our children this way.

Judicious spankings substitute for real-world negative effects. They do not bruise or inflict lingering pain. They get children's attention and cause them to abort inappropriate behavior. Like real-world effects, they are unpleasant. Unlike real-world consequences, they are harmless when administrated correctly. They do not waste children's time, and they enable parents and children to move on.

We just need to observe nature to appreciate the effectiveness of spankings. Mother bears cuff their cubs when they become a nuisance. The bear cubs disengage and life goes on. Most mammals want their parents' approval. When parents take the time to correct bad behavior and demonstrate that they are willing to back up their requests with a spanking, children respond. And the sooner children learn to coexist with authority and rules, the faster they develop, the more opportunities they have, and the more they actualize.

If I recall correctly, I spanked each of our two boys about five times. Once they learned I was willing to back my wife's and my requests with a spanking, I no longer needed to administer them. Upon making a reasonable request and failing to receive an appropriate response, I counted "one, two, three" aloud slowly, giving our sons time to register that an unacceptable response to our request had consequences. After failing to respond to this count a few times and receiving a spanking, the count elicited the desired effect, and the need to administer spankings ended. When penalties for inappropriate behavior are timely and consistent, children adjust their behavior.

Spankings are only effective with children between the ages of two and seven years of age. For children over age seven, a three-step discipline process is more effective. Before describing the process, I cannot emphasize enough the importance of communicating reasonable rules, boundaries, and penalties to children. If the rules and boundaries are too many, unclear, or unreasonable, the discipline process will break down.

The three-step discipline process works as follows. The first violation of a boundary results in a gentle warning. The second violation results in a stern verbal or written warning. The third violation results in a loss of privileges and/or the person's removal from their peer group for a period. The penalties for future infractions should be communicated during the first and second warnings. The loss of privileges or isolation period may be 3 minutes, 30 minutes, the rest of the day, or up to 3 days depending on the violator's age, the seriousness of the offense, and the frequency of the violation.

With older children, violations of the rules and authority are teaching moments. They are opportunities to teach children about the real-world consequences of such actions. They are times to express our disappointment with their behavior and indicate that we believe that they will avoid such behavior in the future.

*The **Keys of Effective Discipline** are (a) reasonable rules that are in everyone's interest, (b) clear communication of the rules and penalties, (c) reasonable consequences for violations of the rules, and (d) the consistent application of the rules and consequences.*

The goal of discipline is to help people form the habits of self-control, deferred gratification, and self-discipline and make people self-governing. Discipline minimizes the need to confront, warn, and punish children repeatedly. The best parents, teachers, coaches, and leaders understand that they should encourage children much more than criticize them and that the effectiveness of such rewards and penalties increases with their immediacy and consistency.

Children who have self-control, the ability to defer gratification, and self-discipline enjoy many actual successes and develop real self-esteem. They are more considerate of others, acquire strong education and work ethics, and finish what they start. They make friends more easily and function better on teams. Smoking, drinking, and drugs are unattractive to them. They have better educational, marital, and work opportunities, and they raise more well-adjusted, able children.

Literacy and Education

Along with nurture and discipline, we must place an immense value on literacy and education. People's health, freedom, living standards, and well-being follow their level of literacy and education without exception throughout the world. Former USAID mission director, scholar, and author Lawrence Harrison wrote in *Jews, Confucians, and Protestants: Cultural Capital and the End of Multiculturalism*:

Illiteracy is the single greatest obstacle to progressive cultural change. It enshrouds the human capacity to learn to change, and it nurtures the perpetuation of traditional culture. Human progress lags the most in societies, above all in Islamic countries and Africa, where illiteracy levels are the highest.[221]

If we cannot read, write, and do basic math, we qualify for the least desirable jobs. We generate interest from the least advantageous mates, permit others to take advantage of us, struggle to equip children, and contribute less to our communities. If we cannot read, write, and do basic math, we limit our ability to think. Literacy and education change this. They transform us from uninteresting and ineffective beings into interesting and able ones, open innumerable doors, and brighten our future.

Parents bear an important responsibility to further their children's literacy, education, and curiosity. Reading interesting stories to children between the ages of 1 and 8 every day expands their world and pays enormous dividends. It increases their knowledge and improves their verbal skills. Later, as children learn to read, listening to them read facilitates their progress. Children work harder when parents recognize their achievements, and they improve their pronunciation, vocabulary, comprehension, spelling, and grammar skills as they read aloud. Parents may think that they do not have time to listen to their children read, but they can make the time. If parents split the load, the commitment amounts to 20 minutes every other day.

Responsible parents also encourage their children to explore, ask questions, and find answers. They help them access inspiring and educational books, TV shows, and movies. They expose their children to courageous and noble heroes and instill in their children a lifelong thirst to learn.

Children benefit greatly when parents take an interest in their teachers, lessons, and homework. When parents insist that children complete their homework after dinner and before they text friends, play video games, or watch television, they do them a great service. Once children develop this habit, they do better in school. The practice of completing one's work before playing will likely remain with them in some form for the rest of their lives.

If we have good parents and access to solid education, it is in our interest to learn from our parents and do well in school. The better we do, the more opportunities and choices we have. If we do not have these advantages, we must take responsibility for our own education much earlier in our lives by:

- Accessing libraries and the people, books, and Internet in them;

- Utilizing free educational opportunities like the Kahn Academy courses available on the Internet;

- Finding work under able supervisors and mentors; and

- Finding books like Stephen Covey's *The 7 Habits of Highly Effective People* and this one that describe winning perspectives, practices, and habits.

Experiences and Challenges

Responsible parents fill their children's time with new experiences and challenges. They provide activities that require gradually increasing amounts of effort and struggle. They present their children with new perspectives that jar them and cause them to grow. English philosopher and physician John Locke wrote:

Encourage therefore [their] inquisitiveness all you can, by satisfying [their] demands, and informing [their] judgement, as far as it is capable. When [their] reasons are any way tolerable, let [them] find the credit and commendation of it . . . without being laughed at for [their mistakes] be gently put into the right; and if [they] show a forwardness to be reasoning about things that come in [their] way, take care, as much as you can, that no body checks this inclination in [them], or mislead it by captious or fallacious ways of talking with [them].[222]

The softer you find your [children are], the more you are to seek occasions at fit times thus to harden [them]. The great art in this is to begin with what is but very little painful, and to proceed by insensible degrees, when you are playing, and in good humor with [them], and speaking well of [them]: and when you have once got [them] to think [that they have] made amends for [their] suffering by the praise given [them] for [their] courage; when [they] can take pride in giving such marks of [their fitness], and can prefer the reputation of being brave and [strong], to the avoiding a little pain, or the shrinking under it.[223]

Chores are an important type of childhood experience. Responsible parents do chores with their children and assign chores to them. They understand chores challenge children; help them develop self-discipline, competencies, and resilience; and cause them to enjoy work as adults. Scott M. Peck, author of *The Road Less Traveled*, wrote:

Life is a series of problems. Do we want to moan about them or solve them? Do we want to teach our children to solve them? . . . Problems call forth our courage and our wisdom; indeed, they create our courage and wisdom. It is only because of problems that we grow mentally and spiritually. When we desire to encourage the growth of the human spirit, we challenge and encourage the human capacity to solve problems, just as in school we deliberately set problems for our children to solve. It is through the pain of confronting and resolving problems that we learn.[224]

Children also need to experience some adversity. Adversity strengthens our bodies and minds. The Israeli Prime Minister Golda Meir wrote:

You'll never find a better sparring partner than adversity.[225]

Adversity creates dissonance between what is and something better. It evokes frustration and causes a transformational desire to take root in us. It forces us to work hard and develop competencies. Adversity that does not overwhelm us seeds dreams, creates confidence, and builds character. Responsible parents understand the story of "The Butterfly" and avoid doing for children what those children can do for themselves.

The Butterfly

One day, a small opening appeared in a cocoon. A nearby couple had watched the butterfly for several hours struggle to emerge from the little hole. All at once, the butterfly seemed to stop making progress. It appeared to have gone as far as it could and could not go any further. They decided to help the butterfly.

They took a pair of scissors and opened the cocoon. The butterfly emerged easily, but it had a withered body and tiny, shriveled wings.

They continued to watch because they expected that the butterfly's body would become firm and the wings would open, enlarge, and expand at any moment. Unfortunately, none of this happened. In fact, the butterfly spent the rest of its life crawling around with a withered body and shriveled wings. It never could fly.

What the couple did not understand was that the struggle required for the butterfly to squeeze through the tiny opening forced fluid from the body of the butterfly into its wings so that it could fly once freed from the cocoon.

Some experiences and challenges cost money, but many of them are free. Books, travel, friends, teachers, and mentors enlarge children's worlds. Visiting grandparents, aunts, uncles, and cousins is inexpensive and expansive. Trips to the library, extra-curricular school activities, and Internet-based educational opportunities like the Khan Academy cost little. Excursions to museums and county, state, and national parks are very affordable. Music lessons further child development when family resources permit them.

Books take children to other times and places, providing alternative views of people and the world. They capture others' insights and explain how the world works. They teach children how their life experiences are the same or different from those of other times and places. Books permit us to learn from some of the most insightful and accomplished people who ever lived.

Taking the time to find the best sources and teachers is worth the effort. Childhood is short and the amount of available information unlimited. Accurate and useful information is worth much more than most of the bombardment that comes our way. A few hours spent reading *Big History* by David Christian, Cynthia Stokes Brown, and Craig Benjamin or *The Power of Habit* by Charles Duhigg benefits young adults so much more than most other books.

Along with books, spending time in other countries brings many new and important perspectives. Had I not traveled so much at a young age, my world would be much smaller and my thoughts more limited. Traveling shatters paradigms and presents innumerable new ideas. When people travel, they never return home the same. Not only do they learn about new places and cultures, they see their communities, country, and culture through the eyes of others, and in doing so, obtain a greater understanding of them.

Our childhood experiences and challenges allow many of our dreams to take root. We never know when, but sometime, somewhere, something sparks our imagination and becomes an important motivation in our life. Some place, some challenge, some person causes us to say, "I want to go there," "I want to do that," "I want to solve that problem," or "I want to be like him or her." These seeds are important. Lots of people, including myself, can tell you the place and time that a dream took root. The self-help author Napoleon Hill wrote:

Cherish your visions and your dreams as they are the children of your soul, the blueprints of your ultimate achievements.[226]

Role Models

Our family and early mentors are important role models who imprint upon us their perspectives, priorities, practices, and taboos. Children are natural mimics who say and do whatever they see their role models say and do. If we want children to become well-adjusted adults, then we need to model constructive behaviors and shun debilitating ones. Hypocrisy undermines our credibility and tarnishes our instruction. We cannot tell children to be honest and then lie. We cannot insist that our children work hard and then not work hard ourselves. Children learn abstract concepts and nuances, but only as they align with the behaviors of their role models.

Children acquire their sense of motherhood and fatherhood from their mothers and fathers. They receive their sense of being a grandmother or grandfather from their grandparents. They gain a sense of marriage from their parents, grandparents, and the married couples with whom they spend time. "Normal" to children is what is around them. Until they experience other influences later in their lives, they speak and act like their parents. They view school, work, authorities, and ethnic groups like their parents do, and they also frequently drive, spend, save, play, and vote like their parents.

Paraphrasing Alexis de Tocqueville, the 19th century French author of the landmark work *Democracy in America:*

Step back in time; look closely at children in the very arms of their mothers and fathers. See the external world reflected for the first time in the yet unclear mirror of their understanding. Study the first examples which strike their eyes; listen to the first words which arouse within them the slumbering power of thought; watch the first struggles which they undergo. Only then will you comprehend the source of children's prejudices, the habits, and the passions which are to rule their lives. The entire child, so to speak, comes fully formed in the wrappings of his or her cradle.[227]

Grandparents

If we become parents, we are likely to become grandparents. And while our culture places few expectations on grandparents, they can affect the development of their grandchildren tremendously and have a wonderful time doing so. Grandparents have perspective, knowledge, experience, and usually time and resources that parents lack. They have lived longer, done more, raised children, paid off their mortgage, and may have substantial savings. While many parents do not have a spare minute or dollar, grandparents generally have both.

Because my grandparents were farmers, I had the good fortune of spending hundreds of hours with them on the farm while growing up—working, caring for horses, gardening, mowing lawns, and doing other chores. And while much of my time with them involved work, it never seemed like work. My grandparents made the work fun and always reserved time for play. We played catch, had squirt gun fights, went to parks, watched baseball games, decorated Christmas trees, watched "The Wonderful World of Disney" together, and enjoyed many meals, donuts, and cookies as well as a lot of popcorn and ice cream.

Optimally, grandparents are important role models, checks on trendy ineffective parenting approaches, patient mentors, and teachers. They provide parents with needed breaks, cheer grandchildren's performances, and console their disappointments. Grandparents read to their grandchildren, listen to them read, and share instructive family histories and stories with them. They teach grandchildren to cook, garden, keep an orderly house, and do the yardwork and home repairs. They take grandchildren to libraries, parks, museums, art and sports performances, and on trips. They reward grandchildren's hard work and accomplishments with visits to the bakery or ice cream store. Grandparents also may help their grandchildren's educational expenses.

Little brings more purpose and joy than seeing our children and grandchildren develop and flourish. While we do not play the leading role in our grandchildren's lives, our supporting role is a lot less work and more fun.

Our children's development occurs in small, daily imperceptible progressions and is only noticed over the passage of weeks, months, and years. When our children are young and completely dependent upon us, we may wonder if we will ever have our lives back. But then one day, our responsibility ends, and they leave home. They grow up and become independent. When this happens, we experience both great loss and satisfaction.

For most people, having children and grandchildren is the greatest privilege, opportunity, and joy in life. It is beyond words and multigenerational. Not understanding this when we are young frequently becomes many people's greatest regret. Time and time again, my senior friends tell me that they wish they had spent less time on their careers and more with their children and grandchildren.

No one loves us like our parents. No one expends as much effort on our behalf, shares as many resources with us, makes as many sacrifices for us, and expects so little in return. No matter how old our parents are when they die, their passing weighs heavily on us. We ache for their presence, warmth, and love. Responsible parents are the foundation of a flourishing people. They positively impact their children, the well-being of our communities and country, and their descendants for generations.

Responsible Parenting – *a lifelong commitment to love one's children and grandchildren unconditionally, nurture and educate them, and share one's time and resources with them. It requires a progeny consciousness; teaching our children self-control, to defer gratification, and self-discipline; being good, lifelong role models; and continuously exposing our children to challenges that enhance their knowledge, competencies, and confidence. Irresponsible parenting, underdevelopment, and depravity are antitheses of responsible parenting.*

Chapter 30

Empowering Habit Formation

Our habits make or break us.

We are creatures of habit. Most of our activity consists of executing a series of learned routines. Wake up, walk to the bathroom, shower, dress, eat breakfast, brush our teeth, and drive to work. Engage in a series of routines at work. Walk from work to the car, drive home, eat dinner, read the newspaper, watch television, put on our pajamas, walk into the bathroom, wash, brush our teeth, and go to bed. We do these and similar routines every day, year after year, in largely the same way.

We form habits both unconsciously and consciously because habits aid survival. Unconscious habit formation occurs simply from doing the same activity over and over, whereas conscious habit formation takes repeated concentration. Organisms that can automate most activities make their conscious bandwidth available for unexpected threats and opportunities.

Forming Empowering Habits

Reason, if consulted with, would advise, that their children's time should be spent in acquiring what might be useful to them when they come to be [adults], rather than to have their heads stuffed with a deal of trash, a great part whereof they usually never do ('tis certain they never need to) think on again as long as they live: and so much of it as does stick by them they are only the worse for.[228]

—John Locke

Sages have commented on the importance of habits throughout history. More recently, Pulitzer Prize winner and author of *The Power of Habit*, Charles Duhigg, presents some of the latest insights regarding habits and defines the following related concepts. [229]

Habits consist of cues, routines, and rewards that cause cravings.

Cues trigger routines. Generally, we do not choose the cues or choose to respond to them.

Routines are series of activities that become automatic over time.

Rewards are pleasures associated with the completion of routines.

Cravings are desires for rewards. They block distractions and drive habits.

Doing the same thing over and over creates neurological pathways in our brains. Like water eroding a canyon, the more we repeat a routine, the stronger the neurological pathways. Repeat something 30 to 90 times; it ingrains itself in our minds. Repeated routines become habit "with or without our permission." Consistent cues and rewards over a few weeks solidify routines; once they are in place, they do not go away. We may alter our behaviors and associated neurological pathways but cannot erase them.

If we watch television each evening before bedtime and go to the kitchen to get a snack during commercial breaks, the commercial becomes the trigger and the routine a habit before long. Drinking and snacking habits form easily, as soda, alcohol, and sweets pleasure our brain. If we want to create a habit to do our homework every night after eating dinner, our cue could be rising from the dinner table. The routine is doing our homework, and the reward is the satisfaction of pleasing our parents and teachers.

Charles Duhigg indicates that "believing a habit makes our lives better" helps us establish the habit as belief amplifies the psychological payoff, especially when those around us reinforce this belief.[230] Duhigg indicates that some habits called "keystone habits" influence the formation of many other habits.[231] Attending school and going to work are examples of keystone habits because they affect the development and exercise of so many other habits.

Keystone Habits *are routines that affect numerous other routines.*

When I was growing up, I was fortunate to have one set of grandparents living in the house next door. This enabled me to see them almost every day. I distinctly remember my grandmother, Metta Bitz, remarking:

Good habits carry us through life's difficult times.[232]

I formed many good habits with the help of my parents and grandparents that helped me throughout my life. All four of my grandparents and both of my parents had amazing habits. The positive effects of these behaviors helped them maintain good health, slowed their aging, and caused them to live to the ages of 88, 90, 93, and 95, and my parents so far to the ages of 88.

What were some of the habits that I learned as a child? Two of the first habits were to say "please" when asking for something and "thank-you," upon receiving it. Another one was that when my parents said "no," they meant it. My parents also created a habit of truth-telling in their children by penalizing lying more severely than any other offense.

My sister, brother, and I were taught to respect our elders and apologize to people we treated poorly. We learned to go to bed at a specified time, rise early, brush our teeth every evening, and have regular dental checkups. We were expected to attend church on Sunday and help others.

There was usually time for play, but our work had to be done first. My parents expected us to do homework and attend school unless we were very sick. Not doing our homework and skipping school were never considerations. My parents taught us that watching television was a waste of time and watching it more than a couple of hours a day was unacceptable.

My parents instructed us to work and save money. If we wanted something special that was relatively inexpensive, we might receive it for our birthday or at Christmas. We were expected to celebrate the birthdays of those in our family. We were to honor our mother and grandmothers on Mother's Day, our father and grandfathers on Father's Day, and our ancestors and veterans on Memorial Day. My parents taught us to follow the laws, pay our taxes, and avoid anything potentially addictive and harmful like cigarettes, drinking, drugs, pornography, promiscuity, and gambling.

Although some might see our childhoods as too structured and might think that the spankings my sister and I received for fighting were harmful, nothing could be further from the truth. I enjoyed my family, friends, play, hobbies, and sports and have never been inclined to fight or strike anyone since childhood.

Our parents, grandparents, and other able and positive mentors filled our childhoods. They were among my greatest blessings in life. They set us on a path to be healthy, successful, and happy. And while I have experienced plenty of adversity, little of it has been self-created. I wish every child could have a similar family and developmental assistance.

My habits today are not identical to the ones my parents gave me. The weekly bath morphed into a daily shower. I stopped attending church in my early 20s and learned to brush and floss my teeth after every meal. Having little physical work, I exercise every day, avoid foods with added salt and sugar, and do not snack. I eat smaller portions, less meat, and more nuts, fruits, and vegetables. In social situations, I drink a glass of wine, and I only have desserts on special occasions. Having some savings now, I spend money a little more freely. Otherwise, the habits that my parents and grandparents helped me form have remained intact for over 50 years.

Empowering habits are Winning Practices that we do so many times that they become automatic routines. Empowering habits enhance our effectiveness and help us through life's difficult times. Previous generations paid much more attention to children's formation of habits at home and in school. John Locke wrote:

> Let me give two cautions. 1. The one is, that you keep them to the practice of what you would have grown into a habit in them by kind words and gentle admonitions, rather as minding them of what they forget, than by harsh rebukes and chiding, as if they were willfully guilty. 2. Another thing you are to take care of is not to endeavor to settle too many habits at once, lest by variety you confound them, and so perfect none. When constant custom has made any one thing easy and natural to them, and they practice it without reflection, you may then go on to another.[233]

Previous generations understood that we form habits whether they yield positive or negative effects. They recognized that we become what we repeatedly do. A much larger cross-section of the population thought about how children spent their time. Idle pastimes and pleasures were discouraged, and productive, skill-building ones were encouraged at all socio-economic levels.

The habits of having a cup of coffee in the morning, a cigarette during breaks, and a drink in the evening form effortlessly because caffeine, tobacco, and alcohol pleasure the brain. On the other hand, the habits of truthfulness, consideration, and punctuality are difficult to form. Their formation requires conscious effort, and we benefit from outside help. These behaviors form more easily when we receive heartening praise for exhibiting them and gentle admonishments from our parents and authority figures for our lapses.

Once we are taught these behaviors and do them often enough, we usually exhibit them in some manner for the rest of our lives. Any effort adults make to develop empowering habits in children is well worthwhile. Children are going to form habits anyway, and we are better off to help them form empowering ones rather than allow them to form debilitating ones.

In the previous chapter, I discussed unconditional love and three forms of discipline—self-control, deferred gratification, and self-discipline. These four behaviors or practices are keystone habits, and I might even go as far as to say cornerstone habits. These four behaviors positively affect everything that we do in life. They are fundamental to our fitness and well-being.

Unconditional Love *involves actively caring about others, accepting and affirming them, sharing our time and resources with them, and having their best interests at heart regardless of how they treat us.*

Self-Control *is the practice of governing our speech and actions. It requires us to check impulsiveness and to speak and act judiciously. It checks disruptive, counterproductive, and shortsighted actions.*

Deferred Gratification *is the practice of exchanging short-term pleasure for a future of more enduring satisfaction. It enables the steady improvement of our organizations and lives.*

Self-Discipline *is the practice of pursuing a chosen course in the face of distraction, competing desires, difficulty, and adversity.*

Unconditional love energizes us. When we feel loved, our will strengthens and our energy increases. We want to do the right thing and have the energy to form empowering habits. Self-control enables us to form other habits successfully. If we wish to form a habit to listen more carefully to others, we need self-control to refrain from saying everything that enters our mind during the conversation.

Deferred gratification enables us to bear the pain for a later pleasure. If we want to develop a Monday-through-Friday jogging habit, we must embrace the unpleasantness of waking up earlier, inclement weather, and exerting ourselves before we can enjoy the resulting endorphin and psychological pleasure of improving our health and well-being.

Self-discipline helps us to finish what we start. We accomplish little without self-discipline. The morning jog does not become a habit until we consciously force ourselves to do it some 30 to 90 times. Without the steely will to embrace the unpleasantness of waking up earlier and exerting ourselves for several weeks, the habit never forms.

Winning Practices of Individuals and Groups

Having employed hundreds of people over the years, I have thought much about how habits influence people's work and well-being; I thus formulated the Winning Practices of Individuals and Groups that comprise Chapters 14 through 26. These practices include Health, Thought, Integrity, Proactivity, Prudence, Excellence, Thrift and Investment, Affiliation, Decency, Understanding, Leadership, Teamwork, and Improvement. When repeated many times, these practices become habits. Parents, teachers, coaches, and other mentors do us great favors when they help us form these habits.

Breaking Habits

Breaking habits is much more difficult than forming empowering ones. The best way to avoid having to break bad habits is not to form them in the first place. If we fall into a bad habit and want to break it, we must become aware of the cues and consciously eliminate them, substitute empowering routines for debilitating ones, or eliminate the opportunity to perform the routine.

If we want to break the snacking habit that television commercials cue, we could eliminate the advertisements and snacking trigger by recording shows and fast-forwarding through the ads. We could watch commercial-free television, or upon seeing an advertisement, we could opt for a stretching routine instead of a trip to the kitchen. Alternatively, we could replace the unhealthy snacks in the kitchen with healthy ones.

Examples of debilitating habits include: dishonesty, laziness, rudeness, borrowing and overspending, absenteeism, tardiness, overeating, smoking, and drug abuse. Common effects of debilitating habits include: reactiveness, weakness, lethargy, discord, alienation, underachievement, poverty, and indebtedness.

The absence of empowering habits and the presence of debilitating ones are the reasons most chronically unemployed people do not find jobs. People who are unkempt, unhealthy, untruthful, inconsiderate, unprepared, frequently absent or tardy, obese, and unfit are not people employers want to hire. Those who are lazy, do substandard work, abuse alcohol, or use illicit drugs are not employable. Any employer will validate these realities.

Our country has millions more unemployable and unemployed people than it should for three primary reasons: (1) some parents fail to develop empowering habit in their children, (2) our social safety net enables people with destructive habits to continue them and to transmit them to their children, and (3) the rest of us do not fix our flawed social safety net nor see that all children form empowering habits.

Ideally, parents assume the responsibility for forming empowering habits in their children, and teachers and other adults reinforce those habits. In practice, however, so many parents no longer understand the importance of empowering habits or even know what they are. And while schools could do much more to help children develop empowering habits, the current permissive, identity-sensitive pedagogies ignore the problem.

Consciously integrating empowering habit formation into our schools would benefit many children. Empowering habit formation does not require curriculum changes. It only requires principals and teachers to expect certain behaviors like not speaking until being called upon in class, doing what teachers and principals ask, telling the truth, completing one's homework on time, being prepared for tests, and being considerate of one's classmates.

Administrators and teachers help children learn self-control and be considerate of others by the behaviors they permit in the classroom. They help children become more responsible and learn self-discipline by insisting that they complete their assignments on time. They help children become more respectful and understanding by teaching them to habitually consider others' views. Were students to master the Winning Practices of Individuals and Groups before leaving school, many more would find good-paying, rewarding jobs. Singapore's Lee Kuan Yew wrote:

> Habits that make for high productivity in workers are the result of the values implanted in them at home, in school, and at the work place. These values must be reinforced by the attitudes of society. Once established, like a language a society speaks, the habits tend to be a self-reproducing, self-perpetuating cycle.[234]

Just as our ancestors and grandparents could not afford to be lax, irresponsible, or careless, neither can we. We live in a competitive world and when our organizations, enterprises, communities, and country underperform, our position weakens. If our parents did not help us form empowering habits as children, it is in our interest to take the time to form them. If we have inadvertently formed debilitating habits, it is in our interests to transform them into empowering habits.

Paraphrasing American jurist Oliver Wendell Holmes, too many people go to their graves with their music unsung. Parents, teachers, and other adults who help us form empowering habits and break debilitating ones counter this tendency and positively shape our lives.

Empowering Habit Formation *– performing routines that yield positive effects some 30 to 90 times so that we perform them unconsciously. Environments of nurture, discipline, modeling, expectation, recognition, and correction facilitate empowering habit formation. Habits involve a cue, routine, and reward. They form from repetition whether they are advantageous or disadvantageous. Good habits yield positive effects and empower us. Bad habits stream negative effects and handicap us. Debilitating habit formation is the antithesis of empowering habit formation.*

Section VI: Winning Practices of Education

Winning Perspectives

Truth	Human Nature
Causality	Culture
Scale	Periodic Disaster
Evolution	Eco-Dependency
Fitness	

Winning Practices

Knowledge

Health	**Universal Education**
Thought	**Parental Choice**
Integrity	**Results-Oriented Education**
Proactivity	
Prudence	Free Enterprise and Markets
Excellence	Responsible Corporate Governance
Thrift and Investment	Prudent Regulation
	Enterprise Competitiveness
Affiliation	
Decency	Government of the People
Understanding	Powers, Prohibitions, and Structure
Leadership	Freedoms, Rights, and Responsibilities
Teamwork	The Rule of Law
Improvement	Inclusion and Meritocracy
	Prudent Taxation
Spouse Selection	Financial Strength
Marriage	Savings Accounts, Social Safety Nets
Responsible Parenting	Consumer-Driven Healthcare
Empowering Habit Formation	Assimilation
	Peace Through Fitness
	Sustainability

Chapter 31

Knowledge

Research brings knowledge, vanquishes ignorance, and makes the impossible possible.

For millennia, our observable world was the savanna and a starry sky around us. While the starry sky remains, scientists have revealed a wondrous and bewildering universe with billions of galaxies, solar systems, and planets beyond the sky. Now, we glimpse a vast and ancient universe, estimated to be 100 billion light years in diameter and 13.7 billion years old.

Scientists also chronicle the 13.7 billion-year evolution of the universe in amazing detail. They describe matter, energy, space, and life on scales significantly beyond anything familiar to us. Detecting and understanding all of this required over 280 thousand human generations, the development of science, and tremendous technological advancements. Astronomer, cosmologist, and best-selling author Carl Sagan wrote:

[Science] is, so far, entirely a human invention. . . . It is not perfect. It can be misused. It is only a tool. But it is by far the best tool we have, self-correcting, ongoing, applicable to everything. It has two rules. First: There are no sacred truths; all assumptions must be critically examined; arguments from authority are worthless. Second: Whatever is inconsistent with the facts must be discarded or revised.[235]

Babylonian, Egyptian, Indian, and Chinese innovators practiced rudimentary science two to four thousand years ago. Greeks developed science-like procedures. Aristotle established the first formal systems of logic and taxonomy in the 4th century BC. Alexander the Great, his student, sent samples of newly discovered plants and animals back to him for classification, transforming myth-based methods into logical ones. Persian scientists made advances in agriculture, medicine, mathematics, physics, optics, and medicine, kept science alive through the Middle Ages, and added a lot to our body of evidence-based knowledge. Francis Bacon, Copernicus, Johannes Kepler, Galileo Galilei, and Isaac Newton formalized the scientific method in the 16th and 17th centuries and made tremendous advances in mathematics, physics, and astronomy.

The Scientific Method

At the heart of science is the scientific method that began when Thales of Miletus, one of the seven Greek sages in the 6th century BC, visited the Egyptians, who worshipped water. Thales fell into a well while observing the night sky and hypothesized that water was the most fundamental material.[236] Thales' early method of inquiry evolved into a series of steps called the scientific method. The scientific method is transparent, explicit, and competitive. It helps us acquire knowledge about our world and works as follows:

1) Observe and ponder what is of interest;
2) Formulate a hypothesis about it;
3) Review what is already known about it;
4) Test the hypothesis through experimentation;
5) Record and analyze the experimental data;
6) Accept the hypothesis if the experimental results support it, and reject the hypothesis if they contradict it;
7) Communicate the findings via conference presentation and publications that summarize the hypothesis, experiment, data, and conclusions, and offer suggestions for follow-up research;
8) Review the feedback from other scientists; and
9) Continue the inquiry if questions remain.

The scientific method and its insistence on transparency, experimentation, the use of controls, and evidence-based conclusions enable scientists to overcome natural human biases and correct, improve, and expand our knowledge base. It places scientists in competitive communities that value rigorous, evidenced-based findings over sloppy, inaccurate, and unreliable ones. Advancing theories in the face of contradictory data and without supporting evidence destroys scientists' reputations.

The results of the application of the scientific method have been astounding. Just since the Copernican Revolution in the 1500s, scientists have dispelled many cultural myths; demonstrated that amulets, horoscopes, incantations, potions, fortune-telling, clairvoyance, spells, witchcraft, ghosts, evil spirits, and bloodletting do not produce the claimed effects; and have caused educated people to expect others to substantiate their claims with evidence. One of the great challenges of understanding the world is that knowing what is true is much more difficult than what is untrue, as millions of supporting observations do not make a hypothesis true, but one contradictory observation makes it false.

The advances of science extend beyond debunking myth and superstition. Science has helped us dramatically reduce infant mortality and double our lifespans. It has helped bring an abundance of food, running water, sanitary sewers, electric lights, roadways, railroads, and airports. It has unlocked the secrets of creating cloth, paper, metal, plastic, and other materials. It facilitated the creation and steady improvement of ships, trains, cars, planes, jets, phones, radios, televisions, microwaves, computers, and the Internet. Science has taught us to harness hydro, fossil, hydraulic, electrical, nuclear, and solar energies and led to the development of vaccines, antibiotics, x-rays, CAT scans, and transplants. It has brought us conveniences, more leisure time, and higher living standards.

Science reveals what exists beyond our everyday experience and dispels misconceptions by exposing the cause-and-effect relationships that underlie everything. For example, we did not know for over 280 thousand generations that we reside on a rotating, spherical mass hurling through space. We did not imagine that the universe, stars, planets, elements, molecules, RNA, amino acids, proteins, cells, plants, and animals self-assemble. Then, as if peeling back the layers of an onion, scientists exposed more of the workings of the universe each year, unraveling the evolution, structure, and interactions of subatomic particles, atoms, molecules, meteorites, comets, planets, solar systems, stars, quasars, black holes, and galaxies. Today, scientists probe the mysteries of proteins, DNA, genes, viruses, bacteria, cells, tissues, organs, plants, animals, and the human body. When they exhaust what is detectable with existing technology, we develop new instruments to understand substances, processes, and relationships on ever larger and smaller scales.

Science encompasses the basic disciplines of mathematics, physics, chemistry, biology, medicine, and a growing list of newer disciplines such as: aeronautics, agronomy, anthropology, astronomy, biochemistry, economics, entomology, forestry, genetics, geology, horticulture, linguistics, meteorology, microbiology, nutrition, paleontology, pathology, psychology, sociology, and veterinary medicine. We practice science so extensively now that new scientific disciplines emerge almost every year.

While science has brought us unparalleled benefits, the science-enhanced life-styles have degraded our habitats, destroyed hundreds of species, and spewed billions of tons of carbon and pollutants into the air each year. Science-enhanced weapons give many nations the means to eradicate much of the life on Earth.

Scientists are human, do err, and serve competing nations. They and their benefactors have agendas. Sometimes, they mistakenly believe something is true when it is false. Self-interest and groupthink are concerns. When data is incomplete and experimental results are ambiguous, scientists' biases may creep into their work. Scientists want to please their benefactors and believe those around them just like the rest of us. Presenting findings that conflict with benefactors' agendas, revered theories, and convention is very difficult.

In 2005, John Ioannidis, a professor of medicine at Stanford University, suggested that about half the results published in peer-reviewed scientific journals were wrong. And since then, researchers have verified that they cannot reproduce the results of many of the studies, adding credence to the professor's claim.[237] Two implications of these findings are: (1) the social psychology that informs education policy may be largely irreproducible and (2) many climate change predictions may be products of unreliable methodologies and groupthink.[238] While there is no doubt many social psychology findings are sound and that greenhouse gas emissions can alter the climate, I have thought for years that many of the changes in public schools and universities were negatively impacting student performance and that scientists do not understand all the variables and interactions related to climate change well enough to make specific predictions regarding temperature and sea-level changes.

Federal agencies, foundations, and scientific journals could further scientific objectivity by (a) requiring scientists to preregister their methodologies before conducting experiments, (b) requiring independent replications of the research, and (c) disseminating the names of those who publish inaccurate findings.

We must always remember that facts and accurate findings representative of reality are the basis of knowledge and underlie our effectiveness. They exist whether we discover, acknowledge, or ignore them. They are unaffected by our hopes. And as Ayn Rand indicated, they are the final arbiter of disagreements:

When I disagree with a rational [person], I let reality be our
final arbiter; if I am right, he [or she] will learn; if I am wrong,
I will; one of us will win, but both will profit.[239]

Scientific laws, theories, and explanations are our best approximations of reality and natural processes. They surpass all other
characterizations. Although imperfect, they yield a vast, reliable, useful
body of knowledge that exponentially expands our ability to understand,
negotiate, and manipulate our world.

Libraries and Databases

Systematically storing science-based knowledge and making it
readily available to our citizens furthers our fitness, effectiveness, and
well-being. An important role exists for government and businesses to
house our knowledge in geographically dispersed public and private
databases. When libraries and books were the primary depositories of
our knowledge before the widespread use of the Internet, Carl Sagan
wrote:

The library connects us with the insights and knowledge,
painfully extracted from Nature, of the greatest minds that ever
were, with the best teachers, drawn from the entire planet and
from all our history, to instruct us without tiring, and to inspire
us to make our own contribution to the collective knowledge of
the human species.[240]

Public access to such knowledge has been limited throughout
history with political and religious leaders controlling people's access to
it. Even today, many governments restrict people's access to information
or invest little in making it available to their citizens. The creation of
public libraries and research institutions early in our country's history
and their continuation make this knowledge available to all our citizens.

With the advent of the Internet, information is more accessible but less curated in our country. The greater accessibility is a step forward and the loss of curation a step backward. The information that our parents and grandparents found in libraries was more reliable than what our children find on the Internet because it was the result of a peer-review process. Most of the information on the Internet is not peer-reviewed. Internet users must assess the reliability of the source or authenticate the information itself.

A federally supported university system, a state-supported county library system, and numerous private sector databases reduce the risk of the corruption and destruction of our knowledge. Such geographical and institutional dispersion and redundancy make it difficult to corrupt or destroy the knowledge. Concentrating our knowledge in one level of government or too few commercial companies would put us at risk.

To reduce the inaccuracy and corruption of our knowledge, federally supported university systems, state-supported libraries, and numerous private sector research facilities should only store and offer peer-reviewed, trusted information. Not only would such a system of clearly identified databases make sources dedicated to accuracy available to the public, but they would ensure that one or a few entities do not control our knowledge.

Our knowledge is precious and should be available to everyone. It has taken hundreds of years and millions of hours to develop. And ideally, it would be a well-organized, cumulative body of factual information, and 100 percent accurate. In practice, however, this is not the case. Most of our information lacks coherence and contains prejudice and error, things we must keep in mind as we use it.

An Education, Research, and Extension System

Some of the least appreciated but most important legislation passed in our country's history was the Morrill Act of 1862.[241] The act established a research and education system to teach agriculture, engineering, and military tactics in several states. Subsequent legislation funded agricultural experiment stations and veterinary research in 1887 and a cooperative extension system in 1914.[242] The experiment stations developed best agricultural and homemaker practices for each state and territory, and the cooperative extension system disseminated these practices throughout rural America.

In 1862, 85 percent of the U.S. population lived in rural areas, and 55 percent were involved in agriculture.[243] The public research, university, and extension system played a critical role in disseminating evidence-based knowledge and empowering practices to generations of rural Americans. Millions of people attended these universities and benefited from the knowledge they developed regarding health, nutrition, child development, plant science, animal nutrition, breeding, animal husbandry, engineering, and business.

The research, education, and extension system facilitated the movement of more than 50 percent of our population out of agriculture, enabling less than 2 percent of it to produce our food. The system fueled tremendous productivity improvements and brought us the lowest-cost food supply in the world. It gave us critical research findings, millions of well-educated professionals, many more well-functioning families, and higher living standards.

While the need for the system to serve rural areas still exists, a tremendous need for such services now also exists in our cities. The poverty rate is 17 percent in rural areas, 11 percent in the suburbs, 16 percent in small metro areas, and 20 percent in large cities.[244] Redirecting some of the system's resources and personnel to small urban populations could yield significant returns. Many low-income people, and especially those receiving public assistance, could benefit from greater access to sound health, nutrition, family, and child-development practices.

A Free and Responsible Press

Libraries and data bases perform an indispensable role to ensure that evidence-based knowledge is available to all citizens, but they cannot be the sole conveyor of factual information. A free and responsible press plays a crucial role in providing us with evidence-based knowledge and accurate information. If we are to make good decisions, we need apolitical, accurate information. We need exposure to perspectives and practices that improve our decisions and effectiveness.

A free and responsible press presents factual, balanced news. It separates political viewpoints and news. It investigates and exposes conflicts of interest to prevent corruption, abuses of power, and the immoral actions of authorities, organizations, and people.

Conflicts of Interest occur when our self-interest competes with our responsibilities to others.

Conflicts of interest were a great concern to past generations and should also concern us. They are only acceptable when those with power have the same downside risk as those without power. One of the most harmful conflicts of interest in our country involves the common practice of businesses, unions, wealthy individuals, and Political Action Committees (PACs) giving campaign support to our representatives in exchange for legislative, monetary, or contractual favors. Such exchanges conflict with the responsibility of representatives to do what is best for their constituents. Although representatives deny that campaign support affects their actions, we all know that it does.

Another conflict of interest, which violates the Constitution's separation of government and press, involves public news organizations. Public news organizations cannot receive money from governments and maintain objectivity toward the elected officials who appropriate the money. National Public Television and Radio should not exist no matter how much we like them, as eventually they will align their news with the views of their benefactors.

To assure greater separation of government and the press and mitigate a couple troublesome conflicts of interest, we should amend our Constitution to forbid (1) government funding of news organizations, (2) government interference with news reporting, (3) government intimidation of news owners, organizations, and journalists, (4) government discrimination among news organizations, and (5) owners, employees, and journalists of news organizations from financially or editorially supporting political campaigns.

Private news organizations also have a conflict of interest in accurately reporting the news and their desire to sensationalize and politicize news to attract viewers and secure advertising revenue. To improve the accuracy, relevance, and balance of our news and ensure that multiple news sources and editorial viewpoints exist in every community, the Federal Trade Commission (FTC) should apply antitrust laws to news organizations just as we do to other corporate concentrations of power and only issue broadcast licenses to news organizations that provide at least 2.5 hours of ad-free, prime time news a day. Moreover, we should insist that our congressional representatives strengthen libel and slander laws, making it easier for citizens to hold news organizations accountable for the information they publish.

We must also expect our news organizations to (a) present news in a balanced and apolitical manner, (b) hire groups of journalists who represent the entire political spectrum, (c) uphold the timeless journalist standards of independence, accountability, respectfulness, honesty, impartiality, fairness, accuracy, completeness, transparency, and excellence, (d) collaborate and substantiate questionable information, (e) presume people innocent until they are proven guilty, (f) present opposing political views, and (g) separate and clearly identify what is news and what is commentary. And if we taught our children to think critically, consider opposing points of view, and boycott news organizations that do not adhere to these standards of journalism, more news organizations would conform to these standards.

Knowledge empowers people, and the lack of it handicaps them. Knowledge impacts our effectiveness at every level of human organization—individual, family, group, education, enterprise, and government. Leaders, scientists, teachers, parents, and everyone else must do their best to develop, disseminate, and use accurate information. Scientific research; science-based libraries and databases; an education, research, and extension system; and a free and responsible press convey immense advantages to those who invest in them. They improve our understanding of our world, our ability to defend ourselves, and our ability to secure territory and resources. They minimize conflicts of interest, check corruption, and increase our fitness, effectiveness, and well-being.

Knowledge – the discovery, collection, and organization of information that accurately describes reality and increases our fitness, effectiveness, and well-being. The scientific method; public libraries and databases; a university research, education, and extension system; and a free and responsible press facilitate the development of knowledge. Ignorance, superstition, bias, and inaccurate information are antithetical to knowledge.

Chapter 32

Universal Education

Whoso fails to learn in his youth, loses the past and is dead for the future. [245]

—*Euripides*

The words of Euripides are as true today as they were over two thousand years ago when he wrote them. Well-educated people do better the world over. Consider the knowledge and skills that:

- Parents need to develop their children;

- Farmers require to feed millions of people;

- Architects and trades-people use to build our infrastructure and homes;

- Teachers and professors need to teach higher mathematics, biology, chemistry, and physics;

- Nurses, doctors, and pharmacists need to keep us healthy; and

- Software engineers and technicians require to design and maintain our computers, Internet, and cellphones.

If education is so important, then why do 10 percent of Asian, 12 percent of White, 22 percent of Hispanic, 25 percent of African American, and 17 percent of all children in the U.S. fail to graduate from high school each year? [246] Perhaps it is because too many neighborhoods are unsafe, too many families are dysfunctional, too many parents and students are unaccountable, too many schools are underperforming, too much of the curriculum is irrelevant, too many immigrants overwhelm many schools, and because we feed the vested interests rather than do what is necessary to provide children an excellent education.

Crime-ridden neighborhoods and broken families expose too many children to poverty, gangs, alcohol, drugs, violence, neglect, abuse, trauma, and abandonment. Many parents do not see that their children are well fed, do their homework, get a good night's sleep, and attend school. Many schools poorly support teachers, cave in to the demands of overprotective and misguided parents, fail to maintain an order conducive to learning, and retain too many poor-performing administrators and teachers. Too much of the curriculum over-emphasizes information, preparation for college, and social issues. It underemphasizes the development of good habits as well as work and life skills. Many students fall behind, become discouraged, and do not grasp the importance of education.

Parent Accountability

If one looks at truancy and reported child abuse in the country, we are not doing well by at least 1 in 6 children. Consider that 6 million children miss more than 10 percent of the school year; the truancy rate runs 7, 13, 17, and 23 percent for Asians, Whites, Blacks, and Native Americans respectively; our authorities receive reports of child abuse on 7.4 million children annually.[247] Children and education are so precious and important to our future that we must create an order where mothers and fathers responsibility advance their children's well-being and education or they lose custody of their children.

To break the growing multigenerational cycle of poor parenting, we must insist that parents see that their children attend school or homeschool them well. When parents are not getting their children to school, are absent from the home, or are not financially contributing to the family, authorities must locate the parents and send them to remedial parenting facilities. Allowing parents to neglect their children fuels generations of difficulty and does not deter other parents from doing the same thing. Sending deadbeat and abusive parents to jail has little rehabilitative value and guarantees that parents will not contribute to their children's development.

To encourage parent accountability, we should create parenting facilities in each county. These facilities must teach negligent parents to be responsible and be able to deal with substance abuse issues. Most mothers and fathers want to be good parents but too often do not know how and/or have substance abuse issues. Many have never had good parental role models, lack employment, and struggle to make ends meet.

10 days of unexcused or 20 days of excused absences by a child in one school year should trigger an investigation by county authorities. If the absences prove to be unwarranted, parents should be given warnings and fined. If the truancy continues, parents should attend a three-day remedial parenting program and pay larger fines. When such absenteeism occurs a third time, parents should revisit the corrective facility for a time commensurate with the severity of neglect and truancy. A responsible family member should be given temporary custody of the children or the children taken care of in an adjunct facility while the parents attend the remedial parenting program.

If such abdication of parental responsibility occurs a fourth time, a responsible family member should be granted permanent custody of the children, and the parents should be required to pay a substantial fine over five years equivalent to the higher of their current annual income or the average of their previous three years of income. If the parent is on public assistance, he or she should receive only 80 percent of those funds for five years. Parents must face consequences for irresponsible parenting, if we ever are to decrease the number of ill-prepared children. Allowing children to remain with negligent parents carries heartbreaking, multigenerational effects.

Enabling negligent parents to receive normal levels of public aid is unconscionable—yet this is exactly what we have done for decades. Delinquent parents deny their children the opportunity to develop into well-adjusted, able adults and cause them lifelong heartache and difficulty. They increase crime and the need for law enforcement, incarceration, and public assistance; spawn future generations of irresponsible parents; and waste critical public resources.

Student Accountability

Around age 13, as children's executive function develops, we must hold both parents and children accountable for the children's performance in school, and we must unapologetically remove unengaged and disruptive children from classrooms. Failing to do this enables a few students to waste their childhoods, burden teachers, and diminish the education of other students. A safe, distraction-free classroom gives students the opportunity to learn self-control, defer gratification, and practice self-discipline, as well as so many other things that will help them in life.

To hold teenagers accountable for their education, we should establish a military-like academy in each county for problem teens. These academies would be staffed with well-trained, caring, and disciplined people who provide the nurture and discipline lacking in many of these children's lives. All the schools in a county could send disengaged and unruly children to these academies for the remainder of any school year. There would be no television, movies, or cellphones at these facilities, and the staff would completely structure the students' time. Computers would be available only for academic work. Students would attend classes, prepare their meals, wash their clothes, clean the facility, and play sports and/or engage in the arts.

When students do well at these facilities, they should be rewarded with certain privileges like recreation time or the opportunity to watch inspiring movies, and participate in field trips. When they do not perform satisfactorily, they should lose privileges. The academies might also pilot withholding an evening meal from unruly students. Periodic fasting, which I do twice a week, is simple, harmless, and uncomfortable enough to cause people to want to avoid the discomfort. Some Native Americans effectively disciplined unruly children by withholding their evening meal, and I suspect this practice, when performed under the guidance of skilled pediatricians, would be an effective behavior modification tool.

Upon satisfactory completion of the program, attendees could return to their normal schools at the start of the next school year. Rather than risk being sent back to the highly-structured military-like academies, most past attendees would approach school more constructively. This is tough love. On the surface, remedial parenting facilities and military-like academies seem a bit extreme. But when you reflect on the problem more deeply, you realize every child in our country should have the opportunity to live a good life, and our current order is unconscionable. Just imagine for a minute the anguish and destroyed lives caused by leaving hundreds of thousands of children in the hands of neglectful and abusive parents and only offering these children a life of failed relationships, alcohol and drug-induced highs, government checks, and the four walls of a jail cell.

Providing remedial training to parents who neglect their children corrects counterproductive behaviors before they do more harm. Providing unruly and disengaged children military academy experiences early in their lives alters their self-defeating behaviors before their public educational opportunities end or they harm others and themselves— whether this means failing to realize their potential or engaging in school fights or shootings.

Real-World Feedback

When we stray a little and life becomes more difficult for us, we change our behavior. When others shield us from the negative effects of our actions or when the adverse impacts of our actions occur years into the future, we do not learn to make good choices. Real-world feedback ensures that people feel the constructiveness or destructiveness of their behaviors. Except in the case of pre-school children, it involves allowing students to experience the effects of their actions and providing them with immediate corrective feedback when the negative effects would occur years into the future.

When parents and teachers discipline children for being disrespectful, they teach them to be respectful of authority. While this may not seem like a big deal at the time, it is important. When the police stop these people for a traffic infraction later in life, they are more likely to respect the police than those who did not learn this behavior as children. Such discipline saves lives. Parents and teachers who tolerate children's disrespectful behavior set them up for future trouble.

Empowering Habit Formation

A few years ago, my dad shared a book with me that Cornell University disseminated to country schoolteachers in the late 1800s. As I read it, I was surprised to find a tremendous emphasis on the formation of good habits in students. The book made me painfully aware that our ancestors' approach to this aspect of education was superior to our current method.

I discuss the Winning Practices of Individuals and Groups in Chapters 14 through 26. For children to acquire these habits and reap their streams of positive effects, they need good role models and help in forming these behaviors. Furthermore, they need people to forewarn them about the negative effects of destructive practices and shield them from those who exhibit these undesirable behaviors.

Parents, teachers, coaches, and prominent people have a special responsibility to exhibit constructive thought, speech, and habits. Their words and actions matter more than most of us realize. Children readily absorb the behaviors around them. Just as the constructive words and actions of good role models impacted us when we were children, so they affect our children. And just as we reaped streams of benefits from mastering the Winning Practices of Individuals and Groups, so will our children.

Children learn the habits of self-control, deferred gratification, and self-discipline simply by being in environments that have enforced rules. Expecting children to follow reasonable rules and be respectful and considerate, then praising them for this, and consistently correcting their lapses cause them to acquire self-control, the ability to defer gratification, and self-discipline. At a young enough age, consistent reminders, along with a few "attaboys" or "attagirls," and gentle reprimands are all that are necessary for children to learn these behaviors.

I discuss truthfulness, an aspect of integrity, in Chapter 16. Truthfulness is a keystone habit. So many things depend on it. Forming this habit is a matter of being honest, expecting honesty, and making dishonesty a more serious offense than other offenses. Truthfulness furthers trust, and trust promotes interpersonal effectiveness. Truthfulness and trust are essential to our freedom, fitness, and prosperity. Studies show that the countries with the highest prevalence of honest people enjoy the highest quality of life.[248]

In past decades, parents and teachers emphasized the habits of good manners, preparation, attendance, and punctuality more than they do today. Manners are habits of consideration. Preparation yields better outcomes. Attendance eliminates the need for others to do our work, and punctuality saves people time.

Completing one's homework on time is a critical habit for children to learn. Homework supplements class time, magnifies its value, requires concentration, and provides opportunities for practice. Regular homework helps students develop self-discipline, time management skills, and the ability to delay gratification. A requirement for children to complete their homework before playing motivates them to do their homework and provides a reward for doing so.

Related to homework, or any type of work for that matter, is the habit of excellence. Excellence involves working to high standards and requires us to pay attention to the details. It is an approach to work that is advantageous to make a habit. Excellence causes things to work better and opens many doors for people throughout their lives.

Ideally, parents would assume the responsibility for forming the Winning Practices of Individuals and Groups in their children, and teachers and coaches would reinforce these practices. Many parents do not do this, however, and schools become the child developers of last resort. As I indicated in Chapter 30, the lack of empowering habits and the presence of destructive ones are shortcomings of most chronically unemployed people. People who are unkempt, untruthful, rude, disrespectful, frequently absent or late, unprepared, and generally unfit are not people whom employers hire and retain. People who misuse alcohol or use illicit drugs are unreliable and sometimes endanger those around them.

Life- and Science-Based Curriculum

Along with empowering habits, schools must convey large amounts of information to children and orchestrate the development of many skills. Teaching children to read, write, calculate, and find needed information prepares them to perform many jobs throughout their lives. Learning about the evolution of the universe and life, history, and culture widens and deepens children's understanding of the world and improves their judgment. Learning employment and family skills assures that the children one day will be able to support themselves, raise able children, and contribute to their communities.

Science-based curriculums are critical to the future of our children because science-based knowledge evolves, expands, and self-corrects; has the most accurate representations of reality; and houses the only expertise that transcends cultures, countries, and time. Teaching scientific methods to small children reinforces the need for us to support our assertions with evidence.

Religious tenants lack these characteristics and generally are anecdotal, impossible to substantiate, and oftentimes contradictory. While some religious teachings make people more aware and considerate of others and improve long-term decision making, many teachings exist simply to unify and advance a group. Because religious teachings are not grounded in evidence, do not self-correct, and usually promote the agendas of groups, they are inappropriate to teach in public schools.

Elementary Curriculum

We want all children to grow into healthy, well-adjusted, and able citizens. We want them to advantageously earn their livelihoods and contribute to their communities and country. Yet we must remember that children do not learn in the same way or at the same rate. If we judge those best-suited for the trades, business, teaching, and the arts in the same manner, we would cause many children to think that they are inept beings without futures. As the adage goes:

Everybody is a genius. But if you judge a fish by its ability to climb a tree, it will live its whole life believing that it is stupid.[249]

As we think about our current education system and the habits, knowledge, and skills required to earn a livelihood and live, it is apparent that we standardize education too much, overemphasize things that do not matter, and underemphasize things that do matter. Schools neglect empowering habit formation. Comfortable childhoods cause many students to avoid the more rigorous fields of engineering, programming, and science. Parents, teachers, and thought leaders glorify college and deemphasize vocational instruction, apprenticeships, and co-ops.

To correct these deficiencies, we need to distinguish between foundational elementary curriculum and individualized secondary education. We want to teach basic habits, knowledge, and skills during the first 6 to 8 years of school and create more individualized tracks of learning during the remaining 5 to 7 years. Elementary school should be a time when children develop the habits of good hygiene, health, eating, exercise, and sleep; master the Winning Practices of Individuals and Groups; learn to read, write, calculate, search libraries and databases, and speak foreign languages; play musical instruments and sports; and learn about the evolution of the universe, life, and culture.

While we tend to think of "history" as a progression of activities by our species in the last 6 thousand years, we should now think of it as the progression of our universe, galaxy, solar system, planet, and all life on Earth over the last 13.7 billion years. Although it has taken humans millions of years to realize this, our history is much more extensive than we ever imagined, and it puts everything in context. Rabbi and best-selling author Chaim Potok wrote:

> Everything has a past. Everything—a person, an object, a word, everything. If you don't know the past, you can't understand the present and plan properly for the future.[250]

Although research skills have always been important for college-bound students, these skills are now valuable for all children with the advent of the Internet. Research skills, or what we now might call "search skills," encompass the techniques necessary to find information on the Internet and the ability to access the information critically. Search engines make finding information easy, but children need to develop the skills associated with finding the most advantageous information and judging the reliability of the source and the content. They need the guidance of parents and teachers to be safe and see the Internet as a tool of effectiveness more than a source of entertainment.

Seven Secondary Tracks

After teaching a common elementary curriculum to children, it would be advantageous to individualize a secondary curriculum that conveys the knowledge and skills necessary to earn a livelihood and personally flourish. Sometime around the age of 12, children should be able to select one of seven tracks with input from their parents, teachers, and counselors. Depending on the size of the school system, each of these tracks might have 1 to 3 levels of difficulty or speeds at which teachers expect students to learn the material. Examples of seven such tracks are as follows.

Leadership – for students preparing to lead for-profit, nonprofit, military, and government organizations.

Professional – for students who want to be doctors, nurses, lawyers, engineers, accountants, and other professions requiring a college education.

Teaching and Research – for students preparing to be professors, teachers, researchers, and scientists.

Trades – for students who plan to be electricians, carpenters, plumbers, heavy-equipment operators, computer and network technicians, or engage in other similar trades.

Arts and Sports – for students who wish to go into music, acting, other arts, cosmetology, and sport-related professions.

Manufacturing – for students preparing to work in factories.

Sales and Service – for students preparing to work in commercial and retail sales and services.

To decide which track and level of difficulty are most appropriate for a child, guidance counselors, parents, and students should work together and consider parent and teacher observations of the student; the student's performance on intelligence, personality, and aptitude tests; the activities for which the student demonstrates strong interest; the student's comparative advantages; the student's preferences; and projected employment opportunities. The discussion should work toward a consensus of the track and level.

Although tracks challenge some American sensibilities, they have proven to be highly effective in several European countries. Germany and Switzerland do this better than just about any other country. When German students are about 12 years old, grades, test scores, teachers' feedback, and parental input influence whether they receive the basic education, prepare for a trade, or prepare for college. Germany retains more manufacturing jobs than the U.S. and most other developed countries due to their emphasis on training their young adults for the trades.

One source indicates that 17 percent of Germans and 33 percent of Americans obtain a college degree, while 75 percent of Germans and 5 percent of Americans undergo vocational training with apprenticeships by age 25. This implies that about 92 percent of Germans compared to 38 percent of Americans are prepared well for the workforce, something which is further reflected in the fact that high school graduates earn 65 percent as much as college graduates in Germany, and only 45 percent as much in the United States.[251] Germany's and Switzerland's approaches to education create higher living standards, a larger middle class, and more competitive trades-related companies.

A system of secondary tracks must be flexible enough to allow students willing to do the necessary remedial work during the summer to change tracks at the start of the subsequent school year for a couple of years. Distilling the content of this curriculum so that it is widely supported would be a challenge. On the other hand, ignoring the benefits of this approach ill-equips large proportions of our population for life.

In addition to preparing students for a career in their chosen field, each track should provide instruction on personal health, marriage, parenting, and financial fitness. We know that it is advantageous for children to have two well-adjusted parents who are committed to one another and their children. If more young adults understood the importance of commitment, the responsibilities of parents, and the practices associated with successful family units, then they would take fewer reproductive risks, enter relationships more cautiously, and better vet marital prospects. If more young adults understood the power of frugality, savings, and investment, they would graduate from high schools, vocational schools, and colleges less indebted and would live more securely and comfortably. If more of our citizens understood how our current educational system fails so many children, they would want schools to pilot new approaches and implement the most effective ones.

Homogeneous Grouping

Homogeneous grouping is the practice of placing children of similar ability in the same classes. It facilitates learning by allowing teachers to introduce material at a pace that engages and challenges most students. Homogenous grouping mitigates the frustration, behavioral issues, and challenges that accompany having slower and faster students in the same classrooms.

Why do we not use this approach today? Homogeneous grouping fell out of favor in the 1960s when many educators felt that parents, teachers, and students perceived that the children in the slower-moving classes were less intelligent. They felt these perceptions undermined the self-image and academic performance of the slower students. Although these concerns have merit, the solution of heterogeneous groupings did not solve the problem and yielded numerous more negative effects. Heterogeneous grouping makes teaching more difficult, school frustrating, and instruction less effective for all students.

A common criticism of heterogeneous grouping is that teachers must teach to the average students' ability and cannot fully meet the needs of the highest and lowest performing students. In practice, however, heterogeneous grouping requires teachers to teach at the pace of the slower students. Heterogeneous grouping makes the disparities between better and poorer students more evident because the variation of ability is greater in each classroom. Educators reduce the contrasts to a certain extent with grade inflation, but grade inflation undermines the learning process by falsifying feedback and mastery. While heterogeneous grouping and grade inflation mask differences in student-learning ability to outsiders, the teachers and students know who the slower students are. Worst of all, the slower students who need the most help never receive it, are passed through the system, develop feelings of inferiority, and all too often, never find their place in the world.

As a student in the 1960s and 70s, I experienced both homogeneous and heterogeneous grouping. When our school switched to the heterogeneous approach, some of us finished our day's work in one-third the time of other students, and this variation in learning presented quite a problem for the teachers. One of my teachers resolved it by sending a couple of us to the library to shelve books each afternoon, while another one kept some of us busy writing "I will not disrupt the classroom" on numerous afternoons.

While we must be careful that homogenous grouping does not result in socio-economic or racial classroom grouping, I know of no competitive organization or sports teams that would ever use heterogeneous grouping to develop their employees or athletes. Heterogeneous groupings and grade inflation are practices with a few positive effects and many negative ones. Moreover, they are contrary to evolution. Nature does not "dumb down" life to accommodate the weakest nor does it provide us with false feedback.

We live in a competitive world. We want arrangements that spur the greatest number to obtain the best education. We do not want groupings and grading geared to the slowest learners. We do not want to neglect the high achievers, to provide students misleading feedback, or to pass students from one level to the next without mastery of the prerequisite material and needed knowledge and skills.

Individualized Learning

Flipped classrooms can help teachers meet the individualized learning needs of students. They are a hybrid learning environment where students receive instruction and complete, assignments, quizzes, and exams on line; and then, teachers use class time to focus on problem areas and work one-on-one with students. Flipped classrooms permit all students to receive instruction from the best teachers and move at a pace corresponding to their abilities. Students can work on their lessons at home and repeat them as many times as necessary. Online metrics give students immediate feedback, allow teachers to gauge student progress, and enable schools to prevent students from advancing without proficiency.

Computers and the Internet permit schools to deliver individualized instruction more cost-effectively than ever before. The Khan Academy and other online offerings provide videos that build on one another on elementary, secondary, and undergraduate subject matter. The online courses incorporate practice exercises and exams. This type of model is already used in some public schools to achieve better results. Flipped classrooms and individualized learning reduce student frustration, feelings of inadequacy, and learning failures.

It is more advantageous for children to master the material and graduate equipped to succeed than it is for children to graduate at a specific age. Mastering critical material at 16, 17, 18, or 19 years of age does not matter. What matters is that students learn about the world and develop empowering habits and skills.

Universal Education – *(a) helping all children acquire critical perspectives, habits, skills, and knowledge that prepare them for work and life, (b) making parents accountable for their children's education, (c) making teens responsible for their education, (d) providing school children with age-appropriate, real-world-like feedback, (e) utilizing homogenous grouping and individualized learning, and (f) offering a life- and science-based curriculum that (i) helps children form constructive habits, (ii) emphasizes reading, writing, math, science, historical and cultural context, search, foreign languages, music, art, and sports opportunities, and (iii) features seven secondary tracks and a family studies curriculum. Ignorance, unequal opportunity, and ill-preparation are antithetical to universal education.*

Chapter 33

Parental Choice

If developing knowledgeable, able, young adults is our objective, then let us create a structure that yields this result.

The National Assessment of Educational Progress report released in April 2016 indicates that 28 percent of U.S. high school seniors lack basic reading skills and 38 percent lack basic math skills.[252] The U.S. Department of Education indicates that we spend on average $12,300 per student for primary and secondary education, roughly 30 percent more than the average Organization for Economic Cooperation and Development (OECD) countries.[253] Something is horribly wrong. We spend much more on education than other developed countries in almost every school district, yet do not provide basic skills to one-third of our children. How can this be?

Equitable County Districts

We currently organize our school districts around townships, villages, and boroughs. This organizational structure creates inequities because school districts serving lower-income communities are less able to attract higher-performing administrators and teachers and must allocate more of their limited resources for safety and discipline issues.

Americans do not support equal outcomes, but they do support equal opportunity. If we are serious about equal opportunity, we need to create a structure that provides it. We must improve the rule of law in many unsafe neighborhoods, open high-performing charter schools, make the public education system more meritocratic, create more relevant curriculums, give parents choices, and close poor-performing public schools.

County governments that surround townships, villages, and smaller cities could merge schools throughout a county aggregating wealthier suburbs with the poorer rural and urban areas, and distributing the best administrators and teachers throughout the county-wide system. States could supplement the poorer counties to reduce the variation in resources among the counties. This county-wide model works well in Florida.

Ending the Public Education Monopoly

Kenneth B. Clark, a black educator and psychologist, summed up the attitude of the school bureaucracy: . . . it does not seem likely that the changes necessary for increased efficiency of our urban public schools will come about because they should. . . . What is most important in understanding the ability of the educational establishment to resist change is the fact that public school systems are protected public monopolies with only minimal competition from private and parochial schools.

Few critics of the American urban public schools—even severe ones such as myself—dare to question the givens of the present organization of public education. . . . Nor dare the critics question the relevance of the criteria and standards for selecting superintendents, principals, and teachers, or the relevance of all these to the objectives of public education—producing a literate and informed public to carry on the business of democracy—and to the goal of producing human beings with social sensitivity and dignity and creativity and a respect for the humanity of others.

A monopoly need not genuinely concern itself with these matters. As long as local school systems can be assured of state aid and increasing federal aid without the accountability that inevitably comes with aggressive competition, it would be sentimental, wishful thinking, to expect any significant increase in the efficiency of our public schools.[254]

—Milton Friedman quoting Kenneth Clark

Monopolies eliminate competition, and people underperform in the absence of it. Monopolies are only advantageous when the economies of scale are so large that the savings overwhelm the other negative characteristics. This is clearly not the case with public education, as it costs more than private education and generally delivers poorer results. Charter school restrictions, union work rules, tenure, and seniority-based compensation insulate teachers and administrators from competition. Public school administrators do not terminate poor-performing teachers nor discover what works best. Teachers work at a more relaxed pace upon receiving tenure, and many deliver mediocre performances.

An Island of Socialism

Many people like to think that our education and enterprise systems can work well without competition, but this is naïve and fanciful. History and experience do not support this. Evolution is clear. We run the race and improve, or we exit the stage. Economist, education reformer, and Nobel laurate Milton Friedman wrote:

> The establishment of the school system in the United States as an island of socialism in a free market sea reflected only to a very minor extent the early emergence among intellectuals of a distrust of the market and of voluntary exchange.[255]

Not only is our public education system a poor-performing, expensive monopoly, but it also cultivates and conveys an anti-competition, anti-free market, big-government, socialistic mindset to our children. Public education is filled with left-leaning, unionized, tenured administrators, professors, and teachers who receive positions and compensation on a seniority basis more than a meritocratic one. Public education is not an arrangement where university and school boards enter win-win arrangements with educational personnel. Rather, it is one where the boards negotiate lose-win arrangements with more powerful state and national unions and the National Education Association, which is the largest labor union in the country, giving 95 percent of their campaign contributions to Democrats.[256]

If we are serious about improving our children's education and equipping them to succeed, we will end the public school monopoly by giving parents vouchers and creating more private educational opportunities. We will insist on administrator and faculty political diversity in our public schools and universities and create a healthy mix of perspectives. If our educational institutions had a healthier mix of conservative and progressive perspectives, they would evolve pedagogies that yield better educational outcomes. They would convey to children more of the Winning Perspectives and Practices that enable people to realize better lives.

Parental Choice and Involvement

The tragedy, and irony, is that a system dedicated to enabling all children to acquire a common language and the values of U.S. citizenship, giving all children equal education opportunity, should in practice exacerbate the stratification of society and provide highly unequal learning opportunities. Expenditures on schooling per pupil are often as high in the inner cities as in the wealthy suburbs, but the quality of schooling is vastly lower.

> In the suburbs, almost all the money goes for education; in the inner-cities much of it must go to preserving discipline, preventing vandalism, or repairing its effects. The atmosphere in some inner-city schools is more like that of a prison than of a place of learning. The parents of the suburbs are getting far more value for their tax dollars than the parents in the inner cities. . . . Schooling, even in inner cities, does not have to be the way it is. It was not that way when parents had greater control. It is not that way now where parents still have control.[257]

> —Milton Friedman

The secrets to cost-effective, high-quality services are competition and choice. We oftentimes take this for granted in our country, but if you spend time in countries where monopolies deliver products and services, you see that they are inferior to ours. The positive effects associated with competition and choice regarding products and services are the same for education as for other goods and services.

When people can choose where they purchase their products and services, they patronize the establishments that offer the best items at the lowest prices. When parents can choose where their children attend school, they do the same thing, forcing educators to improve their offerings or close their schools.

Some private schools are available in our country, but currently the parents who send their children to these schools pay for their children's education twice. They pay local taxes for the public-school system yet they also pay private school tuition. To counter the negative effects of public-school monopolies and the double expense of sending children to private schools, some states license a few charter schools and give them public money for their operations. Karl Zinsmeister, author and Philanthropy Roundtable Editor, wrote:

> Chartering represents one of the great self-organizing movements of our age. It rose up in the face of strong resistance from the educational establishment. It has been powered by independent social entrepreneurs and local philanthropists. It is a response by men and women who refused to accept heartbreaking educational failures that the responsible government institutions showed no capacity to solve on their own.[258]

> Successful charter schools have many distinctive features: longer school days and longer school years, more flexibility and accountability for teachers and principals, higher expectations for students, more discipline and structure, more curricular innovation, and more rigorous testing.[259]

They attract more entrepreneurial principals and teachers into the field of education. School autonomy allows wide experimentation with new ways of education. This same flexibility is used to circumvent bureaucratic obstacles that often block conventional schools from succeeding.

Charters sidestep the dysfunctional labor relations of many urban districts. They erode monopolies and introduce competitive energy into public education. Research shows that charters are more effective at recruiting teachers who graduate in the top third of their college class. Charters give parents who cannot afford private schools, or moving, another choice besides their neighborhood school.[260]

A private, charter, and public education system offers parents choices, creates competition, and has synergistic advantages. Private and charter schools inject competition, quality, affordability, specialized educational options, and innovation into the education system. Competition among the offerings furthers the excellence of each offering. We already have this public-private mix in higher education and benefit greatly from it. Except for a few misstarts, charter schools generally obtain superior results to public schools at a lower cost. Michael Block, cofounder of the BASIS charter school network, wrote:

There's no magic here. It's just a four-letter word: Work. We just work harder.[261]

Our laws enable enterprises to freely enter markets and prohibit one enterprise from monopolizing a market everywhere except in primary and secondary education. If we were serious about offering our younger children and teens affordable, high-quality education, we would take the same approach with our school systems. We would enact laws that allow private companies to freely open primary and secondary schools in our communities and give all parents vouchers to pay for their children's education at public, private, or charter schools.

A parental-choice education system could work as follows: The county gives parents a voucher to cover the cost of educating the child at the closest public school in the county. If the parents chose the public school, they enroll their child in it, and the school receives the funding. If the parents register the child in any other public or private school in the county, then the chosen school gets the funding.

If parents choose a non-public school and the cost of enrollment exceeds the value of the voucher, the parents pay the difference. When parents with incomes above the area median do not send their children to the closest public school, the parents must transport the children to and from the school themselves or pay the public school system a fee to perform this service. In this manner, the public schools have enough of an advantage to enable the better ones to continue.

Some argue that parental choice would create chaos and destroy the public education system. If done correctly, parental choice would produce no more havoc than the opening or closing of a supermarket in a community. The only thing it would destroy is the cozy, self-serving arrangements that the teacher unions have with politicians.

Those protective of the National Education Association union never acknowledge that their monopoly hurts children from low- and middle-income families the most. Upper-income parents have choices. They have the means to reside in the districts with the best schools or send their children to private schools. Low- and middle-income families trapped in rural areas and inner cities do not have these options.

Robert Balfanz, a research professor at Johns Hopkins University School of Education, wrote an editorial for *The New York Times,* in which he said that while more than three million students would receive a high school diploma in 2014, one-third of the nation's black and Hispanic young men would not.[262] When parents are free to choose, schools only continue if they provide children a desirable environment and good education. Milton Friedman wrote:

Violence of the kind that has been rising in public schools is possible only because the victims are compelled to attend the schools that they do. Give them effective freedom to choose and students—black and white, poor and rich, North and South—would desert schools that could not maintain order. Discipline is seldom a problem in private schools that train students as radio and television technicians, typists and secretaries, or for myriad other specialties.

Let schools specialize, as private schools would, and common interest would overcome the bias of color and lead to more integration than now occurs. The integration would be real, not merely on paper.[263]

State Goals and Exams

Our federal government tried to improve education across the country with the No Child Left Behind program. The program gave federal dollars to states to improve teacher quality and student performance. The program required states to set teacher quality standards, improve teacher quality in its schools, create standardized tests, and improve student performance. Well-intended and wonderfully named, this program had two serious deficiencies. First, it did not give parents choices, and second, it forced unwelcomed testing upon teachers.

While we want our schools to operate to a high standard and improve, we can obtain much better results with competition than with a federal government mandate. Rather than using the No Child Left Behind approach that few stakeholders find satisfactory, the federal government should leave education to the states, which is exactly what it did for most of our nation's history. Each state is fully capable of establishing goals and developing tests on its own, and each county can decide how to achieve state educational objectives. Business leaders understand the value of setting goals, measuring them, and letting their reports and business units decide how to reach them, but for some reason few government officials understand the efficacy of this practice.

States could model their programs after the decades-old, highly successful New York State Regents goals and exams. They might set objectives for median and variance exam scores and publish the results for each district and school, enabling county governments, school boards, administrators, teachers, parents, and taxpayers to gauge how their schools perform relative to the others. Fifty states and numerous counties per state would evolve different methods to educate children and learn from one another.

State goals, measures, and tests would prevent educators from deviating from and dumbing down the curriculum. Counties could go beyond the state curriculum, but not neglect it. Most importantly, this approach incentivizes everyone to work hard and steadily improve outcomes in the education system.

The benefits of parental choice are immense. Children stuck in poorly performing schools would have the option to move to excellent schools and receive life-transforming educations. School administrators and teachers would work harder to improve their schools. Those who perform poorly would make career changes. Parents would be more involved in their children's education. Taxpayers and the communities would receive better value. If we truly care about our children and our country's future, we will create an education system that effectively teaches our children the habits, knowledge, and skills necessary to be successful.

Parental Choice – (a) developing a better mix of public and private education, (b) creating equitable county school districts, (c) ending the public education monopoly, (d) ending tenure, (e) implementing merit-based retention and compensation, (f) allowing parents to decide where their children attend primary and secondary school, and (g) ending the federal government's involvement in education. Monopolistic, socialistic, and inequitable education is antithetical to education with parental choice.

Chapter 34

Results-Oriented Education

We spend close to $200,000 to educate each child, yet inadequately prepare one-third of our children for work and life.[264]

Adequately funding schools makes universal education possible. Aligning school curriculums with the needs of children, families, and employers improves resource use and children's learning and preparation for life. Giving parents the ability to choose their children's primary and secondary schools incentivizes administrators and teachers to improve educational outcomes. But we still are not there. Adequately preparing our children for life requires us to benchmark school and district performance, empower administrators and teachers, make them more accountable for results, and populate our schools with a healthy mix of conservative, moderate, and progressive educators.

Benchmarking

When we fly over the ocean in the dead of night, we have no sense of where we are going or how fast we are flying. We have no reference points. So it is in education, business, and government when they operate without performance benchmarks. Reference points and criteria are necessary to determine how we are doing.

Benchmarking is the comparison of our individual, group, or organizational performance to others' performance in meaningful ways. Benchmarking encourages people to do their best, work together, use their resources wisely, and steadily improve.

For benchmarking to work well, leaders must understand the few primary drivers of their organizations' performance. They must develop measures and create goals and incentives reflective of the drivers to align individual and organizational interests. Too many benchmarks create confusion and are as undesirable as too few.

Leaders must be careful about what they incentivize, as eventually the administrators and teachers will deliver it if the incentives are sufficient. When leaders get the drivers, measures, goals, and incentives right, people work toward the objectives. A lack of benchmarks, incorrectly specified goals, and inadequate incentives are common problems in organizations. Examples of critical benchmarks and drivers in education are:

–   The median and variance of scores on standardized tests;

–   Administrators per teacher;

–   Students per teacher;

–   The ratio of special-needs students to resource staff;

–   Expenditures per pupil and per special-needs student per year;

–   The percentage of students successfully forming critical habits; and

–   The median and variance of student scores in reading, writing, mathematics, history, science, and family studies for each grade.

Once school systems identify, measure, and report their results of the most critical education drivers, then state governments, school boards, administrators, teachers, parents, and taxpayers can gauge district, school, and administrator effectiveness and make well-informed decisions. Administrators can identify opportunities for improvement and training needs, make personnel changes, more advantageously allocate the limited resources, adjust compensation, and recognize and reward accomplishment. Teachers learn what they did well and what needs improving. Parents learn which schools perform well, and taxpayers ascertain whether their money is being used wisely.

Recently, the federal government mandated rigorous testing and benchmarking for school districts and schools, which was not received well. Benchmarking terrifies union leaders, administrators, and teachers because it exposes their poor results. While benchmarking is a good thing, the federal government lacks constitutional authority to be involved in public education. The federal government advantageously involved itself in education with the establishment of land-grant universities, but this involvement only amounted to donating surplus federal lands to fund the system. Nonprofit organizations, not the federal government, built and administer the universities.

In truth, few people like the discipline and rigor of bench-marking and competition. Elected officials seek to avoid competition through party rules, gerrymandered districts, and favorable campaign finance laws. Business leaders evade competition with patents, trade secrets, acquisitions, and large market shares. Unions insulate their members from competition with the use of preferential laws and protective work rules. Universally, people try to escape competition, but competition serves us well, and there really is no escaping it. Improvement, prosperity, and continuation are the products of competition. Stagnation, corruption, and relative decline are the inevitable products of the absence of competition.

Administration Empowerment and Accountability

Along with benchmarking, limiting union power would improve children's education in many states. School boards, superintendents, and principals need the authority to hire, compensate, and terminate school personnel on the basis of performance to improve our educational results. School personnel need the same—no less and no more—protections as private sector employees. Although there are many dedicated, high-performing teachers and administrators in our educational system, there are too many poorly performing ones. Attracting, retaining, and incentivizing the best ones are essential practices for providing our children with quality education.

When people propose benchmarking, limiting union power, and enacting performance-based employment and compensation, educators invariably insist that education is different. They want protection from parents and do not want to be penalized for having slower students in their classes. My response to these concerns is "of course."

Boards of education, superintendents, and principals can protect teachers from parents just like airline leaders protect their service agents from angry passengers when they cancel flights. Teachers can be taught to handle and defuse parent disappointment and frustration. Yes, some employee performance is difficult to measure and incentivize in every line of work, but intelligent leaders find ways to measure and appropriately reward every type of work. Benchmarks, goal setting, and incentives require intelligence, sensitivity, and judgment.

One way to create a better balance between school administration and union power is to prohibit unions from aggregating and operating on regional, state, or federal levels. Allowing unions to amass too much power hampers school boards and superintendents, shortchanges students, and unnecessarily costs taxpayers billions of dollars.

Another way to balance school administration and union power is to pass right-to-work laws that prevent union majorities from coercing school personnel to join unions. People should decide to join unions on an individual basis and not be coerced and forced to support others' political agendas. Schools do not exist to enrich union leaders, members, and their political friends. Unions should not have the power to protect people who work hard for a few years, obtain tenure, and then work at a relaxed pace the rest of their lives.

We also must have enough administrators in districts to adequately supervise teachers. As a rule of thumb in relatively complex environments, leaders should have about 8 to 15 direct reports. Teachers, like all people, need training, coaching, recognition, and monitoring. Superintendents must observe and regularly interact with principals, and principals and department heads must observe and regularly interact with teachers and students.

Depending on the state and school district, many superintendents and principals can no longer pick their teams, develop their personnel, affect their reports' compensation, or reward superior performance. Work rules and tenure saddle them with numerous poor-performing teachers. Chief executives in the private sector would not put up with these constraints. Jack Welch wrote:

Tenure is a terrible idea. It keeps [professors and teachers] around forever and they don't have to work hard.[265]

Once we adequately empower school administrations, we must also make them accountable for better educational outcomes. Just as we hold corporate boards and executives responsible for the performance of businesses, we must hold school board members and superintendents accountable for the performance of schools. We must assess the job they do and condition their continuation and compensation on their results.

Teacher Empowerment and Accountability

Schools also must have enough teachers and empower, incentivize, and hold them accountable for what happens in their classrooms. Counterproductive union work rules, difficult parents, and misguided lawsuits have stripped teachers of the freedom to do what is best for students. Ironically, teachers' power in the classroom has declined as their unions have amassed power.

Many teachers can no longer assign homework; give credit for homework; give a C, D, or F for poor work; discipline students; or remove disruptive students from their classrooms. Do we expect students to learn much without homework or students to apply themselves when they can take exams numerous times and receive an A or a B regardless of their effort and number of correct answers on exams? Do we expect students to learn much when they are only in class six hours a day for half the year? Do we expect teachers to be highly motivated when they do not receive extra compensation for superior work, must deal with ongoing disruptive student behavior, and are expected to yield to overprotective parents?

Few people consider the effects that jaded and poor teachers have on children. To gauge them, consider junior high and high school teachers who do the minimum and teach 100 children per year. Over 20 years, each poor performing-teacher negatively affects 2,000 children. Next, compare the school districts where only a small portion of the teachers perform well with those where most teachers perform well. The cumulative difference in the quality of the instruction that the students receive over the course of 13 years in the two districts is staggering. For some children, it is the difference between college, a successful career, and an intact family or a life of drugs, crime, and failed relationships.

How Children Succeed

Almost universally, career, marital, and parental success results from a long series of early successes at home and in school. Figure 22 summarizes several essentials of how children succeed.

Success at home is a function of safe neighborhoods, intact families, responsible parenting, nurture and discipline, and empowering habit formation. Children need to attach to their parents, learn to express themselves constructively, develop self-control, defer gratification, focus, and finish what they start. Parents need to encourage children's natural curiosity and help them build confidence, conscientiousness, winning habits, and executive function.

What is executive function? It is the ability to make good choices. It is a simple concept but a characteristic that takes years to develop in children. Executive function enables children to control their emotions, prioritize their activities, defer gratification, solve problems, and conscientiously fulfill their responsibilities. Executive function is one of the greatest predictors of success.

Figure 22: How Children Succeed

Inputs	Outputs
Success at Home	
Safe Neighborhoods Intact Families Responsible Parenting Nurture and Discipline Empowering Habit Formation	Attachment Self-Control Constructive Expression Ability to Defer Gratification Focus and Follow Through Winning Habits Conscientiousness
Success in Elementary and Junior High School	
Safe Neighborhoods Intact Families Responsible Parenting Nurture and Discipline Empowering Habit Formation Parental Choice Adequate Funding Life and Science-Based Curriculum Results-Oriented Educators	Executive Function Winning Habits People Skills Contextual Knowledge Reading, Writing, Math, Science, and Search Skills
Success in High School	
Safe Neighborhoods Intact Families Responsible Parenting Nurture and Discipline Empowering Habit Formation Parental Choice Student Accountability Adequate Funding Life- and Science-Based Curriculum Results-Oriented Educators Seven Secondary Tracks	Executive Function Winning Perspectives Winning Habits Knowledge of Winning Practices People and Life Skills Contextual Knowledge Vocational or College Preparation
Success in College and Vocational Schools	
Safe Neighborhoods Intact Families Responsible Parenting Nurture and Discipline Empowering Habit Formation Student Choice and Accountability Life- and Science-Based Curriculum Results-Oriented Educators Work Opportunities, Savings, Scholarships	Executive Function Winning Perspectives Winning Habits Knowledge of Winning Practices People and Life Skills Advanced Contextual Knowledge Vocational or Professional Knowledge and Skills Effectiveness
Success at Work, in Marriage, and as Parents	

Success in elementary and junior high school is a function of success at home and access to good schools, which have adequate funding, life- and science-based curricula, and results-oriented administrators and teachers. Success in elementary and junior high school involves the ongoing development of executive function, winning habits, and people skills; proficiency in reading, writing, math, and search skills; and understanding the evolution of the universe and life and the history and nature of their community, state, and country.

Success in high school builds on the foundation that parents and previous schooling provide. It depends on access to good schools that have adequate funding, life- and science-based curricula, and results-oriented administrators and teachers. It involves the ongoing development of executive function, winning habits, and people skills. Success in high school occurs when students learn about and assume responsibility for their health, nutrition, continuing education, financial well-being, and career, marital, and parenting preparation.

Success in college and vocational schools builds on the foundation that parents and schools provide young people. It expects students to choose vocational school or college and to utilize their savings, earnings, scholarships, and family resources to fund their education. It involves mastering vocational and professional knowledge and skills and obtaining greater contextual, career, marital, and parenting knowledge and skills.

Bridging Conservative and Liberal Biases

The unionization of our public schools and universities inadvertently and steadily increases the representation of liberal biases in our schools, causes poorer educational outcomes, and inculcates children with these biases. Union leaders emanate a liberal culture, support liberal administrators who hire liberal teachers, and make life difficult for conservatives. Brent Roberts, a University of Illinois professor, exposes one of the great shortcomings of liberal biases regarding child development. In Paul Tough's book, *How Children Succeed*, Roberts stated:

Researchers prefer to study the things they value. And the people in society who value conscientiousness are not intellectuals, and they're not academics, and they're not liberals. They tend to be religious-right conservatives who think people should be more controlled.[266]

Paul Tough continues:

What intrigues Roberts most about conscientiousness is that it predicts so many outcomes that go far beyond the workplace. People high in conscientiousness get better grades in high school and college; they commit fewer crimes; and they stay married longer. They live longer—and not just because they smoke and drink less. They have fewer strokes, lower blood pressure, and lower incidence of Alzheimer's disease. "It would actually be nice if there were some negative things that went along with conscientiousness," Roberts told me. "But at this point, it's emerging as one of the primary dimensions of successful function across the lifespan. It really goes cradle to grave in terms of how well people do."[267]

Liberals like openness and spontaneity, and they dislike conscientiousness and discipline. Conversely, conservatives *like* conscientiousness and discipline and dislike openness and spontaneity. These are not black-and-white differences but ones of degree.

A primary problem with our public schools and universities is that liberal biases are overrepresented and conservative biases underrepresented, causing schools to be soft on discipline and do a poor job of developing self-control, the ability to defer gratification, and conscientiousness in our children. This is extremely unfortunate, as young people's failure to develop the latter characteristics handicaps them for life.

Too much openness and spontaneity and too much conscientiousness and discipline negatively impact children. Too much openness and spontaneity cause people to be reckless and irresponsible. Too much conscientiousness and discipline cause people to be overly cautious and less creative. Children need to develop and judiciously use all these muscles. They need to be open to all types of law-abiding people and advantageous innovations, unwilling to experiment with illicit drugs and extramarital sex, and conscientious about their work. While we want to be sensitive to many children's difficult circumstances, we must not deny them the opportunity to develop the self-control and conscientiousness needed to overcome their circumstances and succeed in life.

Conservative- and liberal-preferred traits both have their place. Improving our education requires us to populate our public schools and universities with similar numbers of conservatives, moderates, and liberals; nurture openness, spontaneity, and conscientiousness in our children; test competing pedagogies; and do what is best for the children.

―――――――――――

Our current large concentrations of power in education, the isolation of administrators and teachers from competition, seniority-based retention and compensation, and the overrepresentation of liberals in our public schools yield half-hearted effort, inefficiency, ever-higher costs, and poor results. Until we change these realities and become more results-oriented, we will continue to fail millions of children.

Results-Oriented Education – *the understanding that doing well at work, in marriage, and as parents is the product of a series of earlier achievements in our homes and elementary, junior high, and high school, vocational school, and universities. Results-oriented education involves benchmarking; administrator and teacher empowerment and accountability; understanding how children succeed; limiting union power; and populating our schools with similar numbers of conservative, moderate, and liberal educators. Unionized, left-leaning, inconsistent education is the antithesis of results-oriented education.*

Section VII: Winning Practices of Enterprise

Winning Perspectives

Truth
Causality
Scale
Evolution
Fitness

Human Nature
Culture
Periodic Disaster
Eco-Dependency

Winning Practices

Health
Thought
Integrity
Proactivity
Prudence
Excellence
Thrift and Investment

Affiliation
Decency
Understanding
Leadership
Teamwork
Improvement

Spouse Selection
Marriage
Responsible Parenting
Empowering Habit Formation

Knowledge
Universal Education
Parental Choice
Results-Oriented Education

Free Enterprise and Markets
Responsible Corporate Governance
Prudent Regulation
Enterprise Competitiveness

Government of the People
Powers, Prohibitions, and Structure
Freedoms, Rights, and Responsibilities
The Rule of Law
Inclusion and Meritocracy
Prudent Taxation
Financial Strength
Savings Accounts, Social Safety Nets
Consumer-Driven Healthcare
Assimilation
Peace Through Fitness
Sustainability

Chapter 35

Free Enterprise and Markets

When governments provide services, we pay for what majorities want whether we approve or disapprove. When free markets and enterprise provide services, we only pay for what we purchase. Governments are coercive, and free enterprise and markets are voluntary by their nature.

In recent years, many people have focused more on the economic inequalities that free markets and enterprise bring than the higher living standards. Big government and socialist-leaning politicians, journalists, professors, and public-school teachers malign free enterprise. Businesses with large market concentrations and unscrupulous business leaders tarnish it. But rather than malign the voluntary system that improves people's lives like no other, we should understand that a few unsavory people mar every order, and we should use antitrust laws to break up monopolistic companies and privatize more of our government.

Between 1500 and 1965, free enterprise and markets caused living standards in the West to improve to more than 75 times those of China.[268] Free enterprise and markets facilitated the development of sewer systems, vaccines, and healthcare; doubled lifespans; enabled a single farmer to feed hundreds of people; facilitated the growth of low-cost energy and machines; enabled universal education; brought people unprecedented amounts of free time; and spurred the development of affordable computers, cell phones, and the Internet.

Free market transactions are voluntary, mutually beneficial, and efficient. They transform self-interest into common interest; in doing so, they advance the common good. People and businesses earn income as they provide labor, products, and services that others desire. The more they do what others value, the more they earn. People and companies use resources frugally, lower costs, and innovate; if they do not, their customers patronize their competitors. People earn their livelihood, a surplus to invest, and the means to fund government. They form the capital that fuels business and improves living standards. Businesses and people win in proportion to their contributions. Adam Smith wrote:

> Give me that which I want, and you shall have this, which you want, is the meaning of every such offer; and it is in this manner that we obtain from one another the far greater part of those good offices which we stand in need of. It is not from the benevolence of the butcher, the brewer, or the baker that we expect our dinner, but from their regard to their own interest. We address ourselves, not to their humanity, but to their self-love, and never talk to them of our own necessities, but of their advantages.[269]

Free enterprise and markets have moved hundreds of millions of people from subsistence to relative affluence, providing people with lifestyles superior to those of past kings and queens. Detractors would have us believe that free enterprise and markets make people greedy, advance social inequality, and destroy the environment. But human nature and the growth of populations cause these realities, not free enterprise. People are greedy and take advantage of their positions, and growing populations harm the environment regardless of the economic system.

Private Property

Private property is a person's or an organization's money, savings, investments, inventory, assets, and real estate. Governments further their citizens' well-being as they permit them to buy, use, invest, and sell property, and they protect them from fraud, theft, and violence. Private ownership of property advances the responsible use of property more than government and communal ownership because the private ownership conveys more value to its owners than government and collective ownership does to anyone in their populations.

Private ownership, development, and investment of property help everyone. When farmers clear land, till the soil, and plant and harvest crops, we have food. When construction firms buy land and build houses and commercial facilities, we have homes and businesses. When people work hard and save or invest some of their earnings, they fund the operations of banks and companies. As people responsibly use their property, they earn a return and the larger population benefits. As they responsibly maintain their property, they preserve its value, and everyone gains.

When no one owns property, opportunists exploit it. When governments and groups own property, they seldom maintain, improve, or use it in the best manner, as its best use is relatively inconsequential to government and community leaders. Milton Friedman wrote:

> When everybody owns something, nobody owns it, and nobody has a direct interest in maintaining or improving its condition. . . . Nobody uses somebody else's resources as carefully as [they use their] own.[270]

While our founders established laws and institutions to enable us to purchase, hold, and sell property, they did not create them to restrict the government's confiscation of it. Establishing some constitutional limitations on the taxation of property, income, and estates would be advantageous to our citizens and the country. When governments tax personal property too much, economic activity declines. People work less, take fewer risks, and hide income from governments. What is too much? When federal, state, and local government's cumulative taxation of income exceeds 50 percent, people feel they work more for the government than themselves, and when real estate taxes exceed 3 percent, governments significantly devalue people's property.

An important practice related to private property is restitution, which is the practice of compensating others for damaging their property. When governments force people who damage others' property to pay restitution, they make the injured parties whole, cause people to be respectful of others' property, and incarcerate fewer people.

Free Enterprise

The production of goods and services occurs in one of three ways: (1) entrepreneurs and corporations freely provide products and services to others at competitive prices, (2) monopolies offer products and services to others at set prices, or (3) governments provide products and services to others at set prices. The production of goods and services by entrepreneurs and corporations generally is the most advantageous.

The modern corporation, one of the greatest business-related innovations, originated with the creation of the Dutch East India Company in the 1600s and the Joint Stock Companies and Limited Liability Acts of 1844 and 1855 in Great Britain. The Dutch East India Company was the first business to offer shares of ownership on a public exchange. The Joint Stock Companies and Limited Liability Acts were the first legislation to allow business leaders to establish legal corporate entities separate from themselves; shield their investors and themselves from the risk of failure; raise large amounts of capital; and address larger-scale, riskier projects.

A *Corporation* *is a legal entity that can have multiple owners; borrow money; buy, sell, and own property; produce products; provide services; and shield its leaders and owners from liability.*

Except for a couple of specific situations, entrepreneurs and corporations with limited market shares provide products and services more effectively than monopolies and governments. Entrepreneurs and corporations utilize resources more efficiently, are more responsive to market price signals, evolve lower-cost and higher-quality products and services, and are relatively apolitical.

When monopolies and governments provide products and set prices, shortages and surpluses materialize. Price setting creates supply-and-demand imbalances, wastes resources, and makes people wait for products. Monopolies are only desirable when the economies of scale for one entity are much greater than those for multiple entities, such as in the delivery of electricity. In this case, one entity can run the electrical lines and provide the electricity at a much lower cost than multiple entities. Governments must regulate the monopolies, however, or monopolies will exploit their position, take advantage of consumers, and make surplus profits.

Similarly, government-provided goods and services are only desirable in the special situation of public goods.

Public Goods are products and services everyone receives and no one purchases. A country's defense and law enforcement are two examples of public goods. In both cases, everyone receives the service but no one directly pays for it.

When services are public goods, governments must offer them because no private entity would do so. Private entities cannot recover their costs and earn a return when offering public services. On the other hand, when services are not public goods, governments should not furnish them as they use resources inefficiently, provide inferior services at higher prices, and politicize the production and offering of the services.

When entrepreneurs and businesses offer products and services, the entrepreneurs and shareholders own the enterprises. They decide what to produce and who to hire. They and employed professionals lead the enterprises. The type of ownership, amount of owner involvement, and scale of the enterprises guide their behavior. Smaller owner-operated enterprises tend to reflect the character of the owners and are usually more stakeholder-, long-term-, and community-oriented. Publicly-traded companies are much more shareholder- and short-term-oriented.

Both types of ownership have their advantages and disadvantages. Smaller, owner-operated enterprises work best when the company's earnings are volatile, and their customers value personal service. Larger, publicly traded companies work best when capital requirements are high and economies of scale are favorable. Both types of businesses provide people with lower-cost and better-quality goods and services than governments and monopolies.

Free enterprise and markets allow business leaders and employees to enter voluntarily into employer-employee relationships. Governments and unions only need to constrain these relationships when employers violate basic employment, safety, compensation, and benefit standards. Voluntary arrangements that allow employers to select their team and employees to choose their place of employment yield more efficient, effective, and competitive teams. When governments and unions unnecessarily restrict these freedoms, enterprises employ fewer people, products and services cost more, and enterprises sell less and/or relocate to more business-friendly locations.

The free enterprise system works well because it is consistent with evolution and human nature. Like evolution, it creates competition for businesses to provide their customers with desirable, high-quality, low-cost products. Those who successfully do these things profit, employ the best people, continuously improve their offerings, and steadily grow. Those who fail to do them gradually go out of business.

Although we seldom think about it, every government restriction, regulation, fee, tax, and action that is unrelated to securing our lives and rights, providing a public good, or addressing an externality distorts market prices, causes resources to be used inefficiently, lowers living standards, and encroaches on people's freedom. Every government action coerces us to do what the majorities mandate whether the actions benefit us or not.[271]

In my lifetime, I have had the privilege of knowing hundreds of able, effective, and responsible business leaders and have run across a very few irresponsible ones. As hard as it is for some to accept, individual responsibility, the pursuit of self-interest, and the opportunity to profit underlie most people's fitness and well-being. Ayn Rand wrote:

> America's abundance was created not by public sacrifices to the common good, but by the productive genius of free [people] who pursued their own personal interests and the making of their own private fortunes. They did not starve the people to

pay for America's [bounty]. They gave the people better jobs, higher wages, and cheaper goods with every new machine they invented, with every scientific discovery or technological advance—and thus the whole country was moving forward and profiting, not suffering, every step of the way.[272]

Self-interest and the opportunity for profit cause business leaders to work harder and more responsibly than most people. The majority of business leaders work 60 to 100 hours per week and deliver tremendous benefits to their organization, employees, and customers. They assume responsibility for the welfare and performance of their team members and the company's inventories, equipment, facilities, contractual obligations, debt, products, and services. Moreover, they carry this responsibility 24 hours a day, 7 days a week for as long as they lead their organizations. The differences between the most effective leaders and average ones can amount to thousands, millions, or even billions of dollars of shareholder, employee, and consumer value.

Highly motivated and responsible leaders provide us with employment opportunities and superior products at affordable prices. They create and develop life-transforming enterprises like General Electric, Ford Motor Company, Boeing, Walmart, Microsoft, Apple, Google, and Amazon. Competition and the opportunity to profit fuel their excellence.

Profit is the difference between a company's revenue and expenses. Enterprises use profits to operate, modernize, and expand facilities; enhance employee compensation and working conditions; improve their product offerings; reward shareholders; and pay taxes. Profits enable businesses to borrow money and raise equity capital. Enterprises must have many satisfied customers to earn profits over time. People who have investment and retirement accounts own portions of businesses and benefit greatly from their profits.

Some people think businesses should not make profits. They prefer nonprofit companies or want governments to tax companies' profits heavily. History suggests this approach is shortsighted. Eliminate the opportunity to profit, and leaders and their teams do not work as hard. Product quality, innovation, and enterprise competitiveness deteriorate. Businesses relocate to friendlier environments, and employees lose their jobs. The opportunity to profit is undesirable only when companies have large market concentrations and earn excessive profits. If governments use antitrust laws to break up companies with large market concentrations, their earnings decrease to healthy levels.

The free enterprise system works best when five or more entities compete in the market, and few barriers to enter the market exist. It works best when entrepreneurs are ethical, responsible, and industrious, and they prudently consider the short- and long-term needs of their stakeholders. There are four situations where nonprofits work better than for-profits: (1) basic research, (2) aggregation and deployment of donated money, (3) the opportunity to attract and mobilize large numbers of volunteers exists, and (4) employment of disabled people in our communities.

Nonprofits are advantageous for basic research-related organizations when breakthroughs are unpredictable and take years. They are also well-suited for service organizations like the Boy Scouts, Girl Scouts, YMCA, and Nature Conservancy. These are situations where people are willing to donate money and time and it is inappropriate for leaders and employees of the organization to profit from donor charity. Nonprofits also may provide a vehicle to employ disabled and other unemployable people who the private sector cannot cost-effectively utilize.

Free Markets

Free markets coordinate the actions of millions of suppliers and consumers. They register their choices and evolve market-clearing prices. They elevate living standards, channel capital to projects that people value most, and facilitate the creation of trillions of dollars of wealth. Suppliers and consumers do not need approval from governments or central planners to transact business within free markets. Unlike a centrally planned economy, free markets balance the supply of products and services as buyers and sellers adjust prices and voluntarily engage in transactions.

Free markets work because they alter buyer and seller behavior. When sellers run low on a product, they increase its price, expand, and produce more of it. Consumers use less of the product and purchase substitutes. When sellers have too much of a product, they decrease its price, idle production, and produce less of the product. Consumers abandon higher-priced alternatives and purchase more of the product. Buyer and seller self-interests balance the quantities of products bought and sold over time.

Free markets cause businesses to use resources prudently, operate efficiently, innovate, and provide value to consumers. They incentivize organizations to find the optimal structure, scale, and mix of the features, quality, and price of products. They motivate business leaders to work hard to lower their costs and improve the desirability of their products. In a sense, businesses work for their customers as their customers select which products they purchase—and, ultimately, which businesses continue.

The opportunity for profit directs enterprises and employees to engage in activities others value most. At any given time, employers and employees choose among a myriad of alternative activities. As they select the most profitable opportunities, they favor the ones that benefit others and themselves the most. As Adam Smith wrote in *The Wealth of Nations*:

[People are] continually exerting [themselves] to find out the most advantageous employment for whatever capital [they] can command. It is [their] own advantage, indeed, and not that of the society, which [they have] in view. But the study of [their] own advantage naturally, or rather necessarily, leads [them] to prefer that employment which is most advantageous to society .... [They] intend only [their] own gain, and [they are] in this, as in many other cases, led by an invisible hand to promote an end, which was not part of [their] intention.[273]

Free market prices also enable consumers to find the mix of products and services that most satisfies them. The prices contain location and time-specific information about producer costs and consumer preferences. The prices enable consumers to compare their desire for one product with their interest in other products. Consumers do not make all-or-nothing decisions. They choose a little more of this or that, e.g., a little more food or another article of clothing.

Free Trade

Free trade is the voluntary exchange of products and services for money between people of different countries. It moves products and services from those who value them less to people who value them more. It permits each party to specialize in what they do best and to get more of what they want. It furthers efficiencies and economies of scale, enabling firms to achieve lower per-unit costs. It increases the wealth of traders and countries and benefits the wealthy, middle class, and poor. Free trade works because of comparative advantage, where:

Comparative Advantage is the reality that when individuals or countries specialize and trade, each doing what he or she does relatively better, they all benefit. Even when one party does everything more efficiently than the other parties, all parties benefit from doing what they do best, selling some of their products and services, and using the proceeds to purchase what others do best.

Tariffs, quotas, and other trade restrictions reduce the benefits of trade. They benefit some industries and harm others and direct people to produce things that they have a disadvantage in producing, raising the costs of products to producers and consumers. While appearing to protect jobs, they decrease exports, export-related jobs, and our foreign exchange earnings, as well as increase the cost of our imports. Countries gain immensely from free trade even when they unilaterally engage in it.

Leaders enact tariffs, quotas, and other trade restrictions to protect immerging industries, curry favor with special interests, retaliate against other countries' predatory trade practices, and for national security reasons. Retaliation to predatory trade practices and national security reasons are about the only times when trade restrictions are advantageous to a population.

Capital Formation and Investment

People defer consumption, save, and invest their savings to earn a return and prepare for the future. Their deferred consumption and savings form the capital that governments use to build infrastructure, enterprises use to fund their operations, and consumers use to buy things on credit. Equity and debt are two forms of capital. Chapter 20 provided details on several other types of capital.

Once people accumulate some money, they may use it to buy debt and equity instruments. They may loan some of their money to governments, enterprises, or consumers in return for larger cumulative cash-flow streams. These investments offer tremendous opportunity for gain and loss, and they require significant amounts of research, weighing numerous alternatives, exceptional judgment, and patience. In a free-market economy, financial institutions such as banks, leasing companies, and bond, stock, and mutual fund exchanges create markets for various debt and equity instruments. These institutions enable government, enterprises, and people to store and access capital. Without these institutions and investment opportunities, we would form little capital.

Capital formation is best left to private citizens and investors. When governments tax us and invest our money, the returns are frequently less than those of private investment professionals. Although government officials claim that reliable analysis drives their investment decisions, more often than not they invest capital in ways that are popular with their donors and constituents.

While most private investments earn positive returns, some lose money. Much in life is uncertain, and investment outcomes fall into this category. Occasional losses are one of the downsides to investments and trying to make improvements. We do not learn and progress, however, without experimentation and investing in instruments and projects with uncertain outcomes.

———————————

Completely aligned with evolution and nature, free enterprise and markets further a people's fitness and well-being like no other form of economic organization. The voluntary and mutually beneficial nature of free enterprise and markets and their advancement of the common good are some of the great benefits of the system. Free enterprise and markets comprise the engine that powers everything—our defense, infrastructure, education, living standards, and social safety net. Life goes much better as we appreciate, maintain, and use this engine.

Free Enterprise and Markets – *(a) private property, (b) free entry of entrepreneurs and businesses into and out of markets, (c) entrepreneurs and firms voluntarily purchasing supplies from vendors, employing workforces, and creating products and services, (d) voluntary buying and selling of products and services among people, businesses, and governments, and (e) capital formation and investment. Centrally planned economies, government-owned enterprises, monopolies, oligopolies, unions, fixed prices, tariffs, quotas, trade restrictions, and excessive taxation are antithetical to free markets and enterprise.*

Chapter 36

Responsible Corporate Governance

Numerous stakeholders contribute to the success of every enterprise.

Entrepreneurial risk-taking and shareholder capital start businesses; reliable suppliers, competent employees, and satisfied customers fuel them; and supportive communities and healthy environments sustain them. Directors and business leaders, who appreciate the many stakeholders who contribute to their success and seek win-win arrangements with them, create the most successful, desirable, and enduring businesses.

Stakeholder Inclusion

Stakeholder inclusion involves eliciting feedback from interested parties and sharing as much information with one's stakeholders as possible. The more leaders involve stakeholders in their decisions, the more they gain their goodwill. Personal and proprietary data must be kept confidential but leaders can share most other information.

Systematically eliciting stakeholder feedback is as simple as routinely circulating among the stakeholders, meeting with representatives of stakeholder groups, or placing stakeholders on corporate boards. The advantage of each approach depends on the size and geographical footprint of a business. Owner-operated enterprises with few employees have little need for formal board meetings because their leaders associate with the stakeholders during day-to-day activity. Leaders of larger, geographically dispersed businesses have less opportunity for interaction. These leaders must structure and schedule opportunities to interact with stakeholders and representatives of stakeholder groups.

In the largest of my businesses, I met with my managers, walked through our principal facilities, and interacted with most team members every week. I also had lunch with my managers and rotating groups of team members weekly. I led monthly safety committee meetings with representatives from all departments and moderated quarterly company meetings. Quarterly, semiannually, or annually, I met with many vendors and customers. I was active on numerous community boards and had an interest in the environment. This circulation and interaction provided me with an ongoing sense of business and stakeholder concerns. It provided me with a perspective that enhanced my ability to make sound decisions and create win-win arrangements.

Leaders of large organizations must navigate multitudes of stakeholder interests and multi-continent footprints. These leaders need feedback from stakeholders, but the sheer numbers and geographical dispersion of them force leaders to interact with representatives of these groups. Nevertheless, even leaders of large organizations must circulate and interact directly with some stakeholders, or they become captive to the information that the intermediaries feed them.

Stakeholder inclusion works best when the leaders are honest, competent, hardworking, and accountable, and the leaders and team members are subject to the same rules and receive market-rate remuneration. Stakeholder inclusion does not work well when leaders have significant privileges that others lack or if leaders and stakeholders have hidden agendas and take advantage of their positions.

Stakeholder inclusion rejects an "ends justify the means" approach that does not demonstrate concern for people. It requires leaders to employ honorable means, balance the interests of the organization and stakeholder groups, and achieve results. Leaders must make hard decisions, as in the cases of layoffs, terminations, and facility closings, but they can make these decisions in as honest, respectful, and considerate a manner as possible.

Stakeholder Directors

Business leaders tarnish the free enterprise system when they fill their boards with subordinates and friends rather than with independent directors and representatives of stakeholder groups. They harm the system when they overcompensate their directors and themselves, pay themselves bonuses when businesses do poorly, and neglect the interests of other stakeholders. The solution to this problem is not salary caps or a retreat from the free enterprise system, but for leaders of large organizations to put employee-, customer-, community-, and environment-oriented directors on their boards. Having representatives of these stakeholder groups enables broader input without the elimination of a shareholder orientation. Rotating people in these positions every 2 to 4 years improves the input.

A second way to address corporate and director self-indulgence is to require half the directors on boards to be independent and give the consumer-, employee-, community-, and environmental-oriented directors some voting interests. If more of the directors were independent and represented these stakeholders, corporate leaders would advance the stakeholder interests more advantageously and their compensation would be more reasonable.

Shareholders who have their personal resources at risk would retain control in a somewhat diluted form. Taking the control from shareholders would immeasurably harm our enterprises and cause capital to flee our country. Whereas, giving these four stakeholder groups a voice at the corporate table, but not controlling interest, would improve corporate decision-making. Consumers would have safer and better products and services. Team members would have better working conditions and compensation, and companies would be better stewards of their communities and the environment.

Media Reports of Corporate Misconduct

Along with stakeholder inclusion and independent directors, more media focus on corporate conduct would improve it. The press could establish business tip lines, have journalists circulate more among the leaders and team members of major businesses, and increase the investigative reporting of companies. Media reporting of good and bad corporate behavior is the only way consumers learn of it. Such reporting provides consumers the opportunity to signal their approval or disapproval of corporate conduct with their patronage, and in doing so, forces business leaders to be less indulgent and treat their stakeholders more honorably. Adam Smith wrote:

> The real and effectual discipline which is exercised over a [enterprise] is that of [its] customers. It is the fear of losing their [patronage] which restrains [its] frauds and corrects [its] negligence.[274]

Having run several businesses and worked hard to build strong personal and business reputations, I can attest to the truth of Adam Smith's statement and the power of this discipline. Government regulation has much less effect on leaders and enterprises than factual media reports on their conduct. For this approach to work, however, the news media must operate with integrity, corroborate their stories, and stick to the facts as widely circulated solicitous stories would do immense harm to our free enterprise system.

Winning Cultures

Winning cultures are those with a high prevalence of winning perspectives, practices, and prohibitions within them. The best businesses create these cultures. Leaders and senior staff convey these perspectives, practices, and prohibitions to new personnel, and they reinforce them in the performance review criteria as well as hiring and termination decisions.

Winning Culture is the shared beliefs and practices of people that guide their discretionary behavior in ways that are beneficial to individuals, the larger group, and the environment in the short and long term.

Winning cultures not only strengthen enterprises and improve their performance, but they also further responsible corporate governance. Enterprises are largely continuums of interactions, activities, arrangements, and transactions. The Winning Practices of Individuals and Groups—Health, Thought, Integrity, Proactivity, Prudence, Excellence, Thrift and Investment, Affiliation, Decency, Understanding, Leadership, Teamwork, and Improvement—all positively affect the interactions, activities, arrangements, transactions, and governance of enterprises.

People's acceptance into winning cultures must depend on their willingness to learn and utilize the Winning Perspectives and Practices. When winning cultures permeate enterprises, they positively impact the enterprises and their personnel every day. They mobilize their team members to act in ways that precipitate positive effects. People know what to do and do it regardless of the presence or absence of their leaders.

Responsible Corporate Governance – when businesses advance their interests in ways that promote their stakeholders' interests. It involves stakeholder inclusion, independent and stakeholder directors, media focus on corporate conduct, and winning cultures. Exploitive enterprises and corruption are the antitheses to responsible corporate governance.

Chapter 37

Prudent Regulation

The best governments enforce a few sensible laws and otherwise leave enterprises alone. Like good referees, they let the players play the game and do not pick the winners and losers.

Just as we need referees to protect players and monitor sports competitions, countries need governments to protect their citizens and enterprises and monitor their interactions and competitions. Switzerland, one of the freest countries in the world with relatively few laws and regulations, is an example of a country that does this exceedingly well. Venezuela, one of the least free countries in the world with many laws and regulations, does this poorly.

Contract Enforcement

Contracts are essential to enterprise. They give definition to transactions and arrangements, reduce misunderstandings and conflicts, and facilitate business. For contracts to work well, however, they must be straightforward, conflicts must be resolved in a fair and timely manner, and governments must impose penalties on people who violate the terms. Common-sense laws, well-trained attorneys, and an effective judicial and penal system are all essential to contract creation and enforcement.

When these conditions prevail, people readily use contracts and commerce flourishes. When government authorities are unfair, untimely, and ineffective, people do business elsewhere, and commerce suffers. The World Bank's "Doing Business" report assesses the time, cost, and procedural complexity of contract dispute resolution within different countries. The ten best countries for doing business in order of rank are: New Zealand, Singapore, Denmark, South Korea, Hong Kong, the United States, the United Kingdom, Norway, Georgia, and Sweden.[275]

Transparency

Transparency enables people to accurately understand what is going on. In business, it involves providing people with accurate, timely, and complete information so that they may assess the risks and rewards associated with an enterprise or investment. It also involves the use of Generally Accepted Accounting Practices (GAAP) and full disclosure of business and investment information.

Transparency improves understanding, decision-making, and people's conduct, thereby decreasing unlawful actions, conflict, and litigation. It helps people and firms build good reputations, which reduces the premiums people require to transact business, expands business activity, and increases living standards. Businesses and governments that judiciously set and follow transparency standards strengthen their cultures and operations.

Market Share Restrictions

One of the least appreciated and most important roles of government is to maintain competitive market structures. When a few enterprises dominate a market, a few shareholders benefit at the expense of many consumers. When competitive market structures exist, everyone wins. Antitrust laws empower governments to block corporate mergers and break up corporations with large market concentrations.

A Competitive Market Structure exists when at least five parties buy and sell a product or service in a market, and no one entity buys or sells more than 1/3 of the products or services.

Competitive market structures give choices to vendors, enterprises, consumers, employers, and employees, and these choices bring out the best in everyone. No one person or entity dictates the terms of exchange. When markets operate efficiently, people are much less likely to take advantage of one another. Employers treat their employees well or lose them to other companies. Employees perform well or lose their jobs. Enterprises provide desirable products to their customers or else their customers purchase the products from other firms.

When competitive market structures exist, the choices of buyers and sellers discipline the players and reduce the need for regulation. People do the right thing or they suffer. On the other hand, when a few people or companies dominate markets, they take advantage of others consciously and unconsciously until governments forbid the behavior. Competitive market structures require little government intervention and positively affect the behavior of everyone. Regulations cost a lot and only influence the actions of conscientious, law-abiding people.

Once enacted, agencies must enforce the regulations, people must comply with them for decades, and the regulations become incomprehensible over time. Federal, state, and local government regulations run tens of thousands of pages. They are impossible for normal people to know and regulatory agencies to enforce. Too many regulations undermine all the regulations by causing honest people and enterprises to give up trying to comply with them.

Limiting buyer and seller concentration in markets is a superior way to affect the behaviors of buyers and sellers. When competitive market structures exist, the prices of products permit the better enterprises to make enough money to cover their costs, pay employees competitive wages, maintain their facilities, compensate investors with competitive returns, and pay taxes. If profits are high, they do not remain high because enterprises expand and new entrants come into the market. The supply of the products increases, prices decrease, and profits fall. Workers receive competitive compensation, and consumers purchase products at competitive prices. Nobel Laureate Milton Friedman wrote:

The great danger to [consumers] is the monopoly—whether private or governmental. [Their] most effective protection is free competition at home and free trade throughout the world. [Consumers are] protected from being exploited by one seller by the existence of another seller from whom [they] can buy and who is eager to sell to [them]. Alternative sources of supply protect [consumers] far more effectively than all the Ralph Naders of the world.[276]

When competitive enterprise and market structures do not exist, companies earn excess profits. They pay their leaders, directors, and shareholders excessive amounts, while unionized workforces receive excess compensation and benefits. Corporate CEOs and unions influence the political process and gain ever-greater advantages. Three of the least recognized and most important keys to creating a strong middle class and improving living standards are: (1) competitive market structures, (2) right-to-work laws, and (3) the advantageous admission of immigrants and guest workers. The latter two topics are discussed in Chapters 38 and 49.

Debt Restrictions

Prudent governments and central banks restrict the amount of credit that financial institutions issue. They do not allow these institutions to become so large that they must bail them out one day, and in the process of doing this, the governments and central banks encourage irresponsible risk-taking. They do not allow banks, enterprises, and people to borrow more than they can pay back and precipitate prolonged periods of hardship for large portions of the population.

When financial institutions lend $30 or $40 for every dollar they hold in reserve, they unnecessarily risk their depositors' savings and shareholders' investments. When enterprises borrow $8 or $9 for every dollar of assets, they needlessly risk their employees' jobs and shareholders' investments. When people obtain mortgages and do not pay at least 20 percent of the cost of the property upfront, they increase the likelihood of defaults and undercollateralized mortgages during recessions. When investors buy equities and other assets on margin and assets fall in price, many investors must sell their assets to meet margin calls. In all these cases, too much leverage causes enterprises and people to sell more and purchase less during economic contractions, deepening and prolonging the contractions.

We have enough history with the use of debt to know which liabilities-to-assets and principal-and-interest-to-income ratios are sustainable. Banks and financial institutions should use time-tested, proven ratios and not lull themselves into thinking that current circumstances do not warrant such caution. Limiting loan-to-reserve ratios for banks to 10-1, total-liabilities-to-total-asset ratios for businesses and mortgages to 4-1, and equity-to-margin ratios for stock purchase to 2-1 would moderate economic cycles and eliminate many financial crises.

Governments and central banks must also prevent banks from speculative activity outside their savings and loan functions and require them to hold their mortgages to maturity. Banks that limit their leverage and avoid speculative trading do not put their customers' deposits unnecessarily at risk. Banks that hold their mortgages qualify borrowers more carefully and make better loans.

Financial derivatives are instruments that transfer risk from those who do not want it to those who willingly bear it. The risks associated with future contracts and options on equities and commodities are straightforward and understandable, but those related to mortgage-backed securities are largely unknown. They pose a risk to the economy that warrants elimination. Just as governments only permit useful, well-understood, and effective prescription drugs, so they should only allow useful, well-understood, and effective financial derivatives.

Externality Taxation

An externality exists when someone or something's actions affect others who have no say in the activities. Pollution is an externality. Power generators benefit from burning fossil fuels while the public reaps sickness and shortened lifespans. When harmful externalities exist and governments prudently tax them, businesses and people find cost-effective ways to reduce the negative effects of their activities. When governments do not tax harmful externalities and invest in reducing externalities themselves, like the Obama administration did subsidizing the manufacture of solar panels, they make investments that benefit their cronies and forgo the opportunity to incentivize everyone to find cost-effective ways to reduce adverse externalities. Taxing harmful externalities, as in enacting a carbon tax, is an effective use of government power, whereas public investment in private businesses is misguided, corrupting the use of it.

Externalities *are situations where one party's actions create a cost or a benefit to others who have no say in the activities.*

Do No Harm

Although some government interference in our lives is necessary, much is unnecessary. Many intrusions like those in healthcare and education distort market prices, transfer resources from productive citizens to politically favored groups, create special interests, and ensnare people in multigenerational dependency.

Government officials are much less apt to misuse their power when it is divided among the three branches of government and codified into law. Giving government officials and agencies large amounts of discretionary power always results in its eventual misuse. The Internal Revenue Service; Occupational, Safety, and Health Administration; and the Environmental Protection Agency provide examples of Executive Branch agencies that operate in an unconstitutional manner. These agencies create regulations, enforce them, and adjudicate them. Yet, the Constitution only grants Congress the power to create laws and regulations and the federal courts the power to resolve disputes of interpretation. The current unconstitutional actions of these agencies leave people little recourse when the agencies misuse their power.

Governments also should not produce products or provide services that are not true public goods. As indicated in Chapter 35, public goods are those where the consumption of the good by one person does not reduce the amount available for other people. Defense and public roads are public goods. Healthcare for veterans and mail delivery are not public goods. It is advantageous for the government to provide the defense and public roads but not to offer healthcare for veterans and deliver our mail. Private healthcare and delivery services provide better, lower-cost offerings than the U.S. Veterans Administration and the Postal System.

When governments enable union structures to coerce their membership and aggregate power on a state and national level, they seriously harm taxpayers, enterprises, consumers, and their countries. Powerful unions adversely influence the terms of employment. Employers and employees enter and exit work relationships less freely. Seniority-based replaces performance-based compensation, and incentives to "put in time" replace incentives "to do one's best."

Unions are an unavoidable evil that benefit a few people and harm many other people. Employees need the opportunity to organize when owners, administrators, and managers treat them poorly, but they should not have the power to monopolize the labor in an industry or coerce other employees to join a union. Unions raise their members' incomes in the short term, and increase the cost of products and services to other people. They cause enterprises to be less competitive, and eventually to relocate or fail. Decreasing tax rates in exchange for employee-directed savings and curbing the flow of illegal immigrants, practices discussed in Chapters 47 and 49, are better ways to strengthen middle-class incomes.

Governments should not implement production quotas, price controls, or rent controls, as they create surpluses and shortages. An example of this occurred when the federal government fixed the price of fluid milk for years. The high fixed price brought extra income to dairy farmers, but it also raised the cost of milk to consumers. It caused dairy farmers to vote for the politicians who supported the program, but it also cost taxpayers and consumers billions of dollars. Fixing the price of milk created ever-larger milk surpluses for years, which the government sold or donated in the form of powdered milk to foreigners. The government only stopped fixing these prices when the political costs of doing so exceeded the political benefits.

When elected officials interfere with free markets, such as placing tariffs on imported sugar, they favor their political supporters and harm their constituents. They understand the positive political effects and ignore the negative consequences of their actions. Unless restrained by a constitution, majorities and special interests act politically and do not further the well-being of the population.

Doing no harm requires governments to avoid taxing desirable activities—like work and enterprise—and enact an efficient tax-collection system. When governments tax work and enterprise, they increase unemployment, depress wage rates, decrease commerce, reduce economic growth, and lower living standards. When governments create complex tax laws and heavily tax their citizens, they force their citizens to spend billions of hours and dollars every year to comply with the regulations and incentivize them to find ways to avoid paying taxes.[277] Spending inordinate amounts of time and money each year to comply with and evade complex tax laws are not productive behaviors.

Restraining governments from implementing trade quotas, tariffs, and trade bans except to counter state predatory trade practices and for national security avoids harm. Merchants, enterprises, and countries lose comparative advantage and specialization opportunities when governments restrict trade. Unemployment increases and living standards decline.

Doing no harm also involves letting the markets determine interest rates. When central banks set interest rates below normal market rates for prolonged periods, they take income from savers and give it to borrowers, reduce capital formation, slow productivity improvement, and depress economic growth. They cause resource misallocations and speculative bubbles and magnify economic contractions.

Governments also should not routinely engage in deficit spending nor accumulate large debts. Deficit spending and large debts increase interest rates and debase currencies. They decrease productivity gains and economic growth, take resources away from investments in defense and infrastructure, and lower living standards. Governments also should avoid government-run social security systems, as such systems cause people to work and save less. I discuss a superior way to ensure that people have adequate money for retirement in Chapter 47.

Finally, governments should not spend large amounts on social safety nets, except to support the 7 to 9 percent of the population who cannot provide for themselves. Each dollar of social spending crowds out a dollar of savings, which in turn decreases our productivity and living standards, entraps able-bodied people in the social safety net, increases our deficit spending, and indebts our children and grand-children.[278]

Long-Term Incentives

Our short-term orientation that was advantageous in the earlier hunter-gatherer times challenges us today. It takes time to develop the infrastructure, businesses, and products that we require. Governments encourage a longer-term orientation by taxing short-term gains more than long-term ones. Such taxation discourages the short-term buying and selling of financial assets, makes next quarter's numbers less important to business leaders and shareholders, encourages public companies to report their numbers more accurately, and reduces the fluctuations of asset prices and the duration of economic downturns.

Short-term money supply and government taxing, borrowing, and spending adjustments harm long-term outcomes. They distort price signals and negatively affect enterprise and consumer behavior. They increase the use of resources, increase waste, and lower living standards. When governments interfere with businesses and markets, usually their objectives go unrealized and the real effects of the interference harm people in ways that few recognize.

Few people are aware of how much government really costs. Personal income, payroll, sales, and property taxes funded only two-thirds of the cost of our government for the last ten years. The other third was funded by corporate taxes, fees, other taxes, and over $10 trillion of debt. Most people have some sense of the first two-thirds because they pay these taxes but are relatively unaware of latter third and even more unaware that their children and grandchildren will bear this burden.

Taxes and fees on corporations increase the costs of our products and services. Corporations pay these taxes and fees, but they pass these expenses, and their billions and billions of dollars of lobbying and regulatory costs onto consumers. Complying with DOJ, DOL, FDA, USDA, OSHA, EPA, SEC, IRS, and countless other federal, state, and local agency regulations significantly increases the costs of our products and services. Lobbying and tax compliance expenditures alone comprise over 8 percent and 2 percent of GNP respectively.[279]

The Economic Freedom of the World Index (EFW) assesses the degree to which countries (a) protect private property, (b) evenhandedly enforce contracts, (c) have a sound currency, (d) maintain low taxes, (e) utilize free markets, and (f) permit free enterprise and free trade.[280] Countries with the highest EFW increase their living standards the fastest, while those with the lowest EFW that lack natural resources merely subsist. From 2000 to 2015, the U.S. EFW rank fell from 2nd to 16th place in the world![281] Not surprisingly, most people's living standards did not improve throughout this period.

Prudent Regulation – government laws, regulations, and oversight that do not play favorites; effectively enforced contracts; increased transparency; limited market share concentration; restricted risk-taking and leverage in ways that have proven advantageous over time; taxes on harmful externalities; taxes on short-term gains more than long-term ones; and the avoidance of production quotas, price controls, rent controls, price fixing, trade quotas, tariffs, taxes on labor, excessive social spending, easy money, and currency debasement. Playing favorites, ineffectual contract enforcement, poor and misleading information, monopolistic enterprises and unions, unrestrained leverage and speculation, harmful externalities, and most interference with free markets are antitheses of prudent regulation.

Chapter 38

Enterprise Competitiveness

Enterprises, like all of life, successfully compete or perish. They provide appealing and affordable products and services, offer employees competitive compensation, procure inputs at affordable prices, comply with government regulations, give shareholders compelling returns, and do all this a little better every year. If you think this is easy, think again.

By and large, people take enterprises for granted when we think more deeply about them, however, we realize they are the economic engines on which everything depends. Enterprises provide our food, housing, clothing, healthcare, education, public infrastructure, and transportation and communication systems. They equip our military and fund our research, government, social safety net, and the arts. They provide us with thousands of products and services worth trillions of dollars along with the means to purchase all these things each year. Every aspect of our life depends on our enterprises.

Some people dislike enterprise profits and support taxing and regulating them more. And, undoubtedly, there are some bad actors. Yet for the most part, our enterprises and those who they employ operate with integrity, honor millions of commitments, and do an incomprehensible amount of work each year.

Customer Focus

Enterprises exist foremost to fulfill people's needs and desires. They either create something that people value or cease to exist. While this seems obvious, many corporate leaders and employees lose sight of this objective, believing that businesses exist to provide them with high pay and benefits, time off, and a comfortable lifestyle. Warren Buffett wrote:

You need to carefully protect customer interests. When a company finds a way to save costs and cut expenses, they shouldn't pocket all the profits, but rather reduce their prices to protect customers' interests. This is an intangible virtue of reciprocity and if you do that more customers will come, they will buy more from you, and you will increase both your revenue and your profit.[282]

Entrepreneurs and business leaders must have their ear to the ground, interact with their customers, and understand their customers' interests. They must learn and imagine what their customers want and work relentlessly to bring better products, services, and value to them. Failure to focus on customers leads to the demise of many businesses.

A High-Performance and Improvement Culture

For enterprises to be competitive, leaders must cultivate cultures of performance and improvement. They must praise, recognize, reward, celebrate, and promote team members who work hard, improve their knowledge and skills, communicate well, are innovative, approach work with a can-do attitude, get the work done, uplift those around them, and bring in new business.

To succeed and remain competitive, leaders must make sure people know that dishonesty, fraud, unexcused absences, illegal and disruptive conduct, tardiness, poor workmanship, unfulfilled commitments, and insubordination are unacceptable behaviors. Team members of enterprises must understand that this conduct jeopardizes their employment. Furthermore, the leaders and team members must recognize that competitors are improving their own organizations, processes, products, and services and that the technology, methods, and products of today will not be the ones of tomorrow.

Minimal Overhead

Keeping the overhead of an enterprise low is one of the most important practices of enterprise competitiveness. What is overhead?

Overhead is *the labor and assets—the management, maintenance, human resources, accounting, information technology, marketing, sales, and clerical personnel, and the real estate, offices, buildings, and corporate vehicles—not directly involved in the creation of products and services.*

Usually enterprises start lean; the best-led ones remain so. Some enterprises start lean, become very profitable, and live large. Some leaders of these enterprises lose their discipline. They build large, imposing, beautiful corporate offices on prime real estate and use their burgeoning cash flows to fill these offices with people. They might even purchase expensive, nonproductive corporate cars and jets.

Using enterprise cash flows in this manner generally does not sink a business, but it does weaken it and enables unanticipated events to sink it. New competitors materialize, key customers are lost, and/or a recession occurs. Unexpectedly, sales decline, the enterprise has too much overhead relative to its sales, and it loses money. Rather than immediately cutting the overhead, leaders believe better times are just around the corner. They use the enterprise's remaining credit standing to cover their shortfalls with debt. The two Winning Practices that help enterprises avoid this fate are: (1) keeping overhead as low as possible and (2) cutting overhead quickly when sales decline.

Limited Leverage

Starting, operating, and growing enterprises takes a lot of capital. Businesses raise this money from investors, generate it from operations, or borrow it from suppliers, banks, and those who purchase their bonds. Leverage is a measure that compares companies' liabilities and assets.

Leverage is *the ratio of the value of a company's obligations to its assets.*

When enterprises assume obligations or debt judiciously, they improve their competitiveness and profitability. Using debt to purchase real estate, buildings, equipment, and inventory is useful and usually necessary to start and expand enterprises. While debt is used prudently to improve facilities, processes, offerings, market share, and returns, it also is used foolishly to support lavish lifestyles.

In theory, when returns on invested capital are greater than the interest rates associated with loans, enterprises should borrow. The more they borrow, the more profitable they become. In practice, however, this is true only when the seas are calm. When internal or external events shock enterprises and cash flows decline, too many liabilities reduce the ability of companies to capitalize on opportunities and may result in bankruptcy when their cash flows decrease. What constitutes "too much debt" varies from enterprise to enterprise. Oil and gas exploration companies with highly variable cash flows may find liabilities comprising 40 percent of their total assets problematic, while utility companies with highly predictable cash flows may find obligations comprising 80 percent of their assets to be no problem.

All companies should avoid using debt to cover routine expenses or expand unprofitable ones. Companies with inexperienced leaders should use less debt than those with experienced leaders as high levels of debt leave little room for error. When companies assume liabilities, it is advantageous to repay them faster than the depreciation of the underlying asset values. Otherwise, these companies will find themselves with more debt than assets.

Willing- and Able-Workforces

Enterprises flourish with willing and able workforces. Many things influence the drive and quality of workforces. Some of these include the state of our families, schools, and immigrants and the prudence of our government. While most people readily recognize the importance of the first three, they do not grasp the importance of prudent government.

Government policies that strengthen families, give children quality education, and provide young people access to part-time employment facilitate child development and strengthen the workforce. Government policies that allow illegal immigrants to stream into the country, tax labor, and enable people to freeload, however, adversely affect our workforce. I discuss each of these government policies in subsequent chapters.

New York State, where I lived the first 52 years of my life, was once the dynamo of our country's economy. It was home to many Fortune 500 companies, the quality of education and life in the state were excellent, and living standards steadily improved for most people. The state led and prospered in every way.

In the 1960s, however, the leadership of New York State government made several policy mistakes. Some of these mistakes enabled the public sector to unionize, extract too much from the economy, impose dues on union members, give substantial portions of these dues to their bosses, and influence the legislative process too much.

Union work rules hamper enterprise leaders from building high-performing and steadily improving workforces. They limit performance-based compensation, interfere with the discipline and termination of poorly performing employees, and force businesses to overcompensate poorer-performing and undercompensate higher-performing employees. They cause the high-performing employees to slow down or to work somewhere else. Union work rules precipitate cultures of mediocrity and raise the cost of products and services.

Unions negatively affect the private sector and adversely impact the public sector several times over. The negative effects of unions in the public sector are greater because public agencies have monopoly positions. No countervailing competition checks the increase in costs or the deterioration in the quality of the products and services associated with the unionization of public institutions.

Those who promote unions do so with the good-hearted intentions of protecting employees and raising middle-class wages and benefits. While unions shield their employees and improve their wages and benefits in the short term, they also create inefficiencies and divide management and labor in organizations. They force managers to reward seniority at the expense of merit, and in doing so, they further mediocrity, make enterprises less competitive, and frequently cause members to lose their jobs in the long term. Unions raise the prices of products and services and lower non-member living standards. Those who more critically consider the effects of unions ultimately realize that consumer losses and the eventual loss of employees' jobs, related economic activity, and related tax revenue more than offset members' short-term gains.

Inevitably, the cost of doing business in New York State increased on several fronts. Input prices, wages, utilities, and taxes all rose faster in New York State than other states. Then, company after company moved their headquarters, offices, and factories to other states and countries, and many of New York's brightest, most productive, and wealthiest people left the state.

Between 1964 and 2016, New York State's population declined dramatically relative to other states, as demonstrated by the 37 percent decline of its congressional delegation. And not only did New York's population decline relative to other states, but the fitness of its residents declined as well, becoming less entrepreneurial, skilled, and productive; poorer; more dependent on government; and older relative to the populations of other states.

Instead of leading as it once did, New York now lags most other states on many fronts. Government policies that gave too much power to the unions destroyed one of the greatest collections of companies ever assembled in the world, precipitated a steady deterioration in educational outcomes and infrastructure quality, and more than tripled the proportion of the population that depends on social programs.

When governments maintain competitive market structures, control the flow of immigrants into the country, enforce basic work standards, and provide adequate unemployment insurance, workers have protections, temporary support, and alternatives. Workers have little use for unions, and enterprises can avoid the dissension, higher costs, and mediocrity that accompany unions.

While we must give workers the right to organize because unions are the only way to check abusive leaders in enterprises, we should not give unions the power to force people to join them and pay dues to advance their political agendas. History demonstrates that enterprise fitness and economic growth are better in states with right-to-work laws like Arizona, Florida, Georgia, Idaho, Indiana, Iowa, Kentucky, Nebraska, North and South Carolina, Texas, and Utah, where unions cannot do these things.

If unions must exist, governments should prohibit them from organizing beyond the level of individual businesses. They should not be able to aggregate to the level of an industry or organize within the public sector. Just as corporations cannot collude and dominate markets, so unions should not collude or dominate labor markets. When this happens, they cause enterprises to lose competitiveness and oftentimes relocate their operations. They gain too much influence over elected representatives and corrupt the governing processes.

Governments are more representative of their citizens and less representative of special interests when campaign finance laws prohibit corporations, unions, foreigners, political action committees, and lobbyists from contributing to political campaigns. These entities should not exchange campaign support for favorable legislation, work rules, compensation, or other benefits. Elective officials should represent citizens—not corporations, unions, foreigners, political action committees, and lobbyists. Campaign finance laws that only allow citizens to make small contributions to fund campaigns serve us better.

Well-Developed Infrastructure and Enterprise-Friendly Policies

Governments enhance enterprise and reduce the number of people needing assistance when they build critical infrastructure and enact enterprise-friendly policies. Businesses flourish where needed services are most readily available, the cost of doing business is low, and regulations are sensible. Low-cost water, sewers, electricity, natural gas, telephone lines, high-speed Internet, and well-developed roads, airports, railroads, and ports further enterprise. Honest, prudent, and sensible laws and effective law enforcement and judiciaries facilitate business. While this is common sense, many governments do not do these things.

Lee Kuan Yew, the founder and longtime leader of Singapore, understood the importance of enterprise and an attractive business environment. His administration worked hard to build infrastructure and create and enact business-friendly policies. His administration's efforts brought Singaporeans rapidly growing living standards and transformed Singapore from one of the poorest to one of the wealthiest countries in the world.

Minimal Government Burdens

Enterprises flourish in environments of limited government, prudent laws and regulations, and low taxes. They wither in environments with lots of rules, slow bureaucratic processes, and high taxes. The difference between the two settings is the difference between competitiveness and uncompetitiveness, rising and falling government revenues, high employment and unemployment, and rising and falling wages.

Enterprise Competitiveness – the ability of businesses to interest enough customers to purchase their products and be viable, as facilitated by a focus on the customers, a culture of performance and improvement, little overhead, limited leverage, a willing and able workforce, well-developed infrastructures, enterprise-friendly policies, and minimal government burdens. Subsistence, stagnation, and decline are the antitheses of enterprise competitiveness.

Section VIII: Winning Practices of Government

Winning Perspectives

Truth
Causality
Scale
Evolution
Fitness

Human Nature
Culture
Periodic Disaster
Eco-Dependency

Winning Practices

Knowledge
Health
Thought
Integrity
Proactivity
Prudence
Excellence
Thrift and Investment

Affiliation
Decency
Understanding
Leadership
Teamwork
Improvement

Spouse Selection
Marriage
Responsible Parenting
Empowering Habit Formation

Universal Education
Parental Choice
Results-Oriented Education

Free Enterprise and Markets
Responsible Corporate Governance
Prudent Regulation
Enterprise Competitiveness

Government of the People
Powers, Prohibitions, and Structure
Freedoms, Rights, and Responsibilities
The Rule of Law
Inclusion and Meritocracy
Prudent Taxation
Financial Strength
Savings Accounts, Social Safety Nets
Consumer-Driven Healthcare
Assimilation
Peace Through Fitness
Sustainability

Chapter 39

Problems with Democracy

Government is the great fiction through which everybody endeavors to live at the expense of everybody else. [283]

—*Frédéric Bastiat*

For billions of years, the universe has subjected life to the rigors of competition. The will to live, compete for resources, and proliferate is inherent in life's DNA. This is true for simple as well as higher forms of life. It is true for bacteria, fish, flowers, wolves, and humans. It is also true for enterprises, nations, and cultures.

Governance and organization that further our individual and collective interests are essential to our ability to compete. To date, representative democracies have furthered these interests better than monarchies, dictatorships, and aristocracies, enabling large portions of populations to flourish.

Representative democracies are not without their problems, however, and they now face serious competition from an authoritarian, single-party government in China. History provides few examples of long-lived representative democracies. The Roman Republic, Iroquois Nation, Iceland, and the U.S. have had quasi-democracies for 200 to 500 years, but most democracies have lasted for less than 200 years.

Before discussing the Winning Practices of representative democracy, it is important that we understand some of democracy's major shortcomings. Only as we recognize these deficiencies can we mitigate them. Alexander Hamilton, a founding father and coauthor of the Constitution and *The Federalist Papers,* wrote:

It has been observed that a pure democracy, if it were practicable, would be the most perfect government. Experience has proved that no position is more false than this. The ancient democracies in which the people themselves deliberated never possessed one good feature of government. Their very character was tyranny; their figure deformity.[284]

Human Fallibility

The first problem with representative democracies is that most candidates for office size up their audiences and tell them exactly what they want to hear, whether true or untrue. They espouse what is popular, avoid what is unpopular, tout the benefits of policies, conceal the costs, and ignore the adverse effects.

Moreover, most people support candidates with whom they emotionally connect and identify, even if those candidates pass but a few litmus tests of their political party. Generally, people do not weigh the reputations, qualifications, past conduct, and accomplishments of the candidates. Lee Kuan Yew wrote:

> One person, one vote is a most difficult form of government. From time to time, the results can be erratic. People are sometimes fickle. . . . and in a reckless moment, they vote for a change for change's sake. . . .

> The easiest of appeals that can be made to [people] are simple, emotional ones, not economic development and progress and all these other things they do not understand, but simple things, pride in race, in language, in religion, in culture.[285]

Representative democracies only function well when citizens are well-informed and vote for the most qualified, competent candidates, and elective officials represent their constituents rather than their parties. We would never go to doctors who did not complete medical school and their required residencies or who put the interests of the medical community ahead of their patients. Yet we routinely support candidates who have little leadership experience, have few real-world accomplishments, and vote more than 90 percent of the time with the leadership of their party.

Conflicts of Interest

Few [people] have virtue to withstand the highest bidder.[286]

—George Washington

Conflicts of interest occur when people have self-interest that competes with their responsibility to their constituents. Elected officials who receive foreign, business, union, or other campaign contributions and then vote on legislation that affects the donors have serious conflicts of interest. Their self-interest to garner campaign contributions competes with their duty to advance voters' interests. Even when such conflicts of interest do not seem to harm the public, their mere presence should make us uncomfortable and cause us to eliminate them.

Conflicts of interest negatively impact the impartiality of government but also infiltrate the sources from which people learn about government and the world. News organizations and journalists, who select and spin the news to curry political favor and appeal to audience niches, partially and inaccurately deliver news. They betray the public trust. They distort people's perception of reality and people's judgment of candidates, officials, government, and policies.

Special Interests

Special interests are people and representatives of organizations who seek to persuade governments to serve their common interests. While special interests seem relatively benign, the legislative advantages and public resources that they gain from governments at the expense of the public is very harmful to people.

A dictator or monarchy is a special interest of one. An aristocracy is a special interest of a few. The Chamber of Commerce is a special interest of enterprises. The 1199SEIU is a special interest of healthcare workers. The NAACP is a special interest of African Americans. The Christian Coalition is a special interest of Christians.

We do not want governments to prevent those with common interests from meeting, socializing, and learning from one another, but we do want governments to be impartial to special interests. Special interests that provide government leaders with helpful information are benign. Those that give large sums or other forms of support to candidates and political action committees corrupt the government and hurt the public interest.

Lack of Accountability

One of the great challenges of representative government is accountability. When representatives obfuscate and enact convoluted legislation, people have trouble holding their representatives accountable for their actions. The Affordable Care Act of 2010 and our tax code provide excellent examples of unintelligible and convoluted legislation and regulation. When representatives of multiple levels of government share responsibility for initiatives and blame one another for poor outcomes, citizens have trouble holding their representatives accountable for their actions. Education is a case in point. When the federal, state, and local government representatives all have a role in it, they blame the poor results on one another.

Representatives Play Santa Claus

A lady asked Dr. Franklin, "Well, Doctor, what have we got, a republic or a monarchy?" "A republic . . . if you can keep it."[287]

—Benjamin Franklin

Government leaders love to play Santa Claus with the public treasury and credit. Such actions bring them political advantages and few negative repercussions. Each favor costs the public little and means a lot to the recipients. Recipients reward their benefactors during the next election. Former playwright George Bernard Shaw wrote:

A government that robs Peter to pay Paul can always depend on the support of Paul.[288]

The problem with political favors is that they reduce the effectiveness of the government, and their ongoing, cumulative cost ruins democracies. Representative tendencies to play Santa Claus increase taxes and debt. They feed and grow special interests, choke a country's economic engine, and lower people's living standards.

How long the favors and their adverse effects continue depends on the extensiveness of them and a country's economic vitality and credit worthiness. But whether they remain for a short or long time, their aggregate effects harm and bankrupt representative democracies.

Leaders Love Power

Dominance advantages life, and dominating tendencies reside in the DNA of leaders. Leaders love power—authority, wealth, and influence. They always want more of it, especially when their testosterone is high and/or egos large.

Governments give leaders authority, public resources, and influence. Unless institutionally constrained, many leaders abuse their power and misuse public resources. Philosopher and political economist Adam Smith wrote:

The [people] of system, on the contrary, is apt to be very wise in [their] own conceit; and is often so enamored with the supposed beauty of [their own ideal plans] of government, that [they] cannot suffer the smallest deviation from any part of [them]. [They go] on to establish [them] completely and in all [their] parts, without any regard either to the great interests, or to the strong prejudices which may oppose [them]. [They seem] to imagine that [they] can arrange the different members of a great society with as much ease as the hand arranges the different pieces upon a chess-board.[289]

Frank Herbert makes an astute observation about people who cloak themselves with compassion, think they know best, covet power, and really do not believe in democracy. In *God Emperor of Dune*, he wrote:

Liberal bigots are the ones who trouble me most. . . . Scratch a conservative and you find someone who prefers the past over any future. Scratch a liberal and find a closet aristocrat. It's true! Liberal governments always develop into aristocracies.[290]

Short-Term and Group Thinking

Another problem with representative democracies is that most leaders and people think short-term. Short-term thinking is characteristic of human nature but also of our relatively short representative terms. Two-, six-, and four-year terms give Congressional Representatives, Senators, and Presidents corresponding time horizons.

Rather than find real solutions to our problems, our leaders avoid taking risks, pretend to address our issues, and only deal with many of our problems once they become crises. They increase the police in poor neighborhoods rather than fix underperforming schools. They borrow money from the next generation rather than limiting their spending. They allow illegal immigrants to pour into the country rather than controlling the border and admitting immigrants legally.

Few of our leaders and representatives consider and vote in accordance with the long-term interest of their constituents. They absorb the thinking of the political party to which they belong and support short-term fixes. Many citizens are no different about voting in accordance with their long-term interests. Many voters no longer appreciate the need to constrain central governments, the long-term consequences of many policies, and the manipulative nature of candidate appeals.

Majorities Dominate Minorities

Another problem with democracy is that majorities marginalize minorities. We associate and empathize with those who are most like us and distance ourselves from those most different from us.

Rather than enact a pure democracy, our founders created a constitutional, federated, representative democracy. They conceived a Constitution, Bill of Rights, three branches of government, and federal, state, and local levels of government. They created a system of government that periodically requires the consent of the people. In doing these things, our founders formed a system of government that reflects the preferences of the majority and protects minorities.

With enough constitutional restrictions, institutional checks, individual protections, and honest and decent people, representative democracy does work. It aggregates citizen preferences and provides feedback to leaders better than any other form of government. In the next 12 chapters, I discuss the divisions, checks, and protections necessary to assure that our leaders' self-interests do not usurp the public interest.

While we have made several improvements to our Constitution and government, which have expanded the promise of equality before the law to all citizens, we have forgotten the importance of many divisions, checks, and protections, and have allowed our government to grow into a poorly functioning colossus with many special interests coopting the public interest.

To recreate a government of the people, we must appreciate and respect our Constitution, the complementary roles of the three branches and three levels of government, and our laws. We must have access to factual and balanced news and teach our children the practices that yield the best results.

Problems with Democracy Summary

Human Fallibility – the tendencies for leaders to tell their constituents what they want to hear and make emotional appeals and for people to respond to many appeals that are not in their long-term best interests.

Conflicts of Interests – circumstances where people's self-interest competes with their responsibility to their constituents.

Special Interests – groups that seek favors from government.

Lack of Accountability – the tendency for government officials to avoid problems, controversy, and responsibility for their inaction and actions.

Representatives Play Santa Claus – the tendency for government officials to use the public treasury and credit to do favors for their supporters, continuously increase taxes and debt, and suppress the growth of people's incomes.

Leaders Love Power – the tendency for many leaders to abuse their power and misuse public resources.

Short-Term and Group Thinking – the tendency for people to consider what happens in the next week, month, or year and absorb the thinking of the groups to which they belong.

Majorities Dominate Minorities – the tendency for large numbers of similar people to associate with one another and dominate smaller numbers of people who are different from them.

Chapter 40

Government of the People

Government is not benevolence. It is force—dangerous when despotic and welcomed when evenhanded, representative of its citizens, and restrained!

For most of history, the boldest, strongest, and ablest men and women ruled. Allied with other leaders, they used force, public resources, and alliances to maintain their authority. This was the natural order until the Athenian democracy and Roman and American republics. One needs only to read some early American history, the Articles of Confederation, and the Constitution of the United States of America to grasp the significance of the creation of the American government.

The drama of American democracy unfolded on a sparsely populated, resource-rich, remote continent. Highly intelligent, well-educated, and pragmatic business people played the leading roles. Hundreds of thousands of determined souls, who had been subjected to years of hardships and tyrannical indignities, made up the remaining cast. Sensing their historic opportunity and risking everything, this cadre of leaders and hearty souls created a government superior to any past one, enabling people to enjoy previously unimagined freedom and living standards. Two centuries later, Carl Sagan wrote:

When we consider the founders of our nation. . . . we have before us a list of at least ten and maybe even dozens of great political leaders. They were well educated. Products of the European Enlightenment, they were students of history.

They knew human fallibility and weakness and corruptibility. They were fluent in the English language. They wrote their own speeches. They were realistic and practical, and at the same time motivated by high principles. They were not checking the pollsters on what to think this week. They knew what to think. They were comfortable with long-term thinking, planning even further ahead than the next election. They were self-sufficient, not requiring careers as politicians or lobbyists to make a living. They were able to bring out the best in us. They were interested in and, at least two of them, fluent in science. They attempted to set a course for the United States into the far future—not so much by establishing laws as by setting limits on what kinds of laws could be passed.[291]

Our founders were not perfect, but they were sturdier, more visionary, and more realistic than most current-day leaders. They were well-schooled in the Athenian and Roman democratic and republic experiences, the European monarchies and aristocracies, and English jurisprudence. They distrusted power and concentrations of it, and they understood the importance of social cohesion and fitness. They considered the effects of their actions over generations and were willing to make short-term sacrifices for long-term gains. The willingness of their primary leader, George Washington, to disperse and relinquish power was almost unprecedented in history and critical to the formation of our government.

Our founders mistrusted power and sought to create a government "of the people, by the people, and for the people." They did this by grounding the American government in the citizenry, states, and three federal branches of government rather than in divine authority, royalty, aristocracy or party, the military, or a powerful central government. They did this by first creating a Constitution, a permanent delineation of the institutions, powers, and procedures of the federal government and the rights of the citizens for all to reference, defining standards of conduct, and empowering a free press to expose their misconduct. As Thomas Jefferson wrote, they thought a good government:

Shall restrain [people] from injuring one another, shall leave them otherwise free to regulate their own pursuits of industry and improvement, and shall not take from the mouth of labor the bread it has earned.[292]

Our founders separated all levels of government from religion, enterprise, and the press and the federal government from the state governments. They conveyed specific powers to the federal government and left all remaining power to the state governments. They defined the architecture, functions, and processes of the federal government and guaranteed basic rights. They sought a uniform application of law rather than the capricious rule of government officials. They created processes to make leaders compete for office and remove unlawful ones from office.

While this government enabled previously unimaginable levels of freedom and prosperity superior to any the world had seen, it was also imperfect. Despite prescribing many citizen-friendly innovations that yielded spectacular results, it treated Native Americans dishonorably, permitted African American slavery, and prohibited women from voting. Subsequent leaders and justices defined individual rights, abolished slavery, empowered women to vote, and outlawed discrimination by age, gender, race/color, ethnicity, and religion.

Unfortunately, not all the changes that subsequent leaders made have been beneficial. Due to a poor understanding of human nature and history, responding to temporary crises, and seeking political advantage, some of the changes have curtailed practices that our founders put in place to protect us from ourselves. One particularly detrimental change ended the state legislatures' appointment of U.S. Senators, another reinterpreted the Constitution's "general welfare" clause, and others violated legislative, executive, and judicial separations of power.

A Constitution

Our founders had no illusions about human nature and sought to constrain the leaders of our government. One way they did this was by defining our federal government in our brief, easy-to-understand Constitution. Thomas Jefferson wrote:

> In questions of power, let us hear no more of trust in men [and women], but rather bind them down from mischief with the chains of the Constitution.[293]

Time has taught us the importance of well-conceived governments from their outset, as the start of a government is the one opportunity to advantageously define the structure and processes of government, qualifications for citizenship, and requirements to hold office. The birth of a government provides the best chance to specify the amendment and impeachment processes. Once governments form, most elected officials want to expand their power and politicize every government action.

Generally, people perceive the short-term effects of actions but not the long-term ones. This tendency causes politicians and special interests to promote constitutional changes and legislation on the basis of the intended, short-term effects. Only a wisely crafted constitution and adherence to it enable people to avoid manipulation by representative and special interest. Changes to our Constitution must always be made cautiously and thoughtfully. The devil we know is often better than the one we do not know, and we only learn of the long-term effects of changes after they are made.

I cannot emphasize enough the importance of a well-conceived constitution and citizens' dedication to it. Constitutional representative democracies have their problems, as do all forms of government, but well-conceived ones and strict leader and citizen adherence to them mitigate many of these problems. Alexander Hamilton wrote:

If it be asked, "What is the most sacred duty and the greatest source of our security in a Republic?" The answer would be, "An inviolable respect for the Constitution and Laws—the first growing out of the last. . . . A sacred respect for the constitutional law is the vital principle, the sustaining energy of a free government."[294]

Our founders understood the Constitution was imperfect and that it would need amending periodically, but they also knew it provided extremely important restraints on government and should not be easy to change. Article V of the U.S. Constitution states:

The Congress, whenever two-thirds of both houses shall deem it necessary, shall propose amendments to this Constitution, or on the application of the legislatures of two-thirds of the several states, shall call a convention for proposing amendments, which in either case, shall be valid to all intents and purposes, as part of this Constitution, when ratified by the legislatures of three fourths of the several states, or by conventions in three fourths thereof. [295]

The procedure gives us time to consider a change thoroughly and assures widespread support for it. With the advantage of hindsight, however, perhaps our founders set the bar for changing the Constitution a little high, as only 27 amendments have been made to the Constitution in 220 years. The difficulty of amending the Constitution became a challenge during the Great Depression, and it led to the rise of judicial activism. Several examples of judicial activism appeared in Figure 5 in Chapter 2.

Judicial Activism occurs when judges base their rulings on political considerations rather than the facts, laws, and the Constitution.

We want to avoid judicial activism because majorities of the elected representatives of our population, not a few judges, are the only ones who should enact policies that affect us all. And once judicial activism starts, it snowballs. A few changes to the amendment process would lead to a few more amendments, less judicial activism, and a greater rule of law. The changes might include altering: (1) the amendment process of the Constitution from "whenever two-thirds of *both Houses* shall deem it necessary" to "whenever two-thirds of *either House* shall deem it necessary," (2) the ratification requirement from "when ratified by the legislatures of *three-fourths* of the several states" to "when ratified by the legislatures of *two-thirds* of the states," and (3) the approval process of Supreme Court justices as described in the next chapter.

Dispersing and Checking Power

If shielded from competition and unchecked, governments and bureaucracies grow. They promulgate edicts and red tape, consume resources, and suppress enterprise. Many of their leaders, arrogant and separated from the consequences of their actions, advance their interests at the expense of their constituents. The founders of our country understood these tendencies and took extraordinary precautions to disperse power to check them. James Madison wrote:

> The accumulation of all powers, legislative, executive, and judiciary, in the same hands, whether of one, a few, or many, and whether hereditary, self-appointed, or elective, may justly be pronounced the very definition of tyranny.[296]

A government of the people separates (a) government and religion, (b) the executive, legislative, and judicial branches of government, (c) government and the press, (d) government and enterprise, and (e) federal and state governments. It delineates things that the governments cannot do and procedures that it must follow. Smaller scale and decentralized governments and organizations connect people to the consequences of their actions.

Separation of church and state prevents government leaders from exercising ecclesiastical authority, religious leaders from exercising secular authority, and any one religion from obtaining favored status. Guaranteeing freedom of worship and prohibiting religious discrimenation creates competition among religious groups, furthers pluralism, and causes religious leaders to be less exploitive and more considerate of their members.

Creating separate legislative, executive, and judicial institutions to develop, administer, and judge the constitutionality of laws gives citizens recourse and incentivizes government officials to treat people better. Legislators create more constitutional laws. The Executive Branch applies the laws more uniformly. Judiciaries nullify unconstitutional laws and executive actions, protecting citizens from abuses of power.

The Bill of Rights and a free and responsible press check government power by directly prohibiting certain actions, scrutinizing government activities, and keeping everyone informed. The right to bear arms makes it more difficult for governments to wield power unlawfully. The right to due process and a trial by a jury of one's peers make it harder for governments to detain and silence opposition.

Other important divisions and checks include: (a) separation of the power to appropriate and spend money, (b) separation of power to declare and prosecute wars, (c) separation of the military into several branches, (d) creation of three military academies to train officers in different branches, (e) separation of the functions of the military, foreign espionage, and law enforcement, (f) giving the Legislative Branch power to impeach the leaders of the Executive Branch, (g) giving the Judicial Branch power to judge the constitutionality of legislation, and (h) giving the Executive Branch power to veto legislation.

Just as government and religious alliances are undesirable, so are government alliances with industries, corporations, and labor unions, as each alliance creates conflicts of interest, special interests, and abuses of power.

The separation of federal and state governments is one of the most important checks on federal power. Those who control the military and police have an inordinate amount of power, and this separation disperses this control. Initially, our federal government raised an army, each colony had its own militia, and the cities and towns handled law enforcement. While this has changed some over time, the federal government still controls the major defense forces, states have some control over the National Guard and Reserves, and local governments continue to handle most of the law enforcement. Our state governors with their many powers and resources also make it difficult for a president or military leader to take control of the country.

Another important reason to separate federal and state authority and give many powers to the states is that citizens can reside in any state but not in any country. The ability for citizens to choose state residency creates competition among the states. States cannot be oppressive and retain their citizens for long. The current migration of citizens from the high-taxed states to low-taxed ones, like from New York to North Carolina, South Carolina, or Florida and from California to Oregon, Nevada, or Arizona demonstrate this.[297] Competition among states incentivizes them to be lawful and efficient and treat their citizens well.

On the other hand, people's inability to reside in different countries enables national governments to neglect and misuse citizens. Unconstrained national governments corrupt easily. Dwarfing other powers, they encroach on their citizens' freedom and propagate inefficiency. North Korea, Somalia, and Sudan are examples of corrupt, inefficient, and oppressive governments.

The more countries disperse governance among competing units, the more their governments are innovative, efficient, and effective. The more countries concentrate governance, the more corrupt, inefficient, and ineffective governments are. The Soviet Union and the U.S. in the 1950s and 1960s provide excellent examples of the differences in the evolutionary dynamism of centralized and decentralized governments.

A Republic with a Bicameral Legislature

The State governments will, in all possible contingencies, afford complete security against invasions of the public liberty by the national authority. Projects of usurpation cannot be masked under pretenses so likely to escape the penetration of select bodies of [representatives,] as of the people at large. The legislatures will have better means of information.[298]

—Alexander Hamilton

Our founders formed our country to protect the colonies from a superior outside force. Reluctant to cede any more power than necessary to a central government, they created a republic comprised of thirteen colonies. They understood that central powers grow over time and realized the need to disperse and contain power.

The federal nature of our government and its bicameral legislature distinguish it from many other governments. Most people recognize that our bicameral legislature provided a way for our founders to resolve the proportional representation concerns of smaller and larger colonies. Smaller colonies did not want larger colonies to dominate them, and larger colonies thought they should have a greater say than the smaller colonies. A bicameral legislature addressed both concerns. It gave the small colonies equal representation in the Senate and the large colonies proportional representation in the House.

Our early bicameral legislature did something else, however, that few people recognize. It enabled the states to check the power of the federal government. While the residents of each state have always elected their Representatives in the House, they have not always elected their U.S. Senators. State legislatures chose the U.S. Senators until 1913. In giving state governments power over federal legislation, limiting the scope of the federal government, and disincentivizing the formation of powerful special interests, this practice was pure genius. U.S. Senators who were selected by state legislators limited federal borrowing, taxing, spending, and mandates. Their policies limited us less and enabled our living standards to increase faster. Since we removed this constitutional restraint, one can see from Figure 3 in Chapter 2 that the federal government has grown much faster than the economy.

Contrary to current practice, were we to require the federal and state governments to completely self-fund their operations, we would make our representatives more accountable. Mixing sources of income and governing functions makes it difficult to determine which level of government is responsible for the successes, shortcomings, and failures of policies.

Supermajorities and Minority Accommodation

The most effective government and policies align with the preferences of large portions of the population. Monarchs, dictators, aristocracies, oligarchs, and national parties do not create the most effective governments and policies. They have limited intelligence and feedback, and their self-interests dominate the public's interests.

The genius of prudently conceived democratic republics is that as they disperse, limit, and check power and cause representatives to act on the preferences of their citizens. Furthermore, the better ones consider the preferences of supermajorities and provide accommodation to the losing minorities. Passing laws with simple majorities makes sense when the laws are relatively inconsequential. It does not make sense, however, when enacting taxes, spending the public's money, and creating consequential institutions, laws, and policies. To have as many people against as for a tax plan, spending plan, or law is divisive.

For a population to flourish and have social harmony, a large portion must consent to the government's laws, policies, and activities. Requirements for double and triple supermajority support assure that larger portions of a population support a government. Double supermajority requires two-thirds of both Houses of the Legislative Branch to approve legislation. A triple supermajority requires two-thirds of both Houses and two-thirds of the entire population via national referendum to approve legislation before it can become law.

If we (1) required double supermajorities for routine legislation and declarations of war and triple supermajorities for borrowing, taxing, and spending laws, and (2) expected winning majorities to make some accommodation for losing minorities as is the practice in Switzerland, we would have legislation that reflected a much greater proportion of the preferences of our population. We would have less government, a better-quality government, greater freedom, and an improved quality of life.

Journalist and author Walter Lippmann wrote in the *New-York Tribune* in 1940:

The predominant teachings of this age are that there are no limits to [people's] capacity to govern others and that, therefore, no limitations ought to be imposed upon government. The older faith, born of long ages of suffering under [people's] dominion over [people], was that the exercise of unlimited power by [people] with limited minds and self-regarding prejudices is soon oppressive, reactionary, and corrupt.[299]

We have lost much of the wisdom of our founders, as we have not lived under oppressive rulers and governments nor been taught it in our schools. Well-functioning governments of the people have been especially rare and short-lived throughout history. They require visionary, knowledgeable, and pragmatic founders and well-informed, vigilant citizens. Government leaders, the military, the press, and the citizenry must respect well-conceived constitutions, separations of power, and the rule of law.

Government of the People – *(a) representative federal, state, and local governments, where constitutions define the governments, (b) the governing power is dispersed among and checked by different branches and levels of government, (c) federal, state, and local government responsibilities are clearly defined, distinct, and separate, (d) the federal and state governments are required to maintain balanced budgets except in time of war, and (e) the federal government has a bicameral legislature and utilizes double supermajorities to pass laws and go to war, and triple supermajorities to approve borrowing, taxing, and spending legislation. Monarchies, dictatorships, aristocracies, and the rule of special interests are antitheses to a government of the people.*

Chapter 41

Powers, Prohibitions, and Structure

Most governments throughout history deny their citizens basic freedoms and rights, ignore their preferences, confiscate their wealth, and oftentimes misuse them. Preventing governments from doing these things requires the implementation and vigilant defense of several practices.

Our founders understood that a government with too much power is our master rather than our servant. James Madison wrote:

If [people] were angels, no government would be necessary. If angels were to govern [people], neither external nor internal controls on government would be necessary. In framing a government which is to be administered by [people] over [people], the great difficulty lies in this: you must first enable the government to control the governed; and in the next place oblige it to control itself.[300]

Thus, our founders built our government upon a constitution, divided it into three branches, created a bicameral legislature, only gave it a few specified powers, and created an ingenious system of checks and balances. And in doing these things, our founders successfully constrained our federal government and secured our freedom from 1887 to 1913.

Specified Federal Powers

Unconstrained, central governments grow and grow. Our founders constrained our federal government in many ways, one of which was to grant it only a few specified powers in the Constitution. Unfortunately, the Supreme Court shredded this constraint with its reinterpretation of the Constitution's "General Welfare" clause in the 1930s. Central governments serve their populations best when they only govern activities that transcend states and offer services that state and local governments cannot effectively provide, such as:

1. Securing people's lives, rights, and property;

2. Enforcing contracts;

3. Overseeing interstate communication and transportation infrastructures;

4. Ensuring competitive market structures;

5. Maintaining the integrity of the banking system, financial markets, and currency;

6. Establishing lending standards and limiting public and private indebtedness;

7. Providing some funding for university research, education, and extension systems;

8. Establishing standards that protect employees, consumers, and the environment;

9. Taxing and mitigating harmful externalities; and

10. Providing some funding for the exploration of space.

For the first 125 years of our nation's history, our leaders abided by the constitutional constraints placed on the federal government like the state legislature selection of U.S. Senators, the few specified federal powers, and the separation of legislative, executive, and judicial functions. But this changed in the 20th century with the 17th Amendment and the New Deal and War on Poverty legislation. We would be freer, carry less debt, and enjoy higher living standards if we reinstated these constitutional constraints, allowed the states to govern themselves in a manner of their choosing within the federal framework, and created a social safety net more like the one described in Chapters 47 and 48.

Letting the people of each state govern themselves within the federal framework would allow different types of state governments to evolve and provide people with options. For example, if states were responsible for their residents' healthcare, welfare, and retirement systems, they would evolve many different types of systems, and people who want certain types and mixes of systems could move to the state that provided them. The services, cost, and quality of the programs would reflect the majority's preferences of each state, and each state would offer an affordable, desirable mix of programs or lose people to other states.

Prohibitions

Along with granting the federal government a few specified powers, our Constitution prohibits arbitrary searches, arrests, and detainments, and cruel and unusual punishment. Most of us take these prohibitions for granted as we have never experienced life without them. Many governments, especially those with a single-party system, routinely search, arrest, detain, and torture people. They do this without warrants from elected judges, without evidence, and without charging people with a crime. Understanding the importance of due process, Alexander Hamilton wrote:

> The creation of crimes after the commission of the fact, or, in other words, the subjecting of [people] to punishment for things which, when they were done, were breaches of no law, and the practice of arbitrary imprisonments, have been, in all ages, the favorite and most formidable instruments of tyranny.[301]

Our Constitution also forbids many forms of discrimination, recognizing that we should include, exclude, and reward people on the basis of their knowledge, skills, and accomplishments—things they can control—and not on the basis of their age, gender, race/color, or ethnicity—things they cannot control.

While our government has always prohibited arbitrary searches, arrests, and detainments, and more recently discrimination by age, gender, race/color, ethnicity, and religion, we would be wise not to extend these prohibitions to foreign combatants and immigrant applicants. Our government's legitimacy does not arise from foreigners, and we do not need to treat them as if it did. We want limited numbers of refugees and larger numbers of immigrants who support our Constitution and laws, speak English, and have needed skills. We do not want immigrants who intend to commit, or have committed, violent acts or those who are likely to depend on our social safety net.

Communists were a problem during the Cold War. White supremacists, black supremacists, and radical Muslims are a problem today. Like Australia, Canada, Switzerland, and many other countries, we should admit immigrant applicants based on at least one of their parents being an American and their desirability, or in other words, their (a) willingness to uphold our Constitution and laws, (b) ability to speak English, (c) possession of needed work skills, and (d) ability to support themselves. Furthermore, law enforcement agencies must vigorously remove foreigners and immigrants who violate our laws or advocate violence. These people should not be altering our government, civil order, or way of life.

Another challenge is the adverse effects of wealthy people and special interests on citizen preferences. The best solution to this problem is to reduce the influence of special interest groups by decreasing the size and scope of the federal government and many of the state governments. A second-best solution is to prohibit all forms of support for political campaigns except for small individual contributions. Such donations should also be limited per candidate per election cycle to a sum equal to five times the minimum wage per hour. Foreigners, corporations, unions, and other organizations should not be supporting our candidates. We should also limit candidate campaigns to the three months before the election. Candidates and citizens must be able to speak freely, but we also must curtail the self-serving and harmful influence of special interests.

Legislative, Executive, and Judicial Branches

Rather than have one leader or branch of government create, enforce, judge, and interpret laws, our founders created three branches and separated these functions. They created the Legislative Branch comprised of a House of Representatives and Senate to enact laws, levy taxes, appropriate money, and declare war. They created the Executive Branch to defend the country, administer the laws, collect the taxes, spend the money, and conduct foreign policy. They created the Judicial Branch to judge the constitutionality of the laws and resolve interstate disputes.

Our founders gave each branch powers over the other branches. They gave the Legislative Branch the power to: (a) create laws, (b) confirm Executive Branch and judicial appointments, (c) review and monitor Executive Branch agencies, policies, and actions, (d) impeach the president, department officials, and judges, (e) override presidential vetoes, and (f) ratify treaties. They gave the Executive Branch the power to: (a) veto legislation, (b) preside over the Senate, (c) execute the laws, (d) appoint judges, (e) conduct foreign policy, (f) negotiate treaties, and (g) issue pardons. They gave the Judicial Branch the power to: (a) judge the constitutionality of legislation, (b) interpret laws, and (c) settle disputes between states.

Since the beginning of the 20th century, our government has repeatedly violated the separation of powers in our Constitution by creating government agencies like the IRS, OSHA, and EPA with the power to promulgate, enforce, and adjudicate regulations. Placing these three functions in the same agency invites the abuse of power and leaves citizens little recourse when it occurs.

House of Representatives

Our founders set up the House of Representatives to represent the people. The number of Representatives in the House varied over the years until the Reapportionment Act of 1929, which capped the number at 435. Representatives must be at least 25 years old, a resident of the state they represent, and a U.S. citizen for at least 7 years. Representatives serve two-year terms.

The people of a state have representation in the House in proportion to their population. State governments define the districts of their Representatives. By federal law, they must construct districts reflective of the state population that do not discriminate against minorities. In most states, the dominant political party gerrymanders the districts to maximize the number of contests their party wins.

Two changes that would make our Representatives more responsive to the people are term limits and apportioning the voting districts more objectively. Limiting our Representatives to 3 two-year terms would reduce influence of special interests, as roughly one-third of our Representatives would always be completing their last term and would have less need to kowtow to special interests. Requiring states to apportion voting districts along municipal boundaries in such a manner as to minimize the cumulative length of the district boundaries would cause the election outcomes to be more reflective of the citizens' preferences within the district.

Senate

Our founders set up the Senate to prevent larger populated states from dominating smaller ones and enable the states to check federal power. Two Senators from every state, or a total of 100 Senators, comprise the Senate. Senators must be at least 30 years old, a resident of the state they represent, and a U.S. citizen for at least 9 years. Senators serve six-year terms.

As noted in previous chapters, each state legislature elected its two Senators for the first 124 years of our country's history. The 17th Amendment to the Constitution changed this practice in 1913. Now, the citizens of each state elect the two Senators every six years. Senate terms stagger, so challengers contest one-third of the Senate seats every two years.

Two changes that would reduce the ability of special interests to influence Senators and enable the states to check federal power are rescinding the 17th Amendment and limiting each Senator to two six-year terms. State legislature-selected Senators want to limit the federal government's infringement on state powers; state resident-selected Senators want to play Santa Claus with public revenues and credit. Senate term limits would decrease the influence of special interests as half of the Senators would always be completing their last term and would not need to pander to special interests during their second six-year term in office.

The Senate has the power to impeach or remove from office the President, Senators, Representatives, and Justices. The Constitution is vague on what constitutes unacceptable, impeachable behavior. Amending the Constitution as the historian Brion McClanahan suggests would resolve the ambiguity. The non-italicized words in the following passage are those originally written in the Constitution and the italicized words reflect McClanahan's suggested changes.

> The President, Vice President, and all Civil Officers of the United States, shall be removed from office on impeachment for, and conviction of, Treason, Bribery, Incapacity, *Negligence, Perfidy, Peculation, Oppression, Violation of the Oath of Office, Abuse of Power,* or other high crimes and misdemeanors *including violation of the laws of the United States, or the laws of the several states.*[302]

If we clear up this ambiguity, our presidents would find it riskier to lie and/or act unconstitutionally. They would be less inclined to (a) use executive orders and federal agencies to enact regulations, (b) make appointments that require congressional consent without congressional authorization, (c) selectively enforce laws, (d) use federal agencies against their political opponents, and (e) conduct military operations in other countries without congressional authorization.

Executive Branch/Council

The President leads the Executive Branch and our country. If something happens to the President, the Vice President replaces him or her. Candidates for President and Vice President must be natural-born U.S. citizens, residents of the U.S. for at least 14 years, and at least 35 years of age. They can serve 2 four-year terms.

The President also serves as the Commander-in-Chief of the military and is responsible for our country's foreign policy. It is his or her responsibility to "preserve, protect, and defend the Constitution" and "faithfully execute our laws." The Vice President supports the President, stands ready to assume his or her duties, and can break tie votes in the Senate.

Our founders set up the Electoral College to elect our president and vice president. Each state has the same number of Electors in the College as Representatives and Senators. The District of Columbia has the same number of Electors as the least populated state. Citizens choose Electors based on who the Electors support for the presidency. Electors do not have to vote for the candidates to whom they pledge support but they usually do. Candidates win electoral votes state by state, and states award these votes either in proportion to the votes or a winner-take-all basis. The determination of the number of Electors gives smaller states disproportional influence and the winner-take-all approach gives the larger states disproportional influence. These procedures also provide the states with political majorities that fluctuate among elections and exert tremendous influence over election outcomes.

Initially, our Executive Branch was comprised of just 3 departments: State, Treasury, and War. As recently as 1950, it was comprised of 8 departments: Agriculture, Commerce, Defense, Interior, Justice, Labor, State, and Treasury. Currently, 15 departments and numerous other organizations comprise the Executive Branch. The departments are: Agriculture, Commerce, Defense, Education, Energy, Health and Human Services, Homeland Security, Housing and Urban Development, Interior, Justice, Labor, State, Transportation, Treasury, and Veterans Affairs. The other federal organizations are: The National Security Council, Office of Management and Budget, Council of Economic Advisors, Council on Environmental Quality, Office of U.S. Trade Representative, Office of National Drug Control Policy, and Office of Science and Technology Policy. The total federal government workforce—federal employees, contractors, grant employees, active-duty military, and postal carriers—is around 9.1 million.[303]

One of the weaknesses of our current government is that when the President, Senators, and Representatives serve four-, six-, and two-year terms, respectively, there exists little incentive for long-term planning and problem-solving. While the shorter terms ensure that the leadership regularly obtains the consent of the citizenry, they handicap the federal government's ability to focus, plan, and then complete long-term projects. One president initiates domestic and foreign policies and programs that move the country to the right, and the next one supports policies and programs that move the country to the left. One president allies our country with one group of counties and opposes another group, and the next president allies us with the latter group and opposes the former.

Switzerland, one of the oldest and best functioning democracies in the world, is led more by a council rather than a president. The Swiss President is like the chair of a corporate board of directors and the Federal Council is like the corporate board. The Swiss President and Federal Council do not veer so much to the right and left. Their approach is more moderate, incremental, and long-term oriented.

To transform our Executive Branch into a Swiss-style executive council, we should create 5 ten-state groups, one in the Northeastern, Southeastern, North Middle, South Middle, and Western regions of the country. Citizens of each of these 5 regions would elect 1 of the 5 Executive Councilors every 4 years. Then, the Executive Council members would select the country's President, Secretary of State, Secretary of Defense, Attorney General, and Secretary of Treasury from council members every 2 years.

The President of the Executive Council could only be president for two years. His or her executive actions would need the support of two of the other councilors on an ongoing basis, and the four other councilors could remove him or her from office at any time. If the president were incapacitated or died, the Secretary of State would act as president until the unrepresented region elected a new councilor. Although the presidents of the Council would have shorter tenures than our current president, their actions would be more moderate and long-term oriented because of the collegial nature of the council and a reduction in the need to pander to a political base.

Along with creating an Executive Council, we would be wise to specify minimum qualifications for councilor candidates. The quality of our leaders affects over 320 million of us directly and the lives of billions of other people indirectly. Knowledgeable, visionary, responsible, able, lawful, and ethical leaders make all the difference. Well-vetted, proven leaders more successfully lead large, complex organizations than poorly vetted, unproven ones. Our need for effective presidents is too great to take chances on unproven leaders. Candidates for councilor positions should be offspring of two U.S. citizens, at least 35 years of age, and have been a governor of a state or CEO of one of our country's largest 1,000 for-profit and nonprofit organizations for at least four years.

Once created, an Executive Council could streamline the federal government and return many current federal functions back to the states. This would be advantageous to us and future generations. Of the 15 existing departments and 7 other executive organizations, only the following 10 departments and 2 executive organizations engage in necessary federal functions and deliver essential public goods.

Commerce, Defense, Environment, Infrastructure, Justice, Labor, National Security, State, Trade, and Treasury, and

The Council of Economics and The Council of Science and Technology.

To these departments and councils, we could add an advisory Council of Presidents that would be comprised of the former presidents who would engage in strategic and long-term planning for our country by developing five-year and ten-year plans. They would share their work with the leaders of the three branches of government and the unclassified portions of it with the public. Securing one's place in the world and achieving a high quality of life takes real leadership, something our country has lacked for years. Regarding the extraordinary transformation of Singapore from a third- to first-world country, Lee Kuan Yew wrote:

> It is not by accident that we got here. Every possible thing that could have gone wrong, we tried to preempt. That is how we got here, that is why we have substantial reserves. Because if we do not have reserves, the moment we run into trouble. . . . we have got nothing.[304]

Executive Branch Prohibitions and Emergency Powers

I indicated how 20th and 21st century presidents had expanded presidential and federal power and frequently violated their oath to preserve, protect and defend the Constitution in Chapter 2. To encourage our presidents to uphold their oaths of office and discourage these tendencies, Brion McClanahan suggests that we amend the Constitution to limit executive authority more definitively:

The President of the United States shall not issue proclamations, orders, statements, or decrees of a legislative nature or in
regard to foreign policy; create commissions, committees,
boards, regulatory agencies, or appoint "dictators," "czars," or
any other non-elected government official, organization, or
agency unless prescribed by the Constitution for the United
States; submit a budget for the Executive Branch of the
government of the United States; withhold non-classified
information from the Congress of the United States; or
undertake any acts of legislative or judicial nature.[305]

While this amendment would be a step in the right direction, our
history suggests that sometimes presidents need to exceed their
constitutional authority to lead the nation out of a crisis. Certainly, the
Civil War, WWI, the Great Depression, WWII, 9/11, and the Great
Recession are six examples of circumstances where a president needed
additional powers. To accommodate this need, we could amend the
Constitution to enable two-thirds of both Houses of Congress to grant a
president well-defined emergency powers for 90 days in the event of a
crisis. Such an amendment would allow presidents to deal with crises
constitutionally.

The Supreme Court

The Supreme Court interprets laws, judges the constitutionality of
laws, and resolves interstate disputes. It is a body of nine justices. The
President nominates each Justice. The Senate Judiciary Committee
interviews them, and the Senate has the power to confirm or reject them.
Supreme Court Justices serve for life or until they choose to retire. The
Constitution does not specify any qualifications for Supreme Court
Justices.

We could improve the functioning of the Supreme Court by amending the Constitution to require Justices to (a) be a child of two U.S. Citizens, (b) be at least 35 years of age, (c) have a Juris Doctor degree, (d) have been a state or federal judge for at least four years, (e) have been affirmed by a two-thirds Senate supermajority, and (f) retire from office at age 75. These qualifications and this approval procedure would decrease the likelihood of the appointment of activist judges—those who ignore the Constitution, and in effect, legislate policy from the bench. These changes, along with the previously mentioned ones, would make it easier to amend the Constitution and decrease the tendency for the Supreme Court to move from one end of the political spectrum to the other as new judges replace former ones. It would also prevent some older, failing judges from remaining on the Court.

Public Infrastructure

Along with securing our lives, freedom, rights, and property, it is important for central governments to provide critical public goods and infrastructure. Public goods are products and services that, when provided, everyone receives and no one purchases. Defense, roads, and navigable rivers are public goods. I discussed public goods in Chapter 35. Adam Smith wrote of the importance of public goods and infrastructure:

Good roads, canals, and navigable rivers, by diminishing the expense of carriage, put the remote parts of a country more nearly upon a level with those in the neighborhood of the town. They are, upon that account, the greatest of all improvements. They encourage the cultivation of the remote, which must always be the most extensive circle of the country. They are advantageous to the town, by breaking down the monopoly of the country in its neighborhood. They are advantageous even to that part of the country. Though they introduce some rival commodities into the old market, they open many new markets to its produce.[306]

Our federal government has done well providing necessary public goods and infrastructure, and we have benefited immensely from them. As we freed our government from several constitutional restraints, however, it has come to do many things that state and local governments and private enterprise can do more efficiently. For example, the federal government's involvement in healthcare, primary and secondary education, and social services has not brought greater efficiencies, lower costs, or improved service. In each case, I would argue the federal government's involvement has had the opposite effects. These and most other services are more advantageously delivered by states, counties, and the private sector where there exists competition among the public and private entities. The presence or absence of competition affects the efficiency, cost, and quality of services over time. The provision of these services advantages politicians and disadvantages the taxpayers and recipients of the services. Providers and recipients grow dependent upon them and reward the candidates who support them. The government taxes, borrows, and spends incomprehensible sums to pay for them. Our living standards decline, and future generations have large debts thrust upon them.

Powers, Prohibitions, and Structure – (a) giving a few defined powers to the federal government and broad powers to the state governments, (b) forbidding some government actions outright, (c) defining the architecture and processes of the Legislature, Executive, and Judicial branches of government, and (d) defining the House, Senate, Executive Council, and Supreme Court. Oppression, bureaucracy, and corruption are antithetical to powers, prohibitions, and structure.

Chapter 42

Freedoms, Rights, and Responsibilities

A government is the most dangerous threat to [people's] rights: it holds a legal monopoly on the use of physical force against disarmed victims. [307]

—*Ayn Rand*

Many of us who have been fortunate enough to live in a developed democracy the last few decades take for granted our freedoms and rights. We cannot imagine governments that restrict their citizens' movements, suppress their speech, confiscate their property, falsely accuse citizens of crimes, torture them, and sentence them to years of hard labor. We cannot comprehend that some governments prohibit the education of women, discriminate against and sometimes kill minorities, and cause their citizens to flee their countries. These governments exist and have existed throughout all of history.

The freedom, rights, and prosperity that we enjoy are precious given that the default form of government is tyranny, and the default human condition is subsistence. They result from hard-fought battles, the wisdom of our ancestors, divisions of power, and restraints on government. The freedoms and rights that we enjoy give us choices and opportunities. They enable us to author our lives. Securing them took centuries of blood and sacrifice. Russian-born American novelist, philosopher, and playwright Ayn Rand wrote:

At first, [people were] enslaved by the gods. But [they] broke their chains. Then [they were] enslaved by the kings. But [they] broke their chains. [They were enslaved by their birth, by their kin, by their race.] But [they] broke their chains. [They declared to all their brothers and sisters that people have] rights which neither god nor king nor other [people] can take away from [them], no matter what their number, for this is the right of [people], and there is no right on Earth above this right. [308]

Our freedoms, rights, and prosperity are tenuous, though. They are not even safe from decent, well-meaning people. Consider what well-intentioned Communists, Socialists, and Islamic leaders did to the U.S.S.R, Eastern Europe, Cuba, China, North Korea, North Vietnam, Venezuela, Iran, Afghanistan, and numerous other countries. Consider what well-meaning Western leaders have done to Greece, Puerto Rico, and Detroit? Compare the five-page U.S. Constitution and Bill of Rights with the 95,000 pages of the 2016 Federal Register.[309] Or consider that 100 years ago, federal, state, and local government spending was 10 percent of GNP and now it is roughly 36 percent.[310]

Mindful of past bad governments and prescient of future ones, constitutionalist and statesman Daniel Webster wrote:

> Good intentions will always be pleaded for every assumption of authority. It is hardly too strong to say that the Constitution was made to guard the people against the dangers of good intentions. There are men [and women] in all ages who mean to govern well, but they mean to govern. They promise to be good masters, but they mean to be masters.[311]

Freedoms, rights, and prosperity carry responsibilities. They do not just happen. Our forefathers and mothers did their part, but the past and a piece of paper do not secure people's freedoms and rights through time. Everybody wants freedoms, rights, and prosperity, but only a responsible citizenry retains them. Accompanying every freedom and right is a responsibility that we must assume and teach to our children. Otherwise, our freedoms and rights slip away.

Freedoms

We cannot actualize when our parents, schools, government, and culture too tightly dictate our behavior or function so poorly that we have limited opportunities. We only realize our potential when we have choices and opportunities.

People in government like to say that "perception is reality." While this may be true in politics, it is not true regarding our well-being, which depends on reality that in turn depends on the integrity of our people and institutions. Freedom of speech and association provide us with accurate information and help keep our government, citizens, and organizations honest. Benjamin Franklin wrote:

Freedom of Speech is a principal pillar of a free government; when this support is taken away, the constitution of a free society is dissolved, and tyranny is erected on its ruins.[312]

Free speech also helps us find our way and rediscover the path when we lose it. Alan Barth, the former *Washington Post* editor and journalist, wrote:

Thought that is silenced is always rebellious. Majorities, of course, are often mistaken. This is why silencing of minorities is necessarily dangerous. Criticism and dissent are the indispensable antidote to major delusions.[313]

Free speech and association are fundamental freedoms that people should enjoy, but they do not give us permission to ferment hatred and violence. We have the freedoms to assemble, petition the government, and worship, but we only have these freedoms as we do not encroach on others' freedoms. "Our freedoms end where others' freedoms begin."

Four freedoms that the Constitution does not assure are the freedoms of residency, travel, marriage, and procreation. While we have enjoyed these freedoms to date, we should list them in our Constitution to preserve them for future generations.

Rights

Along with the previously listed freedoms, we enjoy the rights to buy, sell, and use property as well as the rights to enter into contracts, engage in enterprise, and choose our place of employment. Although the Constitution does not state the last two rights, they enable us to earn our livelihoods, create desirable products and services, and purchase these products and services at affordable prices. We should also list these rights in our Constitution.

Our Constitution and government guarantee us the rights of self-defense, to possess arms, and to a speedy trial by our peers. The reasonableness of the right of self-defense is self-evident. Were we to lack this right, we would not be here today. Ayn Rand wrote:

> The necessary consequence of [people's] right to life is [their] right to self-defense. In a civilized society, force may be used only in retaliation and only against those who initiate its use. All the reasons which make the initiation of physical force an evil, make the retaliatory use of physical force a moral imperative.

> If some "pacifist" society renounced the retaliatory use of force, it would be left helplessly at the mercy of the first thug who decided to be immoral. Such a society would achieve the opposite of its intention: instead of abolishing evil, it would encourage and reward it.[314]

The right to possess firearms to defend ourselves is a logical extension of self-defense in an age where those who threaten us have firearms. Thomas Paine wrote:

> Arms discourage and keep the invader and plunderer in awe, and preserve order in the world as well as property. . . . Horrid mischief would ensue were the law-abiding deprived of the use of them.[315]

The right to bear firearms has become controversial because it is unconditional as it appears in the Constitution, and what was appropriate in pioneer life is less applicable now. Today, this right must depend on demonstrated irresponsibleness. To possess firearms, people must be of sound mind, of voting age, free of a criminal record, and trained in the proper storage and use of weapons. People who are not all these things should not possess firearms.

To resolve the controversy surrounding the right to bear firearms, it would help if those opposing this right understood that people living in rural areas with slower police response times have a real need for arms, and if those supporting this right, realized that irresponsible people routinely use firearms to kill innocent people in poorer, urban areas.

A commonsense solution that accommodates both these challenges is to limit the possession of firearms to those who fulfill the above criteria. Both banning guns and letting everyone have guns do not make sense. Forbidding guns renders many people defenseless against thugs, drug dealers, and terrorists; prohibiting machine guns, bazookas, stinger missiles, and army tanks—weapons that are unnecessary for self-defense—makes everyone securer. Were guns only sold at licensed outlets and under the condition of satisfactory background checks, fewer guns would end up in the hands of irresponsible people, and responsible people could have guns for self-defense and recreational use.

Along with the right to bear arms, a speedy trial by one's peers is another important right. Many rulers have appointed magistrates to falsely convict their opposition throughout history. Requiring authorities to presume innocence, charge the accused with a crime, and satisfy a high burden of proof before a jury of one's peers help prevent this abuse of power.

The rights to retain at least half our earnings and gift half our estates are two other rights that would be advantageous to state in our Constitution. We receive from and must give to our larger community. When communities expect too much of their members, they oppress them. When they expect too little, they weaken the communities. Over the long term, people flourish as they keep and direct at least half of what they earn and accumulate. As governments guarantee these rights to their citizens, they incentivize people to work and optimize the fitness of their populations.

People who learn, work hard, take risks, and accumulate wealth generally do us great services. Consider Andrew Carnegie, Thomas Edison, Henry Ford, Bill Gates, Steve Jobs, Sergey Brin, Larry Page, and Jeff Bezos. These people have enriched us collectively more than they enriched themselves. They die like the rest of us and typically give their wealth to advance the public interest. They establish universities, research centers, hospitals, museums, and recreational facilities. They fund education and research projects, habitat preservation, and countless other worthwhile things.

Responsibilities

Upon forming a government that grants us individual freedoms and rights, we must remember that evolution suggests life is more about the fitness and well-being of natural habitats and communities than about ourselves. As the character Spock states in *Star Trek II: The Wrath of Khan,* we must remember that:

The needs of the many outweigh the needs of the few.[316]

We are responsible to the many, and for this reason, our freedoms and rights carry corresponding responsibilities. Nelson Mandela, civil rights leader and former president of South Africa, wrote:

I have walked that long road to freedom. . . . I have taken a moment here to rest, to steal a view of the glorious vista that surrounds me, to look back on the distance I have come. But I can only rest for a moment, for with freedom come responsibilities, and I dare not linger, for my long walk is not ended.[317]

If we wish to speak, associate, and exchange information freely, then we must do these things in a respectful and nonviolent manner. If we want to assemble and worship freely, then we must do these things in a civil, noncriminal, and non-treasonous way. If we want to be able to petition our representatives and authorities, then we must not inundate them with petty concerns.

If we desire to live and travel freely, then we must do this lawfully. If we want to marry freely, then we must treat our spouse considerately and lawfully. If we wish to procreate freely, then we must responsibly care for our children from infancy through their adolescent years.

If we want the right to vote, then we must support honest, competent, and capable leaders. If we wish to buy, sell, and use property, we must use and maintain it meritoriously and sustainably. If we want the assurance of lawful agreements, then we must abide by them. If we value the right to engage in enterprise and choose our work, we must honorably do these things.

If we want the rights to self-defense and to bear arms, we must not harm others unnecessarily or leave our weapons unsecured. If we value speedy trials by our peers, then we must tell the truth and willingly serve on juries. If we had the right to retain half our income and gift half our estates, then we would need to use and disperse our wealth responsibly.

We enjoy constitutional prohibitions against arbitrary searches, arrests, detainments, and cruel punishments, but we also have the responsibility to act lawfully. We enjoy protections against age, gender, race/color, ethnicity, and religious discrimination, but we also have the obligation to treat others fairly.

Our freedoms and rights give us the opportunity to author our lives and pursue our dreams, and they are essential to our fitness and well-being. But we only enjoy these freedoms, rights, and protections as we act responsibly, vigilantly defend them, and raise responsible children.

Citizenship Qualifications

Except for those who are intimately acquainted with nature and science, few of us realize that our basic survival unit is not the individual, family, or species, but our country. We further our fitness and well-being as we strengthen and improve our country. While it is advantageous to have allies and assist foreigners, it is more beneficial to take care of our fellow citizens first and help others from positions of strength.

To maintain and improve the quality of our country, we must raise able, well-adjusted children and think more carefully about who becomes a citizen. Typically, our hearts want to invite those in need while our heads seek those most needed. The prudent course is to naturalize a mix of the two.

When people join a highly successful group, it is advantageous for them to undergo an acculturation process. This is beneficial to both the new entrants and the group. New entrants benefit from learning the group's practices, and the group benefits from the entrants' vitality and ideas. If the new entrants do not learn the group's practices, everyone loses.

With an inexhaustible supply of desirable immigrant applicants, it makes no sense to permit people to enter our country illegally or allow people who are unlikely to integrate well into our country. Leaders who want the political support of large illegal immigrant groups and their benefactors and children are the ones who support such immigration.

Except for limited numbers of refugees and those seeking political asylum, prudent people realize that it is advantageous to invite immigrants who have a high probability of contributing to our population and harmonizing with our culture. Prudent people seek immigrant applicants who (a) have not committed criminal or terrorist acts, (b) pledge to uphold the Constitution and laws of the United States, (c) have employment, skills that are in short supply or significant personal wealth, (d) pass a basic English fluency test, (e) agree to live in a community where his or her ethnicity is underrepresented, and (f) are willing to undergo a seven-year acculturation process.

Voter Qualifications

Along with citizen qualifications, we should also think about voter qualifications. Voting is a privilege. Only people who are citizens of the country, 18 years and older, in good standing in their community, not receiving welfare and food stamps, and who can verify their identity should have the right to vote.

Legal and illegal immigrants who are not yet citizens have much to learn. Welfare recipients live at the expense of others. Prisoners have been irresponsible. The interests of these people conflict with the interests of the responsible, hardworking citizens who support themselves and fund the government. Nature does not allow groups with large numbers of freeloaders—those who never contribute and only take from a group—to exist for long. Only those who contribute to making the pie should have a say in its division.

Finally, people must know that the election process is fair and honest for them to accept the outcomes of elections. A process requiring citizens to have photo identification when voting furthers the fair and honest results. If we expect people to have photo identification when they buy alcoholic drinks or stay at a hotel, then it is reasonable to expect it when they vote.

Weighting the Votes of Parents

One of the problems with democracies is that the "one person, one vote" over-weights the interests of the elderly and underweights the interests of children. Anyone looking at our end-of-life healthcare, Medicare, and Social Security expenditures and our beginning-of-life health and childcare expenditures could not help but conclude that seniors have too much power and children too little. To rectify this situation, we should give every parent with children under the age of eighteen one-and-one-half votes. This would provide children better representation. Lew Kuan Yew wrote:

> I am not intellectually convinced that one [person], one vote is the best. We practice it because that's what the British bequeathed us. . . . We would have a better system if we gave every person over the age of 40 who has a family two votes, because he or she is likely to be more careful, voting also for his or her children. He or she is more likely to vote in a serious way than a capricious young person under 30. . . . At the same time, once a person gets beyond 65, then it is a problem.

Between the ages of 40 and 60 is ideal, and at 60 they should go back to one vote, but that will be difficult to arrange.[318]

The current "one adult, one vote" scheme causes our representatives to cater to seniors more than to children. Were parents able to represent children's interests, preschool and full-day kindergarten programs would be more available. We would be less present- and more future-oriented.

Freedoms, Rights, and Responsibilities – delineating in the Constitution's specific citizen freedoms, rights, and responsibilities, as well as citizen and voter qualifications; giving parents an extra half vote for each child under the age of 18; and creating an order where citizens can self-actualize, prosper, and maximize their collective fitness;

Where the freedoms and rights include: self-defense; possession of arms; speech; the purchase, sale, and use of property; residency; work; travel; marriage; notification of offense upon arrest; presumption of innocence and a high burden of proof of guilt; speedy trials by a jury of one's peers; and the retention of half of one's earnings and estate;

Where the responsibilities include: telling the truth; abiding by agreements; treating others respectfully, lawfully, considerately, and honorably; responsibly raising our children; supporting honest, competent, and capable leaders; using property meritoriously and sustainably; and living, working, and dispersing our wealth honorably;

Where the qualifications for immigration include: not having committed criminal or terrorist acts; pledging to uphold the Constitution and laws of the United States; having employment, skills in short supply, or significant wealth; passing a basic English fluency test; agreeing to live in a community where one's ethnicity is underrepresented; and undergoing a seven-year acculturation process;

Where the voter qualifications include: citizen of the country in good standing, 18 years and older, a responsible taxpayer, and with proof of identity; furthermore, parents receive an additional half vote for each child under the age of 18. Oppression and irresponsibility are the antitheses of freedoms, rights, prohibitions, and responsibilities.

Chapter 43

The Rule of Law

Constitutional, easily understood, widely supported, and consistently applied laws enable people to live freely and prosper.

Throughout the modern world, people desire democracy. They associate it with the good life. As Oxford, Harvard, and Stanford historian Niall Ferguson astutely suggests, however, it is property rights and the rule of law that bring freedom and prosperity. It is well-conceived laws, law enforcement, and a justice system that deters crime and creates civility. Compare the Spanish approach in Latin America with the English one in North America, Australia, and New Zealand in the 18th century or visit Hong Kong, Singapore, Taiwan, post-WWII Germany, Japan, and South Korea to affirm this insight. Niall Ferguson writes:

> It was an idea that made the crucial difference between British and Iberian America—an idea about the way people should govern themselves. Some people make the mistake of calling that idea "democracy" and imagining that any country can adopt it merely by holding elections. In reality, democracy was the capstone of an edifice that had as its foundation the rule of law—to be precise, the sanctity of individual freedom and the security of private property rights, ensured by representative, constitutional government.[319]

Our founders had a great reverence for our Constitution and just and wise laws. They understood that freedom and workable orders are only possible with them—that governments must (a) limit their power, (b) codify citizens' rights, (c) define acceptable and unacceptable conduct, (d) establish standards, (e) enact procedures for owning property and other activities, (f) define how they fund themselves, and (g) establish a reciprocity and penal system.

Laws must be impartially and consistently applied, however, to be just. They must be legislatively originated, constitutional, easily understood, few, and widely supported. John Locke viewed laws as:

Standing rules, indifferent, and the same to all parties.[320]

Constitutional, Easily Understood, and Widely Supported

It will be of little avail to the people, that the laws are made by [people] of their own choice, if the laws be so voluminous that they cannot be read, or so incoherent that they cannot be understood: if they be repealed or revised before they are promulgated, or undergo such incessant changes, that no person who knows what the law is today, can guess what it will be tomorrow.[321]

—James Madison

Who would have ever believed that James Madison's words written in 1788 would describe the state of our laws in the United States today? Nevertheless, this is the case Our Federal Register of laws was more than 95 thousand pages in 2016.[322] Our laws are voluminous, incoherent, and sometimes unconstitutional. The representatives who create them no longer author, read, or understand them, and our Supreme Court no longer judges their constitutionality or resolves conflicting interpretations of many of them.

Frequently, our laws are knee-jerk reactions to the bad behavior of a few people or organizations, and they intentionally advantage some constituencies. Using public offices and resources to reward political supporters is unconstitutional, unlawful, unconscionable, and ruinous. Once it starts, it snowballs and erodes our freedom and living standards. Using the legislative and executive pens to attempt to rid the country of bad behavior and force desirable outcomes is naïve and foolish. Governments only need to enact laws and regulations when people are unable to sue to correct injustices. David Brooks wrote:

The failures have been marked by a single feature: reliance on an overly simplistic view of human nature. Many of these policies were based on the shallow social-science model of human behavior. Many of these policies were proposed by wonks who are comfortable only with traits and correlations that can be measured and quantified. They were passed through legislative committees that are as capable of speaking about the deep wellsprings of human action as they are of speaking in ancient Aramaic. They were executed by officials that have only the most superficial grasp of what is immovable and bent about human beings. So of course, they failed. And they will continue to fail unless the new knowledge about our true makeup is integrated more fully into the world of public policy, unless the enchanted story is told along with the prosaic one.[323]

Requiring all laws and policies to have a two-thirds supermajority support would yield better laws. It would generate fewer, more intelligible, and widely supported laws and regulations. Using simple majorities to select government leaders who have limited tenure is one thing but using them to enact legislation that affects everyone for decades is problematic.

When there are no laws, the strong oppress the weak, and the ruthless take advantage of the decent. When there are too many narrowly supported complex laws, people selectively comply with them, and they waste people's time and resources. When the laws are constitutional, easily understood, and widely supported, people respect them, live freely and civilly, and have opportunities.

Collegial Improvement

The universe, Earth, and life continuously change, and consequently, some of our laws and policies must also change. If we do not adapt fast enough to our environment and life's changes, we become less fit. If we adjust too quickly to them, we risk precipitating our demise.

Thus, natural selection has created populations of people with conservative, moderate, and progressive inclinations. Collegial improvement recognizes that people with each of these tendencies add value to the improvement process.

Collegial Improvement is the practice of progressives, conservatives, and moderates appreciating one another's roles in the optimization of change and working together to find the best path forward, where: (a) progressives identify potential improvements and push for their implementation, (b) conservatives defend the status quo and identify the adverse effects of the proposed changes, and (c) moderates pilot the proposed changes, examine the effects, tweak the changes to minimize and mitigate any adverse impacts, and support the changes that prove advantageous.

When conservatives, progressives, and moderates each perform their roles during the legislative process, we preserve the most advantageous laws, pilot potential improvements, and legislate beneficial laws. We obtain fairer, more effective, and more widely supported outcomes for individuals, the larger group, and the environment in the short and long term. Appendix C lists several conservative and progressive positions and the syntheses of them utilized in this book.

Legislatively Originated

For thousands of years of human history, monarchs, dictators, and priests held the power, made the laws, and often arbitrarily applied the laws. Over time, we took power from these leaders and devised a better system of government. We separated the creation of laws from their execution and interpretation. We created legislative bodies, representative of the people, to enact laws and regulations. We created executive departments to administer them, and we created courts to judge their constitutionality and interpret them.

Our Constitution specifies these separations but several Congresses, Presidents, and Supreme Courts in the 20th and 21st centuries ignored the separations. The Justice Department, National Labor Board, Internal Revenue Service, and Environmental Protection Agency violate these three separations of power. Several recent Presidents also have violated these separations by creating laws via executive order, allowing the Executive Branch to interpret poorly written laws and promulgate thousands of pages of regulations. Several of these unconstitutional violations are listed in Figure 4 in Chapter 2.

If we are to have constitutional, easily understood, widely supported, and consistently enforced laws, then we must insist that the Supreme Court enforce the separation of powers requirement in the Constitution and invalidate the laws that the Executive Branch issues. We must demand that the Legislative Branch impeach and the media expose those who violate these separations.

Piloted, Beneficial, and Stakeholder-Oriented

Pilots of laws are critical to the improvement of laws because they provide the opportunity to discover their effects on a small scale before implementing them on a large one. It would be beneficial for our representatives to pilot all new laws as a standard practice in a few states before implementing them nationally. Upon completing the pilots, bipartisan committees could interview the affected parties and assess the short- and long-term effects of the laws. Then, they could recommend national implementation, modify the laws, or reject them.

How much better would it have been to pilot Welfare, Medicare, Medicaid, and the Affordable Care Act and learn of their ill effects before thrusting the programs on the entire nation? Unfortunately, our representatives are interested in gaining special interest and popular support more than they are in implementing effective policies.

Cost-benefit analysis is another important aspect of the legislative process. Laws and regulations that create more costs than benefits are undesirable. Many times, the only way to know this before their widespread implementation is to pilot them and measure their real costs and benefits. Laws that have only slightly greater benefits than costs are not desirable because people overestimate the benefits and underestimate the costs of laws and regulations, and laws and regulations have unapparent adverse cumulative effects.

Just as the best enterprises solicit input from their stakeholders, the best governments seek input from those most affected by proposed laws, as when they considered feedback from nutritionists, manufacturers, retailers, and consumers during the creation of nutritional labeling laws. People are also more apt to comply with laws and regulations when they help shape them, and those most impacted by the laws and regulations foresee the positive and negative consequences of them better than most lawmakers.

Stakeholder inclusion depends on our representatives, especially those in the majority. It depends on their willingness to solicit input from all the affected groups and not just those that politically support them. When those in the majority fail to seek stakeholder input, the minority representatives and the press must advocate for an inclusive process.

Impartial and Consistently Applied

Fed up with the arbitrary rule of monarchs, nobility, popes, cardinals, and sheriffs in Europe, our founders sought to create a government where no one was above the law, and no person or group received special treatment. While our founders did well to eliminate the arbitrary rule by a few, they did not eliminate the arbitrary rule of white men over women, Native Americans, and African Americans.

We only corrected this disparate treatment with the passage of the Emancipation Proclamation in 1863, which freed the slaves; the 13th Amendment, which banned slavery in 1865; the 15th Amendment, which guaranteed people of all races and color the right to vote in 1870; the 19th Amendment, which gave women the right to vote in 1919; and the Civil Rights Act of 1964, which outlawed discrimination and segregation on the basis of age, gender, race/color, and ethnicity.

Discrimination is a difficult problem. Universally, people are comfortable with those most like themselves. It is in our DNA and usually culturally reinforced. Discrimination is too subtle for laws to curtail it completely. Laws can only eliminate the most blatant forms of discrimination. Overcoming people's discriminatory tendencies requires ongoing education and strong cultural prohibitions.

It took a civil war, numerous amendments to the Constitution, civil rights demonstrations, and some 200 years to create a set of laws that apply equally to everyone. And just as we made some real inclusion progress, many of the formerly excluded groups became angry about the past, turned against the Constitution, and pressured the government to treat women, African Americans, and Hispanics more favorably than white males. John Kennedy's and Lyndon Johnson's Executive Orders 10,295, 11,246, and 11,375 required government agencies and private employers to advance women and minorities regardless of merit. Other executive orders and Section 342 of the 2010 Dodd-Frank Act require government agencies to give substantial portions of its business to companies owned by women and minorities. The Grutter v. Bollinger Supreme Court decision in 2003 upheld the common practice of preferentially admitting minorities to universities.

The coalition supporting government favoritism toward women, African Americans, and Hispanics also supports government favoritism toward illegal immigrants. Thus, we now have laws that provide Medicaid, food stamps, nutritional assistance (WIC), public housing, unemployment benefits, financial aid, government loans, and tax credits to illegal immigrants who have children in the U.S.[324]

Not only have our government leaders applied laws to their citizens unequally, but they also have exempted themselves from some of our laws. They exempted themselves from the Affordable Care Act until there was a public outcry, and they now exempt themselves from the Freedom of Information Act, investigatory subpoenas, the requirements to post worker rights notices and train employees about worker rights, and prosecution for retaliating against employees.[325] Since the beginning of the 20th century, our leaders also have used the law to advantage unions, attorneys, seniors, farmers, corporations, and many other groups. And they illegally, unjustly, and routinely use the law, public treasury, and public credit to punish their political opposition and reward their political supporters.

Besides impartially enacting laws, our representatives should only pass laws that they can and will consistently enforce. Laws that are unenforceable, not enforced, or inconsistently enforced diminish people's respect for the law. One example of this involves the federal law to arrest and deport illegal immigrants. In the last term of the Obama administration, the federal government selectively enforced this law, and numerous cities defied it.[326] A second example is the federal law prohibiting the sale and possession of marijuana. The federal law stands, yet states openly defy it by legalizing its sale, possession, and use. Selective enforcement of laws erodes the civil order. As people observe others violating laws, they start to ignore the ones that inconvenience them.

Justice

Along with easily understood, widely supported, and consistently applied laws, the rule of law requires just resolution of violations of the law. Justice involves the expeditious and accurate determination of the innocence or guilt of people, the effective administration of penalties for violations of laws, and making injured parties whole as much as practically possible.

Fair, accurate, and expeditious process, or due process, requires: (a) authorities to inform the accused of their violations of the law, (b) impartial judges to try defendants within a reasonable time, (c) courts to utilize proven processes to determine a defendant's innocence or guilt, (d) prosecutors to define the crime and present evidence of it, and (e) judges or a jury of one's peers to decide a defendant's innocence or guilt.

Unfortunately, our current system of justice allows too much lawlessness to go without penalty, especially in our inner cities. It incarcerates too many people, rehabilitates too few, is expensive, and permits countercultures of idleness, sex, drugs, and crime to flourish in prisons.

Justice also is as much about making injured parties whole, rehabilitating people, and deterring future crime as it is about arresting people and determining their innocence or guilt. Requiring nonviolent offenders to make injured parties whole is one of the more advantageous forms of punishment as it permits the offenders to remain with their families, avoids incarceration costs, and compensates victims.

We would also find it advantageous to send more nonviolent, youthful offenders to a military academy-type detention center, where they would be safe, disciplined, and mentored, and learn empowering habits and skills. Discipline, caring, practical instruction, and positive role models are absent in the lives of so many of those who break the law.

Piloting a system of progressive fines and corporal punishment for some violations of the law and the death penalty for large-scale drug dealers also might prove beneficial. Singapore, a city-state of over 5.5 million people, uses these approaches. The country has some of the lowest crime, drug abuse, and incarceration rates in the world. [327] Singaporeans feel safe throughout the city-state, day or night, and very few are ever victims of crime.

Subjecting people, particularly young people, to the debilitating culture of idleness, crime, sex, and drugs in our prisons is crueler and more counterproductive than a system of progressive fines and judiciously administered corporal punishment. We could test the validity of this idea by giving those convicted of nonviolent offenses a *choice* between the approaches. If people choose fines and corporal punishment over prison sentences, we would have evidence that they do not consider judiciously-administered corporal punishment to be a cruel and unusual punishment. If rehabilitation rates improved and crime rates decreased, we would have evidence that these penalties are more effective deterrents of some crimes than prison sentences.

Periodic Review

Along with uniformly and consistently applying the laws to everyone and justly resolving violations of the law, the periodic review of laws and regulations furthers the rule of law. Well-crafted laws and regulations create awareness and help people form new habits. Once people develop this awareness and the new habits, the usefulness of many laws and regulations pass. Other times, laws and regulations result from political motivations and overreaction. If our laws and regulations had sunsets and expired after five or ten years, then we would not have such an incomprehensible and sometimes conflicting body of laws.

Reviews of laws by different people at a different time is an effective way to terminate unnecessary, poorly crafted laws and regulations and eliminate ongoing enforcement and compliance costs. Continuously simplifying and improving our laws and regulations gives people and businesses time to engage in more productive activities than spending time complying with them.

Judicious Litigation

Just as referees of games must ensure competition is fair, safe, and civil to keep the play moving, so governments must maintain a fair, safe, and civil order to permit people to live their lives freely. While it is in everyone's interest to punish bad actors and deter bad behavior, it is in no one's interest to burden people with thousands of pages of laws and regulations.

Judicious litigation enables plaintiffs to take trespassers to court. It allows them to receive compensatory remuneration from those who harm them. It empowers plaintiffs to litigate, but also penalizes frivolous litigation as too little or too much litigation is undesirable. Too little litigation permits incompetence, carelessness, and duplicity. Too much litigation unnecessarily harasses people; increases the cost of insurance, products, and services; makes people and enterprises risk-averse and suppresses their activity; and causes businesses to move offshore.

Our justice system must penalize plaintiffs who bring petty and fraudulent lawsuits to discourage frivolous litigation as well as compensate defendants who are falsely accused. It must require plaintiffs of senseless suits to pay the defendant's and court's expenses. To find the most advantageous level, a commission of retired judges and business leaders could review litigation activity in the country every couple of years and set guidelines for frivolous suit penalties, plaintiff awards, and litigators' share of the awards. Rather than viewing laws as the behavioral modifier of choice, we would be wise to see them as the modifiers of last resort.

Along with relying on judicious litigation to discourage bad behavior and compensate injured parties, several other alternatives exist to costly laws and regulations. Some of these options include improved parenting and education, minority inclusion, and stigmatizing harmful behaviors.

An effective rule of law protects the innocent, deters crime, and creates opportunity. It reduces the loss of life associated with those driving under the influence of alcohol and drugs, children losing their parents, and parents losing their children. An effective rule of law reduces the loss of life and opportunity that occurs when drug dealers peddle their poison and gangs terrorize neighborhoods.

It is shocking to travel to large cities like Dubai, Geneva, Zurich, Singapore, and Tokyo, which have an effective rule of law, and then visit many U.S. cities where the rule of law is less effective. We do immeasurable harm to people when we inconsistently apply laws and/or create bad ones. If we strengthened the rule of law in our country with the practices discussed in this chapter, hundreds of thousands of more people would act more lawfully and avoid prison, and hundreds of thousands would no longer be victims of crime. Insurance premiums would decline and products and services would cost less. Employment would increase, and we would pay fewer taxes. Many more people would realize more of their potential, and we would be less divided, more civil, fitter, and more prosperous.

The Rule of Law – *government mandates that are (a) few, (b) constitutional, (c) easily understood, (d) widely supported, (e) collegially created, (f) legislatively originated, (g) stakeholder-oriented, (h) piloted, (i) cost-effective, (j) consistently enforced, (k) justly administered, (l) periodically reviewed, and (m) augmented with judicious litigation. Harm, loss, death, anguish, and subsistence are antitheses of the rule of law.*

Chapter 44

Inclusion and Meritocracy

Reality #1: We will not truly flourish until most Americans feel a part of our country, pull hard on the oar, and benefit accordingly. Reality #2: We make small inclusive, meritocratic choices every day, or one day we will regret it.

All mammals have natural tendencies to discriminate against those who are different from them. One need only observe the way birds flock, animals herd, or people congregate to see this. Consciously and unconsciously, we live and work with those most like us and choose similar people for our teams, recognitions, and promotions.

For millions of years, or as much as 99 percent of human history, families and extended families formed tribes and shared a common geography, race, and ethnicity. They found strength in numbers and more successfully competed for territory and resources. Each tribe developed varying beliefs and traditions and saw other tribes as threats. The more cohesive tribes and the ones able to demonize other tribes dominated the landscape, embedding these inter- and intra-tribal tendencies into our DNA. Unless we spend time with those who are different from us and are taught not to discriminate, this long tribal history causes us to naturally favor those most like us. If you want to feel the natural unease of being among different people, make yourself a minority of one among a group of a different race, religion, or ethnicity.

Ethnic Sensitivity and Appreciation

We find species, racial, and ethnic insensitivity, discrimination, and abuse throughout human history. Just consider the Punic War, the Crusades, the numerous expulsions of Jews in Europe, the Inquisition, the Cromwellian conquest of Ireland, the Balkan Wars, the Bolshevik treatment of the Cossacks, the Sino-Japanese War, and Nazi annihilation of the Jews. Closer to home, our ancestors eliminated most of the indigenous people of North America, enslaved African Americans, and expelled thousands of Mexicans from Texas. And today, we destroy hundreds of plant and animal species every year. If we learn anything from history, we should learn that we all have the capacity to embrace those within our tribes and demonize those outside our tribes.

Those of us who are part of dominant majorities usually do not appreciate what life is like for the minorities in our midst. While we may empathize with minorities some, we never fully realize their challenges until we find ourselves alone among them or in their circumstances. Not until I found myself in rural Kentucky, South Chicago, Guatemala, Honduras, Columbia, communist Russia, and on an Islamic flight from the Middle East did I gain a sense of what it was like to be a minority. Not until I felt the resentment, hostility, and discrimination of white males by women did I genuinely realize the challenge of our tribal tendencies.

Racial, ethnic, and gender understanding run contrary to many of our instincts and are a tremendous challenge to multicultural societies in the modern world. It is easy to be above them and critical of others when the frictions are distant, but it is much harder to recognize and overcome them when the frictions involve us. Consider the powerful and eloquent words of Anglican Bishop Desmond Tutu and former South African President Nelson Mandela regarding racial discrimination and their struggles to overcome it.

> I am fifty-two years of age. I am a bishop in the Anglican Church, and a few people might be constrained to say that I was reasonably responsible. In the land of my birth, I cannot vote, whereas a young person of eighteen can vote. And why? Because he or she possesses that wonderful biological attribute—a white skin.[328]
>
> —Desmond Tutu

I had no epiphany, no singular revelation, no moment of truth, but a steady accumulation of a thousand slights, a thousand indignities and a thousand unremembered moments produced in me an anger, a rebelliousness, a desire to fight the system that imprisoned my people.[329]

—Nelson Mandela

It has taken me years to see, but the cause of so many of our current problems stems from our failure to include many African Americans in our population. Civil rights activist and leader Martin Luther King, Jr., expressed the problem:

[People] often hate each other because they fear each other. They fear each other because they don't know each other, and they don't know each other because they cannot communicate with each other, and they cannot communicate with each other because they are separated from each other.[330]

Our country has been comprised of people of different races, religions, and ethnicities from its beginning. As Americans, we are all in the same boat, incredibly connected, and either struggle or flourish together. We must become aware of our natural discriminatory tendencies, not see people as stereotypes, and recognize the importance of inclusion and social cohesion in our schools, organizations, and communities.

We all must learn about the four main cultural groups of our country—African Americans, Asians, Caucasians, and Hispanics—and develop friendships with people belonging to each group and adopt many of the Singaporean practices that further social cohesion as discussed in the next section. The practices of all the chapters in the Winning Practices of Government section matter far more than most of us realize. When we fail to be impartial and meritocratic, integrate and assimilate, include, and control immigration, then life becomes much more challenging.

Integration

Our ancestors gave us a fantastic start, but they did not do well with Native Americans. Some synthesis usually occurs when civilizations collide, yet this was not the case when the English and Native Americans competed for the continent. European diseases and technology enabled European colonists to completely overwhelm the Native Americans. Had there been more synthesis, we might have adopted more of the Native American reverence for the environment and preserved more of our habitats; consequently, we'd face fewer environmental challenges today.

Our ancestors also did not do well by African Americans either. Had we not enslaved them and lived apart for decades, we would have avoided the Civil War, decades of racial strife, and the ongoing hard feelings and hardships. We would have fewer broken families, greater numbers of well-parented children, less drug abuse and crime, a more productive workforce, and fewer people dependent on public support. We would have a smaller government, higher living standards, and greater social cohesion. Martin Luther King, Jr., underscored the importance of the integration in the following passage:

> There is no separate black path to power and fulfillment that does not intersect white paths, and there is no separate white path to power and fulfillment, short of social disaster, that does not share that power with black aspirations for freedom and human dignity. We are bound together in a single garment of destiny. The language, the cultural patterns, the music, the material prosperity, and even the food of America are an amalgam of black and white.[331]

Our failures to integrate the Native Americans, African Americans, and many Hispanics are tragic and major causes of so many of our problems. Singapore, perhaps more than any other country, demonstrates the advantages of making integration a national priority. Being roughly three-quarters Chinese, one-eighth Malay, and one-tenth Indian, Singaporeans have worked hard to integrate these groups.

Article Twelve of the Constitution of Singapore guarantees to all people equality before the law. The Presidential Council of Minority Rights exists to ensure that legislation does not discriminate against any race or religious community. The Singaporean government requires its five major boroughs, schools, and universities to accommodate residents and students in proportion to the national demographics. It requires schools to teach children the cultural heritage of each of its major ethnic groups, and it created a national Racial Harmony Day holiday. The Singapore government wants its citizens, and especially its youth, to understand and appreciate the varying cultural heritages of its citizens.

Mitigating our natural tendencies to discriminate requires proactive and ongoing effort. It needs nurture, laws, and a justice system to overcome human nature. While most of the Singaporeans with whom I have interacted do not say there is no racial or religious discrimination in Singapore, they indicate that their government's efforts to combat discrimination and integrate the boroughs have paid immense dividends and that Singaporeans generally live and work well together.

In our country, most people agree that non-meritorious forms of discrimination are unfair, counterproductive, and hurtful. They support minority inclusion but disagree on the means to achieve it. Not surprisingly, those in the majority tend to dislike affirmative action, seeing it as a form of reverse discrimination; those in the minority tend to like it, seeing affirmative action as a necessary remedy to inequality.

The solutions to minority inequality and underrepresentation in many organizations depend on the circumstances and their severity. When the inclusion of underrepresented minorities elevates the performance of organizations, integration occurs relatively easily once a few minorities gain admittance and the organizations discover that their addition is advantageous. This occurred when African Americans gained entrance to collegiate and professional sports. It happened when Asians obtained admittance to universities and colleges. When the minority inclusion elevates group performance, the solution to discrimination is for leaders and the press to shame the perpetrators of discrimination.

When the inclusion of underrepresented minorities lowers the performance of groups, however, the best solution is to address the causes of the underperformance and implement remedial programs. For example, when minorities from inferior primary and secondary schools apply to college and do not gain admittance representative of their numbers, we should improve the inferior schools and provide these students remedial opportunities. Unlike our current admission of unqualified minorities into colleges, this is a real solution. Lowering admission standards, dumbing down curriculum, and passing underperforming minorities through academic programs poorly equips the graduates, causes others to question their competence, and dilutes the quality of everyone's education.

While improving inner-city schools and offering remedial opportunities are a good start, I do not believe that they alone will bridge our racial and ethnic divides. Real inclusion and social cohesion will only come when majorities and minorities live, study, and work together, and our government incentivizes people to do this. Not knowing the best way to further this kind of inclusion in our country and wanting equality before the law, I suggest that three states pilot a program to incentivize the racial and ethnic representation to reflect the national demographics in our schools and municipalities.

Currently Caucasians comprise 60 percent, Hispanics 18 percent, African Americans 13 percent, and Asians 5 percent of our population.[332] The program that I propose would be voluntary and accessible to all U.S. citizens. It would be funded by a 5 percent tax placed on fossil fuels at the retail level. The program would make one-time $10,000 cash payments to those who (a) complete an undergraduate degree at a university or (b) who relocate to a community for five years where they are racially or ethnically underrepresented. People would receive only one of these payments in their lifetimes. The payments would be made on a first-come-first-serve basis each year until the revenue was spent.

Meritocracy and Comparative Advantage

The universe and life both work in the manner that what is most suited to the times continues and what is least suited withers away. In this sense, evolution is meritocratic, and so we must be meritocratic. If we avoid meritocracy and insulate citizens, educational institutions, enterprises, country, and culture from competition, they become unfit, and we enable competing cultures and countries to bury us. Those best adapted to the times continue and those poorly suited to them fade away.

Meritocracy involves assigning the most able people to positions and compensating them in accordance with their qualifications and performance. Meritocracy causes people to develop their skills, prepare, work hard, and perform at high levels. It yields fitter individuals and organizations more than using gender, age, race, ethnicity, religion, political affiliation, seniority, or need to assign positions and set compensation. Meritocracy was discussed in detail in Chapter 8.

Those who see meritocracy as heartless and other types of determinations as fairer should think more deeply. Non-meritocratic assignments hurt conscientious, hardworking people, the very people and attributes on which a well-functioning order depends. Non-meritocratic determinations advance irresponsible, incompetent, lazy people who cause our organizations and communities to work poorly. Non-merit-based organizations eventually lose to meritocratic ones.

People, institutions, and countries only flourish when they compete and operate meritocratically. This was the case in the United State until recently; in West Germany, Japan, and Hong Kong throughout the second half of the 20th century; and in South Korea, Taiwan, and Singapore currently. People, businesses, organizations, and countries struggle when they operate in non-meritocratic ways, as was the situation in post-WWII East Germany, Czechoslovakia, Poland, North Korea, Cuba, and the Soviet Union. Meritocracies optimize. Comparative advantage assures that niches exist for everyone. If people fail to receive one position, they need only to prepare better and try again or find assignments that better suit them and interest others less.

Equal Opportunity

Our sense of fairness counters our tendency to discriminate. I suspected for years that nature embedded a sense of fairness within us, but it took a YouTube video—"Equal Pay for Monkeys"—for me to fully register this reality.[333] In the video, a researcher gives two monkeys in side-by-side cages a piece of cucumber each time one of the monkeys gives him a pebble. The researcher conducts the pebble-cucumber trade several times, and both monkeys are content with the exchange. Then, the researcher gives one monkey a grape for the pebble and the other monkey a piece of cucumber. Monkeys like cucumbers, but they like grapes more. The unequal treatment causes the second monkey to become upset with the researcher and to throw the piece of cucumber back at him.

Besides being hilarious, the video demonstrates that monkeys have a strong sense of fairness. We see this same desire for fairness in our children and ourselves. When a person or organization treats someone else better than us, we are unhappy about it. This instinctual sense of fairness gives socialism and communism traction. People's sense of fairness and jealousy are realities that advocates of democratic capitalism must recognize and accommodate.

The importance of meritocracy and our sense of fairness gave rise to the concept of equal opportunity, and they incentivize us to create circumstances where everyone has a chance to succeed. They remind us to see people as individuals rather than stereotypes and let competition and merit determine outcomes. Furthermore, they should encourage us to provide all citizens with access to food, clothing, shelter, healthcare, daycare, K-12 education, higher education, and a social safety net. Meritocracy and equal opportunity are two of the best antidotes to discrimination. They are fair, motivate people to do their best, align with evolution, and yield spectacular results.

Goldilocks Minimum Wages

The more . . . competitiveness in society, the higher the total performance. If winner takes all, competition will be keen, but group solidarity will be weak. The more . . . rewards [are] evenly distributed, the greater the group solidarity, but the weaker the total performance because of reduced competition.

To maintain social cohesion, we buffer the lowest 20 to 25 percent, the weaker achievers, from the tough competition of the marketplace. . . . We support the lower-income workers with extra income. . . . All this aims for a fair and just society.
334

—Lee Kuan Yew

Australia has a very high minimum wage and a high and steadily growing living standard. Every full-time employee over age 21 earned a minimum of $37,000 in 2018.[335] With such a high minimum wage, one would expect unemployment to be high and the economy to struggle. This is not the case, however, primarily because the Australian government is smart about its business climate and immigration. The Australian government does not overburden businesses with regulations and taxes, set the minimum wage so high as to negate its otherwise friendly business environment, nor let illegal immigrants flow freely into the country and oversupply its labor market.

Like most good economists, I normally oppose a minimum wage. Minimum wages distort market price signals, result in resource misallocations, and increase unemployment. Upon seeing Australia's success with a high minimum wage and realizing our need to be meritocratic and fair, however, I advocate what I call a "Goldilocks Minimum Wage" under certain conditions. When our need for fairness forces us to choose between the alternatives of progressive taxation and a Goldilocks Minimum Wage, the Goldilocks Minimum Wage is the superior option.

Goldilocks Minimum Wages are minimum wages that are high enough for people to earn enough to live on, save some money, and pay some taxes but not so high as to make a country's businesses uncompetitive. A Goldilocks Minimum Wage works well when:

– It only applies to people between the ages of 21 and 65;

– States independently set their minimum wage;

– A universally strong education system exists;

– Incentivized savings programs like the one discussed in the next chapter exist;

– Everyone, except those on public support, pays income taxes or taxes on carbon and non-essential goods;

– The country has prudent laws and regulations, free enterprise and markets, responsible fiscal and monetary policies, well-developed infrastructure, and relatively low taxes; and

– The government advantageously controls the flow of immigrants.

Goldilocks Minimum Wages yield streams of benefits. They enable most people to earn enough to purchase their necessities as well as pay some taxes. They transfer assets and wealth to those who can fend for themselves but are not able to realize much of a standard of living. And unlike our current system that incentivizes people not to work and collect public assistance, Goldilocks Minimum Wages incentivize people to work.

Allowing each state and city to set its minimum wage is superior to a national minimum wage because the cost of living varies across the country, and minimum wages should vary accordingly. Lower-minimum-wage states would have more job opportunities; higher-minimum-wage states would have better-paying jobs. Competition and migration among the states would cause each to find the most advantageous Goldilocks Minimum Wage for its circumstances.

A Can-Do Attitude

> In a time of universal deceit, telling the truth becomes a revolutionary act.
>
> —Author Unknown

One of the things my father taught me was never to feel sorry for myself. If something did not go my way and I started to cry, my father would say, "Stop crying, or I will give you a good reason to cry." The good reason was a spanking. While this seems insensitive and harsh, my father only said this when I was feeling sorry for myself without good reason.

My father was wise enough to know that we cannot have everything we want. He understood that feeling sorry for oneself does not help one move forward. It is better to let go of a disappointment and move on than dwell on it. My father also told me as a child that "there is no such word as 'can't'," and "when the going gets tough, the tough get going." If something was worth doing, I should get at it and do it.

In our family, my mother consoled my siblings and me, and my father stretched us. Today, most people want to console and no one wants to be tough. More people see themselves as victims rather than proactive, able beings. It took me some years to appreciate my father's tough love, but I am ever so thankful for it as well as the occasional teacher, coach, mentor, and friend who did not put up with self-pity.

If there is one message that I would like to convey to those who believe they are victims, it is: "Let it go and move on." Self-pity, a victimhood mentality, and playing the sympathy card may bring small, short-term wins—but like telling lies, they become a habit and diminish our lives in the long term. A victimhood mentality attributes one's condition to the actions of others and conveniently excuses personal irresponsibility, inaction, and incompetence.

Consider journalist and author Bill O'Reilly's thoughts on the damage that the victimhood mentality causes many African Americans:

> Young black men commit homicides at a rate ten times greater than whites and Hispanics combined. . . . Right now, about 73 percent of all black babies are born out of wedlock.

> When presented with damning evidence like that, and like the mini-holocaust in Chicago where hundreds of African Americans are murdered each year, the civil rights industry looks the other way or makes excuses.[336]

Bill O'Reilly suggests that rather than seeing African Americans as victims and making excuses, the civil rights community should define the problem of African American poverty correctly and address its causes, which in his view are the lack of involvement of many African American fathers in their children's lives, dysfunctional schools, and the local environment of gangs, hustling, and drugs. I agree with his assessment. We must work together across the racial and political spectrum to restore the rule of law in many neighbor-hoods, discourage unwed pregnancies, encourage fathers to be involved in their children's lives, and restore discipline and educational excellence in many public schools.

John McWhorter, an African American senior fellow at the Manhattan Institute, agrees with the idea that many African Americans need to stop seeing themselves as victims and start seizing the many available opportunities. In his book, *Losing the Race,* he argues:

> African Americans are pursuing a self-destructive strategy by promoting a "victim" self-image, racial separatism, and the view that education doesn't matter.[337]

Wall Street Journal editorial board member and African American Jason Riley concurs:

Martin Luther King, Jr., and his contemporaries demanded black self-improvement despite the abundant and overt racism of their day. King's self-styled successors, living in an era when public policy bends over backwards to accommodate blacks, insist that blacks cannot be held responsible for their plight so long as someone, somewhere in white America, is still prejudiced.

The more fundamental problem with these well-meaning liberal efforts is that they have succeeded, tragically, in convincing blacks to see themselves first and foremost as victims. Today there is no greater impediment to black advancement than the self-pitying mindset that permeates black culture. . . . Blacks ultimately must help themselves. They must develop the same attitudes and behaviors and habits that other groups had to develop to rise in America. And to the extent that a social policy, however well-intentioned, interferes with this self-development, it does more harm than good.[338]

Human development requires nurture, discipline, instruction, encouragement, honest feedback, and challenges. Ultimately, it requires each of us to take responsibility for our life and proactively learn, work, and seize the opportunities around us. A can-do attitude furthers our development and well-being while an attitude of victimization stifles us.

African Americans have suffered horrible indignities over the centuries. Overcoming past abuses, separation, and discrimination are tremendous challenges for all of us. Most Americans recognize that separation and discrimination are wrong and that we must move beyond the past. Although most people in the majority today had nothing to do with the past injustices, we need to acknowledge them, be sensitive to them, and certainly not perpetuate them. And while we must remember this sad history so that it is never repeated, it is not advantageous to let it consume the present or future. It does no American good to see themselves as separate or a victim. Separation and victimhood mentalities are losing, not winning practices.

A can-do attitude is a Winning Practice. It acknowledges potential and pursues accomplishment. If we focus and work at something, usually we can do it. With our cultural norms forcefully shunning unlawful discrimination, the current government protects against it. And with the recent accommodations made for minorities by most schools and universities, people who shed victim mentalities and utilize winning ones can overcome their circumstances and others' discriminatory actions.

Inclusion and Meritocracy – *practices that cause people to feel a part of a group and optimize its function, which include: (a) appreciation of diversity, (b) integration and free remedial education, (c) advancement of the fit over the unfit, (d) comparative advantage, (e) equal opportunity, (f) a Goldilocks Minimum Wage, and (g) a can-do attitude. Exclusion and mediocrity are antithetical to inclusion and meritocracy.*

Chapter 45

Prudent Taxation

Taxation is legalized theft of people's property. Responsible elected officials exercise this power and the use of confiscated resources impartially and wisely.

Taxes are necessary. Governments need them to function. The effects of taxes can be positive or negative depending on their magnitude, where leaders apply them, and how those leaders use the proceeds. People do not like paying taxes and go to great lengths to avoid paying oppressive taxes. Most government officials tax their opposition and enrich their supporters and themselves. Given these realities, how do we prudently, uniformly, and consistently levy taxes? How do we realize the positive effects of taxation and avoid the negative ones? How do we minimize representative misuse of their taxation power and people's tendency to avoid paying taxes?

Disincentivize the Undesirables

Taxes are natural disincentives, discouraging the use and suppressing the value of the things on which they fall. Tax real estate, and buyers pay more and sellers receive less. Tax energy, and consumers pay more, producers receive less, and consumers use less. Tax capital, and borrowers pay more, savers receive less, and borrowers use less. Tax labor, and employers pay more; workers receive less and work fewer hours.

Prudent governments do not tax what is desirable. They tax things that are unnecessary, undesirable, and/or harmful, things like non-essential goods and services, sugar, trans fats, alcohol, tobacco products, and fossil fuels.

Prudent governments do not tax business inputs like property, labor, and capital. They do not tax people's income or enterprises' profits because they want to encourage employment and increase personal income, savings rates, investment, and productivity. They recognize that taxes on property, labor, capital, income, and profit cause (a) enterprises to hire fewer people, pay lower wages, make fewer productivity-enhancing investments, and produce lower-quality, higher-cost products and services, (b) people to work, save, and spend less, and (c) exports to decrease and imports to increase. Prudent governments also tax activities with harmful externalities—situations where one agent's actions create a cost or a benefit to another agent who did not choose to bear the cost or receive the benefit—like the use of fossil fuels and the clearcutting of forests.

In the cases of using fossil fuels and clearcutting forests, the public bears the adverse effects of the activities in the form of sickness, disease, shortened lifespans, and climate change. Taxation of undesirable externalities is a critical function of government that our founders did not foresee or make provisions for in the Constitution. It would be advantageous to amend the Constitution to empower and direct the federal government to tax activities that create undesirable externalities.

Sales Taxes on Nonessentials

While the taxation of undesirable things is advantageous to the public, generally it does not generate enough revenue. When this is the case, governments may raise additional revenue by taxing non-essential consumer products and services. These taxes are superior to taxes on property, labor, capital, income, and profit because they do not penalize domestic production and advantage imports. Governments should not tax essential products and services like basic foods, clothing, healthcare, education, and the materials and labor in homes because taxing them hurts lower-income people.

When governments tax non-essential items, they increase the cost of these products and services, and people purchase less of them. This is advantageous on a crowded planet. Funding governments with taxes on unnecessary, undesirable, and harmful things maximizes a population's competitiveness and well-being and reduces its environmental footprint. It eliminates the need for income taxes, an Internal Revenue Service, and the time and resources businesses and people waste complying with incomprehensible tax codes. Alaska, Florida, Nevada, South Dakota, Texas, Washington, and Wyoming do not have state income taxes, and they are all thriving relative to other states.

Transitioning from our current mix of taxes to a more advantageous one requires leaders to hold the line on total tax revenue collections and make many small incremental changes over time. Most government officials have strong inclinations to play Santa Claus with the public treasury and increase revenues rather than just change the sources of them. Moreover, changing the mix too rapidly would negatively impact the economy.

Uniform Application of Taxes

Special treatment generally is not a problem when we are the ones receiving it but is a problem when we are not its recipients. The uniform application of taxes is a critical type of equality before the law that avoids treating some people more favorably than others and causes citizens to respect and support their government.

The uniform application of taxes does not mean that everyone pays the same amount of tax, but rather that the government taxes every citizen and organization in the same manner. It means that over 90 percent of the citizens pay taxes and have an interest in how the government uses their money. The taxation of unnecessary, undesirable, and/or harmful things are three examples of taxes that apply to everyone, and the taxes people pay varies directly with their purchases of unnecessary and/or undesirable things.

A progressive income tax and earned income tax credits are two examples of laws that do not apply to everyone. When governments deviate one iota from the uniform application of taxes, they open a Pandora's box of corrupting exchange between government officials, special interests, and the citizenry.

Besides uniformly applying taxes, it is important for governments to apply them consistently over time. Frequent changes to tax laws create uncertainties; alter people's use of credit, goods and services; and harm the economy.

Spending Restraints

History indicates that majorities tyrannize minorities and that most democracies end in bankruptcy. Four practices that help prevent these outcomes include: (1) a Bill of Rights, (2) state legislator selection of U.S. Senators, (3) the requirement for the approval of two-thirds of the House, Senate, and general population to enact taxes and fees, and (4) constitutionally limiting the federal government's spending to 10 percent of a country's GNP.

Throughout history, every population that significantly improved its living standards did so when its government spending, relative to its GNP, was comparatively low. This was true for Australia, Canada, Japan, Hong Kong, New Zealand, Singapore, South Korea, Taiwan, the U.K., the U.S., and many other countries. When governments become too large relative to their country's private sector, they choke their economies. They stifle innovation and productivity, diminish competitiveness, and reduce employment. They cause real wages and living standards to stagnate. Just as enterprises with too much overhead become top-heavy and uncompetitive, so do countries with too much government.

Without a Bill of Rights and taxing and spending restraints, majorities impose their will on minorities, and government officials reward their supporters. Over 500 years ago French Minister of Finance Jean-Baptiste Colbert cynically suggested that:

The art of taxation consists in so plucking the goose as to obtain the largest possible amount of feathers with the smallest possible amount of hissing.[339]

This age-old, simple metaphor describes what governments do. They tax, and they tax, and they tax. They tax property, purchases, and income as well as energy, businesses, and utilities. They enact user fees and tax estates. The world over, governments pass endless arrays of taxes, leaving their citizens unable to register the magnitude of the taxation and eventually causing wealthy people to flee their jurisdictions.

To combat governments' propensity to spend our money, it would be advantageous to (a) only allow Congress to enact taxes and fees, (b) require a triple, two-thirds supermajority to enact taxes and fees, (c) limit federal spending to 10 percent of the country's GNP, and (d) make elected officials who violate the 10 percent spending limit ineligible for reelection and federal pensions.

Giving Congress the sole authority to enact taxes provides a check on the Executive Branch. Requiring a two-thirds majority of both houses and the public via referendum to enact taxes assures that the taxes are acceptable to most people. Limiting federal spending to 10 percent of the country's gross national product keeps the government lean and enables the economy to grow faster. Making elected officials who violate the 10 percent spending limit ineligible for federal pensions and reelection checks their inclination to play Santa Claus with our country's tax revenues and credit.

Prudent governments disincentivize the undesirable and harmful. They apply taxes simply, uniformly, and consistently over time. They fund the government in a manner that enhances the lives of their citizens and does not create reams of complex tax laws and oppressive tax agencies.

__Prudent Taxation__ – (a) not taxing desirable things, (b) taxing undesirable and harmful things, nonessential consumer products and services, and externalities, (c) applying taxes uniformly and consistently over time, (d) prohibiting the Executive Branch from enacting fees, (e) requiring triple supermajorities to enact taxes and fees, and (f) constitutionally limiting federal spending. Undesirable, partial, incomprehensible, erratic, and excessive taxation are antithetical to prudent taxation.

Chapter 46

Financial Strength

Opportunities abound for us when our country is free and financially strong. We can enjoy good healthcare and education, live securely and peacefully, travel freely, and pursue our dreams. We can care for the disadvantaged, elderly, and environment. We may conduct basic research and explore new worlds.

Throughout much of the 20th century, our population was largely healthy and financially strong. Then, our successes went to our heads, and we became soft, less-disciplined, entitled, and foolish. Today, we borrow and spend too much. We incentivize freeloading and weakness, choke our economic engine, hurt our living standards, and harm future generations. Financial strength is no longer much of a priority. What is financial strength?

Financial Strength is having the means to meet more than one's current and future obligations.

Privatization

There is a sweet spot for the size of the government and public sector. Too small and the economic engine lacks octane. Too large and it lacks oxygen. Prudent people understand this and insist that central governments only perform what they do better than state and local governments, while state and local governments merely do what they do better than the private sector.

Privatization furthers competitiveness, economic growth, and financial strength. Private enterprises are efficient and productive. Government agencies lack competitors and are bureaucratic. Government personnel do not have the same incentives to work and innovate as those in the private sector, and the services they provide cost more and are usually inferior to those offered by the private sector.

Privatization involves having private enterprises provide all the products and services except those that the federal and state governments can offer more advantageously.

Free Enterprise and Free Markets

Some economic structures yield greater financial strength and prosperity than others. A free enterprise and market structure occurs when governments permit businesses, employees, and consumers to voluntarily make exchanges and they limit concentrations of market power.

Free enterprise and free markets incentivize people advantageously. Businesses work to attract the best employees, and employees work to secure the most favorable work and compensation arrangements. Enterprises work to satisfy their consumers who work to procure the best values. In short, people generally do their best and reap what they sow. Products and services improve, costs decline, living standards rise, and government revenues increase.

Three alternative economic structures exist, but each one trades voluntary, mutually beneficial exchanges for less optimal, bureaucratic ones. Each alternative creates surpluses, shortages, waste, and economic stagnation.

The first structure is where governments sell services to their citizens. The government or public agency projects the quantities of goods and services that people require and sets the prices. This alternative creates surpluses, shortages, and waste. The former Soviet Union, its communist satellites, and the U.S. Postal Service provide examples of this alternative.

The reasons for surpluses, shortages, and waste under this structure are that civil service employees are not omniscient and have self-interests that are unaligned with their patrons' interests. Civil service employees make politically favorable decisions and benefit from the expansion of bureaucracy. They profit when their budgets, staffs, and salaries grow. Civil service employees do not benefit when the costs of government services decrease or the quality of their services improves.

The U.S. Postal Service is an example of what happens when governments sell services to their citizens. The agency is overstaffed, has too many small post offices, and is slow to innovate and modernize. The only reason the quality and cost of its services seem reasonable is that taxpayers routinely cover billions of dollars of Postal Service losses.

The second structure is where governments purchase products and services from private companies and provide them free of charge to people. The U.S. Medicaid Program exemplifies this arrangement. People go to doctors for services, pay nothing for them, and the government reimburses the doctors. These arrangements incentivize providers to charge governments as much as possible for the services and consumers not to worry about finding the best value. When the government compensates doctors for their services below market rates, the better doctors do not take Medicaid patients, patients wait for the services, and the doctors who treat Medicaid patients support candidates for elective office who expand and enrich the program.

The third structure to free enterprise and markets and the one that propagates the greatest number of adverse effects is where governments provide services free of charge. Our Veterans Health Administration is an example of this arrangement. Veterans' medical centers have monopoly positions. They have little incentive to be efficient, affordable, and quality-oriented because they have patients regardless of how they perform. Veteran administrators earn more as they increase their budgets and staffs. The "free" offering of the services creates overuse and forces the medical centers to ration the services by making people wait for them. The unionized workforces and work rules make the institutions inefficient, expensive, and unresponsive.

Competition is the meritocratic and innovative way of nature. While most people and organizations try to insulate themselves from competition, it is in their interests to embrace it. The competition inherent in the free enterprise and markets serves us well, and the lack of it in the alternative structures yields adverse effects, something that many people fail to appreciate. When government representatives control transactions and prices, the first things they buy are special interest support and the votes of the citizens. When people and organizations receive substantial funds from governments, they spend more time trying to influence the governments than being productive.[340]

Transparency and Good Information

For a country to be financially healthy, people must have reliable information. Markets must discover and report prices in an efficient and timely manner, and governments and public corporations must report their performance, worth, and prospects accurately and completely.

Without good information, entrepreneurs, investors, and consumers cannot anticipate outcomes or make good decisions nor hold government and business leaders accountable for their actions. Entrepreneurs start fewer companies, invest less in their enterprises, and employ fewer people. Consumers buy fewer goods. Capital flees to other countries, and economic activity declines when governments and businesses withhold and distort information.

Financial progress and strength depend on transparency and good information. They are products of honest and competent people, institutions, and cultures that expose dishonesty, incompetence, and inaccuracy. While our government has required publicly traded and other regulated enterprises to use Generally Accepted Accounting Principles (GAAP) to disclose their financial circumstances for years, the federal government and many state governments do not use these standards. They shrewdly hide healthcare, pension, Social Security, Medicare, and other material future liabilities from the public.

Sound Money

The greatest civilizations have benefited from sound money for intermittent periods of their history, and wise leaders and economists have understood the importance of sound money for centuries. Unfortunately, most governments gradually erode the value of their currency to reduce their debt obligations and postpone recessions.

*Money is a medium used for transactions and a store of value, consisting of cash, checks, and credit. **Sound Money** is money that maintains its value over time.*

***The Federal Reserve,** or Central Bank, is a system of 12 banks that manages the supply of money. In 1913, Congress gave the Federal Reserve the mandates to maximize employment, maintain stable prices, and moderate long-term interest rates. In 2009, Congress gave the Federal Reserve additional mandates to regulate the banks and maintain the stability of the financial system.*

Economists typically refer to the Federal Reserve's approach to these mandates as monetary policy.

***Monetary Policy** describes the Federal Reserve actions with regard to: (a) the federal funds rate or the interest rate that the Federal Reserve pays and charges banks for deposits and loans, (b) the reserve requirements or the amount of deposits that the Federal Reserve requires banks to hold for every dollar they lend, and (c) the Federal Reserve's purchase and sale of financial assets.*

The Federal Reserve increases the supply of money as it decreases the federal funds rate, lowers the reserve requirements of banks, or buys financial assets. It reduces the supply of money as it increases the federal funds rate, raises the reserve requirements of banks, or sells financial assets.

While the Federal Reserve is a critical institution, the political nature of its mandate and the appointment of its governors are problems. The Swiss central bank's mandate "to ensure price stability, while taking due account of the economic developments," is superior to our central bank's mandate because it provides one clear apolitical mandate.[341] Our central bank's dual mandate of price stability and full employment politicizes the institution.

Central banks can maintain the value of money and stabilize financial institutions, but they cannot do these things and maximize employment. They can nudge economic activity and employment up or down, but employment is more a function of people's education and skills, competition, immigration, changes in technology, relative tax rates, government spending, and the social safety net.

Attempts by central banks to maintain full employment distort market prices, denying critical feedback to leaders, businesses, consumers, and voters. Such monetary manipulations enable governments, businesses, and people to borrow and spend foolishly and mask the adverse effects of the healthcare, social welfare, immigration, and tax policies of many governments. Central bank actions to maintain full employment distort free-market signals, destroy people's incentive to save, create speculative bubbles, erode the value of money, and transform small corrective recessions into major depressions.

When the Federal Reserve increases or decreases the supply of money faster than enterprises increase or reduce the amount of goods and services, it changes money's value, causing inflation or deflation.

Inflation is a general increase in the prices of products and services. It occurs when the growth of money and credit is greater than the growth of products and services. The Federal Reserve creates inflation when it increases the money supply to decrease unemployment.

The Federal Reserve attempts to moderate business cycles by decreasing interest rates to spur the economy during sluggish times and increasing them to temper the economy during booming times.

Short-Term Business Cycles are natural three- to five-year cyclical fluctuations in the growth of the GNP that result from the changes of private and public sector purchases relative to the production of goods and services. When purchases exceed production and gradually deplete inventories, the economy expands. When production exceeds the purchases and inventories grow, the economy contracts.

The downside of this approach is that the Federal Reserve stimulates more than it restricts, steadily increasing prices, devaluing our currency, stealing purchasing power from savers, and giving purchasing power to borrowers. The Fed's actions have eroded our dollar's value by 85 percent over the last 50 years.[342] As Milton Friedman observed:

Inflation is taxation without legislation.[343]

Inflation undermines government credibility, currencies, domestic savings, and foreign investment. It causes people to work less and spend more time protecting their money. If people understood that better ways exist to increase employment than monetary policy and that business cycles are natural, necessary, and self-correcting, they would insist that their governments maintain the soundness of the currency, stop distorting free-market price signals, and start propagating streams of positive effects. They would require that their governments avoid inflation by matching the growth of their money supplies to the growth of their production of goods and services.

Deflation is the opposite of inflation and is less common. It occurs when consumers slow their spending, businesses make fewer investments, and prices decline. It follows periods of increasing debt and growth. Bankruptcies and layoffs accompany deflation.

Deflation is a general decrease in the prices of goods and services. It occurs when the growth of money is slower than the growth of goods and services. It usually occurs at the end of long-term debt cycles.

Deflation can do a lot of damage. Declining business revenues and large amounts of debt make it difficult for many businesses to cover their expenses and obligations. Corporations cut their staff, and if possible, renegotiate the terms of their loans. People with jobs find that their money buys more but their fear of losing their jobs causes them to spend less and save more. Lower prices increase exports. Employed people increase their spending over time and the deflation runs its course.

Long-term debt cycles are multigenerational changes in the growth rate of the GNP caused by changes in personal, enterprise, and government use of debt.

***Long-Term Debt Cycles** are two- to three-generation fluctuations in the growth of GNP that arise from the increase of personal, enterprise, and government debt relative to the production of goods and services. Economies expand when the aggregate debt grows faster than the production of goods and services. They contract when aggregate debt increases more slowly or decreases. Changing lending standards, altering appetites for debt, and irresponsible monetary and fiscal policies fuel long-term debt cycles.*

Long-term debt cycles work as follows: The economy is healthy and banks have ample deposits so they lower their lending standards. Governments, enterprises, and people live beyond their means and steadily take on debt. Eventually, the governments, businesses, and people reach a point where their prospects for paying back additional debt are uncertain. Financial institutions no longer lend to them so governments, businesses, and consumers buy less. Inventories build. Enterprises lay people off and produce less. Bankruptcies ensue. Prices fall. The economy contracts, and a depression occurs. Then, financial institutions tighten their lending standards. Governments, businesses, and individuals save and invest. Prices stabilize and employment steadily improves. Banks have ample deposits, the economy heals, and the long-term debt cycle starts over.

Although the severe economic contractions are largely preventable, few countries avoid them. People and governments have short memory spans. When times are good, they loosen up, lower their standards, work less, and play more.

Central banks are critical when people lose confidence in financial institutions. They prevent small crises from becoming large ones. But when central banks provide liquidity for financial institutions to meet their short-term obligations, they should do so in exchange for collateral and penalty interest. If a bank or financial institution does not meet these obligations, the central bank should encourage stronger banks to take over the insolvent bank. Financial institutions will only act responsibly when their irresponsible behavior has consequences.

Prohibiting central banks from buying their government's debt forces government leaders to be more responsible and live within their means. When central banks buy government debt, they do so because investors will not buy it, they want to avoid a recession, and they want to increase employment. The downsides of their actions are that they enable government leaders to borrow, tax, and spend irresponsibly and remain in office. They exchange mild, relatively harmless recessions for severe and harmful depressions.

Sound Lending Practices

Though the principles of the banking trade may appear somewhat abstruse, the practice is capable of being reduced to strict rules. To depart upon any occasion from these rules, in consequence of some flattering speculation of extraordinary gain, is almost always extremely dangerous, and frequently fatal to the banking company which attempts it.[344]

—Adam Smith

One of the most misguided and unfortunate policies in our nation's history was the Housing and Community Development Act of 1980 initiated by President Carter and accelerated by President Clinton. By tying the government's permission for banks to expand to the number of loans they extended to poor people, the act pressured banks to lower their lending standards and eventually caused millions of people to lose their homes. The desired effects of the heavy hand of government are seldom the actual ones, and it was no different with this act. Although they took 25 years to manifest, the Housing and Community Development Act eventually caused the prevalence of home ownership in the country to fall to the lowest level in decades.

Sound lending practices require leaders to uphold age-old proven lending standards. Borrowers must have adequate income and resources to repay loans. A requirement to pay at least 20 percent of the cost of assets upfront prevents the underlying assets from becoming worth less than the loans. Keeping the terms of loans to less than the life of the underlying assets and requiring borrowers to have incomes at least four times their principal and interest payments mitigate the risk of borrowers defaulting on their loans.

Requiring financial institutions to maintain reserve-to-loan ratios of 10 to 20 percent and maintain the reserves in some combination of gold, cash, and high-quality government and corporate bonds are other critical risk management practices. Financial institutions that hold less than 10 percent reserves and junk bonds, which decline in value during economic difficulties, are inadequately collateralized to cover potential depositor withdrawals.

Sound financial systems and lending practices also involve having the federal government prevent financial institutions from acquiring predatory market shares and becoming so big that their missteps jeopardize people's livelihoods and savings, the whole financial system, and national economies.

Balanced Budgets and Limited Indebtedness

It is incumbent on every generation to pay its own debts as it goes. A principle, which if acted on would save one-half the wars of the world.[345]

—Thomas Jefferson

Families balance their budgets, enterprises and most organizations balance their budgets, state governments balance their budgets, but our federal government spends more than it collects year after year. Figure 23 shows that we have increased our public debt as a percent of GNP from 40 to 106 percent during the 45 years from 1967 through 2017. History provides many examples of the steady erosion of the financial and economic well-being of countries when their debt becomes greater than their GNP.

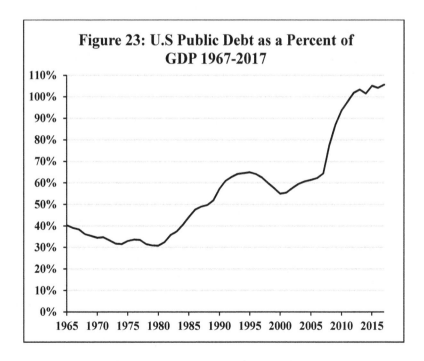

Figure 23: U.S Public Debt as a Percent of GDP 1967-2017

Federal Reserve of St. Louis, https://fred.stlouisfed.org/series/GDP

Squandering the hard work of our ancestors is shortsighted and borrowing from our children is immoral. Yet, this is what we have done. Untethered from our Constitution, our leaders and representatives borrow more and more from future generations. James Buchanan, the 15th President of the United States, wrote:

> Borrowing allows spending to be made that will yield immediate political payoffs without incurring an immediate political cost.[346]

Debtors must repay their creditors, and no person, organization, or country can incur debt at increasing rates indefinitely. Indebtedness that increases faster than productivity crushes people and diminishes the lives of their children.

To restrain our representatives' propensity to borrow, it would be advantageous to amend the U.S. Constitution to require our representatives to: (a) maintain balanced budgets, (b) keep federal debt less than 25 percent of GNP, (c) require the consent of two-thirds of the House and Senate to borrow money, and (d) make elected officials who violate the borrowing limit ineligible for reelection and federal pensions.

Except in times of crises, able leaders in families, enterprises, nonprofits, and governments create surpluses and pay down debt, while incompetent and irresponsible ones create deficits and add debt. Steadily increasing indebtedness gives us more today but less tomorrow. It diminishes our future opportunity. As George Washington wrote:

> We must consult our means rather than our wishes.[347]

WWII Allied Commander and President Dwight Eisenhower wrote:

As we peer into society's future, we—you and I, and our government—must avoid the impulse to live only for today, plundering for our own ease and convenience the precious resources of tomorrow. We cannot mortgage the material assets of our grandchildren without risking the loss also of their political and spiritual heritage. We want democracy to survive for all generations to come, not to become the insolvent phantom of tomorrow.[348]

Prudent Taxation, High Productivity, and Full Employment

People have been led to believe that reducing taxes during recessions increases employment and decreases the severity of recessions. They think this because this is a common fiscal policy that conservatives favor every recession. What is fiscal policy? What increases employment? How do we avoid recessions?

Fiscal Policy refers to the approach taken by the President and Congress to taxation and spending, where a decrease in taxation or increase in spending stimulates economic growth, and an increase in taxation or decrease in spending slows economic growth.

Fiscal policy is a companion to monetary policy. It originates from the work of John Maynard Keynes and the Great Depression in the 1930s. In theory, governments may use fiscal policy to temper business cycles, reduce the severity of economic contractions, and spur employment. In practice, however, most governments only use fiscal policy to justify borrowing large sums and increasing spending during recessions. Governments only decrease spending and pay off small amounts of debt when conservative majorities control them. Just as the Federal Reserve harms the economy with monetary policy in the long term, the President and Congress harm the economy with fiscal policy in the long term.

Except for extreme economic contractions, it is advantageous to set tax rates and leave them alone. Tax rate adjustments to shorten recessions generate more negative than positive effects.

So what increases employment and incomes? As an undergraduate and graduate economics major and someone who has employed hundreds of people in my businesses over the years, I have thought a lot about this. Free enterprise, business-friendly environments, and productivity improvements increase employment and incomes. Companies create products and services, employ people, and create wealth. Governments confiscate this wealth and spend it mostly on the military and social programs. Limited government, privatization, accurate information, sound money, sound lending practices, balanced budgets, and little indebtedness create business-friendly environments conducive to enterprise, employment, productivity gains, and rising incomes. Mandates, regulations, taxes, and social program spending reduce productivity, employment, and incomes.

Productivity is the work per unit of time that people do. One measure of it is the amount of GNP per citizen.

Our individual and collective productivity is the primary key to incomes, and many things affect our productivity. People's health, fitness, attitude, sense of responsibility, education, and skills influence it. The quality of people's parents and schools and the winning or losing nature of their perspectives, habits, and practices affect their productivity. The accessibility and quality of healthcare and the comfortableness of the safety net also impact productivity.

Technology also affects productivity. Just think about the improvements in people's productivity with the advent (a) steam, electricity, gasoline, diesel, and jet engines, (b) vaccines, commercial breeding, nutrition, herbicides, pesticides, and antibiotics, (c) light bulbs, transistors, radio and cellular communication, (d) computer chips, software, and the Internet. Power equipment, agricultural and medical advances, electricity, the computer, and the Internet have tremendously enhanced our productivity.

Basic and applied research yields continuous streams of new technologies. Education conveys knowledge and skills that make people more productive. Well-developed water, sewer, road, canal, railroad, airport, subway, telephone, and Internet infrastructures improve health, mobility, resource and product flows, communication, and our productivity.

Steady investment in public and private infrastructure yields tremendous benefits. Extra investment in public infrastructure during recessions can increase employment and shorten the severity of recessions. Were governments to build reserves, plan infrastructure projects, and expand infrastructure spending during recessions, they could mitigate some of the adverse effects. Reserves and ready-to-go projects would work so much better than perpetual deficits, no planned projects, and ad hoc monetary and fiscal policies.

In summary, (a) the free enterprise system, (b) business-friendly environments, (c) people's health, fitness, attitude, and sense of responsibility, (d) research and technology, (e) people's knowledge and skills, (f) infrastructure investment, and (g) immigration levels are the major determinants of employment and income. Monetary and fiscal policies of central banks and governments only affect the employment and income of small portions of populations temporarily for brief intervals.

Capital Formation

Capital formation is a vital aspect of financial strength. It occurs when individuals and enterprises spend less than they earn and invest their surplus.

Capital is money used to buy property, bonds, and equity, and fund the inventory and receivables of enterprises. Capital fuels productivity, improvement, growth, and financial strength.

Taxes siphon capital from enterprises and citizens. When governments use taxes to fund healthcare, education, research, and infrastructure, they transform private capital into public capital. If deployed well, they improve our productivity, competitiveness, and living standards. When governments use taxes for their operations and social services, they deplete our capital and diminish our future productivity, competitiveness, and living standards.

With the advent of Social Security in the 1930s; Medicaid, Medicare, Food Stamps, and welfare in the 1960s; and mandated healthcare in 2010, the amount of capital that our citizens and enterprises form has decreased and the amount borrowed from foreigners has increased. During the last recession, the Federal Reserve even had to cover capital shortfalls by buying our government's bonds from banks with electronic cash that did not exist before the purchases. The purchases swelled the bank reserves and enabled the capital-depleted banks to function. Several rounds of these acquisitions, or quantitative easing as it was called, occurred between 2007 and 2014, increasing the paper assets that the Federal Reserve held from one to four trillion dollars.[349]

Once governments create plush social safety nets, capital formation and its benefits decline. Increases in productivity, employment, and income slow, and we as a country become less competitive and financially weaker. When people save money and invest it, they create their own safety net, form capital, and improve their living standards. Our ancestors, post-WII Europeans, and the Japanese did this, and post-1990 Chinese, Vietnamese, and Singaporeans still do this.

———————————

Democratic governments make choices. They do not naturally do the right things or make countries financially strong unless they are tethered by a well-conceived constitution, prudent citizenry, and a free and responsible press. Professors and economists James Gwartney, Dwight Lee, and Richard Stroup wrote in *Common Sense Economics*:

The intellectual folly of our age is the view that democratic elections alone will establish an environment conducive to economic progress. Both history and political theory indicate that this view is false. If government is going to be a positive force for economic prosperity, the rules of the political game must be designed to bring the self-interest of voters, politicians, and bureaucrats into harmony with economic progress. This will require that the scope of government be limited and remain neutral among the various subgroups of citizens.

When government is unconstrained—when everything is up for grabs within the political process—divisive and predatory activities will abound. Individuals will spend more time organizing and fighting over slices of the economic pie and less time producing the pie. As a result, output will be smaller than would otherwise be the case. Animosity, distrust, and even hatred among factions will grow, while production stagnates. Life in a highly politicized economy is not an attractive scene.[350]

Financial Strength – when the means of a person, organization, or country exceed their current and future obligations. It is the product of (a) limited government, (b) free enterprise and markets, (c) transparency and good information, (d) sound money, (e) sound lending practices, (f) balanced budgets, (g) little indebtedness, (h) prudent taxation, (i) employment, (j) productivity, and (k) capital formation. Financial weakness, stagnation, and unrealized potential are the antitheses of financial strength.

Chapter 47

Savings Accounts and Social Safety Nets

In my youth, I travelled much, and I observed in different countries, that the more public provisions were made for the poor, the less they provided for themselves.[351]

—*Benjamin Franklin*

Providing for those without means always has been a challenge for communities and governments. Every healthy, well-functioning popular-tion has people experiencing temporary hardship and a small percent of its members who are unable to provide for themselves. We wish to help those going through rough patches and those who cannot make it on their own, but we do not want able people to become dependent upon the government.

When assisting those in need, some approaches work better than others. Centralized bureaucratic approaches provide people relief but usually further dependency and burden the population. People dependent on public programs do not fully realize their potential and detract from the larger community. Centralized bureaucratic methods are expensive and spawn special interests. They saddle us with taxes and debt and consume resources that are better spent on education, infrastructure, research, and sustainability. As author, philosopher, and naturalist Henry David Thoreau cautioned decades before our federal government commenced its war on poverty:

There are a thousand hacking at the branches of evil to one who is striking at the root, and it may be that he who bestows the largest amount of time and money on the needy is doing the most by his mode of life to produce that misery which he strives in vain to relieve.[352]

Savings policies that incentivize people to prepare for rainy days and decentralized assistance work better and cost less than national bureaucratic social safety nets. Savings policies empower people, strengthen communities, and spawn fewer special interests. Decentralized support spurs innovation, allows state and county providers to learn from one another, and evolves more effective, lower-cost forms of assistance.

I have observed in several mammalian populations that about 5-7 percent of the individuals cannot fend for themselves. Natural reproductive processes seem to create able organisms about 93 to 95 percent of the time. This insight helps one gauge the health of a population and desirability of its social safety net. When more than 7 percent of a population depends on a safety net, it is likely flawed.

Avoiding Socialism and the Redistribution of Wealth

> To relieve the misfortunes of our fellow creatures is concurring with the Deity; it is godlike, but if we provide encouragement for laziness, and supports for folly, may we not be found fighting against the order of God and Nature. . . . Whenever we attempt to amend the scheme of Providence . . . we had need be very circumspect, lest we do more harm than good.[353]
>
> —Benjamin Franklin

Many people believe that the redistribution of wealth is the way to create a vibrant middle class and alleviate inequality. History does not bear this out. While the redistribution of wealth lessens the variance of incomes, it also makes most people poorer, weaker, less free, and more vulnerable. When governments give a substantial portion of our income and the profits of businesses to others, they disincentivize work and waste 10 to 20 percent of the money on the administrative process. They confiscate people's hard work, make enterprises less competitive, and reduce employment. They increase interest rates, debase currencies, decrease foreign exchange earnings, and increase the cost of imports.

Socialism is all about the redistribution of wealth. It appeals to people's sense of fairness but weakens individuals and populations. Stealing from the productive and giving to the unproductive diminishes the former, multiplies the latter, fuels decline, and burdens future generations. To confirm this, one only needs to note the ill effects of the wealth redistribution by the powerful central governments of the former Soviet Union, its Eastern European satellites, Communist China, Greece, Italy, Portugal, and Spain.

To understand why the redistribution of wealth lowers people's living standards, consider what happens when a teacher announces at the beginning of the school year that she will redistribute some of the students' scores on exams. Some of the A and B students' correct answers will be credited to the D and F students. A, B, C, and D students all will receive a C. The A, B, D, and F students realize that they will get a C whether they do the homework, study for tests, and learn the material or not, so they do none of these things. Giving the D and F students Cs does nothing to improve their competency. And while the redistribution of student scores lessens grade inequality, it causes the A and B students to learn less and makes it difficult to match students' ability with the available opportunities.

Substitute the government for the teachers and work for the homework, and we have what happens when governments transfer large sums from high-income to low-income people. Once the transfers begin, the high- and low-income people work less, governments collect less tax revenue, and everybody becomes poorer. Just as the teacher's grade subsidies cause students to learn less, government wealth subsidies cause people to work less.

Now, by our very nature, most of us prefer to part with a portion of our surplus and provide people basic shelter, nutrition, healthcare, and education than retain all of our surplus and be haunted by their hardships.

If governments transfer resources freely to those who make poor decisions and have bad habits, however, they enable them to continue their current behavior. Even worse, they oftentimes (a) incentivize those receiving the transfers to have children and multiply their poor decision-making and habits, (b) enable greater numbers of adults to abandon their spouses and children, and (c) result in greater numbers of children dropping out of school and more people becoming alcoholics and drug addicts.

Consider the words of American Revolution leader Samuel Adams, *Declaration of Independence* author Thomas Jefferson, political thinker and historian Alexis de Tocqueville, economist and Nobel Laureate Milton Friedman, former Prime Minister Margaret Thatcher, and *Dune Series* author Frank Herbert regarding the redistribution of wealth.

The utopian schemes of leveling and a community of goods are as visionary and impracticable, as those which vest all property in the Crown, are arbitrary, despotic, and in our government, unconstitutional.[354]

—Samuel Adams

If we can but prevent the government from wasting the labors of the people, under the pretense of taking care of them, they must become happy.[355]

—Thomas Jefferson

Democracy extends the sphere of individual freedom, socialism restricts it. Democracy attaches all possible value to each [person]; socialism makes each [person] a mere agent, a mere number. Democracy and socialism have nothing in common but one word: equality. But notice the difference: while democracy seeks equality in liberty, socialism seeks equality in restraint and servitude.[356]

—Alexis de Tocqueville

There is all the difference in the world, however, between two kinds of assistance through government that seem superficially similar: first, 90 percent of us agreeing to impose taxes on ourselves to help the bottom 10 percent, and second, 80 percent voting to impose taxes on the top 10 percent to help the bottom 10 percent. . . . The first may be wise or unwise, an effective or ineffective way to help the disadvantaged—but it is consistent with belief in both equality of opportunity and liberty. The second seeks equality of outcome and is entirely antithetical to liberty.[357]

—Milton Friedman

Socialist governments traditionally do make a financial mess. They always run out of other people's money. It's quite a characteristic of them. They then start to nationalize everything, and people just do not like more and more nationalization. They're now trying to control everything by other means. They're progressively reducing the choice available to ordinary people.[358]

—Margaret Thatcher

Right from the first, the little people who formed the governments which promised to equalize the social burdens found themselves suddenly in the hands of bureaucratic aristocracies. Of course, all bureaucracies follow this pattern, but what a hypocrisy to find this even under a communized banner. Ahhh, well, if patterns teach me anything it's that patterns are repeated.[359]

—Frank Herbert

If socialism and redistributing people's wealth are undesirable, how do we grow the middle class? There is no simple solution, as it is the widespread use of numerous winning practices that creates a vibrant people.

The Winning Practices in this book create fit people and a strong middle class. Health, thought, integrity, proactivity, prudence, excellence, thrift and investment, along with affiliation, decency, understanding, leadership, teamwork, and improvement enhance individual and group effectiveness. Prudent spouse selection, marriage, responsible parenting, empowering habit formation, knowledge, universal education, parental choice, and results-oriented education empower young adults. Free enterprises and markets, responsible corporate governance, prudent regulation, and enterprise competitiveness enable people to actualize, earn a good living, and access an abundance of low-cost goods and services.

Government of the people; defined powers, prohibitions, and structures; freedoms, rights, and responsibilities; the rule of law; inclusion and meritocracy; prudent taxation; financial strength; savings accounts; state social safety nets; and consumer-driven healthcare, assimilation, peace through strength, and sustainability create an environment for people to flourish. Strong middle classes and vibrant populations are not the product of government but rather the product of an able people employing Winning Practices.

Savings Accounts

In Chapter 44, I discussed the benefits of a Goldilocks Minimum Wage under certain conditions. One of these conditions was for the government to incentivize individual savings accounts. Singaporeans benefit immensely from these savings accounts. While savings accounts are compulsory in Singapore, our government could provide incentives for them and make them optional in our country.

These savings accounts have brought Singaporeans incredible benefits in the form of low-cost, high-quality healthcare, the highest home ownership rate in the world, and relatively low taxes. The savings accounts also provide Singaporeans with one of the world's highest and fastest-growing living standards. When people save, they use fewer government services. The country forms its own capital, borrows less from foreigners, imports cost less, the economy thrives, incomes grow, and governments require less tax revenue.

The savings accounts in Singapore work much like our 401(k) retirement plans. The only differences are that there are three accounts and employers must withhold money from their employees' paychecks and deposit some of it into each employee's accounts. The first savings account is for health insurance and health-related expenses, the second is for education and housing costs, and the third is for retirement.

Singaporeans save and invest a whopping 36 percent of their income.[360] This compares to roughly a 6 percent savings rate for Americans.[361] Singaporeans save 7 percent of their earnings for health insurance and health-related expenses, 23 percent for education and housing, and 6 percent for retirement. The money they save they invest and use for the previously noted purposes.

The benefits of these savings accounts cannot be overstated. Unlike many Americans, most Singaporeans do not have a negative net worth or live from paycheck to paycheck. They have money to purchase health insurance and directly pay for healthcare. Their children do not have large amounts of debt when they complete their education, and 90 percent of Singaporeans own their own home. Were such a system of savings in place in our country, we could transform our extremely expensive healthcare system into a more functional, affordable, consumer-driven one. More of us would own our own homes, be financially secure, and have much higher retirement incomes.

Many people's first reaction to these savings accounts is: "They would never work in our country. We are free people and do not want our government telling us what we need to save." Well, what if our government permitted younger individuals to transition from publicly provided to self-provided healthcare, welfare, and retirement in exchange for lower income taxes? I think many young people would welcome this opportunity.

Employee 401(k) and IRA investment accounts are already common throughout the U.S. and work well. What needs to change is that employers should deposit the Social Security money that they and their employees pay to the federal government into a regulated employee savings account. The federal government has proven to be extremely irresponsible with our money. Rather than saving and investing our retirement money, our federal government runs a Ponzi scheme—promising payouts, spending the money it receives, and not having the funds to make good on its promises as our demographics change.

We are better stewards of our wealth than the federal government. We could invest the additional savings just as millions of us responsibly invest our 401(k) money. Bonded and qualified financial professionals help people protect their savings from inflation and double its value every 10 to 15 years. The money would be available to us at retirement regardless of the demographics and politics of our country. Employers would act as gatekeepers of the accounts, assuring that we use the money for the intended purposes.

With this approach, we would steadily increase our net worth and form capital to grow our living standards. We would temper business and debt cycles and have less severe recessions. We would lend to foreigners rather than borrow from them and have foreign exchange surpluses rather than deficits.

State Social Safety Nets

We have arranged help, but in such a way that only those who have no other choice will seek it. This is opposite of attitudes in the West, where liberals actively encourage people to demand entitlements with no sense of shame, causing an explosion of welfare costs.[362]

—Lee Kuan Yew

We do need a social safety net for those requiring temporary and ongoing assistance. Sometimes, family or medical difficulties prevent us from working, or for any number of reasons, we lose our jobs. Some people are born unable to provide for themselves. The question is not whether we should address these realities but how we should address them.

First, the Constitution of the United States does not grant the federal government the power to provide social programs. James Madison, a primary author of the Constitution, wrote:

> The government of the United States is a definite government, confined to specified objects. It is not like state governments whose powers are more general. Charity is no part of the legislative duty of the government. . . .

> I cannot undertake to lay my finger on the article of the Constitution which granted a right to Congress of expending, on objects of benevolence, the money of their constituents. [363]

Second, the federal government is too inefficient and likely to politicize and expand social programs to task it with providing them. When the federal government implements social programs, special interests mobilize to grow the programs and enrich themselves. No countervailing force exists to check the expansion, abuse, and cost of federal social programs.

Since Lyndon Johnson declared the "War on Poverty" and the federal government has spent trillions of dollars on social programs, four things about the programs have become painfully apparent: (1) they do not decrease the poverty rate, (2) they increase the dependent portion of the population, (3) they increase the proportion of children raised by single parents, and (4) they increase the percentage of children living in poverty. Harvard public policy professor Robert Putman notes that since the 1950s:

The opportunity gap has widened dramatically, partly because affluent kids now enjoy more advantages than affluent kids then, but mostly because poor kids now are in much worse shape than their counterparts then.[364]

Most poor children in the U.S. do not have two able parents to provide resources, form constructive habits, spend time with them, act as positive role models, and advocate for them. They often grow up in cultures and environments of dysfunction, limited opportunity, victimization mentalities, gangs, and addiction. Many do not have good eating habits nor access to quality daycare and schools. Few participate in organized extracurricular activities, attend vocational school or college, or find good jobs. When more than 7 percent of a population permanently depends on a social safety net, most likely the population is either unfit or the safety net is flawed.

When the federal government works with state governments to provide services, neither level of government is accountable for the programs. We see this with public education, welfare, and Medicaid. The federal and state governments mandate while county and local school boards execute. Increasing portions of the population collect public assistance at the same time families, neighborhoods, and schools deteriorate. Children learn less and people pay outrageous taxes. The federal government blames the state and local governments; the state and local governments blame the federal government.

A better way to help those needing ongoing assistance is for each county to employ private organizations to provide the support. The only role for state governments is to supplement the funding for services in the counties with poorer tax bases and higher costs-of-living.

With no federal government and little state involvement, counties would compete more with one another, establish work requirements for able-bodied people, and evolve lower-cost, higher-quality services. If one county's programs were too austere or dysfunctional, area voters would elect new leaders. If they were too lavish, poor people would inundate the county, and those paying for the programs would relocate.

While our current social service programs assist those in need, they also steal life from those who become unnecessarily dependent on them, those who become victims of the crimes of program recipients, and those who pay for the programs. Current social programs increase the incidence of illiteracy, teen pregnancy, single-parent families, abortions, alcoholism, drug abuse, and crime, and they burden hardworking people and waste scarce public resources.

To minimize the dependence-creating nature of public assistance, political support for the flawed programs, and their many other ill-effects, we should not allow those on welfare to vote. Only those who fund the pie should divide it and create the policies to assist others. Taxpayers and those dependent on social service programs have conflicting interests. Taxpayers want effective programs and recipients seek lavish ones.

We should also incentivize people not to have children while they receive public assistance. The priority for able-bodied people on public assistance is to obtain an education, marketable skills, and work. Children of people receiving public assistance face unrelenting uphill battles with disproportionate numbers ending up on public assistance or in prisons. Thousands of other people become victims of their crimes, and millions of other hardworking people pay billions of dollars to support, educate, and provide healthcare to them and billions of more dollars to arrest, try, and incarcerate many of them. If we examine our current approach to public assistance more closely, we realize it is largely insane.

We could discourage public assistance recipients from having children by reducing recipient benefits 20 percent for one year each time recipients have a child. Some people will say this is callous, but I would suggest that it is less cruel than continuing with the current system, turning our back on its shortcomings, and subjecting millions of children to their current opportunity void, and debilitating circumstances.

Our government should also track and cap the public assistance that able-bodied welfare recipients receive throughout their lives. No able-bodied person should receive unlimited benefits. Public resources are too scarce; when we spend resources exhaustively on one person, we do not have resources to devote to the health, education, and well-being of others.

Employment of the Unemployed

We do have some safety net programs that function reasonably well. Currently, states require employers and employees to purchase unemployment and workers' compensation insurance to provide income to unemployed and injured people. State governments and private sector companies handle this portion of our social safety net; not surprisingly, it is relatively effective.

The only changes that I would make to these programs are to: (a) have employers and employees share the cost of the unemployment, workers' compensation, and disability insurance, (b) privatize these insurances completely, and (c) require people to work for their benefits when unemployed. It makes sense for employers and employees to share the cost of unemployment, workers' compensation, and disability insurance because the conduct of both the employer and employee affects people's need for them. Privatizing the insurance is advantageous because private insurers operate less politically and more efficiently and cost-effectively than public agencies.

Requiring unemployed people to work for their benefits helps recipients maintain good work habits and their fitness. Such a program is easier to administer than we have been led to believe. With a higher Goldilocks Minimum Wage, states could enact programs that enable employers to hire unemployed people under the minimum wage and have private insurers make up the difference. Private insurers writing unemployment insurance could competitively solicit offers to employ the unemployed workforce, whereas participating employers would bid an hourly wage that they would pay whomever they hire from the pool of unemployed candidates.

States could mandate that unemployed people received 80 percent of the minimum wage. If the minimum wage was $15 per hour, then unemployed people would receive $12 per hour. Employers participating in the program might agree with an insurance company to hire 10 unemployed people for a year at $7 per hour per employee. The contracting firm would cover $7 of the $12-wage rate, and the insurance company would use its premiums to cover the remaining $5.

Implementing a program that requires unemployed people to work for their benefits would yield many benefits. Unemployed people would earn enough to live on, would not drop out of the workforce, and would have an ongoing incentive of at least $3 per hour to find regular work. They would maintain their fitness and continue to pay taxes. The cost of unemployment insurance would decrease significantly, and our enterprises and country would become more competitive.

Savings Accounts and Social Safety Nets – *(a) minimizing the need to redistribute wealth, (b) incentivizing people to contribute regularly to personal healthcare, education and housing, and retirement savings accounts, (c) having the states via county government provide public assistance to those who are born unable to provide for themselves, and (d) requiring employers and employees to purchase health, unemployment, disability, and injury insurances. Lower living standards, dependency, and dysfunction are the antitheses of savings accounts and social safety nets.*

Chapter 48

Consumer-Driven Healthcare

Of all the forms of inequality, injustice in healthcare is the most shocking and inhumane.[365]

—*Martin Luther King, Jr.*

Our country has two primary problems with healthcare: access and affordability. A small portion of our population cannot access quality healthcare, and a significant portion cannot afford it. Numerous secondary problems underlie these realities, some of which include third-party payment for healthcare, monopolistic concentrations of market power, unwarranted litigation, American obesity, and excessive end-of-life care. Consumer-driven healthcare is an approach where consumers pay large portions of the costs of healthcare directly. This approach is used in Singapore and Switzerland and has been found to produce the best outcomes for patients and other stakeholders in the healthcare system.

The cost of healthcare has been escalating at an outrageous rate. Figure 24 shows the increase in the cost of healthcare insurance for a family of four relative to median family income, and Figure 25 lists the drivers of the escalation of the healthcare costs. In 2001, the average cost of health insurance was $8,400, and median family income was $51,400. In 2017, the cost increased to $26,900 and family income rose to $75,900. The cost of health insurance amounted to 16 percent of a family's income in 2001 and 35 percent in 2017.[366] Think about this. Health insurance for a family of four now consumes over a third of their income!

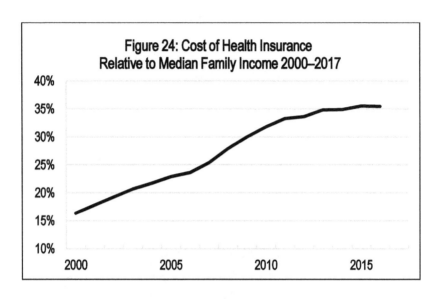

Figure 24: Cost of Health Insurance Relative to Median Family Income 2000–2017

https://fred.stlouisfed.org/series/MEFAINUSA646N
http://www.milliman.com/mmi/

Figure 25: Seven Drivers of the Escalation of Healthcare Costs

Consumers do not pay directly for their healthcare services;

The government allows providers to have near monopolies;

FDA regulatory bureaucracy and pharmaceutical-tiered pricing;

Inactivity and obesity of one-third of the U.S. population;

Large end-of-life expenditures;

Excessive malpractice awards and unnecessary testing; and

Widespread fraud within the current third-party-pay system.

These problems have been widely reported in the news and are easy to substantiate. I will not take time to discuss them now but will discuss transforming our third-party-pay, special-interest-driven healthcare system to a consumer-driven one and several other related Winning Practices in the upcoming chapters. Preceding generations of Americans benefited from many of these Winning Practices, and current generations in Singapore and Switzerland benefit from them now.

Harmful Medical Intervention

Today, when we go to the doctor an array of surgical procedures, physical therapies, prescriptions, and over-the-counter treatments exist for everything. If you are a doctor and want to feel, appear, and be perceived by the patient as being helpful, you intercede. If your living depends on your intervention and the conditions whether you should intervene are gray and opaque, you intervene. Yet oftentimes, what we need is just to relax, rest, be patient, and let our bodies heal themselves. Highly effective and proven natural responses to harm and disease have been worked out by nature over billions of years. For all but the most acute and life-threatening ailments, relaxation, rest, limited activity that improves our circulation, and patience are our best responses to bacterial and viral infections and aches and pains.

Nobody talks about this, but doctors and pharmaceutical companies present an agency problem. What is an agency problem?

Agency Problems occur when the interests of service providers conflict with the interests of their clients.

The good feelings, patient esteem, and fees that accompany medical intervention conflict with the insurer and patients' needs to conserve resources and allow natural processes time to heal the body. The interests of doctors and pharmaceutical companies always conflict with the interests of patients. Regulatory agencies, the public, pharmaceutical companies, and doctors need to be made much more aware of this, and doctors should receive extensive training about when to intervene.

We must also make people aware that regulatory agencies approve drugs because they have been found to be effective treatments for groups of people and not because they help every individual in the group. Some drugs work with some genomes and not with others. If you are elderly and taking ten different medications, some of them may not be helping you and all of them may be creating unpleasant and/or harmful side effects.

When I was raising millions of turkeys, I learned that we could grow much healthier turkeys with far fewer medical interventions by adjusting their diets and improving their environments. And it is no different with people. Were more people to improve their diets, maintain healthy weights, and improve their habits and surroundings, our population would be much healthier, fitter, and happier.

End-of-life treatment is another serious problem. Why do we extend the life of people who have no life? The life of my mother provides an example of misguided end-of-life extension that is dear to my heart. She started having serious dementia problems in her late 60s. She did not know anyone at age 83 could only communicate like a two-year-old at age 85. Why did she receive a pace maker, several ongoing medications, rounds of antibiotics, and numerous other medical interventions between the ages of 83 and 88? Why did my father spend more than $500,000 for nursing home care for the last five years of her life? The answer is because he and my mother's doctors thought that they should do everything possible to prolong life, and they did not want others to think poorly of them for just letting nature take its course.

Situations like my mother's play out millions of times a year across our country. Medical intervention and technology have brought us to the point that we need to view the end of our lives differently. Like the Native Americans, we need to think more about not burdening our families and our tribe at the end of our lives. We must take steps to refuse, and empower our family members to resist, medical interventions on our behalf as soon as our quality of life and healthspan start to seriously deteriorate. We also should pass legislation to restrict the federal and state governments from spending large sums on end-of-life care. One recent study suggests that prohibiting the federal government from covering the cost of any life-extending healthcare medications and services for people over the age of 80 would reduce our healthcare costs by as much as 50 percent.[367]

When we have lived some 75 years, twice as long as most of our ancestors, it is advantageous for us to accept the infirmities of old age and exit the world gracefully. If people want to use their personal resources to prolong their lives past the age of 80, this should be their choice. But we should not expect the government or others to use their resources to extend our lives after this age. And we certainly should not place large amounts of debt onto future generations to postpone our death for one to two years.

When we use public resources to extend our lives beyond 80 years, we have fewer resources to develop children, improve people's lives in general, and solve species-threatening problems like pandemics, climate change, and asteroid impacts. We slow our progress developing life-enhancing technologies and colonizing space.

We should treat all non-emergency medical interventions with skepticism. We should always ask medical professionals: Are you treating my symptoms or the actual disease? Is this intervention necessary? What are the risks of no treatment and the treatment? If you were in my situation, what would you do? Medical interventions should only occur when there are large payoffs and the benefits more than offset the costs and ill-effects.

Advantageous Immigration and Judicious Litigation

To have universal and affordable healthcare, several things must happen. Our government must control our borders and prevent illegal immigrants from overwhelming our labor markets and social safety net.

In 2010, illegal immigration lowered low-income wages by an estimated 6 percent.[368] In 2014, illegal immigration in California brought the state $3.5 billion in tax revenue and cost it an estimated $25.3 billion of its entire $108 billion state budget.[369] I discuss controlling our borders and advantageous immigration in the next chapter.

Enacting legislation to discourage frivolous lawsuits and limit medical malpractice awards is necessary for making healthcare more affordable and accessible. Doctors are human like the rest of us and make mistakes. We cannot allow litigators to prey on them as much as they currently do. A few lawsuits and reasonable awards against the negligent, sloppy, and repeat offenders strengthen the system. They weed out the poorly performing administrators, doctors, and nurses as well as incentivize the remaining ones to function at a high level.

A Harvard School of Public Health study estimated that large malpractice awards transfer $10 billion from the public to a small cadre of litigators annually and incentivize another $46 billion of paperwork and medical testing.[370] Judicious litigation was discussed in more detail in Chapter 43.

Goldilocks Minimum Wages and Savings Accounts

Our state governments need to set Goldilocks Minimum Wages for adults between the ages of 21 and 65 to ensure that people earn enough to purchase healthcare insurance and can pay some healthcare expenses out-of-pocket. I discussed the Goldilocks Minimum Wage in Chapter 44. People also need to have healthcare savings accounts to purchase health insurance and pay some out-of-pocket healthcare expenses. Governments can encourage these by giving adults a choice between making contributions to such accounts or paying an equivalent amount in taxes to a state Medicaid-like health insurance program. Savings accounts were discussed in the previous chapter.

Universal Coverage

As Martin Luther King, Jr., passionately advocated, every citizen in an affluent country should have access to quality healthcare. Pregnant mothers need prenatal care. Young children need immunizations and other medical services, and most people require some healthcare throughout their lives to maintain their health. Like elementary and secondary education, healthcare is a prudent investment in people. Other countries like Singapore and Switzerland make universal coverage work, and we can as well.

An amendment to the Constitution done in the correct way would further people's access to healthcare and health. Such an amendment would need to: (a) prohibit health insurers and providers from discriminating against people on the basis of age, sex, race, ethnicity, religion, genetic predisposition, and preexisting conditions, (b) allow health insurers and providers to give people discounts for maintaining proper weights and avoiding harmful activities, and (c) prohibit the federal government from covering the cost of end-of-life medical interventions for those over age 80.

Advantageous immigration, Goldilocks Minimum Wages, health savings accounts, state social safety nets, and prohibiting discrimination enable universal coverage. Allowing health insurers and providers to give discounts to fit people with good practices incentivizes fitness and good habits. Incentive discounts and limits on end-of-life expenditures would make healthcare insurance and healthcare much more affordable. If we want people to make healthy choices, we need to reward these decisions. We cannot allow people to make bad choices and then pass the costs of them to everyone else.

Consider the problem of obesity. Before people were relatively affluent and inactive, obesity was limited to chieftains and royalty, as obesity is a function of inexpensive, sugary, high-caloric foods, affluence, and inactivity. The development of sound eating and exercise habits take effort, time, and dedication. Most of us are short-term oriented and need more immediate rewards than the promise of better health 3 to 30 years from now. Allowing health insurers and providers to give fit people discounts provides immediate rewards.

Patient Choice

If we are to offer affordable, universal care to our citizens, we must harness the power of free enterprise and free markets. We must reap the benefits of competition. When consumers drive the healthcare system and governments keep insurers and providers from gaining too much market share, healthcare becomes efficient, affordable, and responsive. Consumers compare insurance plans and buy the most advantageous ones while insurers work hard to provide good plans at affordable prices. Consumers compare healthcare providers and select the best providers; providers and professionals work hard to provide high-quality services at affordable prices. Consumers come to trust their doctors and are less likely to sue them.

On the other hand, when health insurers, hospitals, and pharmaceutical companies gain large market shares, they raise prices. Health insurers increase the cost at more than the rate of inflation every year. Labor unions like the United Healthcare Workers 1199SEIU raise wage rates. Hospitals charge whatever they need to compensate their employees well and cover their costs. Pharmaceutical companies sell their products in the U.S. at much higher prices than they do elsewhere. Concentrations of market power and pharmaceutical pricing hurt patients as they increase inefficiency, raise costs, and stifle innovation.

Streamlining drug approval processes and allowing health insurers to offer a greater variety of insurance plans would also increase patient choices and lower healthcare costs. New drugs should not cost a billion dollars to bring to market.[371] Health insurers should be able to offer plans that (a) cover most of the expenses or only the major ones, (b) utilize private providers, health maintenance organizations, preferred provider organizations, or community clinics, and (c) address women's different childbearing preferences.

Out-of-Pocket Payments

In Singapore and Switzerland, healthcare is consumer-driven as opposed to insurer- or government-driven. Their healthcare is some of the most accessible, affordable, highest-quality healthcare in the world. People can buy lower-cost health insurance with relatively high copays and pay significant amounts out of their own pockets. This lowers the cost of the insurance, incentivizes consumers to spend their healthcare dollars wisely, makes the system more responsive to patients, and reduces fraud.

When governments, insurance companies, or other third parties make healthcare decisions and pay most of the expenses then insurers, providers, pharmaceutical companies, and unions gain large market shares and extract monopolistic returns. Consumers must accept what the insurers and providers offer. The system becomes inefficient, unaffordable, and unresponsive.

In the U.S., President Obama, deeply indebted to the 1199SEIU Union, attempted to increase access and lower healthcare costs with a 12-million-word National Health Care Act. The Democratic Party and main stream media supported the act without reading or understanding it, and Congress passed it with about as many representatives opposing it as supporting it. Not surprisingly, the Act: (a) created additional bureaucracy, (b) incentivized doctors to set up concierge practices and retire early, (c) brought consumers fewer choices, lower-quality care, and increased wait times, (d) escalated costs, and (e) suppressed employment and investment in our country.

Consumer-Driven Healthcare – *(a) control of our borders and advantageous immigration to avoid overwhelming our social safety net, (b) limit malpractice awards, (c) create Goldilocks Minimum Wages and healthcare savings accounts, (d) prohibit healthcare insurers and providers from discriminating against patients on the basis of age, sex, race, ethnicity, religion, genetic predisposition, and preexisting conditions, (e) incentivize people with healthcare discounts to be fit and avoid harmful activities, (f) refuse unnecessary, low benefit-to-risk, and end-of-life medical interventions, (g) limit end-of-life public expenditures, and (h) provide patients with more insurance and provider choices. Inefficient, poor-quality, inaccessible healthcare is antithetical to consumer-driven healthcare.*

Chapter 49

Assimilation

Many of our Winning Perspectives and Practices slip away when we fail to orchestrate the flow and assimilation of immigrants into our country.

What does it mean to be an American? In the past, an American was someone who valued truth, freedom, and decency; the Constitution, Bill of Rights, representative democracy, and the rule of law; family, community, and country; and honesty, education, hard work, and free enterprise. An American was forgiving, aspirational, and generous, someone who saw people as individuals, and who welcomed legal immigrants.

Americans were a "can do" people. Our schools, businesses, and government worked well. Our infrastructure was cutting-edge, and our living standards steadily improved. We did not want the government to intrude in our lives, treat some people better than others, or give able people a free ride. We rejected lawlessness, corruption, crime, and violence. But what does it mean to be an American today?

From Many, One

America, the home of the free and the brave, is now America the home of Caucasians, Hispanics, African-Americans, Asians, and Native Americans. American values of truthfulness, lawfulness, civility, hard work, and *E Pluribus Unum* are subordinated to political narratives, multiculturalism, entitlement, and open borders by those wanting to increase the power of minorities and the Democratic Party. And hypocrisies of hypocrisies, as leaders of these groups accuse outsiders of bigotry and discrimination, they seek special treatment and demonize and discriminate against anyone who sees things differently.

While numerous African Americans, Hispanics, and Muslims assimilate well and contribute mightily to our country, many do not and live apart. Without better assimilation and inclusion, substantial numbers of minorities develop American subcultures. Without greater selectivity, greater dispersion, and gaining control of illegal immigration throughout the country, Hispanic, black, and Muslim immigrants enlarge these subcultures and increase the divisions within the United States.

Jason Riley, an African American, senior fellow at the Manhattan Institute, and a columnist for *The Wall Street Journal,* addresses the tendency for large numbers of African Americans to reject the mainstream American culture and embrace a very different subculture:

Here were two young black girls, seven or eight years old, already linking speech patterns to race and intelligence. They already had a rather sophisticated awareness that, as blacks, white-sounding speech was not only to be avoided in their own speech but mocked in the speech of others.

Eighty percent of the black kids in New York public schools are performing below a grade level. And a big part of the problem is a black subculture that rejects attitudes and behaviors that are conducive to academic success. . . . Another big part of the problem is a reluctance to speak honestly about these cultural shortcomings. Many whites fear being called racists. And many black leaders have a vested interest in blaming black problems primarily on white racism, so that is the narrative they push regardless of the reality. Racism has become an all-purpose explanation for bad black outcomes, be they social or economic.

If [we] want to help reverse these crime trends, [we] would do better to focus less on supposed racial animus and more on ghetto attitudes towards school, work, marriage, and childrearing. As recently as the early 1960s, two out of three black children were raised in two-parent households. Today, more than 70 percent are not, and the number can reach as high as 80 or 90 percent in our inner cities. For decades, studies have shown that the likelihood of teen pregnancy, drug abuse, dropping out of school and other bad social outcomes increases dramatically when fathers aren't around.[372]

Jaime Ruvalcaba, a former Hispanic migrant worker and Marine Corps lieutenant colonel, affirms that we need to pay much more attention to the limited assimilation of Latinos into mainstream America. He writes:

After analyzing the Latino legal and illegal immigration flows, education levels, welfare utilization, gang involvement, incarceration rates, and costly parasitic. . . . subculture that prevents Latino youth from assimilating into mainstream society, I conclude that it is of the highest national priority that assimilation of Latinos be vastly accelerated. The social and economic costs are too high to continue to tackle this challenge piecemeal. Accordingly, the government, religious organizations, media, corporate sector, and first and foremost, Latino families must come together to address this threat to Latino youth—and to American identity.

The motto on our national seal reads "E Pluribus Unum." This motto needs to be the guiding theme for our immigration policy and especially our assimilation philosophy—not the multiculturalism that is without core values. Although I acknowledge the value of ethnic diversity, we must exercise caution in espousing the multiculturalist perspective that states that all cultures are equal—regardless of evidence to the contrary, and the costs with which it burdens society.[373]

Frank J. Gaffney Jr., president and CEO of the Center for Security Policy, raises some serious concerns regarding certain Muslim populations' intent to live apart and their failure to assimilate in Europe and the United States. He writes:

Such cohorts typically adhere rigidly to the authorities of Islam's totalitarian and supremacist doctrine of Shariah. They are, therefore, susceptible to domination and exploitation by Muslim Brotherhood organizations and operatives seeking to infiltrate and subvert unsuspecting Western societies "from within."

Matters are made worse by the blind spot that has been created with regard to this ideological wellspring of the Muslim Brotherhood and the Global Jihad Movement thanks to a systematic purge of all official U.S. government training curricula and vocabulary that might prove "offensive" to Muslims. Among the proscribed materials are accurate descriptions of the inspirational sources of Islamic terror to be found in the doctrine, law, and scriptures of Islam.

One consequence of this willful blindness is that the federal immigration system welcomes increasing numbers of Muslim immigrants, asylum seekers, and refugees whose commitment to becoming true Americans is not even discussed, let alone systematically factored into decisions about who to admit. Moreover, as entire regions of the Middle East and other parts of the world descend into chaos, the ability of immigration officials to conduct proper vetting of applicants by verifying places of origin, political orientation, criminal records, or even basic identity, is all too often non-existent.

The magnitude of the disaster being invited is . . . evident in Western Europe where the results of misguided "multicultural" experiments, lax immigration policies, and indifference to assimilation has produced entire neighborhoods in many countries that are essentially Muslim ghettos, where Shariah prevails, outsiders rarely venture and even police and emergency responders need armed protection to carry out their duties. We are on notice, especially insofar as tables across the Islamic world . . . openly proclaim their intent to conquer the West from within through the process of Muslim migration.[374]

What is happening to many immigrants and Hispanic and African American groups in our country now is very different than what happened with the millions of European and Asian immigrants who came to this country in the past. Europeans and Asians brought more traditional American perspectives and practices with them and largely cut their ties with their mother countries. Within one or two generations, they took on an American identity. They brought and adopted more of the Winning Perspectives and Practices that I describe in this book. They did not force the language of their mother country upon their children and required little or no public assistance. They took what work was available, steadily improved their living standards, and contributed mightily to our communities and country.

United We Stand, Divided We Fall

A tribe including many members who, from possessing in a high degree the spirit of patriotism, fidelity, obedience, courage, and sympathy, were always ready to aid one another, and to sacrifice themselves for the common good, would be victorious over most other tribes.[375]

—Charles Darwin

United we stand, divided we fall. Trite? I think not. Anybody who has ever struggled to overcome an enemy in war, a rival in business, or another sports team understands the truth of this statement. A shared mission, values, agenda, and trust unify groups and enable them to perform well and persist.

High-functioning groups are comprised of individuals who *differ* and are *similar in meaningful ways.* Some lead, some inspire, some plan, some organize, some innovate, some teach, some raise children, and some just do whatever needs to be done. Moreover, most of the people in high-functioning groups share a common history, language, purpose, set of practices, and an agenda. The differences create synergy, and the similarity creates cohesion, two essential ingredients of high-performing groups. Countries are just larger groups that work best when their citizens share a common culture or at least a common language and common values, perspectives, practices, prohibitions, and mission.

Numerous cultures and orders work in a country. Sorting out the best mix requires a lot of learning, deliberation, and work. So, we depend on our leaders to identify and articulate a common language, values, perspectives, practices, prohibition, and mission. Every winning perspective and practice that we employ improves our social cohesion, fitness, and well-being.

English as the National Language

In an established national society, one of the fundamental qualifications for joining that national society is an adequate knowledge of the unifying language of that society. It was this language qualification that ensured for the Americans that basic unifying force. Racially, the immigrants started as Germans, Italians, Spaniards, and even Japanese. But the fact that the American state insisted on an adequate command of the American version of English before accepting the immigrants as citizens of the state ensured the unifying force of one common language in the people.[376]

—Lee Kuan Yew

How is it that a man halfway around the world understood the importance of a unifying language, and particularly English, to our country's success when so many of our current leaders do not understand it? How is it that this man incentivized Singaporeans to make English their primary language even though most Singaporeans spoke Mandarin, Malay, or Tami? The answer is Lee Kuan Yew was the top student in all of Malaysia in 1939 and was later educated at Cambridge University. He saw firsthand what our country did for Japan after WWII, understood that most of the business in the world at that time was conducted in English, and recognized the importance of social cohesion and the unifying role of language.

One language unifies. Multiple languages divide. One only needs to visit countries like Belgium, Canada, India, and South Africa to understand the divisiveness and never-ending accommodations that citizens of multilingual countries make to accommodate all the major subcultures. Moreover, when a language like English dominates the world, people who do not speak it are at distinct competitive disadvantages. Not making instruction in English widely available and free—and permitting many immigrants and their children to speak their native language in school and workplaces—handicaps many people for life.

Impervious Borders

The primary responsibility of a country's leadership is to look out for the well-being of its citizens, a duty that includes securing the country's borders and ensuring an orderly flow of immigrants into the country. When immigrants come into the country illegally, gangs, criminals, and terrorists enter the country. Low-end wages stagnate. People's relative income and upward mobility decrease. People's respect for the government and law diminish, and order breaks down. Immigrants overwhelm the infrastructure, schools, healthcare, and social services. Governments heavily tax their citizens, run out of money, and people's quality of life deteriorates.

The U.S. Census Bureau reports that 4.7 million people—or some 63 percent of the total non-citizen households—receive welfare.[377] Federal, state, and local government welfare expenditures for these households were an estimated $134.9 billion in 2017.[378] Depending on how one looks at it, this amounts to a $1,100 annual burden on every working American citizen or an additional $134.9 billion of debt that we place on our grandchildren every year.[379]

When immigrants enter a country illegally and concentrate too much in a geographic area, most people react to the dilution of American perspectives and practices in one of three ways. First, cultural relativists do not care because they maintain that all cultures are equally valid . . . at least until you ask them about radical Islam. Second, partisans celebrate if their political power increases with the greater numbers of immigrants. Everyone else? Well, they get it. They oppose the violation of the law, dilution of our culture, displacement of American workers, and public support of foreigners who have never paid taxes.

Our laws, institutions, and policies do not operate in isolation. Changes in one of them affect other things. Immigration policies and practices affect the labor supply, wage rates, and the demand for social services. Permitting many people to enter our country and improve their lives makes sense until it depresses the wages of our citizens and overwhelms our infrastructure, healthcare system, and social safety net.

Advantageous Immigration

First-generation immigrants do not fully absorb their new country's culture. They dilute it to some extent and never fully assimilate. Countries only preserve their cultures and assure second-generation assimilation as they limit immigrant numbers and disperse them throughout their populations. If a 5-percent concentration of immigrants noticeably dilutes a culture, immigrants average 25 years in age, and they live another 50 years on average, then immigrants should only enter well-functioning countries at an annual rate of 1/10 of a percent of the population. This would work out to about 320 thousand immigrants a year for a country with a population of 320 million like the United States. Richard Estrada of the *Dallas Morning News* wrote:

> The problem in which the current immigration is suffused is, at heart, one of numbers; for when the numbers begin to favor not only the maintenance and replenishment of the immigrants'

source culture, but also its overall growth, and in particular growth so large that the numbers not only impede assimilation but go beyond to pose a challenge to the traditional culture of the American nation, then there is a great deal about which to be concerned.[380]

Countries cannot maintain their cultures when scores of foreigners dilute them, sustain their rule of law when large numbers of illegal immigrants undermine it, and maintain the integrity of their elections when illegal immigrants vote. They cannot increase wage rates when large numbers of immigrants increase the supply of labor faster than their enterprises create jobs. They cannot provide a high level of social services for their citizens who need them when scores of immigrants overwhelm the providers.

We would find it advantageous to do as most other countries in the world do and as Harvard University researcher and lecturer Lawrence Harrison suggests:

– End illegal immigration by enforcing the laws on employment and strengthening our control of our [borders].

– Calibrate legal immigration annually to (1) the needs of the economy and (2) past performance of immigrant groups with respect to assimilation and contribution to our society.

– Declare our national language to be English and discourage the proliferation of Spanish-language media.

– End birthright citizenship, limiting citizenship by birth to children with at least one parent who is a citizen.

– Provide immigrants with easy-to-access education services that facilitate assimilation, including English language, citizenship, and culture.[381]

Five percent of the U.S. population was foreign-born in 1965 compared to 14 percent, or approximately 45 million people, in 2015.[382] Over 10 million of the 45 million foreign-born people were illegal immigrants.[383] We are accepting immigrants too fast and poorly vetting them. We are significantly diminishing the prevalence of our Winning Practices in our culture, the quality of our institutions, our living standards, and the social cohesion of our country.

Limiting the flow of immigrants to levels that assimilate well would lessen the burden on our public infrastructure, healthcare system, and social safety net. It would reduce social welfare spending, government deficits, and the amount of debt that we pile on future generations. Limiting citizenship by birth to children with at least one parent who is an American citizen would end the practice of people just coming to the U.S. to have children, and then taking advantage of numerous social services. Varying the flow of immigrants into the country inversely with the unemployment rate would mitigate business cycles and increase low-end wages. Giving preference to those who already speak English, have needed skills, and are most likely to contribute to our country would enhance the social cohesion and well-being of all the people in our country.

Assimilation – (a) recognizing that strength accrues to groups who have different perspectives and aptitudes and common values and objectives, (b) accepting immigrants on the basis of their values, skills, and willingness to assimilate, (c) making English the national language and the primary language of instruction in all schools, (d) securing our borders, and (e) creating a legal and advantageous flow of immigrants into our country. Division, racial and ethnic strife, and weakness are antitheses of assimilation.

Chapter 50

Peace Through Fitness

There is nothing so likely to produce peace as to be well prepared to meet the enemy.[384]

—*George Washington*

In the middle of war-torn Europe, Switzerland has remained free from war for over 150 years. This is because they are fit, prepared to meet the enemy, and mind their own business. Men in Switzerland serve one year in the military. After basic training, they do annual three-week retraining courses until age 30. Those who are found unfit to serve must perform alternative service. Women serve on a voluntary basis. Those who serve in the military keep weapons in their homes throughout their lives.

The notions held by some that one world government and global disarmament ensure peace and a desirable world order are erroneous. One world government would yield factions vying for power and perpetual corruption. Power corrupts when it concentrates in the absence of competition. We only need to study the rule of past popes, kings, queens, and dictators to understand this. Humans are predatory. In the absence of government, the strong dominate the weak, and in the lack of a strong defense, other countries take advantage of your country. World-renowned biologist E.O. Wilson writes:

Are human beings innately aggressive? . . . The answer is yes. . . . Only by redefining the words "innateness" and "aggression" to the point of uselessness might we correctly say that human aggressiveness is not innate.[385]

Animals use aggression as a technique for gaining control over necessities . . . that are scarce or are likely to become so. . . . They intensify their threats and attack with increasing frequency as the population around them grows.[386]

Ultimately, people, tribes, and countries compete for territory, resources, and influence through wars. The winners of the wars control the landscape and divide the resources and spoils. Natural laws apply to countries and human life, just as they apply to plants, animals, and businesses. Countries, corporations, and people either are fit or they become subservient to others and gradually exit the stage. Peace is ideal, but without constitutionally and institutionally limited government, social cohesion, preparation, and fitness, the realities are corruption, conflict, and subservience. Historians Will and Ariel Durant estimate that only 268 of the past 3,421 years have been free of major wars.[387]

Seven Levels of Human Fitness

Peace requires constitutionally and institutionally limited government, social cohesion, preparation, and fitness, which in turn depend on the widespread use of Winning Perspectives and Practices on all seven levels of human organization: individual, family, group, education, enterprise, government, and culture.

Individual, family, group, and education Winning Practices develop healthy, honest, thoughtful, able people and leaders who work together, perform at a high level, and continuously improve their families, communities, education, enterprise, government, and culture. Enterprise-related Winning Practices create an efficient, cost-effective, and innovative economic engine to fund our institutions and lives. Government-related Winning Practices create a free, orderly, and opportunity-rich environment. Culturally-related Winning Practices identify and propagate the Winning Perspectives and Practices throughout the population and across generations.

Financial Strength

Financial strength is essential to peace. It occurs when the current and future means of people, organizations, and their nation exceed their obligations. It is the product of limited government, free enterprise, good information, sound money, sound lending practices, balanced budgets, little indebtedness, prudent taxation, full employment, high productivity, and healthy capital formation.

Much is possible when countries are free and financially healthy. People have ample territory and resources and do not need to attack other countries. People have excellent healthcare and schools. They interact and travel freely, actualize, and enjoy life. They have the resources to care for the young, disadvantaged, elderly, and the environment. The citizenry conducts basic research and explores new worlds.

A financially strong population has little need to take other people's resources. People may buy them. The country has the wherewithal to prepare for and deter war. Enterprises have the means to innovate. The government's leaders can attract allies, resolve conflicts, and shape a civil and prosperous world order.

Law Enforcement and Justice

In every population, some people bully, steal from others, and prey on others. A free and just order requires effective law enforcement, judiciary, and penal systems. A police force must round up those who violate laws, a network of courts must determine their guilt, and a penal system must punish violators to incentivize lawfulness. If we do not do these things and do them well, lawlessness takes root and grows.

Law enforcement starts with prudent laws and impartial and competent policing. The police must have high-integrity, be well-trained, and be paid well to minimize corruption and crime. National law enforcement agencies must monitor local ones and remove any bad apples on an ongoing basis. People must respect and honor their officers. Putting one's life on the line every day is worthy of respect and honor.

One of the things that our culture no longer does well is to correct and discipline poorly-parented males who are particularly prone to unlawful behaviors. As Niall Ferguson writes:

Civilization is partly about restraining the male of the species from engaging in the violence of the hunter-gatherer period.[388]

Many people who break laws, particularly young males, never had parents who loved and disciplined them. They never learned self-control, to defer gratification, or self-discipline. They never had the opportunity to actualize and contribute. Rather than cage these young people like wild animals when they break our laws, it would be advantageous for them to attend rehabilitation centers like the academies described in Chapter 32 to learn empowering perspectives, practices, and work skills. Giving our judges the option of sending first-time offenders convicted of minor crimes to such centers would improve many lives, dramatically reduce our prison populations, and be superior to housing first-time offenders with criminals who transmit felonious perspectives and practices to them.

Such rehabilitation centers would provide their residents a positive environment, one of nurture, discipline, and structured time. Residents would do chores, attend classes, and participate in sports or arts-related activities. If they did not behave satisfactorily, the centers could withhold their evening meal. Just as the early Native Americans disciplined their unruly youth in this way, we should try disciplining first-time offenders in this manner. Periodic fasting is good for us and uncomfortable enough to change people's attitudes and behaviors.

Community service, monetary fines, and capital punishment are also penal options. Community service and monetary fines work well for minor offenses. Applying the death penalty to large drug dealers, terrorists, sex traffickers, those killing police, and serial killers protects the innocent, deters crime, and civilizes the gene pool over time. We must counter misguided sentiments and recognize, as Adam Smith wrote:

Mercy to the guilty is cruelty to the innocent.[389]

Military, Cyber, and Intelligence Strength and Restraint

We are all capable of believing things which we know to be untrue, and then, when we are finally proved wrong, imprudently twisting the facts to show that we were right. Intellectually, it is possible to carry on this process for an indefinite time: the only check on it is that sooner or later a false belief bumps up against solid reality, usually on a battlefield.[390]

—George Orwell

Little is more terrifying or ugly than war to those who love life. The separation of families, tremendous amounts of melee and carnage, and loss of loved ones cause us to want to avoid war at all costs. Yet, it is our preparation for war and willingness to go to war that free us from it. History is clear on this.

Most wars are avoidable and won or lost before the fighting starts. Those who are better led, better prepared, and more disciplined win. We learn this from the Swiss. Nations can avoid war when they diligently prepare for them, deal honorably with others, avoid entangling alliances, and fight when necessary. Others only attack us when they believe there is more to gain than lose. The great Chinese general Sun Tzu wrote:

To secure ourselves against defeat lies in our own hands, but the opportunity of defeating an enemy is provided by the enemy himself. [391]

Evolution and history demonstrate that the world is a rough place and not for the faint of heart. Challenging opponents who are weak or hesitant to fight is profitable. We are strong, fit, and prudent or we submit and die. All forms of life outstrip their available territory and resources at some point, identify other poorly-defended territory and resources, and take them. Humans are no different. We make ourselves undesirable targets or we must fight one day for our territory, resources, and lives.

Avoiding war does not require superior strength. It only requires enough strength to inflict sufficient damage on one's adversaries to make other targets more attractive and their aggression unprofitable. Every avoided war and subdued enemy resulted from positions of strength that were not created overnight. A position of strength is a function of numbers, resources, preparation, technology, and will. State-of-the-art armies, navies, air and space forces, cyber defenses, and intelligence service are essential components of a position of strength.

The state of our Army, Navy, and Air Force has fluctuated with our presidential administrations over the years. Four to eight years of buildup followed by four to eight years of cuts is wasteful, demoralizing, and foolish. Predictable cycles create vulnerabilities and opportunities for aggressors and incentivize foreigner governments to interfere with our elections. Transforming the leadership of the Executive Branch from a single president to a council, as I suggest in Chapter 41, would lessen these fluctuations and the adverse effects associated with them. We also need to allocate more talent and resources to defend our computers, Internet, and satellites, especially as our competitors identify their vulnerabilities and have more access to space.

Foreign intelligence has always been incredibly important and is even more important today. Just as coaches assess opposing teams, countries must evaluate their competitors. There is no substitute for knowing the strengths, weaknesses, plans, methods, technology, and actions of our competitors. Enterprises, institutions, and governments must use sophisticated technologies to collect, analyze, and exploit oceans of information. Being able to defend and penetrate our competitors' computing technology, information systems, and space-based assets are now primary forms of strength.

To increase our strength, we would be wise to follow the example of the Swiss and require all young, fit males to serve for one year in the military and then serve in the reserves for three weeks a year until age 30. Men who are found unfit to serve in the military could perform alternative forms of community service.

This practice would deter foreign aggression. It would immerse young men in a culture of discipline and further their maturation. Providing this opportunity to women, but not requiring it, would give women the same opportunities as men. It would allow women to serve or establish their careers and have children, something that is necessary for the continuation of our population and culture. Soldiers and other people who risk their lives to defend our communities and country are precious. We want to employ rules of engagement that minimize the likelihood of harm to them and honor their service.

A comfortable and secure order requires strength and knowing when to use our power. James Madison wrote:

In no part of the Constitution is more wisdom to be found than in the clause which confides the question of war or peace to the legislature and not to the executive department.

War is in fact the true nurse of executive aggrandizement. In war a physical force is to be created, and it is the executive will which is to direct it. In war the public treasures are to be unlocked, and it is the executive hand which is to dispense them. In war the honors and emoluments of office are to be multiplied; and it is the executive patronage under which they are to be enjoyed. It is in war, finally, that laurels are to be gathered, and it is the executive brow they are to encircle. The strongest passions, and most dangerous weaknesses of the human breast—ambition, avarice, vanity, the honorable or venial love of fame—are all in conspiracy against the desire and duty of peace.[392]

And Sun Tzu cautioned:

[Those who wish] to fight must first count the cost.[393]

Wars involve much more than winning battles. They completely alter thousands and thousands of people's lives and their repercussions last generations. It is not enough to fight a war and win. Engaging in war carries at least six additional responsibilities: (1) honoring the fallen and the veterans of conflicts, (2) integrating the veterans into civilian life, (3) supporting the children and families of fallen and disabled veterans, (4) repaying any accumulated debts, (5) rebuilding armed forces, and (6) helping the ravaged and displaced populations get back on their feet. These actions are necessary to incentivize people to defend our country in the future, reestablish the country's financial strength, prepare for future conflicts, and transform enemies into allies.

Wars maim and kill countless people. They orphan children. They consume resources and increase indebtedness. They generate transgenerational hatred and sow the seeds of future conflicts. We only should engage in war to defend ourselves and secure essential territory, resources, and interests after exhausting all reasonable economic, political, and diplomatic options. Requiring two-thirds of the support of both the House and Senate to declare and appropriate funds for war reduces a country's involvement in wars and separates the decision to enter war from the decision to execute it. It prevents leaders from going to war to gain political support and limits our involvement in wars to the rare instances when an overwhelming majority of our representatives believe it is necessary.

Military complexes are also dangerous. They are drawn to war, and they maim people, consume resources, and accelerate arms races as well as protect and liberate people. They may consume resources needlessly as well as protect them. James Madison wrote:

> The means of defense against foreign danger have been always the instruments of tyranny at home. Among the Romans, it was a standing maxim to excite a war, whenever a revolt was apprehended. Throughout all Europe, the armies kept up under the pretext of defending, have enslaved the people.[394]

War is the parent of armies; from these proceed debts and taxes; and armies, and debts, and taxes are the known instruments for bringing the many under the domination of the few.[395]

Those who are to conduct a war cannot in the nature of things, be proper or safe judges, whether a war ought to be commenced, continued, or concluded. They are barred from the latter functions by a great principle in free government, analogous to that which separates the sword from the purse, or the power of executing from the power of enacting laws.[396]

Not only must we separate the declaration and funding of wars from their execution, but we must also only entrust the presidency and positions of military leadership to those who have the greatest character and respect for the Constitution. In all cases, we must seek candidates who have a higher regard for our country, Constitution, and laws than they have for their political agendas. To help curb the discretionary, cursory use of the military by presidents, we should amend the Constitution to allow them to deploy the military only in the event of an attack or with a majority consent of the members of both the Senate and House.

The successful execution of war requires the support of the President, Legislative Branch, citizens, military leaders, and soldiers. Our leaders must define the objectives of war and *the plan to exit from the war* before our representatives commit us. They do not have to share the details with the public or our enemies, but they must create the plan. Our Executive Branch needs to enlist allies and plan a war, and our Legislative Branch should adequately fund it. When we decide to fight, we must act with decisiveness, employing overwhelming force, as people have no appetite for protracted wars. If we are well-prepared, financially and militarily strong, judicious, and willing to crush our enemies, we seldom will need to fight.

Allies and Limited Treaty Powers

There is strength in numbers, but we must carefully choose the leaders and governments with whom we ally. Most leaders of countries retain power for a few years and our most helpful and enduring allies are the countries with leaders, governments, and cultures most like our own. Just as enduring friendships among people require commonality, respect, nurture, and reciprocity, so do enduring relationships with nations.

We earn others' trust by being trustworthy, and we should only trust those who demonstrate trustworthiness. We must help others in their hour of need, and expect, but not count on, others to help us in our time of need. We should not expect our allies to do whatever we want nor should they expect us to do whatever they want. Moreover, we should not spy on our closest allies nor allow them to spy on us.

We also must limit the ability of our presidents to make treaties with foreign governments by making it clear in the Constitution that all treaties with foreign governments must have Senate approval before becoming law and that no treaty can violate the authority of the Constitution of the United States.

Democratic Realism

Isolationism, internationalism, realism, and democratic globalism are four common approaches to foreign policy. Libertarians tend to favor isolationism, liberals internationalism, conservatives realism, and some liberals and conservatives democratic globalism. A fifth, and the best approach, democratic realism, is a mix of realism and democratic globalism.

Isolationism is an approach to foreign policy that avoids becoming involved in the affairs of other countries. It is a live and let live approach. Isolationism makes sense for fledging countries but not for those able to create a lawful international order and whose well-being depends on international trade.

Isolationism involves withdrawing from the world and staying out of other countries' affairs.

Internationalism is indifferent to national interests and sensitive to humanitarian interests. It is nice in theory but does not work in practice. Internationalism's insistence upon multilateralism prevents countries from defending themselves and advancing their interests. It ignores the realities that countries compete for territory, resources, and influence; countries advance their self-interests first and others' second; and power concentrates and corrupts in the absence of competition.

Internationalism seeks to abolish national interest, advances international norms, and expects governments to act in a humanitarian and multilateral manner.

Realism understands that people and countries are predatory. It recognizes that international organizations are too disparate in their values, norms, and interests to maintain a workable order. China, Russia, Iran, and the U.S. are examples of four influential countries in the world with very competing values, norms, and interests. There is little social cohesion among the leaders and people of these countries. While these countries may work together to facilitate trade, they constantly work to outmaneuver one another for territory, resources, and/or influence.

Realism understands that those who share values, norms, and interests must defend them. The downside of realism is that countries are less able to develop and utilize soft power or the power that comes from universal aspirations for freedom, self-determination, and prosperity.

Realism is rooted in an understanding of human nature. It recognizes that our well-being depends on competition and the defense of our citizens' shared values, norms, and interests.

Democratic globalism is an alternative to realism. It seeks to proliferate our values and norms as we advance our interests, capitalizing on people's aspirations for freedom, self-determination, and prosperity. Democratic globalism uses soft power to attract allies and hard power to control foes. The problem with democratic globalism is its open-ended commitment. We have limited resources and no appetite for casualties, and we cannot bring freedom, self-determination, and prosperity to everyone in the world.

Democratic Globalism preserves and proliferates our values, and it sees freedom as the supreme value. The objective is not power, but rather to protect and advance a population's values.

Democratic Realism is a foreign policy that Charles Krauthammer developed from Realism and Democratic Globalism. He defines it as follows:

> We will support democracy everywhere, but we will commit blood and treasure only in places where there is a strategic necessity—meaning, places central to the larger war against the existential enemy, the enemy that poses a global mortal threat to freedom.

> Where does it count? Fifty years ago, Germany and Japan counted. Why? Because they were the seeds of the greatest global threat to freedom in midcentury—fascism—and then were turned by nation-building, into bulwarks against the next great threat to freedom, Soviet communism.

> Where does it count today? Where the overthrow of radicalism and the beginnings of democracy can have a decisive effect. [397]

To Charles Krauthammer's Democratic Realism, I would add a corollary that we will only nation-build where the Confucius, Buddhist, Jewish, and Protestant cultures have preceded us and there is the opportunity to be successful. Preserving our territory, freedom, and culture is natural and necessary. Crushing aggressive and troublesome regimes and changing their leaders is much more doable than holding their territory and nation-building, which are long, arduous, expensive, and risky propositions. The likelihood of their success depends on the culture and conditions that precede us.

Democratic Realism (a) preserves our territory, freedom, and culture, (b) protects our interests in the face of the countervailing interests, (c) supports democracy everywhere but only commits "blood and treasure" in places of strategic necessity, and (d) only nation builds where Confucianism, Buddhism, Judaism, and Christianity precede us.

Peace Through Fitness – (a) avoiding violent conflict by preparing for it and dealing with others honorably, (b) the widespread use of Winning Practices on all seven levels of human organization, (c) financial strength, (d) law enforcement and justice, (e) military and cyber strength, (f) foreign intelligence, (g) prudent alliances and limited treaty powers, and (h) democratic realism. Insecurity, war, heartache, and decline are antitheses to Peace Through Fitness.

Chapter 51

Sustainability

We increase the opportunities for future generations when we live more sustainably.

When our numbers were few and our lifestyles more natural, we were a harmless presence on Earth. This is no longer the case. Now, we are many, and whether we are aware of it or not, our lifestyles degrade natural habitats. Most of us live, commute, and work in manufactured buildings, cars, and communities in suburban and urban centers of grass and concrete. If we experience a natural habitat, we experience it on a rare visit to a county, state, or national park.

Apart from nature, we deforest land, drain wetlands, and dam rivers. We irrigate crops and lower water tables. We douse the soil and groundwater with fertilizers, herbicides, and pesticides. We cover fields and forests with highways, commercial centers, suburban communities, and cities. We spread salt on roads and contaminate the groundwater in the winters. We harvest immense quantities of coal, oil, natural gas, and minerals from the earth. We burn vast amounts of fossil fuels, releasing tremendous amounts of greenhouse gases into the atmosphere and increasing our atmosphere's retention of heat. We bury mountains of municipal waste and radioactive material, creating hazards for generations.

Herbicides, pesticides, chemical fertilizers, and medicines find their way into our streams, rivers, lakes, coastal waters, and oceans. They change the alkalinity of coastal waters, destroy oyster and coral reefs, and harm other wildlife. Our activities destroy land and sea-based habitats, eliminate hundreds of species every year, and our populations and harmful activity increase. Unless we reverse these trends, we will soon overwhelm the Earth and life that supports us. E.O. Wilson writes:

Few will doubt that humankind has created a planet-sized problem for itself. No one wished it so, but we are the first species to become a geophysical force, altering Earth's climate, a role previously reserved for tectonics, sun flares, and glacial cycles. We are also the greatest destroyer of life since the ten-kilometer-wide meteorite that landed near Yucatan and ended the Age of Reptiles sixty-five million years ago.[398]

Water, Air, and Land

Water covers about 70 percent and land about 30 percent of Earth's surface.[399] About 40 percent of the land is cultivated, 30 percent is forests, and 30 percent is deserts, mountains, or covered with ice.[400] If Earth was the size of a basketball, its atmosphere would fill a squash ball, the oceans a large marble, and its fresh water a BB.[401] Although air and water cover all or most of Earth's surface, paradoxically there are not much of them.

The diameter of Earth is eight thousand miles, and its atmosphere is only five to ten miles thick. The atmosphere seems plentiful to us, but there is not much of it. Its thickness is only $1/1,000^{th}$ of Earth's diameter. Its composition is approximately 78 percent nitrogen, 21 percent oxygen, and 1 percent carbon dioxide and water vapor.[402] Plants preceded animals by hundreds of millions of years. Plants use the sun's energy to convert carbon dioxide and water into oxygen and carbohydrates. Animals cannot exist without plants. All the oxygen that animals breathe comes from plants. When plants die and layer into the earth, vast amounts of carbon accumulate on the surface.

Our oceans cover most of Earth's surface but are only about 2 miles deep or $3/10,000^{ths}$ of Earth's diameter. They house immense amounts of algae, other photosynthesizing plants, and fish, some of our primary sources of oxygen and protein. What about our fresh water? All fresh water on Earth evaporated from the oceans and fell back as rain or snow, and more than 99 percent of our fresh water is frozen.[403]

If we want to leave our children and other lifeforms a habitable planet, we must become better stewards of our air, oceans, freshwater, forests, arable land, and wetlands, improving the quality of our air, water, and land. We must use agricultural methods that preserve topsoil and protect groundwater and cluster our homes, workplaces, shopping centers, and recreational areas. We must do these and so many other things to reduce our impact on the air, oceans, lakes, rivers, streams, forests, farmland, and the land we occupy.

Ecosystem Conservation and Biodiversity

We depend on plants for oxygen, food, and habitats; bacteria and animals for nutrients and the degradation of waste; and wetlands to filter water. Many of the plants and animals that we consume rely on the grasslands, arable land, forests, mangroves, coral reefs, and seas.

To date, human activity has destroyed an estimated 50 percent of the world's forests, 65 percent of the wetlands in Europe, 50 percent of the wetlands in the United States, 40 percent of the world's coral reefs, and 35 percent of the world's mangroves.[404]

Stuart Pimm, a conservation ecologist at Duke University, and his colleagues estimate that less than one species per million went extinct annually before modern humans evolved 200 thousand years ago; since then, about 500 species per million go extinct annually.[405] Current lifeforms have been over 3 billion years in the making. They and our planetary ecosystems are precious.

This and other ecological data suggest that we have reached the point where increases in the human population on Earth are undesirable. We cannot sustain our population and culture, however, and unilaterally decrease them. I discussed this dilemma in detail in Chapter 8, stating:

We can no more unilaterally decrease our procreative . . . power as our nuclear power. Just as we only decrease our nuclear arsenal when our primary competitor, Russia, decreases its arsenal, so we must only decrease our procreation only as China, India, Brazil, and the Islamic countries decrease their procreation.

So how might we resolve this dilemma? We can solve it with contraceptives, education, negotiation, incentives, and innovation. The history of all countries shows that family sizes dramatically decrease as contraceptives become available and women are educated. To see this, one only needs to compare the average family size in Yemen, where women are poorly educated, with the average family size in the United Arab Emirates, where women are well-educated. These countries had similar family sizes and cultures until the leaders of the United Arab Emirates made the education of women a priority a couple of decades ago. The education of women decreases family size and civilizes the society. Radical ideologies do not thrive in countries with well-educated women. Decreased population growth is achievable with the availability of contraceptives, the education of women, and negotiation.

Limiting population growth, restoring lost habitats, and preserving the planet's biodiversity require leadership, education, and negotiation. They require individual, for-profit, nonprofit, and government initiatives. Science-based environmental groups must make us more aware of the need to alter our lifestyles. Schools must teach children how to live sustainably. People and enterprises must adopt greener technologies and lifestyles. Governments must prohibit environmentally harmful activities and incentivize sustainable living patterns. They must tax labor and capital less and the activities that degrade our ecosystems and planet more. They must work domestically and internationally to limit habitat and wildlife destruction.

Ecosystem and biodiversity conservation require us to consume less, utilize more renewable energy, recycle more, and responsibly dispose of our waste. The Japanese, Scandinavians, and Swiss lead the world in living sustainably. We can learn much from them.

Responsible Resource Use, Recycling, and Waste Disposal

Until we have access to extra-planetary resources and habitats, more purposeful production, consumption, and more recycling are three of the best ways to assure that future generations have hospitable habitats. Environmental groups increase our awareness of the importance of conservation, recycling, and disposal programs when they sponsor related initiatives. Governments reduce waste streams when they make it easy for citizens to recycle, and tax activities and products that harm the environment. Consumers reduce waste streams when they buy higher-quality, longer-lasting products. Parents and schools help future generations conserve resources and reduce waste streams when they teach children to purchase less and recycle more.

When enterprises reduce waste from their processes, they save money, lower resource use, and shrink their waste streams. When they eliminate energy from their processes, they save money, decrease energy consumption, and reduce greenhouse gas emissions. When they minimize their overhead, they eliminate waste and operate more sustainably. Responsible resource use, recycling, and proper waste disposal make enterprises more profitable in the long term. They give us purpose, create competitive advantages, and improve our well-being.

Clean Energy

For decades, scientists and entrepreneurs have sought low-cost, environmentally friendly sources of energy. Numerous forms of clean, sustainable energy exist, but currently they cost more than fossil fuels. Substituting natural gas for other fossil fuels is the most cost-effective way to reduce carbon emissions in the short term. Hydro power is an age-old, low-cost, and sustainable form of clean energy, but opportunities for it are few. Solar cells, wind turbines, and tidal generators are higher-cost clean energy alternatives. Ongoing improvements in these and related technologies are promising approaches on the horizon. The electrolysis of water is another possible form of clean energy.

Photosynthetic processes of plants capture, transform, and store solar energy. Scientists actively seek to commercialize this natural process throughout the world. Oil from algae utilizes photosynthesis to provide a carbon-neutral substitute for oil.

Several nuclear sources of energy emit no greenhouse gases but have some downsides. Nuclear fission of uranium and plutonium is carbon-neutral but produces deadly waste streams. Energy from the fission of thorium generates waste that stabilizes in just a few hundred years rather than tens of thousands of years. Energy from the fusion of hydrogen produces no undesirable waste, but the technology eludes us.

Government investment in research and development of renewable energy sources and the taxation of greenhouse gas emissions are the two best ways to further clean energy. Public investment in basic energy research that enterprises avoid can yield important breakthroughs. Taxes on carbon incentivize enterprises to develop clean-energy alternatives, allow free markets to efficiently orchestrate our transition from fossil fuels, and cause everyone to use less fossil fuel.

Population Growth

If we have the will to confront the politics of the world's population and environmental degradation, there are ways to reduce them. In Chapter 8, I wrote:

Like medieval Christianity, most expressions of Islam are extremely Darwinian. They encourage their practitioners to have large families. We can see this from Islamic teachings and by examining the growth of Islamic populations over time. Islamic populations have grown from 0 to 1.8 billion people and one-quarter of the world's population in just 1,400 years. No other religious group has achieved such growth so quickly.

At current growth rates, Islamic populations will grow to 5.9 billion people and almost half of the world's population in 100 years. Without immigrants, the U.S. population shrinks.[406] With immigrants, the U.S. population grows from 325 to 650 million people and remains at about 5 percent of the world's population.

The unstated and underlying aim of most expressions of Islam is population growth. Most adherents are taught to maintain their faith and distinctive dress, disperse throughout the world, have large families, convert other people to their faith, and gradually change the ethnic mix, culture, and laws of a country. The Islamic threat to the non-Islamic world is not terrorism, but demographic and cultural in nature.

Islamic population growth makes up 70 percent of the total world population's growth. While it is unlikely their populations will sustain their current growth rates for 100 years, learning about their growth and the antidotes to them—readily available contraceptives and the education of women, as discussed earlier in this chapter—is instructive.

Slowing population growth and reversing environmental degradation are not things we can do alone. We must work with other countries and leverage our efforts. One way to do this would be to place mutually agreed-upon tariffs on imports from countries that have high population growth rates, high deforestation rates, and high per-capita greenhouse gas emissions. As I discussed in Chapters 35 and 37, tariffs create inefficiencies and are generally undesirable. The benefits of using them to incentivize nations to decrease their population growth, deforestation, and greenhouse gas emissions, however, would overwhelm their other economic adverse effects in this instance. Most African, Islamic, and developed countries as well as China would be on this list—the African and Islamic countries because of their high population growth rates, and the developed countries and China because of their high per-capita greenhouse gas emissions. Such an arrangement of tariffs would be in everybody's interest.

Prudent growth and sustainability involve increasing our numbers at rates like those of competing populations while keeping the world population under 80 percent of Earth's carrying capacity given existing technologies. Individuals, organizations, and governments reap a steady stream of positive effects from investments in sustainability. They avoid future difficulties with each step toward sustainability. Mark Tercek, CEO of the Nature Conservancy, wrote in *Nature's Fortune:*

> Now the scale of human activities is no longer dwarfed by the planet itself; the planet has limits, and we are nearing them and in places exceeding them. Every farmer knows you should not eat your seed corn, and every banker knows you should not spend your principal. Yet that is exactly what we are doing.
>
> The good news: investing in nature is a great deal. Even if you set aside the benefits to nature and take a steely-eyed look at the bottom line, the opportunities are too good to pass up.
>
> More good news: investing in nature transforms the way people see their place in it. Time after time, people—farmers in Iowa, sugarcane growers in Colombia, jet-setting corporate executives—who absolutely do not think of themselves as environmentalists have come to realize that their lives and livelihoods depend on healthy natural systems. They are attracted to an investment in nature for the specific practical returns they hope to receive from it. . . .
>
> A new valuation of nature, one that integrates conservation values and human development, science and economics means seeing things whole; if we want a successful business, a livable city, a green, diverse, and vibrant planet, we must take nature into account, and recognize the real value of the services nature provides.[407]

Sustainability *– living in a manner that enables future generations to live that involves: (a) maintaining our air, fresh water, land, and ocean quality, (b) conserving and restoring our biodiversity and ecosystem, (c) responsibly utilizing resources, recycling, and waste disposal, (d) using clean energy, and (e) prudently growing our population. Pollution, environmental disaster, and death are the antitheses of sustainability.*

A Note on the Winning Practices of Government

I recognize the political difficulty of implementing many of the Winning Practices in this section and transitioning from current federal, state, and local government practices to winning ones is beyond the scope of this book. Nevertheless, I have presented the most advantageous collection of Winning Practices that I know for two reasons. First, our culture continuously evolves. If our leaders and citizens understand the most advantageous Winning Practices, they are more likely to adopt and move toward them. We only hit the bull's eye when we can see it. Secondly, governments and empires fail, and new ones form periodically as the Soviet Union and several Eastern European governments did in the 1990s. Having the most advantageous collection of Winning Practices delineated to help form new governments has tremendous value.

Chapter 52

Toward Truth, Freedom, Fitness, and Decency

If we make up our minds that this is a drab and purposeless universe, it will be that, and nothing else. On the other hand, if we believe that the Earth is ours, and that the sun and moon hang in the sky for our delight, there will be joy upon the hills and gladness in the fields, because the Artist in our souls glorifies creation. Surely, it gives dignity to life to believe we are born into this world for noble ends, and that we have a higher destiny than can be accomplished within the narrow limits of this physical life.[408]

—Helen Keller

Our lives depend on a habitable planet, territory, resources, a larger community, a home, a workplace, parents, a healthy set of genes, other family members, and friends. Beyond these things, our lives depend on Winning Perspectives and Practices. Winning Perspectives describe our context. They suggest our means and end, as well as a need for an aspirational philosophy of life aligned with reality, nature, and human nature. Winning Perspectives help us identify Winning Practices.

Truth, Freedom, Fitness and Decency

The Winning Perspectives and our history suggest that Truth, Freedom, Fitness, and Decency are four crucial Winning Perspectives and Practices, where:

> *Truth* accurately approximates reality, natural processes, and depictions of current and past events.
>
> *Freedom* is the ability to fulfill our needs, think, speak, associate, travel, work, marry, have children as we choose, author our lives, and actualize.
>
> *Fitness* is the ability of organisms to procure resources, live, reproduce, and flourish relative to other organisms.
>
> *Decency* involves treating others who mean us no harm with respect and consideration and as we want them to treat us.

Fitness is our end; Truth, Freedom, and Decency are our means. Truth enables us to understand our context, trust one another, and work together. Our initial perceptions are only a start in the quest for truth. Freedom allows us to author our lives. Our freedoms end where others' freedoms start. Fitness is the underlying aim of life. It furthers health, performance, affiliation, and happiness. It brings the esteem of others, desirable mates, and offspring. Decency endears us to others, enables us to work with others, and furthers specialization, trade, win-wins, and synergy.

Our most potent understanding of truth comes from science, freedom from our country's founders, fitness from nature, and decency from our Judeo-Christian heritage. Together, these noble means and end enable us to multiply our strength and persist through time. Devotion to this end and means furthers our effectiveness and well-being, strengthens our population, helps us bridge our cultural divides, and gives our lives meaning.

The 9 Winning Perspectives and 37 Winning Practices discussed in this book describe our context and how we flourish in it. The Winning Practices address individuals, groups, families, education, enterprise, and government, and they comprise an unusually practical approach to life. Figure 26 lists the 9 Winning Perspectives and 37 overarching Winning Practices. Appendix D lists all the Winning Perspectives and Practices discussed in this book.

Helen Keller was the first *blind, deaf, and mute* person to earn a Bachelor of Arts degree. She was also an accomplished author, political activist, and lecturer. It is hard for us to imagine her early life and all she overcame. It is also difficult to fathom the difference her life has made in the lives of all subsequent disabled people.

It would have been easy for Helen Keller to have despaired and found her life meaningless, but her parents and teacher Anne Sullivan did not permit this. They worked hard to free Helen Keller from her handicaps. And so it is for us. Although we find no intention in nature or extrinsic purpose, we may fill our lives with intent and meaning "beyond the narrow limits of this life" as perceptive, able, imaginative beings. The Winning Perspectives and Practices help us do this. They describe our context and what matters and reveal how we may flourish and persist!

Looking Within and Without

While I try to incorporate conservative, moderate, and progressive views into my thought, I utilize conservative views more than progressive ones. The reason for this is that the past order has served us well for the most part, whereas most proposed changes are unproven and often do not work out. Progressives assure us that their proposals will improve the current order, but this is only occasionally the case. Approaches that have withstood the test of time are more likely to work than new approaches. New methods must be piloted and only adopted when there is compelling evidence that they truly improve our lives in the long term.

Figure 26: Winning Perspectives and Practices

Winning Perspectives

Truth
Causality
Scale
Evolution
Fitness

Human Nature
Culture
Periodic Disaster
Eco-Dependency

Winning Practices

Knowledge

Health
Thought
Integrity
Proactivity
Prudence
Excellence
Thrift and Investment

Affiliation
Decency
Understanding
Leadership
Teamwork
Improvement

Spouse Selection
Marriage
Responsible Parenting
Empowering Habit Formation

Universal Education
Parental Choice
Results-Oriented Education

Free Enterprise and Markets
Responsible Corporate Governance
Prudent Regulation
Enterprise Competitiveness

Government of the People
Powers, Prohibitions, and Structure
Freedoms, Rights, and Responsibilities
The Rule of Law
Inclusion and Meritocracy
Prudent Taxation
Financial Strength
Savings Accounts, Social Safety Nets
Consumer-Driven Healthcare
Assimilation
Peace Through Fitness
Sustainability

We must be more cautious. Modernity brought us physical comfort, but it also brought us broken families, dysfunctional schools and communities, polluted air and water, weapons of mass destruction, and exploding populations. We must look within and without, reflect on life, and utilize what works best. Most Singaporeans and Swiss are fitter and enjoy a higher quality of life than most Americans because Winning Perspectives and Practices are more prevalent in their populations. The Singaporeans, Swiss, Japanese, and Scandinavians live more sustainably than we do. We have much to learn from them and other societies. It would be advantageous for our leaders to travel to other countries with an open mind, identify perspectives and practices that appear to work well, pilot them in our country, and make people aware of the superior ones. Our country still radiates a lot of light, but the light is dimmer than in the past, and many people throughout the world now draw their inspiration from other countries.

Seven Levels of Human Organization

We must think more about what works best for individuals, groups, families, education, enterprise, our country, and our culture for future generations to flourish. We highly value individuals and enterprise but do we value our families, education, communities, country, culture, and future generations enough? What we cherish only persists as our families, schools, communities, country, and culture of Winning Perspectives and Practices continue. Our ancestors understood this. They pursued self-interest, but they also sought the public interest and made immense sacrifices for their families, education, communities, country, culture, and future generations. Are we as focused on these things as previous generations? Lee Kuan Yew observed:

The ideas of individual supremacy . . . when carried to excess, have not worked. They have made it difficult to keep American society cohesive. Asia can see it is not working. Those who want a wholesome society where young girls and old ladies can walk in the streets at night, where the young are not preyed upon by drug peddlers, will not follow the American model . . . . To have, day to day, images of violence and raw sex on the picture tube, the whole society exposed to it, it will ruin a whole community.

When Asians visit the U.S., many are puzzled and disturbed by conditions there: law and order out of control, with riots, drugs, guns, muggings, rape, and crimes; poverty amid great wealth; excessive rights of the individual at the expense of the community as a whole; and criminals regularly escape punishment.

In the U.S., the community's interests have been sacrificed because of human rights of drug traffickers and drug consumers. Drug-related crimes flourish. Schools are infected. There is high delinquency and violence amongst students, a high dropout rate, [and] poor discipline and teaching, producing students who make poor workers. So, a vicious cycle has set in.[409]

Individual preferences and our pursuit of happiness only serve us well to the extent that they help families, groups, education, enterprise, country, culture, and future generations. This is not an optional reality. It is deeply embedded in the fabric of life. Adam Smith expressed this as follows:

When the happiness or misery of others depends in any respect upon our conduct, we dare not, as self-love might suggest to us, prefer the interest of one to that of many. The [person] within immediately calls to us, that we value ourselves too much and other people too little, and that, by doing so, we render ourselves the proper object of the contempt and indignation of our [brothers and sisters].[410]

As a people, we must consider what is best for our spouses, children, schools, businesses, communities, country, and future generations. We may want to have an affair with someone, but is that best for our marriage and children? We may want to drop out of school, but will doing this negatively impact our ability to be a good parent, employee, and citizen? We may disparage others or cut ahead of them in line, but does this create a world in which we want to live? We may want the protections and benefits of a strong union, but is this best for our enterprises and others? We may want tremendous compensation or a monopolistic market share, but is this best for our colleagues and customers? We may want lots of money for our campaign, but does this further our ability to represent our constituents? We may want higher audience ratings, but does pandering to our audience and sensationalizing the news serve the public interest? We may want to avoid military or public service, but do such choices jeopardize our freedom, communities, country, and culture?

Winning

Life requires us to win as individuals, families, businesses, and countries, and across generations. We must secure territory, resources, and mates as well as raise children and work. Then and only then do our children, communities, country, and culture have a future. Evolution is very clear. Life outstrips the available territory and resources, and then it must either find more or compete for it. Thus, we secure territory and resources, proliferate, and locate more territory and resources, or we exit the stage.

Winning takes the form of win-win and win-lose. While winning is the most critical part of the two alternatives, winning and peacefully coexisting with others is advantageous when there are ample resources. Win-wins are more civil and synergistic than win-loses. Win-wins do not antagonize others and invite retaliation. Rather, win-wins create allies, multiply strength, and enable specialization, exchange, economies of scale, and synergies.

When territory and resources are scarce or others mean us harm, however, we must utilize win-lose approaches. We must defend ourselves and defeat others before they harm us. We engage in win-lose, or we perish. This is inevitable, and we will avoid this fate only by: (1) stabilizing the world's population growth, (2) living sustainably, and (3) colonizing space.

The Winning Perspectives and Practices in this book advance win-win approaches. They further truth, freedom, fitness, decency, specialization, exchange, economics of scale, synergies, and abundance. We are resourceful, efficient, and innovative. We conduct ourselves honorably and play within the rules, but we also are realistic, prepared to defend our turf, and look out for our interests. Naivety, ignorance, untruthfulness, coercion, weakness, and cheating, theft, freeloading, and misusing others are antithetical to Winning Practices.

Winning in these times requires effective individuals, groups, families, education, enterprises, government, and culture. Winning individuals must populate families, schools, groups, enterprises governments, and cultural institutions. They marry and raise able, well-adjusted young adults who continue this cycle. Winning families provide us with safe refuges, love, discipline, and purpose. Winning families and schools develop knowledgeable, skilled, able, and well-adjusted young adults. Winning groups and communities enable us to satisfy our social needs and accomplish things that we cannot achieve on our own. Winning enterprises employ and compensate us; provide us with low-cost, high-quality infrastructure, homes, products, and services; and create the wealth that funds our governments. They also deploy capital alongside us and increase our productivity so that we need not toil from sunup to sundown, seven days a week, and during our senior years.

Winning governments create safe, orderly, and just countries. They secure borders and advantageously admit new entrants. They support governments of the people everywhere, but only commit blood and treasure in places of strategic necessity. They minimize their intrusion into our lives and allow us to live freely and enjoy the fruits of our labor.

They create a few, widely supported laws and regulations and consistently apply them to everyone. They build the necessary infrastructure and facilitate free enterprise and markets. They create high minimum wages for adults between the ages of 21 and 65 and do not redistribute wealth or create entitlement mentalities. They do not formulate policies that treat some people, groups, and businesses more favorably than other ones.

The Prevalence of Winning Perspectives and Practices

I defined Winning Perspectives and Practices in Chapters 3 and 13. Let's review their definitions and consider their antitheses, Losing Perspectives and Practices.

Winning Perspectives are accurate perceptions of reality and conditions of existence. Substantial evidence exists for them. They further our effectiveness and help us identify Winning Practices.

Losing Perspectives are inaccurate perceptions of reality and the conditions of existence. They are fiction. They decrease our effectiveness and hinder our identification of Winning Practices.

Winning Practices are actions that positively affect individuals, groups, and/or the environment in the short and long term. They place us and future generations in strong positions.

Losing Practices are actions that negatively affect individuals, groups, and/or the environment in the short or long term. They place us and future generations in weak positions.

Truth and Fitness are examples of Winning Perspectives. Superstition and Apathy are examples of losing ones. Marriage and Responsible Parenting are examples of Winning Practices. Promiscuity and Irresponsible Parenting are examples of losing ones. If Winning Perspectives and Practices are much more desirable than losing perspectives and practices, why don't more cultures of the world utilize them?

Winning Perspectives and Practices are not obvious and instinctual. Knowledge, technology, and patterns of life have changed so much in the last three thousand years and the effects of both winning and losing perspectives and practices are invisible, indirect, and delayed. The perspectives and practices required for success in the modern world are more involved than those of the past. They call for tremendous amounts of learning, discipline, habit formation, and hard work.

Some people and groups acquire and employ more Winning Perspectives and Practices than others, and it is the prevalence of these perspectives and practices within a population that determine its fitness and well-being. Life in a country where 90 percent of the population employs Winning Perspectives and Practices is very different from life in a country where only 10 percent of the population employs them. Such a contrast of prevalence exists between the populations of Switzerland and Haiti today.

The politically correct concept of cultural relativism would have us believe that no culture is more desirable than another and that we have no basis to judge the perspectives and practices of other cultures. While this concept is thought to further intercultural harmony and make people feel better about themselves, the concept simply is not true. If we want to flourish, we must distinguish between winning and losing perspectives and practices and recognize, acquire, and employ the winning ones.

Circle of Influence

Each of us can make a difference and improve the lives of those around us. Let us strive to be the best students, employees, spouses, parents, leaders, teachers, and mentors that we can be. Let us strive to improve the enterprises, institutions, organizations, communities, and country to which we belong.

Moreover, each of us affects our children, grandchildren, friends, and colleagues, and we can use this influence to share the Winning Perspectives and Practices with them. We may also condition our support of charter and private schools upon the inclusion of Winning Perspectives and Practices in their curriculums and advocate for their use in the curriculums of our public schools. Our population is polarized and many of our educational and governmental institutions function poorly. We must use our circle of influence to strengthen our families, groups, education, enterprise, country, and culture.

Leadership and Service

The difference between excellent and poor leaders can be the difference between subsistence and abundance as well as existence and nonexistence. The decisions and actions of high-integrity, competent, caring leaders yield so many more positive effects than those of dishonest, incompetent, ruthless ones. The more we pay attention to the past practices and results of leaders and the more carefully we select them, the more we flourish.

Moreover, we do not need to be a leader to improve our world. We affect those around us immeasurably when we are good spouses, raise good children, do good work, are loyal friends, and encourage others. We reap what we sow and are fulfilled as we serve, and the benefits of our actions ripple for years, decades, centuries, and millennia.

Winning Culture

If knowing the Winning Perspectives and Practices increased their prevalence and use, many more people would flourish in our country and around the world. As is the case with most everything, knowing is a necessary but not a sufficient condition for obtaining improvement. Improvements are only made as our desire for them overwhelms the inertia of the present and our contentment with it.

Who blocks the changes that would cause far greater portions of our population to flourish? Who prevents the perspectives and practices that precipitate predominantly positive effects in the long term? Who prefers a declining culture and living standards over rapidly ascending ones? Who prefers gradual irrelevance to relevance?

The answer is the intelligent and powerful people who comfortably occupy the current order and who would have to work harder in the new one. Who are these people? They are (a) many of the people who occupy our educational institutions, dominant enterprises, and governments, (b) civil service and unionized employees, (c) people currently being treated preferentially by the government and our institutions, (d) people receiving government assistance, and (e) illegal immigrants. Who would be interested in creating an order where people reap more of what they sow and less of what they commandeer from the government? Well, this is most of the people who pay for the current order.

Looking within and without is the first step. Recognizing our individual, family, education, business, national, cultural, and generational interests is the second step. Understanding the role competition plays in life and our need to win is the third step. Learning about the Winning Perspectives and Practices and sharing them with our children, grandchildren, friends, and colleagues is the fourth step. Selecting better leaders and overcoming the special interests that utilize and champion losing practices is the fifth step. In the end, we only flourish and persist as we unite in purpose and employ Winning Perspectives and Practices.

What we do echoes in eternity.[411]

Toward Truth, Freedom, Fitness, and Decency – *(a) looking within and without, (b) being individual-, family-, community-, education-, business-, country-, and culture-oriented, (c) understanding the role competition plays in life and our need to win, (d) learning about Winning Perspectives and Practices, (e) sharing Winning Perspectives and Practices with our children, grandchildren, friends, and colleagues and increasing their prevalence in our population, and (f) being a good spouse, raising able, well-adjusted children, doing our work well, being a loyal friend, encouraging others, and carefully selecting our leaders.*

Postscript

In comparing how Americans are doing relative to other flourishing populations, documenting how we lost our way and became so divided, describing the cards nature deals us, contrasting our instinctual operating system with the one needed for success in the modern world, and inventorying many Winning Perspectives and Practices, I hope to make people more aware of our need to be evolutionarily fit, and most importantly, to increase the prevalence of Winning Perspectives and Practices in our population. Please help with this endeavor!

And finally, the Winning Perspectives and Practices discussed in this book do not describe "the" conditions for people to flourish, only "some of the best-known ones." Improved variations and collections of Winning Perspectives and Practices will evolve.

Acknowledgments

It is impossible to name all the people who directly and indirectly influenced my thinking. Included are some of the greatest leaders, thinkers, explorers, and innovators in history. Their thoughts and work enable us to realize the best of what life offers. Figure 13, Appendix B, and the Endnotes provide the names of many of these people. Though many have provided feedback to me concerning the content of this book, their mention here does not mean that they endorse all the perspectives and practices in it.

In the preparation of this book, I thank my beautiful and ever-supportive wife, Leokadia, my sons, Karl and Asher, daughters-in-law, Kristi and Kalee, and my extraordinary mother and father. I thank my faithful and talented administrative assistant, Sherri Woods; insightful and encouraging editors, Deborah Grandinetti, Jill Hernandez, Samantha Mason, and Angela Panayotopulos; energetic and able social media publicists, Autumn Glading and Rebecca Daneault; publishing freelancer, Vanessa Anderson; graphic artist, Patty Schuster; artist, Katiana Robles; photographer, Michelle Reed; the brave and thoughtful members of my advisory board, Susannah Adelson, Sheila Marshman, Roxanne Parmele, Barb Quijano, and Russ Smith; CEO mentor, Steve Pond; publicist, Jane Wesman; and bestselling author, Harvey McKay. I also want to thank John Ingram of Ingram Content Group and Rachael Brandenburg, Elizabeth Chenette, Steven Elizalde, Corrin Foster, Tanya Hall, Jay Hodges, Carrie Jones, April Murphy, Pam Nordberg, Daniel Pederson, and Chelsea Richards of Greenleaf Book Group.

I thank longtime friends and supporters Rolly Anderson, Bill Burrows, Joe Coleman, John Doyle, Evan Dreyfuss, Brian Dunsirn, Bill Ellis, Tom Ewert, Dan Fisher, Verne Freeman, Had Fuller, Jim Howe, Michael Korchmar, Amy Lockhard, Ken Lockhard, Steve McMahon, Jean Merrell, Carole-Ann Miller, Mark Nielsen, Isabelle Nüssli, Rosemary Perez, Steve Pond, Jack Reinelt, Ed Telling, Bob Vanourek, Jennifer Lehmann Weng, Carl Youngman, and Karl Zinsmeister. I thank Jon Carroll, Jim Cohen, Mark Danni, Katherine Davies, Paul de Lima, Tom Embrescia, Gary Fenchuk, Dick Glowacki, Clint Greenleaf, Cordia Harrington, Suzanne Heiligman, Richard, Kaufman, Deborah Keller, Jim Jameson, Christina Keeley, Steve McConnell, Bill Morton, Dr. Story Musgrave, Lori Ruhlman, Ed Samek, Ed Schifman, Lindsay Schlauch, Mitch Sill, Haisook Somers, and Rollie Strum for their input and/or encouragement.

I thank Diana Anastos, Chip Hyde, Bella Stahl, and the exceptional team members of CNY Feeds, the dedicated staffs of the Syracuse YMCA, Northwest YMCA, and Florida Nature Conservancy, and the staffs and members of the International YPO and CEO organizations. I am also appreciative of all the people who spent hours developing Google, Wikipedia, and Wikiquote. Their efforts made finding and recalling information so much easier and ultimately enriched the content of this book immeasurably.

Appendix A: Alternative Types of Investments

Certificates of Deposits and Money Market Funds function much like traditional bank savings accounts. In the case of certificates of deposit (CDs), investors loan fixed sums of money to banks for specified periods. The banks return predetermined quarterly interest payments to the investors throughout the certificate's term and the invested sum at the end of the term. In the case of money market funds, investors loan financial institutions money for as long as the investors desire, and the institutions pay the investors periodic interest payments that vary with the institution's returns from their investment of the funds. The federal government guarantees CDs and money market funds up to $250,000 per person per financial institution. Generally, CDs and money market fund investments fluctuate and return less than other investments.

Debt Instruments are loans to others in return for the periodic interest payments and the repayment of the loan at the end of the term. Terms vary from 30 days to 30 years. Professionals call debt instruments with less than 10-year terms "Notes" and those with more than 10-year terms "Bonds." Debt instruments pay fixed rates of interest that are called "Coupon Rates." Debt instruments also have yields-to-maturity, which are calculations of the percentage the debt instruments' return annually to purchasers over the instruments' lives. Yields-to-maturity consider the current price of debt instruments, interest to be paid, term of the loan, and amount of the loan. Debt instrument prices fluctuate in accordance with their supply and demand.

When held to maturity, quality debt instruments generally provide predictable cash flows and pay higher returns than certificates of deposit and money market funds. The disadvantage of notes and bonds is that investors do not always receive the promised interest and loaned funds back. The value of debt instruments also fluctuates more than certificates of deposit and money market funds.

Real Estate Investments refer to people's purchases of land, buildings, and homes. Usually, buying a home is more advantageous than renting when people plan to reside in the same home for several years. Real estate investments, however, are more difficult investments for most people. The relatively high cost of buying, selling, and owning real estate often exceeds the appreciation in value. Only when people purchase homes and real estate at depressed prices and/or where demand grows rapidly for years are real estate investments profitable.

Most people borrow money or assume a mortgage to purchase their homes. Home mortgages are advantageous when we have sufficient earnings, the mortgage is less than 80 percent of a home's value, the mortgage rate is fixed, the interest on the mortgage is less than the cost of renting, and home prices are not at cyclical highs.

The only debt that most of us should ever incur are modest student loans, home mortgages, and business-related loans. Using debt to buy cars and for consumption-related purchases lowers our living standards. Maintaining modest lifestyles enables us to largely avoid debt, create surpluses, and invest the surpluses. Modest lifestyles and prudent investment make our lives more secure and enjoyable.

Common Stock represents some fractional ownership of a company. Investors buy and sell these shares privately or on public exchanges. Common stock prices reflect the total value of a company divided by the number of outstanding common stock shares. Investors owning more than 50 percent of a company's common stock control the company. They may hire and fire the leadership, set its policies, and determine how the company uses its cash flows.

The keys to investing in common stocks are to identify a few well-managed profitable companies with excellent growth prospects, buy them at discounted prices, and hold the common stock for years. Investors profit from the appreciation of share prices and the periodic payment of dividends. Not all companies pay dividends, and unlike interest payments of debt instruments that are defined legal obligations, companies may increase, decrease, or curtail dividend payments.

To determine the expected returns of a common stock or its yield relative to other investments, look at their "Earnings before Interest, Taxes, Depreciation, and Amortization," or EBITDA, relative to their Enterprise Value. In a sense, investments in companies have expected yields just like investments in certificates of deposit and debt instruments. Though the expected yields are unstated and unknown, we can estimate them or find a brokerage firm or financial website that does this for us. I include this important measure because most people are not aware of it and overpay for equities.

Company profitability and growth rates affect this measure, but generally equities of well-managed, growing companies with EBITDA / EVs of 10 percent or greater are reasonable values, and those having 15 to 20 percent or greater yields are excellent values.

EBITDA/EV is the annual Earnings before Interest, Taxes, Depreciation, and Amortization of a company divided by its Enterprise Value, where EV is the Enterprise Value of a company or its Market Capitalization plus Debt and Preferred Equity less its Cash and Cash Equivalents. Market Capitalization is the product of a company's number of outstanding shares of stock and its market price.

If we buy over-valued assets, frequently trade, and sell at distressed prices, all things that inexperienced investors typically do, we waste our hard-earned capital. Wise investing requires method, research, and patience. When evaluating equities as investments, we want to consider numerous other characteristics and performance measures of the underlying companies besides EBITDA/EV. Four other important criteria include the company's (1) Sales Growth Rate, (2) EBITDA Growth Rate, (3) Current Liability to Asset Ratio, and (4) Long-Term Liability to Asset Ratio. In short, we want to purchase well-managed, financially strong, growing, and profitable companies with enduring competitive advantages at discounted prices.

The common stocks of such companies that have histories of paying increasing dividends are my favorite investments. Historically, these investments have been reliable and profitable, and they have protected people's reserves against inflation or the erosion of the value of our currency. When I do not need my invested money for more than seven years or only need the dividend streams from it, I invest in the common stocks of 12 to 20 good dividend-paying companies.

Preferred Stock is a hybrid of debt instruments and common stock. Like debt instruments, preferred stocks pay to their owners defined quarterly amounts or dividends that do not change. Unlike debt instruments, companies can start and stop the quarterly payments at will, though they must make up the preferred stock payments before paying any common stock dividends. Preferred stock does not convey voting rights or any control to its owners. Preferred stock prices fluctuate in accordance with the supply and demand of the shares. The underlying growth, earnings, and financial strength of companies and interest rates affect preferred stock values. Preferred stocks pay streams of reliable cash flows that usually return and fluctuate more than those of debt instruments and less than those of common stocks.

Exchange Traded Funds (ETFs) provide purchasers ownership of a collection of certificates of deposit, debt instruments, preferred stocks, real estate companies, or common stocks. In the case of debt instrument ETFs, the collections are usually of similar types and maturities. In the case of common stock ETFs, the collections may comprise the common stocks defined by an index, sector, exchange, or country. ETFs offer investors a low-cost way to own small quantities of numerous assets and diversify their holdings. They eliminate the risk of owning individual financial instruments in exchange for average returns on the underlying collection of instruments. Well-managed ETFs are excellent investment vehicles for most people.

Appendix B: Special Sources

Giants

The Ten Commandments	Moses
The Art of War	Sun Tzu
The Apology of Socrates	Plato
The New Oxford Annotated Bible with the Apocrypha	
Ninety-Five Theses; Catechisms; Letor on the Papacy	Martin Luther
and on Temporal Authority	
The Principia[a]	Isaac Newton
The Declaration of Independence	Thomas Jefferson et al.
An Inquiry into the Nature and Causes of the Wealth of Nations	Adam Smith
The Pennsylvania Constitution of 1776	Benjamin Franklin et al.
The Constitution of the United States of America	Hamilton, Madison, Morris,
and the Bill of Rights	Washington et al.
The Federalist Papers	Hamilton, Jay, Madison
On the Origin of Species	Charles Darwin
General Relativity and Special Relativity[b]	Albert Einstein
I Have a Dream	Martin Luther King, Jr.
Lee Kuan Yew: The Grand Master's Insights on China,	Lee Kuan Yew
The United States, and the World[c]	

Significant

Berkshire Hathaway Annual Reports	Warren Buffett
The 7 Habits of Highly Effective People	Stephen Covey
Principles	Ray Dalio
Life Evolving	Christian de Duve
A Universe of Consciousness	Gerald Edelman
Capitalism and Freedom; Free to Choose	Milton Friedman
Jews, Confucians, and Protestants	Lawrence Harrison
Cosmos; Dragons of Eden; The Demon-Haunted World	Carl Sagan
The Black Swan; Antifragile; Skin in the Game	Nassim Taleb
Winning[d]	Jack Welch
The Ants; On Human Nature; Consilience;	E. O. Wilson
The Future of Life; Half Earth	

[a] *The Clockwork Universe*, Edward Dolnick
[b] *Einstein*, Walter Isaacson
[c] By Graham Allison, Robert Blackwill, Ali Wye, and Henry Kissinger
[d] By Jack & Suzy Welch

Very Helpful

As a Man Thinketh	James Allen
Big History	Benjamin, Brown, Christian
The Unexpected Legacy of Divorce	Blakeslee, Lewis, Wallerstein
The Little Book of Common Sense Investing	John Bogle
The One Minute Manager	Blanchard, Johnson
How to Win Friends and Influence People	Dale Carnegie
The Richest Man in Babylon	George Clason
Good to Great	Jim Collins
Aerobics	Kenneth Cooper
Jews, God, and History	Max Dimont
Leadership Is an Art	Max De Pree
The Power of Habit	Charles Duhigg
The Lessons of History; Fallen Leaves	Ariel and Will Durant
Civilization: The West and the Rest	Niall Ferguson
Common Sense Economics	Gwartney, Lee, Stroup
Sapiens; Homo Deus; 21 Lessons	Yuval Harari
The Story of Earth	Robert Hazen
Dune; Dune Messiah; Children of Dune	Frank Herbert
How the Scots Invented the Modern World	Arthur Herman
Culture and Organizations	Hofstede, Hofstede, Minkov
Men Are from Mars, Women Are from Venus	John Gray
Being There	Erica Komisar
Life Ascending	Nick Lane
9 Presidents Who Screwed Up America	Brion McClanahan
The Diversity Delusion	Heather Mac Donald
The Dirty Dozen	Levey and Mellor
Democracy	David Moss
The Road Less Traveled	M. Scott Peck
Brand Luther	Andrew Pettegree
Enlightenment Now	Steven Pinker
The Chosen; My Name is Asher Lev	Chaim Potok
Our Kids	Robert Putnam
The 5000 Year Leap	W. Cleon Skousen
Nature's Fortune	Jonathan Adams, Mark Tercek
The Outsiders	William Thorndike, Jr.
How Children Succeed	Paul Tough

Appendix C: Drawing from the Right and the Left

Approach of the Right	Approach of the Left	Winning Approach
Military Strength	Humanitarianism, Diplomacy, Economic Sanctions, and Negotiation	Peace through Fitness; Diplomacy, Economic Sanctions, and Negotiation; Selective Engagement in Accordance with National Interest and Realistic Opportunity
Rule of Law, Live and Let Live, Personal Responsibility, and Laissez-Faire Government	Social Justice, Wealth Redistribution, and Extensive Social Programs	Rule of Law, State Social Programs, Universally Safe Neighborhoods, Universally Excellent Education, Equal Opportunity, Free Remedial Education, Conscious Inclusion, Goldilocks Minimum Wage, Incentivized Savings, Vibrant Economy, Upward Mobility
Limited Immigration	No Borders	Opportunistic and Humanitarian Legal Immigration that Increases with Decreasing Unemployment and Decreases with Increasing Unemployment
Laissez-Faire Government with Respect to Free Enterprise and Markets	Ever More Government Regulation and Service	Government Enforcement of Competitive Market Structures, Judicious Litigation, and Limited Government Regulation
A Monetary Policy of Sound Money and a Fiscal Policy that Balances the Budget	A Monetary Policy and Fiscal Policy that Spur Employment	A Monetary Policy of Sound Money and a Fiscal Policy that Balances the Budget; Pro Enterprise and Labor Policies; Money Set Aside in Good Times to Invest in Infrastructure during Recessions
An American Identity	Multiculturalism	An American Identity and Respect for All Cultures

Approach of the Right	Approach of the Left	Winning Approach
Judgmentalism	Nonjudgmentalism	Nonjudgmentalism of People; Judgmentalism of Perspectives, Practices, and Taboos
Faith Community Values	Humanistic Values	A Cultural Council and Winning Perspectives and Practices
Pro-Life	Pro-Choice	Readily Available Birth Control; Choice for the First 4 Months of Pregnancy; Minimizing Extra-marital Sex
Only Marital Sex	Free Sex	No Children out of Wedlock and No Fooling Around While Married
Conscientiousness and Discipline	Openness and Empathy	Conscientiousness, Discipline, Openness, and Empathy
Non-Unionized Education	Unionized Public Education	Competition—Private, Charter, and Public Education with Parental Choice
Laissez-Faire	Forced Inclusion	Education and Conscious Inclusion
Realistic News with Mostly Right-Leaning Viewpoints	Narrative News from the Left	Realistic News that Presents Opposing Political Viewpoints
No Global Warming and/or Unknown Outcomes	Global Warming with Predictable Outcomes	Steady Movement Toward Sustainability
Organic Population Growth	Zero Population Growth	Contraceptives, Education, and Negotiated Population Growth

Appendix D: Perspectives, Practices, and Concepts

Three of the Most Desirable Places to Live

Singapore, Switzerland, and the U.S.

Crime, Corruption, and Poverty
Health and Longevity
Income and Financial Security
Carbon Emissions

Losing Our Way

Inclusion Failures
Change in the Election of U.S. Senators
Presidential Constitutional Failings

Supreme Court Constitutional Failings
Special Interests
Less Faith-Community Relevance

Less Integrity, Responsibility, and Civility
Promiscuity and the Decline of Marriage
Poorly Parented Children

Unionization and Liberalization of Education
Social Justice Missteps
Cultural Relativism, Nonjudgmentalism, and
   Multiculturalism

Declining Discipline, Poor Habits, Less Learning
Oligopoly and Monopoly
Offshoring

Entitlement
Consumerism and Debt
Easy Money

Hubris and Nation Building
Immigration Failures
Distorted News and Political Polarization
Separation from Nature

Winning Perspectives

Truth

Causality

Fallacy, Correlation, Necessity, Sufficiency
The Inanimate and Animate Worlds

Scale

Evolution

The Evolution of the Universe
The Evolution of Life
Competition and Comparative Advantage
Natural Selection and Gradualism
Interrelated Products of the Past

Fitness

Meritocracy
Procreation
The Underlying Aim of Life

Human Nature

Individual Nature
Familial Nature
Social Nature
   Superorganism
Environmental Alignment

Culture

Cultural Relativism
The Path of Fitness
Operating System I
Operating System II

Periodic Disaster

Eco-Dependency
Externalities

Winning Practices

Individual Level
Group Level
Family Level
Education Level
Enterprise Level
Government Level
Winning Practices
Collegial Improvement

Health

Hygiene
Nutrition
Periodic Fasting
Sleep
Exercise
Avoiding Harm

Medical and Dental Care
DNA Fidelity
Reflection
Purpose and Social Interaction
Balance

Thought

Assimilation
Visualization
Creativity
Reverse Engineering

Research
Choice and Alignment
Focus
Rehearsal
Mentors

Integrity

Truthfulness
Honorableness
Reliability
Priorities
  The Effects Test

Proactivity

Purpose
Responsibility
Constructive Speech and Action

Preparation
Work
Fitness-Related Service

Prudence

Fitness, Courage, Knowledge, Discipline
Symmetry and Nonlinearity
  Asymmetry
Antifragility
  Black Swans
  Fragility
  Robustness
Prohibitions
Optionality and Judicious Risk-Taking
Practical Experience
Accomplished Souls, Collective Wisdom
Being Slow to Make Important Decisions

Excellence

Extra Thought, Focus, Effort, and Time
Near-Perfect Practice and Perseverance
High Standards and Attention to Detail
Facilitators and Impediments

Thrift and Investment

Minimizing Expenditures
Automated Investment
Financial Tools
  The Rule of 69
  Present Value and Future Value
  Present and Future Value of Annuities
Investments
Advantageously Buying and Selling Assets
  Business Cycles
  Long-Term Debt Cycles
Minimizing Taxes
  The Keys to Wealth

Affiliation
Accountability
Attendance
Punctuality
Appearance and Congeniality
Independent Thought
Friendship

Decency
Abundance, Decency, Scarcity, Ruthlessness
Ally Acquisition
Respectfulness
Consideration and Appreciation
The Modified Golden Rule
Apology and Forgiveness
Expenditure of Time, Energy, Resources

Understanding
Humility
Trust
  Emotional Bank Account
Listening
Clarification
Shared Experience

Leadership
Good Decisions
Mission, Vision, and Strategy
Structure and Stakeholder Inclusion
Goals, Budgets, and Plans
Accountability and Assignments
Incentives and Evaluations
Winning Practices of Individuals and Groups
Realism, Courage, Passion, and Perseverance
Culture of Success

Teamwork
Winning Practices of Individuals and Groups
Leader Selection and Retention
Member Selection and Retention
Beneficial Diversity
Equal Opportunity and Meritocracy
Skin in the Game
Win-Win
Cooperation, Specialization, Coordination, Synergy
Associations

Improvement
Evolution and Competition
Trials and Pilot
Research and Development

Continuous Improvement
Collegial Improvement
Sustainability-Related Improvement
Winning Practices

Spouse Selection
Differences between Men and Women
Vetted Love

Deferred Sex
Necessary Marital Attributes
Family Decision-Making

Marriage
Love and Accommodation
Family Centeredness and Specialization
Commitment and Fidelity

Responsible Parenting
Progeny Consciousness
Nurture and Discipline
  Unconditional Love
  Keys of Effective Discipline

Literacy and Education
Experiences and Challenges
  The Butterfly
Role Models
Grandparents

Empowering Habit Formation
Forming Empowering Habits
  Habits, Cues, Routines, Rewards, Cravings
  Keystone Habits
  Unconditional Love
  Self-Control
  Deferred Gratification
  Self-Discipline

Winning Practices of Individuals and Groups
Breaking Habits

Knowledge
The Scientific Method
Libraries and Databases
Education, Research, Extension System
A Free and Responsible Press
    Conflicts of Interest

Universal Education
Parent Accountability
Student Accountability
Real-World Feedback
Empowering Habit Formation
Life- and Science-Based Curriculum
Elementary Curriculum
Seven Secondary Tracks
Homogenous Grouping
Individualized Learning

Parental Choice
Equitable County Districts
Ending the Public Education Monopoly
An Island of Socialism
Parental Choice and Involvement
State Goals and Exams

Results-Oriented Education
Benchmarking
Administration Empowerment and Accountability
Teacher Empowerment and Accountability
How Children Succeed
Bridging Conservative and Liberal Biases

Free Enterprise and Markets
Private Property
Free Enterprise
    Corporations
    Public Goods
    Profit
Free Markets
Free Trade
    Comparative Advantage
Capital Formation and Investment

Responsible Corporate Governance
Stakeholder Inclusion
Stakeholder Directors
Media Reports of Corporate Misconduct
Winning Cultures

Prudent Regulation
Contract Enforcement
Transparency
Market Share Restrictions
    A Competitive Market Structure
Debt Restrictions
Externality Taxation
Do No Harm
Long-Term Incentives

Enterprise Competitiveness
Customer Focus
A High Performance and Improvement Culture
Minimal Overhead
    Overhead
Limited Leverage
Willing- and Able Workforces
Well-Developed Infrastructure
Enterprise-Friendly Policies
Minimal Government Burdens

Problems with Democracy
Human Fallibility
Conflicts of Interest
Special Interests
Lack of Accountability
Representatives Play Santa Claus
Leaders Love Power
Short-Term and Group Thinking
Majorities Dominate Minorities

Government of the People
A Constitution
    Judicial Activism
Dispersing and Checking Power
A Republic with a Bicameral Legislature
Supermajorities and Minority Accommodation

Powers, Prohibitions, and Structure
Specified Federal Powers
Prohibitions
Legislative, Executive, and Judicial Branches
House of Representatives
Senate
Executive Branch/Council
Executive Prohibitions, Emergency Powers
The Supreme Court
Public Infrastructure

Freedoms, Rights, and Responsibilities
Freedoms
Rights
Responsibilities
Citizenship Qualifications
Voter Qualifications
Weighting the Votes of Parents

The Rule of Law
Constitutional, Understood, Widely-Supported
Collegial Improvement
Legislatively-Originated
Piloted, Beneficial, Stakeholder-Oriented
Impartial and Consistently Applied
Justice
Periodic Review
Judicious Litigation

Inclusion and Meritocracy
Ethnic Sensitivity and Appreciation
Integration
Meritocracy and Comparative Advantage
Equal Opportunity
Goldilocks Minimum Wages
A Can-Do Attitude

Prudent Taxation
Disincentivize the Undesirables
Sales Taxes on Nonessentials
Uniform Application of Taxes
Taxation and Spending Restraints

Financial Strength
Privatization
Free Enterprise and Free Markets
Transparency and Good Information
Sound Money
  Money
  The Federal Reserve
Monetary Policy
  Inflation
  Short-Term Business Cycles
  Deflation
  Long-Term Debt Cycles
Sound Lending Practices
Balanced Budgets, Limited Indebtedness
Prudent Taxation, Productivity, Employment
  Fiscal Policy
  Productivity
Capital Formation

Savings Accounts and Social Safety Nets
Avoiding Socialism and the Redistribution of Wealth
Savings Accounts
State Social Safety Nets
Employment of the Unemployed

Consumer-Driven Healthcare
Harmful Medical Interventions
Advantageous Immigration and Judicious Litigation
Goldilocks Minimum Wages and Savings Accounts
Universal Coverage
Patient Choice
Out-of-Pocket Payments

Assimilation
From Many, One
United We Stand, Divided We Fall
English as the National Language
Impervious Borders
Advantageous Immigration

Peace through Fitness
Seven Levels of Human Fitness
Financial Strength
Law Enforcement and Justice
Military, Cyber, Intelligence Strength and Restraint
Allies and Limited Treaty Powers
Democratic Realism
  Isolationism
  Internationalism
  Realism
  Democratic Globalism

Sustainability
Water, Air, and Land
Ecosystem Conservation and Biodiversity
Resource Use, Recycling, and Waste Disposal
Clean Energy
Population Growth

Toward Truth, Freedom, Fitness, and Decency
Truth, Freedom, Fitness, and Decency
Looking Within and Without
Seven Levels of Human Organization
Winning
The Prevalence of Winning Perspectives and Practices
  Winning and Losing Perspectives and Practices
Circles of Influence
Leadership and Service
Winning Culture

Endnotes

[1] "The World Factbook," Central Intelligence Agency, 2018 (2015 Data), https://www.cia.gov/library/publications/the-world-factbook.

[2] FRED Economic Data, Federal Reserve of St. Louis, Filters: Gross Domestic Product, Per Capita, Purchasing Power Parity, Haiti, and Singapore, https://fred.stlouisfed.org/series/PPCGDPHTA620NUPN.

[3] "GDP per capita, Current U.S. Dollars," The World Bank, 2018 (2017 Data), https://data.worldbank.org/indicator/NY.GDP.PCAP.CD?end=2015&start=1960.

[4] "The World Factbook: Country Comparison: GDP – Per Capita (PPP)", Central Intelligence Agency, 2018, (2017 Data), https://www.cia.gov/library/publications/the-world-factbook/rankorder/2004rank.html#sn.

[5] "List of Countries by International Homicide Rate," Wikipedia, 2017 (2016 Data), https://en.wikipedia.org/wiki/List_of_countries_by_intentional_homicide_rate, and "World Prison Brief," Institute for Criminal Policy Research, Birkbeck, University of London, World Prison Data, 2017, http://www.prisonstudies.org.

[6] "Corruption Perceptions Index 2017," Transparency International, 2018, https://www.transparency.org/news/feature/corruption_perceptions_index_2017.

[7] Ibid.

[8] Max Fisher, "Map: How 35 Countries Compare on Child Poverty (The U.S. is Ranked 34th)," The Washington Post, April 15, 2013, https://www.washingtonpost.com/news/worldviews/wp/2013/04/15/map-how-35-countries-compare-on-child-poverty-the-u-s-is-ranked-34th/?noredirect=on&utm_term=.a4371997c797.

[9] "List of Countries by Intentional Homicide Rate," Wikipedia, 2018 (2016 Data), https://en.wikipedia.org/wiki/List_of_countries_by_intentional_homicide_rate.

[10] "Corruption Perceptions Index 2017," Transparency International, 2018 (2017 Data), https://www.transparency.org/news/feature/corruption_perceptions_index_2017.

[11] Max Fisher, "Map: How 35 Countries Compare on Child Poverty (The U.S. is Ranked 34th)," Washington Post, April 15, 2013, https://www.washingtonpost.com/news/worldviews/wp/2013/04/15/map-how-35-countries-compare-on-child-poverty-the-u-s-is-ranked-34th/?noredirect=on&utm_term=.a4371997c797.

[12] "The World FactBook," People and Society: "Obesity," Central Intelligence Agency, 2018 (2016 Data), https://www.cia.gov/library/publications/resources/the-world-factbook/.

[13] "The World FactBook," People and Society: "Health Expenditures," Central Intelligence Agency, 2018 (2015–2016 Data), https://www.cia.gov/library/publications/resources/the-world-factbook/.

[14] "The World FactBook," People and Society: "Life Expectancy," Central Intelligence Agency, 2018 (2017 Data), https://www.cia.gov/library/publications/resources/the-world-factbook/.

[15] "The World FactBook," Economy: "GDP – per capita (PPP)," Central Intelligence Agency, 2018 (2017 Data), https://www.cia.gov/library/publications/resources/the-world-factbook/.

[16] "The World FactBook," Economy: "Gross National Saving," Central Intelligence Agency, 2017 (2017 Data), https://www.cia.gov/library/publications/resources/the-world-factbook/.

[17] "The World FactBook," Economy: "Public Debt," Central Intelligence Agency, 2018, (2017 Data), (The number for the U.S. includes state debt and U.S. Treasury borrowing from Social Security, Medicare, Disability, Unemployment, and other Trusts), https://www.cia.gov/library/publications/resources/the-world-factbook/.

[18] "CO2 Emissions," (Metric Tons Per Capita), The World Bank, 2014, https://data.worldbank.org/indicator/EN.ATM.CO2E.PC?view=chart.

[19] "List of Countries with Universal Healthcare," Wikipedia, 2017, https://en.wikipedia.org/wiki/List_of_countries_with_universal_health_care.

[20] World Bank Economic Indicators, 2012, https://data.worldbank.org/indicator/.

[21] World Bank Economic Indicators, 2012, https://data.worldbank.org/indicator/.

[22] "The World FactBook," Economy: "GDP – per capita (PPP)," Central Intelligence Agency, 2018 (2017 Data), https://www.cia.gov/library/publications/resources/the-world-factbook/.

[23] "The World FactBook, Economy: Public Debt," Central Intelligence Agency, 2017, (The number for the U.S. includes state debt and U.S. Treasury borrowing from Social Security, Medicare, Disability, Unemployment, and other Trusts), https://www.cia.gov/library/publications/resources/the-world-factbook/.

[24] "List of Countries by Home Ownership Rate," Wikipedia, 2013–14, https://en.wikipedia.org/wiki/List_of_countries_by_home_ownership_rate.

[25] Calculated using data from The World Factbook, Central Intelligence Agency, 2015, https://www.cia.gov/library/publications/the-world-factbook.

"Singapore," International Monetary Fund, 2015, https://www.imf.org/external/np/sta/ir/IRProcessWeb/data/sgp/eng/cursgp.htm.

"Switzerland," International Monetary Fund, 2015, https://www.imf.org/external/np/sta/ir/IRProcessWeb/data/che/eng/curche.htm.

"United States," International Monetary Fund, 2015, http://www.imf.org/external/np/sta/ir/IRProcessWeb/data/usa/eng/curusa.htm#I.

[26] World Bank Economic Indicators, 2010, https://data.worldbank.org/indicator/.

[27] "China GDP Per Capita," Trading Economics, 1960-2018, (GDP Per Capita: China $132 and $7,329 and the U.S., $17,036 and $53,129 in 1960 and 2017), https://tradingeconomics.com/china/gdp-per-capita.

[28] Alexander Hamilton, James Madison, and John Jay, *The Federalist Papers*, No. 45, Edited by Clinton Rossiter, (New York: Signet Classics), 2003, 289.

[29] Gerhard Peters and John T. Woolley, "Executive Orders," *The American Presidency Project*, Edited by John T. Woolley and Gerhard Peters, Santa Barbara, California, 1999-2018, http://www.presidency.ucsb.edu/data/orders.php.

"Executive Orders Disposition Tables: Franklin D. Roosevelt," Federal Register, National Archives, https://www.archives.gov/federal-register/executive-orders/roosevelt.html.

"Executive Orders Disposition Tables: Lyndon B. Johnson," Federal Register, National Archives, https://www.archives.gov/federal-register/executive-orders/johnson.html.

"Executive Orders Disposition Tables: George W. Bush," Federal Register, National Archives, https://www.archives.gov/federal-register/executive-orders/wbush.html.

[30] "Obama Encourages Illegals," The Washington Times, Washington, D.C., November 18, 2009, http://www.washingtontimes.com/news/2009/nov/18/obama-encourages-illegals/.

[31] Brion McClanahan, *9 Presidents Who Screwed Up America*, (Washington, D.C.: Regnery History), 2016, 172.

[32] Ibid., 274.

[33] James Madison, Speech at the Virginia Convention to ratify the Federal Constitution, June 6, 1788, *Debates in the Several State Conventions on the Adoption of the Federal Constitution*, edited by Jonathan Elliot and J.B. Lippincott, Philadelphia, 1836, v.3, 87.

[34] James Madison, "Letter to James Robertson," April 20, 1831, Wikisource, https://en.wikisource.org/wiki/James_Madison_letter_to_James_Robertson.

[35] Robert Levy and William Mellor, *The Dirty Dozen: How Twelve Supreme Court Cases Radically Expanded Government and Eroded Freedom*, (Washington D.C.: Cato Institute), 2008, 50–66.

[36] Ibid., 19–36.

[37] Ibid., 181–197.

[38] Ibid., 20–49.

[39] Ibid., 67–85.

[40] Ibid., 143–154.

[41] Ibid., 67–85.

[42] Ibid., 198–214.

[43] Ibid., 155–168.

[44] Carol Tucker, "The 1950s—Powerful Years for Religion," USC News, June 16, 1997, https://news.usc.edu/25835/The-1950s-Powerful-Years-for-Religion/.

Kelly Shattuck, "7 Startling Facts: An Up Close Look at Church Attendance in America," Church Leaders, April 10, 2018, http://www.churchleaders.com/pastors/pastor-articles/139575-7-startling-facts-an-up-close-look-at-church-attendance-in-america.html.

[45] "Alcohol Facts and Statistics," National Institute on Alcohol Abuse and Alcoholism, August 2018, http://www.niaaa.nih.gov/alcohol-health/overview-alcohol-consumption/alcohol-facts-and-statistics.

[46] "National Survey of Drug Use and Health," National Institute on Drug Abuse, https://www.drugabuse.gov/national-survey-drug-use-health.

[47] "Statistics," American Sexual Health Association, http://www.ashasexualhealth.org/stdsstis/statistics/.

[48] Aggressive Driving and Road Rage," American Safety Council, http://www.safemotorist.com/articles/road_rage.aspx.

[49] "Corruption Perceptions Index 2017," Transparency International, https://www.transparency.org/news/feature/corruption_perceptions_index_2017.

[50] Crime Index for Country, 2018 Mid-Year, NUMBEO, http://www.numbeo.com/crime/rankings_by_country.jsp.

[51] Julissa Cruz, "Marriage: More Than a Century of Change," Bowling Green State University, Bowling Green, Ohio, 2013, https://www.bgsu.edu/content/dam/BGSU/college-of-arts-and-sciences/NCFMR/documents/FP/FP-13-13.pdf.

[52] Ibid.

Robert Putman, *Our Kids: The American Dream in Crisis*, (New York: Simon & Schuster), 2015, 70.

[53] Robert Putman, *Our Kids: The American Dream in Crisis*, (New York: Simon & Schuster), 2015, 63.

[54] Ibid., 70.

[55] Ibid., 78.

[56] David Brooks, "The Cost of Relativism," *The New York Times*, March 10, 2015, https://www.nytimes.com/2015/03/10/opinion/david-brooks-the-cost-of-relativism.html.

[57] Bradley Sawyer and Cynthia Cox, "How Does Health Spending in the U.S. Compare to Other Countries?" Peterson-Kaiser Health System Tracker, December 7, 2018, https://www.healthsystemtracker.org/chart-collection/health-spending-u-s-compare-countries/#item-start.

[58] Graham Alison and Robert D. Blackwill, *Lee Kuan Yew: The Grand Master's Insights on China, The United States, and the World*, The MIT Press, Cambridge, MA, 2013, 34.

[59] "Debt Outstanding by Sector," Board of Governors of the Federal Reserve System, December 7, 2017, https://www.federalreserve.gov/releases/z1/current/html/d3.htm.

[60] "U.S. Treasury securities held by the Federal Reserve: All Maturities," FRED, Economic Research, Federal Reserve Bank of St. Louis, https://fred.stlouisfed.org/series/TREAST.

Board of Governors of the Federal Reserve System, www.federalreserve.gov.

"Employment," U.S. Bureau of Labor Statistics, https://www.bls.gov/ces/.

[61] "Modern Immigration Wave Brings 59 Million to U.S., Driving Population Growth and Change Through 2065," Pew Research Center, September 28, 2015, http://www.pewhispanic.org/2015/09/28/modern-immigration-wave-brings-59-million-to-u-s-driving-population-growth-and-change-through-2065/.

[62] Jack Welch, *Encyclopedia.com*, "http://www.encyclopedia.com/topic/Jack_Welch.aspx.

[63] Jack Welch, *Jack Straight from the Gut*, (New York: Warner Books), 2001, 4.

[64] Winston Churchill, Speech in the House of Commons, *Royal Assent*, HC Deb, 17 May 1916, v. 82, cc 1578.

[65] Dale Carnegie, *How to Stop Worrying and Start Living*, "Thomas Edison," Pocket Books, Kindle eBook, August 24, 2010, 36.

[66] Carl Sagan, "Wonder and Skepticism," Skeptical Enquirer, Volume 19.1, January / February 1995.

[67] Carl Sagan, *The Demon-Haunted World: Science as a Candle in the Dark*, Ballantine Books, New York, 1996, 28.

[68] Will Durant, *The Story of Civilization, Volume 1: Our Oriental Heritage*, (New York: Simon & Schuster), 1954: 263–264.

[69] Annie Dillard, *Pilgrim at Tinker Creek*, (New York, Bantam Books, Inc.), 1975, 9–10.

[70] "Abiogenesis," Wikipedia, http://en.wikpedia.org/wiki/Abiogenesis.

[71] Ibid.

[72] "Timeline of Evolutionary History of Life," Wikipedia, https://en.wikipedia.org/wiki/Timeline_of_the_evolutionary_history_of_life.

[73] Rachel Brazil, "Hydrothermal Vents and the Origins of Life," Chemistry World, April 16, 2017, https://www.chemistryworld.com/feature/hydrothermal-vents-and-the-origins-of-life/3007088.article.

[74] "Evolution," Wikipedia, http://en.wikipedia.org/wiki/Evolution.

[75] Ibid.

[76] "Timeline of the Evolution of Life," Wikipedia, http://en.wikpedia.org/wiki/Timeline_of_evolutionary_history_of_life.

[77] Ibid.

[78] Ibid.

[79] Charles Darwin, On the Origin of Species, 1859, (New York: Signet Classics), 2003, 61.

[80] Ibid., 278.

[81] "Origin of the Domestic Dog," Wikipedia, https://en.wikipedia.org/wiki/Origin_of_the_domestic_dog.

[82] E.O. Wilson, On Human Nature, (Cambridge, MA: Harvard University Press), 1978, 88.

[83] Will Durant, "The Map of Human Character," Lecture broadcast over WGN, Chicago, November 18, 1945, http://www.theimaginativeconservative.org/2012/05/map-of-human-character.html.

[84] "Total Fertility Rate of the United States," Wikipedia, https://en.wikipedia.org/wiki/Total_fertility_rate, "United States."

[85] Jared Diamond, Guns, Germs, and Steel, (New York: W.W. Norton), April 17, 1999, 429.

[86] Thomas Jefferson, "The Declaration of Independence of the United States of America," The Declaration of Independence and the Constitutions of the United States of America, Cato Institute, Washington D.C., 9–10.

[87] E.O. Wilson, On Human Nature, (Cambridge, MA: Harvard University Press), 1978, 84.

[88] Ibid.

[89] David Brooks, "Social Animal: How the New Sciences of Human Nature Can Help Make Sense of Life," The New Yorker, January 17, 2011.

[90] Geert Hofstede, Gert Jan Hofstede, and Michael Minkov, *Cultures and Organizations: Software of the Mind*, (New York: McGraw-Hill), 2010: 3–12.

[91] Ibid., 12–14.

[92] Ibid., 53–88.

[93] Lawrence Harrison, *Jews, Confucians, and Protestants*, (Plymouth, U.K.: Roman & Littlefield Publishers, Inc), 2013.

[94] Donald Hebb, *The Organization of Behavior*, (New York: John Wiley and Sons), 1949.

[95] "Extinction Events," Wikipedia, http://en.wikipedia.org/wiki/Extinction_event.

[96] "World Population," Wikipedia, http://en.wikipedia.org/wiki/World_population.

[97] "List of Famines," Wikipedia, http://en.wikipedia.org/wiki/List_of_famines.

[98] Ibid.

[99] Carl Sagan, *Pale Blue Dot: A Vision of the Human Future in Space*, (New York: Random House), 1994, 371.

[100] "Used Fuel Storage and Nuclear Waste Fund Payments by State," Nuclear Energy Institute, 2017, https://www.nei.org/resources/statistics/used-fuel-storage-and-nuclear-waste-fund-payments.

[101] Norman Myers, *Gaia Atlas of Planet Management*, (Hamburg, Germany: Anchor Publishing), 1992, 159.

[102] David Biello, "How Much Is Too Much? Estimating Greenhouse Gas Emissions," Scientific American, April 2009.

[103] Carl Sagan, *Cosmos: A Personal Voyage*, 1980, Episode 6, 58 min, 56 sec.

[104] Nick Lane, *Life Ascending*, (New York: W.W. Norton & Co), 2009, 282.

[105] Anahad O'Connor, "Fasting Diets Are Gaining Acceptance," Food Section, *The New York Times*, March 7, 2016

Dr. Mercola, "Intermittent Fasting Extends Longevity in the Same Way as Exercise," TapNewsWire, March 2016, http://tapnewswire.com/2016/03/intermittent-fasting-extends-longevity-in-the-same-way-as-exercise/.

[106] Ibid.

[107] Melinda Smith, Lawrence Robertson, and Robert Segal, "Sleep Needs," Help Guide.org, October 2018, https://www.helpguide.org/articles/sleep/sleep-needs-get-the-sleep-you-need.htm.

[108] Kenneth Cooper, M.D., M.P.H., *Aerobics,* (New York: Bantam Books), 1969, 37-53.

[109] Nick Lane, *Life Ascending,* (New York: W.W. Norton & Co, 2009), 36-37.

[110] Stephen Covey, *The 7 Habits of Highly Effective Families,* (New York: St. Martin's Griffin), 1997, 301.

[111] Marcus Aurelius, *Wisdom for the Soul,* Compiled and Edited by Larry Chang, (Washington, D.C: Gnosophia), 2006, 52.

[112] Dewey Bunnell and Gerry Beckley, "America," *Holiday Collection,* Warner/Chappell Music Ltd, WB Music Corp, 1974, http://www.azlyrics.com/lyrics/america/tinman.html.

[113] Gerald M. Edelman and Giulio Tononi, *A Universe of Consciousness: How Matter Becomes Imagination,* (New York: Basic Books), 2000, 38.

[114] "Human Brain," Wikipedia, http:/en.wikipedia.org/wiki/Human_brain.

[115] Gerald M. Edelman and Giulio Tononi, *A Universe of Consciousness: How Matter Becomes Imagination,* (New York: Basic Books), 2000, 38.

[116] Marcus Aurelius, *Meditations,* Book II, Chapter IX, Translation by Jeremy Collier, https://en.wikiquote.org/wiki/Talk:Marcus_Aurelius.

[117] James Allen, *As a Man Thinketh,* (New York: Grosset & Dunlap), 2001, 61.

[118] Stephen Covey, *The 7 Habits Study Guide/Private Victory,* https://en.wikibooks.org/wiki/Seven_Habits_Study_Guide/Private_victory.

[119] Frank Herbert, *Dune,* (New York: Berkley Books), 1984, 262.

[120] James Allen, "Your Mental Attitude," *Above Life's Turmoil,* http://www.jamesallenlibrary.com/authors/james-allen/above-lifes-turmoil/your-mental-attitude.

[121] Stephen Covey, *The 7 Habits of Highly Effective People,* (New York: Simon & Schuster), 1989, 46.

[122] Thomas Jefferson, "The Letters of Thomas Jefferson: To Peter Carr," (Paris, August 19, 1785), Yale Law School Lillian Goldman Law Library, 2008, http://avalon.law.yale.edu/18th_century/let31.asp.

[123] Albert Einstein, Letter to the Editor of The New York Times, May 1, 1935, Princeton University, https://www.agnesscott.edu/lriddle/women/EinsteinNYTLetter.pdf.

[124] Sometimes attributed to Socrates and sometimes considered an Arab Proverb. The origin of the triple filter appears to be unknown.

[125] Nellie Bitz, Plainville, New York, 1977.

[126] Geert Hofstede, Gert Jan Hofstede, and Michael Minkov, *Cultures and Organizations: Software of the Mind,* (New York: McGraw Hill), 2010, 82-86.

[127] Ibid., 85-86.

[128] Christopher Reeve, "Christopher Reeve: A Hero Onscreen and Off," Interview by Alanna Nash, *Reader's Digest,* New York City, October 2004.

[129] Stephen Covey, *The 7 Habits of Highly Effective People,* (New York: Simon & Schuster), 1989, 157.

[130] Ibid., 161.

[131] Ibid., 98.

[132] David Brooks, *The Well Kept Secret,* (North Carolina: Lulu Press), 2011, 215.

[133] Jim Bickford, "Joseph Sugarman," *American Comeback* (Las Vegas: American Comeback Publishing) 2013, 46.

[134] Donovan Leitch, Lyrics for the "Brother Sun, Sister Moon," theme song in Franco Zeffirelli's movie, *Brother Sun, Sister Moon,* 1972.

[135] Albert Einstein, *Living Philosophies,* (New York: Simon & Schuster), 1931, 3–7, https://www.aip.org/history/exhibits/einstein/essay.htm.

[136] Leo Tolstoy, *Anna Karenina,* Translated by Richard Pevear and Larissa Volokhonsky, (New York: Penguin Group), 2002, 465.

[137] Although this quote is attributed to Sun Tzu, I could find no translation that attributes it to him.

[138] Nassim Nicholas Taleb, *Antifragile,* (New York: Random House), 2016, 20–21.

[139] Ibid., 175–186.

[140] Ibid., 268–289.

[141] Ibid., 6–7.

[142] Ibid., 92–93.

[143] Ibid., 20–27.

[144] Ibid., 20–27.

[145] Ibid., 20–27.

[146] Ibid., 169–186.

[147] Ibid., 161–162.

[148] Ibid., 217–240.

[149] "Excellence," Ronnie Oldham, 1998, http://ronnieoldham.com/excellence.htm.

[150] Vince Lombardi, as quoted in "First Team Meeting as the Packers Coach (1959)," *Game of My Life: 25 Stories of Packers Football* by Chuck Carlson, (Champaign, IL: Sports Publishing L.L.C.), 2004, 149.

[151] Warren Buffett, "Homespun Wisdom from the 'Oracle of Omaha'" by Amy Stone, Business Week, June 5, 1999, https://en.wikiquote.org/wiki/Warren_Buffett.

[152] Warren Buffet, Berkshire Hathaway Annual Meeting, 2004, https://en.wikiquote.org/wiki/Warren_Buffett.

[153] Warren Buffett, "Rules That Warren Buffett Lives By," Stephanie Loiacono at Yahoo Finance, February 23, 2010, https://en.wikiquote.org/wiki/Warren_Buffett.

[154] Warren Buffett, Berkshire Hathaway Chairman's Letter, 1990, https://en.wikiquote.org/wiki/Warren_Buffett.

[155] Warren Buffett, Interview in Forbes Magazine, November 1, 1974, https://en.wikiquote.org/wiki/Warren_Buffett.

[156] Warren Buffett, *Berkshire Hathaway, Inc: An Owner's Manuel,* 1999, https://en.wikiquote.org/wiki/Warren_Buffett.

[157] "China GDP Per Capita," Trading Economics, 1960–2018, (GDP Per Capita: China $132 and $7,329 and the U.S., $17,036 and $53,129 in 1960 and 2017), https://tradingeconomics.com/china/gdp-per-capita.

[158] George Washington, Letter to Bushrod, January 15, 1783, *Life of Washington: In the Form of an Autobiography,* (Boston: Charles Upham), 1840, Vol. II, 94, https://books.google.gr/books?id=SDFPAAAAYAAJ&lpg=PP7&ots=7MKPe7wXFQ &dq=Life%20of%20Washington%3A%20In%20the%20Form%20of%20an%20Aut obiography%2C%20(Boston%3A%20Charles%20Upham&pg=PP7#v=onepage&q =Life%20of%20Washington:%20In%20the%20Form%20of%20an%20Autobiograp hy,%20(Boston:%20Charles%20Upham&f=false.

[159] Dale Carnegie, *How to Win Friends and Influence People,* (New York: Pocket Books), 1981, 66.

[160] Ibid., 83.

[161] Ibid., 54.

[162] Ibid., 29.

[163] Ibid., 14.

[164] Ibid., 5.

[165] Ibid., 117.

[166] Ibid., 124.

[167] Dale Carnegie, *How to Stop Worrying and Start Living,* Pocket Books, Kindle eBook, August 24, 2010, 118.

[168] Ibid., 111.

[169] Abraham Lincoln, "The President's Remarks at a Union Meeting in Washington, August 6, 1862," *The Political History of the United States of American During the Great Rebellion,* Edward Mcpherson, Second Edition, (Washington D.C.: Philp & Solomons), 1865, https://books.google.gr/books/about/The_Political_History_of_the_United_Stat.html.

[170] Marcus Aurelius, as quoted in *The Spiritual Teachings of Marcus Aurelius,* by Mark Forstater, (New York: Harper Perennial), 2001.

[171] Clay Christensen, *How Will You Measure Your Life?* (New York: Harper Collins), 2012, 72–73.

[172] Martin Luther King, Jr., "Loving Your Enemies," Sermon Delivered at Dexter Avenue Baptist Church, Montgomery, Alabama, November 17, 1957, http://kingencyclopedia.stanford.edu/encyclopedia/documentsentry/doc_loving_yo ur_enemies/.

[173] Stephen Covey, *First Things First,* (New York: Free Press), 2003, 203.

[174] Stephen Covey, *The 7 Habits of Highly Effective People,* (New York: Simon & Schuster), 1989, 188–199.

[175] Jim Collins, "Appendix 3: Fannie Mae and the Financial Crisis of 2008," *How the Mighty Fall,* (New York: Harper Collins), 2009.

[176] Stephen Covey, *The 7 Habits of Highly Effective People,* (New York: Simon & Schuster), 1989, 98.

[177] Jack and Suzy Welch, *Winning,* (New York: Harper Collins), 2005, 69.

[178] Jack Welch. with John Byrne, *Jack: Straight from the Gut,* (New York: Warner Books), 2002, 83.

[179] Peter H. Diamandis, "Peter's Laws: Supercharging Your Attitude," Google+, April 26, 2013, https://plus.google.com/+PeterHDiamandis/posts/evNhPNVjpf4.

[180] Jack Welch, "Jack Welch: An Oral History," Diane Brady, Bloomberg, August 28, 2012, https://www.bloomberg.com/news/articles/2012-08-28/jack-welch-an-oral-history.

[181] Stephen Covey, *The 7 Habits of Highly Effective People,* (New York: Simon & Schuster), 1989, 58.

[182] George Bernard Shaw, "Back to Methuselah, Act I," *Selected Plays with Prefaces,* 1949, vol. 2, p. 7, http://www.bartleby.com/73/465.html.

[183] Thomas Edison, as quoted by Deborah Headstrong, *From the Telegraph to the Light Bulb with Thomas Edison,* Deborah Headstrong, (Nashville, TN: B&H Publishing Group), 2007, 22.

[184] Jim Collins, *Good to Great,* (New York: Harper Collins), 2001, 62.

[185] Max DePree, *Leadership Is an Art,* (New York: Doubleday), 1989, 17.

[186] Nassim Nicholas Talab, *Skin in the Game,* (London: Penguin Random House), 2018, 3-6.

[187] Ibid., 6.

[188] Alan Greenspan, "Remarks by Chairman Alan Greenspan at the Federal Reserve Bank of Chicago's Money Smart Conference," Chicago, May 13, 2004, http://www.federalreserve.gov/BoardDocs/speeches/2004/20040513/default.htm.

[189] Alexis de Tocqueville, *Democracy in America and Two Essays on America,* 1835, (New York: Penguin Books), 2003, 596.

[190] Edward W. Deming, "Dr. Deming's 14 Points for Management," Point 4, The W. Edwards Deming Institute, https://deming.org/explore/fourteen-points.

[191] Philip Crosby, *Quality Is Free,* (New York, Penguin Books), 1980, 152–169, 181–191.

[192] Edward W. Deming, "Dr. Deming's 14 Points for Management," Point 11, The W. Edwards Deming Institute, https://deming.org/explore/fourteen-points.

[193] Ibid., Points 6 and 13.

[194] Philip Crosby, *Quality Is Free,* (New York: Penguin Books), 1980, 169–181.

[195] Ibid., 169–178.

[196] Ibid., 218–220.

[197] Edward W. Deming, "Dr. Deming's 14 Points for Management," Point 9, The W. Edwards Deming Institute, https://deming.org/explore/fourteen-points.

[198] Philip Crosby, "The Six Stages of Change," Philip Crosby Associates, http://technacon.com/philip-crosby-quality-management-philosophy/the-six-stage-of-change-or-the-6-cs.htm.

[199] Philip Crosby, *Quality Is Free,* (New York: Penguin Books), 1980, 110.

[200] Ayn Rand, *The Fountainhead,* 1943, (New York: Plume), 1993, 710.

[201] Raphaelle Chaix, Chen Cao, and Peter Donnelly, "Is Mate Choice in Humans MHC-Dependent?" Plos Genetics, San Francisco, CA, September 12, 2008, https://journals.plos.org/plosgenetics/article?id=10.1371/journal.pgen.1000184.

[202] M. Scott Peck, M.D., *The Road Less Traveled,* (New York: Simon & Schuster), 1978, 84.

[203] Julissa Cruz, "Marriage: More than a Century of Change," Bowling Green State University, Bowling Green, Ohio, 2013, https://www.bgsu.edu/content/dam/BGSU/college-of-arts-and-sciences/NCFMR/documents/FP/FP-13-13.pdf.

[204] Robert Putnam, *Our Kids: The American Dream in Crisis,* (New York: Simon & Schuster), 2015, 70.

[205] Sandra Blakeslee, Julia Lewis, and Judith Wallerstein, *The Unexpected Legacy of Divorce,* (New York: Hachette Book Group), 2000, xxviii–xxix.

[206] Robert Putnam, *Our Kids: The American Dream in Crisis,* (New York: Simon & Schuster), 2015, 78–79.

[207] Nick Lane, *Life Ascending,* (New York: W.W. Norton & Co), 2009, 36-37.

[208] M. Scott Peck, M.D., *The Road Less Traveled,* (New York: Simon & Schuster), 1978, 88.

[209] John Gray, *Men are from Mars, Women are from Venus,* (New York: Harper Collins), 1992, 159.

[210] Ibid., 159.

211 Felice Dunas and Philip Goldberg, *Passion Play,* (New York: Penguin Putnam, Inc.), 1997, 167.

212 United States Census Bureau, Topics, Population, Data, More Population Data, Families and Living Arrangements, Detailed Tables, Table AD-3, by Age Group (5tables), https://www.census.gov/data/tables/time-series/demo/families/marital.html.

213 "Marriages and Divorces 1900-2012," Infoplease, http://www.infoplease.com/ipa/A0005044.html.

214 United States Census Bureau, Topics, Population, Data, More Population Data, Families and Living Arrangements, Detailed Tables, Table AD-3, by Age Group (first table), https://www.census.gov/data/tables/time-series/demo/families/marital.html.

215 Robert Wright, *The Moral Animal: Why We Are the Way We Are: The New Science of Evolutionary Psychology,* (New York: Vintage Books), 1994, 130-131.

216 Stephen Covey, *7 Habits of Highly Effective People,* (New York: Simon & Schuster), 79–80.

217 Nick Lane, *Life Ascending,* (New York: W.W. Norton & Co), 2009, 36–37.

218 John Gray, http://www.prweb.com/releases/karen-leckie-MarsVenusNow/relationshipsteleclass/prweb9065757.htm.

219 Erich Fromm, *The Art of Loving,* (New York: Harper Collins), 2006, 48.

220 M. Scott Peck, M.D., *The Road Less Traveled,* (New York: Simon & Schuster), 1978, 15-18.

221 Lawrence Harrison, *Jews, Confucians, and Protestants: Cultural Capital and the End of Multiculturalism,* (New York: Rowman & Littlefield Publishers, Inc.), 2013, 173.

222 John Locke, *Some Thoughts Concerning Education,* 1693, Section 122, https://en.wikipedia.org/wiki/Some_Thoughts_Concerning_Education.

223 Ibid., Section 115.

[224] M. Scott Peck, M.D., *The Road Less Traveled*, (New York: Simon & Schuster), 1978, 16.

[225] "Selected Quotes from Golda Meir, Golda Meir Center for Political Leadership," Metropolitan State University of Denver, https://www.msudenver.edu/golda/goldameir/goldaquotes/.

[226] Napoleon Hill, in *Diamond Power: Gems of Wisdom from America's Greatest Marketer* by Barry Farber, (Franklin Lakes, NJ: Career Press), 2004, 53.

[227] Alexis De Tocqueville, *Democracy in America and Two Essays on America*, "Volume 1: Author's Introduction," Part, 1, Chapter 2, (New York: Penguin Books), 2003, 37.

[228] John Locke, *Some Thoughts Concerning Education*, 1693, Section 94, https://en.wikipedia.org/wiki/Some_Thoughts_Concerning_Education.

[229] Charles Duhigg, *The Power of Habit*, (New York: Random House), 2014, 31–59.

[230] Ibid., 97–126.

[231] Ibid., 60–93.

[232] Metta Bitz, Plainville, NY, 1971.

[233] John Locke, *The Works of John Locke*, The Fifth Edition, Volume III., Printed for S. Birt, D. Browne, T. Longman, J. Schuckburgh, C. Hitch and L. Hawes, J. Hodges, J. Oswald, A. Millar, J. Beecroft, J. and J. Rivington, J. Ward, and M. Cooper, 1751, 20, https://books.google.com/books?id=fGRZAAAAYAAJ&printsec=frontcover&dq=Jo hn+Locke,+The+Works+of+John+Locke&hl=en&sa=X&ved=0ahUKEwjtvKWAxaPf AhWud98KHX3RBlkQ6AEIMDAB#v=onepage&q=John%20Locke%2C%20The%2 0Works%20of%20John%20Locke&f=false.

[234] Lee Kuan Yew, as quoted by Graham Alison and Robert D. Blackwill, *Lee Kuan Yew: The Grand Master's Insights on China, The United States, and the World*, (Cambridge, MA: The MIT Press), 2013, 90.

[235] Carl Sagan, *Cosmos*, (New York: Random House), 1980, 333.

[236] "Thales of Miletus," Wikipedia, https://en.wikipedia.org/wiki/Thales_of_Miletus.

[237] Peter Wood and David Randall, "How Bad Is the Government's Science?", The Wall Street Journal, April 17, 2018, A17.

[238] Ibid.

[239] Ayn Rand, *Atlas Shrugged,* (New York: Plume), 1993, 1023.

[240] Carl Sagan, *Cosmos,* (New York: Random House), 1980, 282.

[241] "Morrill Land-Grant Acts," Wikipedia, https://en.wikipedia.org/wiki/Morrill_Land-Grant_Acts.

[242] Ibid.

[243] Fred Brown, "The Morrill Act of 1862: Morrill Land-Grant Act Transformed American Agriculture," October 2012, Colorado State University Libraries, http://www.colostate.edu/morrillact/.

[244] Elizabeth Kneebone, "The Changing Geography of US Poverty," February 15, 2017, The Brookings Institution, https://www.brookings.edu/testimonies/the-changing-geography-of-us-poverty/.

[245] "Euripides," Phrixus, Frag. 927, https://en.wikiquote.org/wiki/Euripides.

[246] "Public High Schools Graduation Rates, 2014-2015," National Center for Educational Statistics, https://nces.ed.gov/programs/coe/indicator_coi.asp.

[247] "Chronic Absenteeism in the Nation's Schools," U.S. Department of Education, 2013-2014 data, https://www2.ed.gov/datastory/chronicabsenteeism.html.

"National Child Abuse Statistics," American Society for the Positive Care of Children, 2018, https://americanspcc.org/child-abuse-statistics/.

[248] "Corruption Perceptions Index 2017," Transparency International, https://www.transparency.org/news/feature/corruption_perceptions_index_2017.

[249] Many people attribute this quote to Albert Einstein on the Internet, but I could find no evidence that he said or wrote it.

[250] Chaim Potok, *Davita's Harp,* (New York: Fawcett Books), 1985, 10.

[251] Simon Janssen and Edward Lazear, "Germany Offers a Promising Jobs Model," The Wall Street Journal, New York, September 9, 2016, A11.

[252] Leslie Brody, "Just 37% of U.S. High School Seniors Prepared for College Math and Reading, Test Shows," The Wall Street Journal, April 27, 2016, https://www.wsj.com/articles/just-37-of-u-s-high-school-seniors-prepared-for-college-math-and-reading-test-shows-1461729661.

[253] "The Condition of Education, Letter from the Commissioner, Education Expenditures by Country," U.S. Department of Education, Institute of Education Sciences, National Center for Education Statistics, Updated May 2018, Washington, D.C., https://nces.ed.gov/programs/coe/indicator_cmd.asp.

[254] Kenneth Clark, as quoted by Milton Friedman in *Free to Choose,* (New York: Harcourt, Inc.), 1990, 172.

[255] Milton and Rose Friedman, *Free to Choose,* (New York: Harcourt, Inc.), 990, 154.

[256] "Recipients: Among Federal Candidates, 2012 Cycle," OpenSecrets.org, National Education Assn, http://www.opensecrets.org/orgs/recips.php?cycle=2012&id=D000000064.

Perry Chiaramonte, "96 percent of Ivy League Professors' Donations Went to Obama", November 28, 2012, FoxNews.com, http://www.foxnews.com/politics/2012/11/28/ivy-leaguers-overwhelmingly-supported-obama-in-campaign-contributions.html.

[257] Milton and Rose Friedman, *Free to Choose,* (New York: Harcourt, Inc.), 1990, 158.

[258] Karl Zinsmeister, "The Charter School Performance Breakout," The Wall Street Journal, Saturday, March 29, 2014.

[259] Ibid.

[260] Ibid.

[261] Michael Block, as quoted in *From Promising to Proven* by Karl Zinsmeister, (Washington D.C.: Philanthropy Roundtable), 2014, 44.

[262] Carl Bistany and Stephanie Gruner Buckley, *Last Bell: Breaking the Gridlock in Education Reform,* (London: Profile Books), 2015, 15.

[263] Milton and Rose Friedman, *Free to Choose,* (New York: Harcourt, Inc.), 1990, 165–166.

[264] Endnotes 251 and 252.

[265] Jack Welch, Interview on CNN with Piers Morgan that was aired June 11, 2011, http://www.cnn.com/TRANSCRIPTS/1106/11/pmt.01.html.

[266] Brent Roberts, as quoted in *How Children Succeed* by Paul Tough, (Boston, MA: Mariner Books), 2012, 70.

[267] Ibid., 71.

[268] Calculated using the World Bank's Development Indicators online database, http://databank.worldbank.org/data/reports.aspx?source=2&country=&series=NY. GNP.PCAP.CD&period=.

[269] Adam Smith, *The Wealth of Nations,* edited by Edwin Cannan, (New York, Bantam Classic), 2003, bk 1, ch ii: 23–24.

[270] Milton Friedman, "On Freedom and Free Markets," Public Television Interview, October 1, 2000, http://www.pbs.org/wgbh/commandingheights/shared/minitext/int_miltonfriedman.html.

[271] James Gwartney, Dwight Lee, and Richard Stroup, "Part III: Economic Progress and the Role of Government," *Common Sense Economics,* (New York: St. Martin's Press), 2005, 79-119.

[272] Ayn Rand, "What is Capitalism?" as quoted in *Capitalism: The Unknown Ideal with Additional Articles* by Nathaniel Branden, Alan Greenspan, and Robert Hessen, (New York: Signet), 1967, 29, http://www.amazon.com/Capitalism-Ideal-Ayn-Rand/dp/0451147952/.

[273] Adam Smith, *The Wealth of Nations,* edited by Edwin Cannan, (New York: Bantam Classic), 2003, bk iv, ch ii, 569–570.

[274] Ibid., bk 1, ch ii, 178.

[275] "Doing Business in 2018," World Bank, 2018, http://www.doingbusiness.org/content/dam/doingBusiness/media/Annual-Reports/English/DB2018-Full-Report.pdf.

[276] Milton Friedman, *Free to Choose: A Personal Statement,* (New York: Houghton Mifflin Harcourt), 1990, 226.

[277] James Gwartney, Dwight Lee, and Richard Stroup, "Part III: Economic Progress and the Role of Government," *Common Sense Economics,* (New York: St. Martin's Press), 2005, 87.

[278] Reshma Kapadia, "Alan Greenspan on What Trump Gets Wrong and Sweden Gets Right," Barrons, New York, October 16, 2018, https://www.barrons.com/articles/alan-greenspan-interview-1539635388.

[279] James Gwartney, Dwight Lee, and Richard Stroup, "Part III: Economic Progress and the Role of Government," *Common Sense Economics,* (New York: St. Martin's Press), 2005, 87.

U.S. Government Publishing Office, http://www.gpo.gov/fdsys/pkg/ECONI-2001-12/html/ECONI-2001-12-Pg1.htm.

Kelly Phillips, "Report: Americans Spend More than 8.9 Billion Hours Each Year On Tax Compliance," Forbes, June 20, 2016, https://www.forbes.com/sites/kellyphillipserb/2016/06/20/report-americans-spend-more-than-8-9-billion-hours-each-year-on-tax-compliance/#402da9af3456.

[280] "Economic Freedom of the World: 2015 Report," Cato Institute, http://www.cato.org/economic-freedom-world.

[281] Ibid.

[282] Warren Buffett, as quoted in *Berkshire Beyond Buffet: The Enduring Value of Values,* by Lawrence Cunningham, (New York: Columbia Business School), 2014.

[283] Frederic Bastiat, *The State, Journal des Debats,* 1848, par. 5.2.

[284] Alexander Hamilton, Speech in New York Urging Ratification of the U.S. Constitution, June 21, 1788, https://www.thefederalistpapers.org/founders/hamilton/alexander-hamilton-on-democracy-speech-in-new-york-urging-ratification-of-the-u-s-constitution-june-21-1788.

[285] Lee Kuan Yew, as quoted in *Lee Kuan Yew: The Grand Master's Insights on China, The United States, and the World* by Graham Allison and Robert Blackwill, (Cambridge, MA: The MIT Press), 2013, 119.

[286] George Washington, Letter to Major-General Robert Howe, August 17, 1779 published in *The Writings of George Washington, 1778–79,* Vol. VII, Edited by Worthington Chauncey Ford, 1890, http://oll.libertyfund.org/titles/2348.

[287] Benjamin Franklin, as quoted by James D. Best, (At the close of the Constitutional Convention of 1787 in the notes of Dr. James McHenry), http://www.whatwouldthefoundersthink.com/a-republic-if-you-can-keep-it.

[288] George Bernard Shaw, *Everybody's Political What's What,* Constable, London, 1944, 256, https://books.google.com/books?id=aQaGAAAAMAAJ&q=everybody%27s+political+What%27s+what&dq=everybody%27s+political+What%27s+what&hl=en&sa=X&ved=0ahUKEwiluaeH_uHgAhWOk1kKHYAyC7kQ6AEIKTAA.

[289] Adam Smith, *Theory of Moral Sentiments,* VI.II.42, Lexington, KY, 2015, 204.

[290] Frank Herbert, *God Emperor of Dune,* (New York: Penguin Group), 1981, 152.

[291] Carl Sagan, *The Demon-Haunted World: Science as a Candle in the Dark,* (New York: Ballantine Books), 1996, 428.

[292] Thomas Jefferson, Inaugural Address, Washington, DC, March 4, 1801, http://ahp.gatech.edu/jefferson_inaug_1801.html.

[293] Thomas Jefferson, "The Kentucky Resolutions of 1798, The Annals of America," Mortimer Adler, et al., eds., Encyclopedia Britannica, Chicago, 1968, v. 4: 65–66.

[294] Alexander Hamilton, Essay in the American Daily Advertiser, August 28, 1794, https://www.thefederalistpapers.org/founders/alexander-hamilton.

[295] *The Declaration of Independence and the Constitution of the United States of America,* Cato Institute, Washington, D.C., 35.

[296] Alexander Hamilton, James Madison, and John Jay, *The Federalist Papers,* No. 78, Edited by Clinton Rossiter, (New York: Signet Classics), 2003, 298.

[297] Wendell Cox, "The Migration of Millions: 2017 State Population Estimates," NewGeography.com, http://www.newgeography.com/content/005837-the-migration-millions-2017-state-population-estimates.

[298] Ibid., No. 28, 177.

[299] Walter Lippmann, "Today and Tomorrow," The New York Herald Tribune, September 19, 1940.

[300] Alexander Hamilton, James Madison, and John Jay, *The Federalist Papers,* (New York, Signet Classics), No. 51, 319.

[301] Ibid., No. 84, 511.

[302] Brion McClanahan, *9 Presidents Who Screwed Up America,* (Washington D.C., Regnery History), 2016, 277.

[303] Chase Gunter, "How Big is the Federal Workforce, Really?", FCW, October 5, 2017, https://fcw.com/articles/2017/10/05/federal-workforce-volker-size.aspx.

[304] Lee Kuan Yew, as quoted in *Lee Kuan Yew: The Grand Master's Insights on China, The United States, and the World* by Graham Alison and Robert D. Blackwill, (Cambridge, MA: The MIT Press), 2013, 132.

[305] Brion McClanahan, *9 Presidents Who Screwed Up America,* (Washington D.C., Regnery History), 2016, 277.

[306] Adam Smith, *The Wealth of Nations,* edited by Edwin Cannan, (New York: Bantam Classics), 2003, bk 1, ch xi, pt.1, 202–203.

[307] Ayn Rand, "Man's Rights," *The Virtue of Selfishness,* (New York: Signet Books), 1964, 108.

[308] Ayn Rand, *Anthem,* (New York: Mockingbird Classic), 2015, ch.12, par. 16.

[309] Clyde Wayne Crews, "Trump Regulations: Federal Register Page Count Is the Lowest in Quarter Century," Competitive Enterprise Institute, December 29, 2017, https://cei.org/blog/trump-regulations-federal-register-page-count-lowest-quarter-century.

[310] "What is the Total Government Spending in Percent GDP?" usgovernmentspending.com, https://www.usgovernmentspending.com/percent_gdp.

[311] Daniel Webster, A Blueprint for Judicial Reform, edited by Patrick McGuigan and Randall Rader, Free Congress Research and Education Foundation, Inc., Washington D.C., 8.

[312] Benjamin Franklin, "On Freedom of Speech and the Press," Pennsylvania Gazette, November 17, 1737, https://en.wikiquote.org/wiki/Freedom_of_speech.

[313] Alan Barth, The Loyalty of Free Men, (New York: The Viking Press), 1951.

[314] Ayn Rand, "Chapter 14: The Nature of Government," The Virtue of Selfishness, (New York: Signet Books), 1964, 126.

[315] Thomas Paine, "Thoughts on Defensive War," The Writings of Thomas Paine, Volume I, Chapter XII, 1774-1779, Edited by Moncure Daniel Conway, G.P. Putman's Sons, 1906, 56, https://books.google.com/books?id=_Ffv6zVfnTYC&pg=PA55&dq=Thomas+Paine,+%E2%80%9CThoughts+on+Defensive+War,%22+The+Writings+of+Thomas+Paine&hl=en&sa=X&ved=0ahUKEwiAnqS9u7XfAhWGVN8KHVhODLIQ6AEIMDAB#v=onepage&q=Thomas%20Paine%2C%20%E2%80%9CThoughts%20on%20Defensive%20War%2C%22%20The%20Writings%20of%20Thomas%20Paine&f=false.

[316] Spock, Star Trek: The Wrath of Khan, 1982. www.imdb.com/title/tt0084726/Quotes.

[317] Nelson Mandela, Long Walk to Freedom, (New York: Little Brown and Co), 1995, 751.

[318] Lee Kuan Yew, as quoted in Lee Kuan Yew: The Grand Master's Insights on China, The United States, and the World by Graham Alison and Robert D. Blackwill, (Cambridge, MA: The MIT Press), 2013, 120.

[319] Niall Ferguson, *Civilization: The West and the Rest*, (New York: The Penguin Press), 97.

[320] John Locke, *Second Treatise of Government*, Chapter VII, Section 87–89, 1690, https://faculty.history.wisc.edu/sommerville/367/Locke%20DecIndep.htm.

[321] Alexander Hamilton, James Madison, and John Jay, *The Federalist Papers*, No. 62, Edited by Clinton Rossiter, (New York: Signet Classics), 2003, 379.

[322] "Federal Register Pages Published (1936-2017)," Federal Register.gov, https://www.federalregister.gov/uploads/2018/03/pagesPublished2017.pdf.

[323] David Brooks, *The Social Animal: The Hidden Sources of Love, Character, and Achievement*, (New York: Random House), 2012, xii.

[324] James Hirby, "Why Is It That Illegal Aliens Get Free Food Stamps, Health Insurance and Pay No Taxes?" The Law Dictionary, http://thelawdictionary.org/article/why-is-it-that-illegal-aliens-get-free-food-stamps-health-insurance-and-pay-no-taxes/.

[325] "Congress Exempt from Several Federal Laws," Fox News, Published February 3, 2012 by the Associated Press. http://www.foxnews.com/us/2012/02/03/congress-exempt-from-several-federal-laws.html.

[326] "Obama Encourages Illegals," The Washington Times, Washington, D.C., November 18, 2009, http://www.washingtontimes.com/news/2009/nov/18/obama-encourages-illegals/.

[327] Michael Teo, "Singapore's Policy Keeps Drugs at Bay," The Guardian, June 5, 2010, http://www.theguardian.com/commentisfree/2010/jun/05/singapore-policy-drugs-bay.

[328] Desmond Tutu, Guardian Weekly, London, April 8, 1984, https://en.wikiquote.org/wiki/Desmond_Tutu.

[329] Nelson Mandela, *Long Walk to Freedom: The Autobiography of Nelson Mandela*, (New York: Little Brown and Company), 2008, 95.

[330] Martin Luther King, Jr., Dr. Martin Luther King's visit to Cornell College, October 15, 1962, http://news.cornellcollege.edu/dr-martin-luther-kings-visit-to-cornell-college/.

[331] Martin Luther King, Jr., *Where Do We Go from Here: Chaos or Community?* 1967, https://en.wikiquote.org/wiki/Martin_Luther_King,_Jr.

[332] U.S. Department of Commerce, United States Census, 2017, https://factfinder.census.gov/faces/tableservices/jsf/pages/productview.xhtml?pid=ACS_17_5YR_DP05&src=pt.

[333] Frans de Waal, "Moral Behavior in Animals," TEDx Peachtree, November, 2011, https://www.ted.com/talks/frans_de_waal_do_animals_have_morals.

[334] Lee Kuan Yew, as quoted in *Lee Kuan Yew: The Grand Master's Insights on China, The United States, and the World* by Graham Alison and Robert D. Blackwill, (Cambridge, MA: The MIT Press), 2013: 123–125.

[335] "Minimum Wage Law by Country," Wikipedia.org, July, 2018, https://en.wikipedia.org/wiki/Minimum_wage_law#Historical_rates.

[336] Bill O'Reilly, The O'Reilly Factor, Fox News, July 28, 2013, http://nation.foxnews.com/2013/07/22/must-watch-talking-points-president-obama-and-race-problem.

[337] Lawrence Harrison, J*ews, Confucians, and Protestants: Cultural Capital and the End of Multiculturalism,* (New York: Rowman and Littlefield Publishers, Inc.), 2013, 168.

[338] Jason Riley, "Race Relations and Law Enforcement," Imprimis, Hillsdale College, January 2015, Vol 44, No 1.

[339] Credited to Jean-Baptiste Colbert, a minister of finance to Louis XIV in Seventeenth-Century France, https://en.wikipedia.org/wiki/Jean-Baptiste_Colbert.

[340] James Gwartney, Dwight Lee, and Richard Stroup, *Common Sense Economics,* "Part III: Economic Progress and the Role of Government," (New York: St. Martin's Press), 2005.

[341] "Swiss National Bank," Wikipedia, https://en.wikipedia.org/wiki/Swiss_National_Bank.

[342] U.S. Inflation Calculator, http://www.usinflationcalculator.com/.

[343] Milton Friedman, Comment on President Carter's plan to raise taxes to reduce inflation, 1979, http://www.policyofliberty.net/quotes6.php.

[344] Adam Smith, *The Wealth of Nations*, edited by Edwin Cannan, (New York: Bantam Classics), 2003, bk. V, ch. I, pt. III, art. 1, 1959.

[345] Thomas Jefferson, Letter to Antoine Louis Claude Destutt de Tracy, December 26, 1820, http://www.monticello.org/site/research-and-collections/chain-email-10-jefferson-quotations.

[346] James Buchannan, *The Deficit and American Democracy*, (Memphis, P.K. Seidman Foundation), 1984.

[347] George Washington, Letter to Marie-Joseph-Paul-Yves-Roch-Gilbert Du Motier, Marquis de Lafayette, October 30, 1780, http://founders.archives.gov/documents/Washington/99-01-02-03745.

[348] Dwight Eisenhower, "Farewell Address," January 17, 1961, http://www.americanrhetoric.com/speeches/dwightdeisenhowerfarewell.html.

[349] "What is Quantitative Easing?", The Economist, March 9, 2015, http://www.economist.com/blogs/economist-explains/2015/03/economist-explains-5.

[350] James Gwartney, Dwight Lee, and Richard Stroup, "Part III: Economic Progress and the Role of Government," *Common Sense Economics*, (New York: St. Martin's Press), 2005, 114-115.

[351] Benjamin Franklin, "On the Price of Corn and Management of the Poor," Founders Online, November 29, 1766, https://founders.archives.gov/documents/Franklin/01-13-02-0194.

[352] Henry David Thoreau, *Walden*, (UK: CRW Publishing Limited), 2004, 83, https://books.google.com/books?id=49qWhJ0gjZQC&pg=PA83&lpg=PA83&dq.

[353] Benjamin Franklin, *The Writings of Benjamin Franklin*, edited by Albert Henry Smyth, (New York: Macmillan), 1905–07, v. 3, 135.

[354] Samuel Adams, "Vol. 1, Chapter 6, Document 6: House of Representatives of Massachusetts to Dennis De Berdt," (Jan 12, 1768), *The Founders' Constitution*, The University of Chicago, 1987, http://press-pubs.uchicago.edu/founders/documents/v1ch16s6.html.

[355] Thomas Jefferson, Letter to Thomas Cooper, November 29, 1802, *The Thomas Jefferson, Papers Series 1, General Correspondence*, 1651–1827, Library of Congress, http://memory.loc.gov/cgi-bin/ampage?collId=mtj1&fileName=mtj1page027.db&recNum=500.

[356] Alexis De Tocqueville, as quoted in *The Road to Serfdom* by F. A. Hayek, (Chicago, IL: The University of Chicago Press), 1994, 29.

[357] Milton Friedman, *Free to Choose*, (New York: Harcourt, Inc.), 1980, 140, https://books.google.com/books?id=F5z1B5SwGUEC&printsec=frontcover&dq=Milton+Friedman,+Free+to+Choose&hl=en&sa=X&ved=0ahUKEwj00bnKvbXfAhUBmVkKHU47BjQQ6AEIKjAA#v=onepage&q=Milton%20Friedman%2C%20Free%20to%20Choose&f=false.

[358] Margaret Thatcher, Thames Television, This Week program, February 5, 1976, http://www.snopes.com/politics/quotes/thatcher.asp.

[359] Frank Herbert, *God Emperor of Dune*, (New York: Ace Books), 1981, Ch. 13, https://books.google.com/books?id=oTgvJWFmjOoC&printsec=frontcover&dq=Frank+Herbert,+God+Emperor+of+Dune&hl=en&sa=X&ved=0ahUKEwi8xcDmvbXfAhWyuVkKHdQSACAQ6AEIKjAA#v=onepage&q=Frank%20Herbert%2C%20God%20Emperor%20of%20Dune&f=false.

[360] Yuen Chung Kwong, "What You Need to Know About Singapore's Compulsory Saving Scheme," Singapore Business Review, Singapore, August 10, 2012.

[361] "U.S. Personal Savings Rate," Trading Economics, 2018, https://tradingeconomics.com/united-states/personal-savings.

[362] Lee Kuan Yew, as quoted in *Lee Kuan Yew: The Grand Master's Insights on China, The United States, and the World* by Graham Alison and Robert D. Blackwill, (Cambridge, MA: The MIT Press), 2013, 124.

[363] James Madison, Speech to Congress, Annals of Congress, House of Representatives, 3rd Congress, 1st Session, January 10, 1794, 170, https://en.wikiquote.org/wiki/James_Madison.

[364] Robert Putman, *Our Kids: The American Dream in Crisis*, (New York: Simon & Schuster), 2015, 29.

[365] Martin Luther King, Jr., "Three-Pronged Assault Planned for Hospitals," Call and Post, Cleveland, April 16, 1966.

[366] The United States Census Bureau, 2017 https://www.census.gov/data/tables/time-series/demo/income-poverty/cps-finc/finc-01.html2016.

Milliman Medical Index, May 2016, http:/www.milliman.com/mmi/.

[367] T.R. Reid, "How We Spend $3,400,000,000,000, The Atlantic, June 15, 2017, https://www.theatlantic.com/health/archive/2017/06/how-we-spend-3400000000000/530355/.

[368] "The Watercooler ~ Illegal Immigration Costs California Taxpayers $25.3 Billion Per Year," RedState, http://www.redstate.com/diary/westcoastpatriette/2014/07/01/watercooler-illegal-immigration-costs-california-taxpayers-25-3-billion-year/.

[369] George Borjas, "Immigration and the American Worker," Center for Immigration Studies, April 9, 2013, http://cis.org/immigration-and-the-american-worker-review-academic-literature.

[370] Rick Ungar, "The True Cost of Medical Malpractice – It May Surprise You," Forbes Magazine, September, 7, 2010, https://www.forbes.com/sites/rickungar/2010/09/07/the-true-cost-of-medical-malpractice-it-may-surprise-you/#1924dd312ff5.

[371] "Costs to Bring a Drug to Market Remain in Dispute," Managed Care, September 14, 2017, https://www.managedcaremag.com/news/20170914/costs-bring-drug-market-remain-dispute.

[372] Jason Riley, as quoted in "Race Relations and Law Enforcement," *Imprints*, Hillsdale College, 2014.

[373] Jamie Ruvalcaba, *Jews, Confucians, and Protestants*, by Lawrence Harrison, (New York: Rowman and Littlefield Publishers, Inc.), 2013, p. 159–160.

[374] Frank Gaffney, Jr., as quoted in *Refugee Resettlement and the Hijra to America* by Ann Corcoran, Center for Security Policy, Washington D.C., 2015, pp. 7–8.

[375] Charles Darwin, *The Descent of Man,* (New York: American Dome Library Company), 1902, 179, https://books.google.com/books?id=bhEqAAAAYAAJ&printsec=frontcover&dq=Ch arles+Darwin,+The+Descent+of+Man,&hl=en&sa=X&ved=0ahUKEwinuay1vrXfAh USx1kKHaJmAiAQ6AEIKjAA#v=onepage&q=Charles%20Darwin%2C%20The%2 0Descent%20of%20Man%2C&f=false.

[376] Lee Kuan Yew, as quoted in *Lee Kuan Yew.: The Grand Master's Insights on China, The United States, and the World* by Graham Alison and Robert D. Blackwill, (Cambridge, MA: The MIT Press), 2013, p. 112.

[377] Paul Bedard, "Census Confirms: 63 Percent of 'Non-Citizens' on Welfare, 4.6 Million Households," Washington Examiner, December 3, 2018.

[378] Matt O'Brien and Spencer Raley, "The Fiscal Burden of Illegal Immigration on United States Taxpayers," FAIR Federation for American Immigration Reform, September 27, 2017, https://fairus.org/issue/publications-resources/fiscal-burden-illegal-immigration-united-states-taxpayers.

[379] "Number of Full-time Employees in the United States from 1990 to 2017," Statista: The Statistics Portal, https://www.statista.com/statistics/192356/number-of-full-time-employees-in-the-usa-since-1990/.

[380] Richard Estrada, Columnist for the Dallas Morning News, Letter to Lawrence Harrison, January 13, 1991.

Lawrence Harrison, J*ews, Confucians, and Protestants: Cultural Capital and the End of Multiculturalism,* (New York: Rowman and Littlefield Publishers, Inc.), 2013, 147.

[381] Lawrence Harrison, J*ews, Confucians, and Protestants: Cultural Capital and the End of Multiculturalism,* (New York: Rowman and Littlefield Publishers, Inc.), 2013, 160.

[382] "Modern Immigration Wave Brings 59 Million to U.S., Driving Population Growth and Change Through 2065," Pew Research Center, September 28, 2015, http://www.pewhispanic.org/2015/09/28/modern-immigration-wave-brings-59-million-to-u-s-driving-population-growth-and-change-through-2065/.

---

[383] "Immigration," Pew Research Center, http://www.pewresearch.org/data-trend/society-and-demographics/immigrants/.

[384] George Washington, Letter to Elbridge Gerry, January 29, 1780, http://www.mountvernon.org/george-washington/quotes/6/.

[385] E.O. Wilson, *On Human Nature,* (Cambridge, MA: Harvard University Press), 1978, 99.

[386] Ibid., 103.

[387] Will and Ariel Durant, *Lessons of History,* (New York: Simon & Schuster), 2010, 81.

[388] Niall Ferguson, Interview by Tom Templeton, The Guardian, London, January 17, 2009.

[389] Adam Smith, *Theory of Moral Sentiments,* II.II.21, Lexington, KY, 2015, 74.

[390] George Orwell, "In Front of Your Nose," Tribune, London, March 22, 1946, http://orwell.ru/library/articles/nose/english/e_nose.

[391] Sun Tzu, *The Art of War,* translated by Lionel Giles, (Irving, CA: Xist Publishing), 2014, 17.

[392] Alexander Hamilton, John Jay, and James Madison, "Letters of Helvidius, No. IV," *The Federalist on the New Constitution,* 1788, 550, https://books.google.com/books?id=m3ZqDwAAQBAJ&printsec=frontcover&dq=Al exander+Hamilton,+John+Jay,+and+James+Madison,+the+federalist+papers+iv& hl=en&sa=X&ved=0ahUKEwjdiLq2v7XfAhWBmVkKHbblASwQ6AEIKjAA#v=onepa ge&q&f=false.

[393] Sun Tzu, *The Art of War,* translated by Lionel Giles, (Irving, CA: Xist Publishing), 2014, 6.

[394] James Madison, Speech at the Constitutional Convention, June 29, 1787, https://www.thefederalistpapers.org/founders/james-madison-quotes.

[395] James Madison, "Political Observations," April 20, 1795; https://en.wikiquote.org/wiki/James_Madison.

[396] James Madison, "Helvidius," *The Federalist on the Constitution,* No. 1, August 24, 1793, http://oll.libertyfund.org/quote/396.

[397] Charles Krauthammer, *Things That Matter,* (New York: Crown Forum), 2013, 348.

[398] Edward Wilson, *Consilience: The Unity of Knowledge,* (New York: Vintage Books), 1999, 303–304.

[399] "Earth," Wikipedia, https://en.wikipedia.org/wiki/Earth.

[400] "Unit 7: Agriculture // Section 2: Earth's Land Resources," Annenberg Learner, https://www.learner.org/courses/envsci/unit/text.php?unit=7&secNum=2.

[401] "Earth," Wikipedia, https://en.wikipedia.org/wiki/Earth; "Water Distribution on Earth," Wikipedia, https://en.wikipedia.org/wiki/Water_distribution_on_Earth; Frauenfelder, Mark, "All the Water and Air on Earth Gathered into Spheres and Compared to the Earth," http://boingboing.net/2008/03/11/all-the-water-and-ai.html.

[402] "Earth," Wikipedia, https://en.wikipedia.org/wiki/Earth.

[403] "Water Distribution on Earth," Wikipedia, https://en.wikipedia.org/wiki/Water_distribution_on_Earth#Distribution_of_saline_and_fresh_water.

[404] "Forests," Conservation International, http://www.conservation.org/what/pages/forests.aspx?gclid=CjwKEAjwpaqvBRCxzIGoxs6v2TkSJADel-MlzLaasYxMDs2xaLsXLoK_pBTFK6VClcbY4Dtff6TSexoCo9_w_wcB.

"Habitat Destruction," Wikipedia, https://en.wikipedia.org/wiki/Habitat_destruction.

[405] Christine Dell'Amore, "Species Extinction Happening 1,000 Times Faster Because of Humans?" National Geographic, May 30, 2014, http://news.nationalgeographic.com/news/2014/05/140529-conservation-science-animals-species-endangered-extinction/.

[406] "Total Fertility Rate of the United States," Wikipedia, https://en.wikipedia.org/wiki/Total_fertility_rate.

[407] Mark Tercek and Jonathan Adams, *Nature's Fortune: How Business and Society Thrive by Investing in Nature,* (New York: Basic Books), 2013, 196–197.

[408] Helen Keller, "Dreams That Come True," *Personality,* American Foundation for the Blind, December 1927.

[409] Lee Kuan Yew, as quoted in *Lee Kuan Yew: The Grand Master's Insights on China, The United States, and the World* by Graham Alison and Robert D. Blackwill, (Cambridge, MA: The MIT Press), 29-30.

[410] Adam Smith, *Theory of Moral Sentiments,* III.III.47, Lexington, KY, 2015, 114.

[411] Maximus Decimus Meridius, as quoted in Gladiator, *written by David Franzoni, John Logan, and William Nicholson; Directed by Ridley Scott; Scott Free Productions and Red Wagon Entertainment; 2000.*

Index

Abundance and Decency, 208
Accommodation, 269–71
Accomplished Souls, 181
Accountability, 201–2, 228–29
Acknowledgments, 563
Adams, Samuel, 494
Administration Empowerment and
    Accountability, 349–51
Advantageous Immigration, 509,
    522–24
Affiliation, 201–6
Agency Problem, 507
Allen, James, 137, 143, 144, 570
Allies, 534
Ally Acquisition, 208–10
Antifragile, 167
Antifragility, 173–77
    Concentration of Power, 174
    Debt, 175
    Dependence, 176
    Individuals vs. Groups, 176
    Regulations, 175
    Skin in the Game, 176
Antitrust, 359, 378–80
Apology, 214–15
Appearance, 203–4
Appreciation, 211–12
Assignments, 228–29
Assimilation, 515–24,
Associations, 243–46
Asymmetry, 169–72
Attendance, 202–3
Attention to Detail, 184
Aurelius, Marcus, 132, 136, 211
Authenticity, 146
Automated Investment, 189

Avoiding Harm, 129
Balance, 134
Balanced Budgets, 482–85
Balfanz, Robert, 343
Barth, Alan, 433
Bastiat, Frederic, 397
Benchmarking, 14, 347–49
Beneficial Diversity, 238–39
Bennis v. Michigan, 27
Biases, 354–56
Bicameral Legislature, 413–14
Biodiversity, 541–42
Bitz, Janice, 143, 463, 508
Bitz, Metta, 143, 299
Bitz, Nellie, 147
Bitz, Robert, 143, 282, 326, 463
Black Swan, 173–77
Blakeslee, Sandra, 259
Block, Michael, 342
Brain, 135–36
Breaking Habits, 303–5
Bridging Conservative and Liberal
    Biases, 354–56
Brooks, David, 35, 93, 157, 442
Buchanan, James, 484
Budgets, 227
Buffet, 143, 193, 236, 387, 569
Bush, George H. W., 20–24
Bush, George W., 20–24
Business Cycles, 195
Buying & Selling Assets, 195–96
Can-Do Attitude, 463–66
Capital Formation, 369-370,
    487–88
Capital and Investment, 369-370

Carnegie, Dale, 143, 210
Carson, Rachel, 109, 143
Carter, Jimmy, 482
Causality, 55–60
Certificates of Deposits, 565
Checking Power, 410–12
Cherokee Proverb, 217
Chevron U.S.A. v. Natural
   Resources Defense Council, 27
China
   Living Standards, 15–17, 359
Choice and Alignment, 140
Christensen, Clay, 212
Churchill, Winston, 51
Circle of Influence, 558–59
Clarification, 219–21
Clark, Kenneth B., 338–39
Clean Energy, 543
Climate Change, 110–12
Clinton, Bill, 20-24, 482
CO2 Emissions, 110–12
Collective Wisdom, 181-182
Collegial Improvement, 124, 251,
   443–44
Collins, Jim, 143, 223, 237–38,
Commitment, 273–77
Common Stock, 566-68
Comparative Advantage, 71–78,
   114, 368, 459
Competition, 71–74, 247–48
Competitive Market Structure,
   378–80
Conflicts of Interest, 317, 399, 404
Congeniality, 203–4
Conscientiousness, 355–56
Conservation, 541–42
Conservative Biases, 355

Consideration, 211–12
Constitution, 408–10
Constructive Speech
   and Action, 161
Consumer Driven Healthcare,
   505–14
Consumerism, 39–40
Continuous Improvement, 250–51
Contract Enforcement, 377
Contributory Condition, 58
Cooperation, 242-43
Coordination, 242-43
Corporate Misconduct, 374
Correlation, 57
Courage, 167, 232–33
Covey, Stephen, 132, 140, 143,
   144, 151, 152, 217, 218, 225,
   231, 275, 289, 569
Creativity, 137–38
Crony Capitalism, 28
Crosby, Philip, 249–50
Cues, 298
Cultural Relativism, 34–35, 97–98
Cultural Suicide, 85
Culture, 95–103, 233–34
   Cultural Relativism, 97–98
   Environments I and II, 102
   High Performance, 388
   Improvement, 242-53, 388
   Judeo, Protestant, Confucius, 98
   Operating System I, 99–102
   Operating System II, 100–102
   Path of Fitness, 98–99
Culture of Success, 233–34
Customer Focus, 387–88
Darwin, Charles, 74, 87, 143, 519
Debt, 39–40
Debt Cycles, 196, 480

Debt Instruments, 565
Debt Restrictions, 380–81
Decency, 207–16, 549
Declining Discipline, 35
Deferred Gratification, 302–3
Deferred Sex, 263–64
Deflation, 479
Deming, W. Edwards, 249–50
Democracy
 Conflicts of Interest, 317-18, 399
 Human Fallibility, 398–99
 Lack of Accountability, 400
 Leaders Love Power, 401
 Majorities Dominate
  Minorities, 403
 Representatives Play Santa
  Claus, 400
 Short-Term,
 Group Thinking, 402
 Special Interests, 27-27, 399-400
Democratic Globalism, 536
Democratic Realism, 534–37
Dental Care, 129
DePree, Max, 143, 237
Diamandis, Peter, 230
Diamond, Jared, 82
Diet, 5:2, 126-127
Differences between Men and
 Women, 260–62
Dillard, Annie, 62
Discipline, 281–87
 3 Step Process, 286
 Keys, 287
Dispersing Power, 410–12
DNA, 130–31
 Shared, 207–8
DNA Fidelity, 130–31
Do No Harm, 382–85
Dog, 76

Drawing from the Right and the
 Left, 571–72
Duhigg, Charles, 143, 292, 298-99
Durant, Will and Ariel, 60, 77,
 143, 526, 570
Earnestness, 147
Earth, Atmosphere, Oceans, 540
Easy Money, 41–42
EBITDA, 567
Eco-Dependency, 109–12
 Climate Change, 110–12
 CO2 Emissions, 110–12
 Externalities, 110–12
 Natural Habitats, 109–10
Ecosystem Conservation, 541–42
Edelman, Gerald, 135–36
Edison, Thomas, 52, 138, 233, 436
Education, 321–36
 Benchmarks, 347-48
 Germany and Swiss
  Education, 332
 How Children Succeed, 352–54
 Parental Choice, 337–45
 Socialistic Organization, 339–40
 Tenure, 351
Education, Research, and
 Extension System, 316
Effects Test, 151, 204
Eisenhower, Dwight, 484-85
Election of U.S. Senators, 18–20
Electoral College, 424
Elementary Curriculum, 329–30
Emergency Powers, 427-28
Emotional Bank Account, 218
Employment, 485
Employing the Unemployed, 502–3
Empowering Habit Formation,
 297–306

English, 520–21
Enterprise Competitiveness, 387–94
Enterprise-Friendly Policies, 394
Entitlement, 38–39
Equal Opportunity, 239–40, 460
Equitable County Districts, 337–38
Ethnic Sensitivity and Appreciation, 453–55
Euripides, 321
Evaluations, 229–31
Everybody Is a Genius, 329
Evolution, 247–48
  Common Ancestors, 78
  Comparative Advantage, 71–74
  Competition, 71–74
  Gradualism, 74–77
  Life, 68–71
  Natural Selection, 74–77
  Universe, 67–68
Excellence, 183–86
Exchange Traded Funds, 568
Executive Branch, 411, 421, 424–27
  Departments, 425
Executive Branch Prohibitions, 427-28
Executive Function, 352-54
Exercise, 128
Expenditure of Time, Energy, Resources, 215
Experiences and Challenges, 289–93
Externalities, 111-112, 381–82, 468
  Taxation, 381–82
Extinctions, 105

Extra Thought, Focus, Effort, Time, 183-84
Facilitators and Impediments, 185–86
Faith-Community Relevance, 28-29
Fallacy, 57-58
Family Centeredness, 272–73
Family Decision-Making, 267–68
Famines, 105
Fear, 159
Fear for Safety, 273
Federal Powers, 417–19
Federal Reserve, 477
Ferguson, Niall, 144, 441, 528, 570
Fidelity, 273–77
Financial Strength, 473-498, 527
Financial Tools, 190–92
  Future Value, 191
  Future Value of an Annuity, 192
  Present Value, 191
  Present Value of an Annuity, 192
  Rule of 69, 190
Fitch, John, 138
Fitness, 79–86, 549
Fitness-Related Service, 164–65
Focus, 141
Foreign Born, 43
Forgiveness, 214–15
Forming Empowering Habits, 297–303
Fragility, 174
Franklin, Benjamin, 144, 400, 433, 491, 492, 569
Franklin, Roosevelt, 21-22, 26, 34
Free and Responsible Press, 317–18

Free Enterprise, 362–66, 474–76
Free Enterprise and Markets,
 359–70
Free Markets, 367–68, 474–76
Free Trade, 368
Freedom, 549-50
Freedoms, 432–33
Freedoms, Rights, and
 Responsibilities, 431–40
Friedman, Milton, 143, 144, 338–
 40, 343, 361, 379, 479, 494,
 495, 569
Friendship, 205–6
From Many, One, 35, 515–19
Fromm, Erich, 283
Fulton, Robert, 138
Future Value, 191
Future Value of an Annuity, 192
Gaffney, Jr., Frank J., 517-18
Generally Accepted Accounting
 Practices, 378
Germ Cells, 78
Giraffe, 76
Goals, 227
Goldilocks Minimum Wage
 Necessary Conditions, 462
Goldilocks Minimum Wages,
 460–63, 510
Good Decisions, 223-24
Good Information, 476
Government
 Cost, 385-86
 Debt, 483-85
 Minimizing Burden, 394
 Of the People, 405–16
Government Spending, 384

Gradualism, 74–77
Grandparents, 294–95
Gray, John, 143, 269, 270, 282
Group Thinking, 402
Grutter v. Bollinger, 27
Gwartney, James, 143, 489
Habit Formation, 297–306
Habits, 298
Hamilton, Alexander, 144, 397,
 408, 413, 419, 569
Harmful Medical Intervention,
 507–9
Harrison, Lawrence, 144, 287-288,
 523
Healthcare, 505–14
 Cost, 505–7
 End-of-Life Treatment, 508
 Out-of-Pocket Payments, 513
 Patient Choice, 512
 Savings Accounts, 510
 Seven Drivers, 506
 Universal Coverage, 511–12
Helvering v. Davis, 27
Herbert, Frank, 142, 143, 144,
 402, 494-495
High Standards, 184-85
Higher Latitudes, 149
Hill, Napoleon, 293
Home Building & Loan
 Association v. Blaisdell, 27
Homogeneous Grouping, 333–35
Honorableness, 146–47
House of Representatives, 422
Housing and Community Act, 482
How Children Succeed, 352–54
Hubris, 42
Human Fallibility, 398–99

Human Nature, 87–94
  Aesthetically Pleasing, 89
  Aversion to Losses, 89
  Develop and Actualize, 88
  Environmental Alignment, 92
  Familial, 90
  Groupthink, 91
  Individual, 119
  Pain Avoiding, 87
  Pleasure Seeking, 87
  Psychological, 88
  Self-centered, 88
  Short-term Oriented, 88
  Social, 90–91
Humility, 217
Hygiene, 125
Immigration, 43, 509-10, 515–24
Impervious Borders, 521–22
Improvement, 247–53
  Collegial, 124, 251, 443-44
  Continuous, 250–51
  Sustainability-Related, 252
Incentives, 229–31
Inclusion, 453–66
Inclusion and Meritocracy, 453–66
Inclusion Failures, 17–18
Inclusion, Stakeholder, 371-72
Independent Thought, 204
Individualized Learning, 335–36
Inflation, 478-79
Infrastructure, 394
Integration, 456–58
Integrity, 145–56
Intercourse, 270-72, 264
Internationalism, 535
Investments, 187-97, 565–68,
  193–94
  Insights, 194
Ioannidis, John, 313
Islamic populations, 81–83, 544-45

Isolationism, 535
Jar and the Rocks, 152–54
Jefferson, Thomas, 86, 144, 145,
  236, 406, 408, 483, 494
Johnson, Lyndon, 20–24, 34
Judicial Activism, 409-10
Judicious Litigation, 451, 509-10
Judicious Risk Taking, 179–80
Justice, 33-34, 448–50, 527–28
Keller, Helen, 549, 551
Kelo v. City of New London, 27
Keynes, John Maynard, 485
Keys of Effective Discipline, 287
Keys to Wealth, 196
Keystone Habits, 299, 302
King, Jr., Martin Luther, 33, 143,
  214, 455, 456, 505, 511
Knowledge, 309–19
Krauthammer, Charles, 144,
  536, 537
Lack of Accountability, 400
Lane, Nick, 126, 130, 143
Law Enforcement, 527–28
Laws
  Constitutional, Easily
    Understood, Widely
    Supported, 442–43
  Impartial and Consistently
    Applied, 446–48
  Judicious Litigation, 451
  Justice, 448–50
  Legislatively-Oriented, 444
  Periodic Review, 450
  Piloted, Beneficial,
    Stakeholder-Oriented,
    445–46
Leader Selection and Retention,
  236–37
Leaders Love Power, 401-02

Leadership, 223–34, 559
Lee, Dwight, 143, 489
Legislative, Executive, and
  Judicial Branches, 421
Leitch, Donovan, 163
Leverage, 389
Lewis, Julia, 259
Liberal Biases, 354–56
Liberalization of Education, 32–33
Libraries and Databases, 314–15
Life- and Science-Based
  Curriculum, 328–29
Life-Based Curriculum, 328
Lighthouse Story, 221
Limited Indebtedness, 483–85
Lincoln, Abraham, 211, 236
Lippmann, Walter, 415
Listening, 218-19
Literacy, 287–89
Locke, John, 143, 289–90, 297,
  301, 442
Long-Term Debt Cycles,
  195-196, 480
Long-Term Incentives, 385
Looking Within and Without,
  551, 553
Losing Perspectives, 557-58
Losing Practices, 557-58
Love, 269–71
Lower Latitudes, 149
Madison, James, 18, 25, 144, 410,
  417, 442, 499, 531, 532
Majorities Dominate
  Minorities, 403
Mandela, Nelson, 143, 436, 455
Market Share Restrictions, 378–80

Marriage, 269–78
  Statistics, 273
McClanahan, Brion, 21, 22, 144,
  423, 427-28
McWhorter, John, 464
Medical Care, 129-30
Member Selection and Retention,
  237–38
Mentors, 142–44
Mercy, 528
Meritocracy, 79–80, 239–40, 453–
  66, 459
Meritocracy and Comparative
  Advantage, 459
Military, Cyber, Intelligence
  Strength, 529–33
Minimizing Expenditures, 187–89
Minimizing Taxes, 196
Minority Accommodation, 414–15
Mission, 224–26
Modified Golden Rule, 213
Monetary Policy, 384, 477
Money, 477–81
  Definition, 477
  Deflation, 479
  Federal Reserve, 477
  Inflation, 478
  Monetary Policy, 477
Money Market Funds, 565
Monogamous Tendencies, 260–62
Monopoly, 36
Mosley, Dr. Michael, 127
Multiculturalism, 34–35
Multiple Vantage Points, 149
Nation Building, 42
National Assessment of
  Educational Progress, 337

Natural Habitats, 109–10

Natural Selection, 74–77

Nature Conservancy, 143,
366, 546

Near-Perfect Practice, 184

Necessary Condition, 58

Necessary Marital Attributes,
265–67

News, 43–44

Nixon, Richard, 21, 22, 34

Nonjudgmentalism, 34–35

Nonlinearity, 171–73

Nonprofit Associations, 244–46

Nurture, 281–87

Nutrition, 126

O'Reilly, Bill, 464

Obama, Barack, 21–24, 34, 382,
448, 513

Obesity, 13

Offshoring, 37

Oldham, Ronnie, 183-84

Openness and Spontaneity,
355–56

Operating System I, 99–102

Operating System II, 100–102

Optionality, 179–80

Orwell, George, 144, 529

Out-of-Pocket Payments, 513

Overhead, 188, 388-89

Paine, Thomas, 434

Parent Accountability, 322–24

Parental Choice, 337–45

Passion, 232–33

Path of Fitness, 98–99

Patient Choice, 512

Peace Through Fitness, 525–37

Peck, M. Scott, 143, 257, 262,
283–84, 283, 290

Periodic Disaster, 105–7
Extinctions, 105
Famines, 105
Natural, 105
Plagues, 105
War, 106–7

Periodic Fasting, 126–27, 352

Perseverance, 184, 232–33

Perspectives, Practices, and
Concepts, 573–77

Pilots, 248

Plagues, 105

Plans, 227

Poland, 2

Political Polarization, 43–44

Polygamous Tendencies, 260–62

Poor Habits, 35-36

Poorly Parented Children, 31

Pope John Paul II, 2-3

Population Growth, 80–85,
544–47

Postscript, 562

Potok, Chaim, 143, 330

Powers, Prohibitions, and
Structure, 417–30

Practical Experience, 180–81

Practices of Effective Individuals
and Groups, 231–32, 235

Preferred Stock, 568

Preparation, 161

Present Value, 191

Present Value of an Annuity, 192

Presidential Constitutional
Failings, 20–24

Prevalence of Winning
  Perspectives and Practices,
  557–58
Price Controls, 383
Priorities, 148–54
  Highest, 151–52
  Jar and the Rocks, 152–54
  Schedule, 152
Private Property, 360–61
Privatization, 473–74
Proactivity, 157–66
  vs. Reactivity, 165
Problems with Democracy, 397–404
Procreation, 80–86
  Islamic Populations, 81–83
Productivity, 486
Profit, 365
Progeny Consciousness, 279–81
Prohibitions, 419–20, 419–20
  Adultry, 178
  Covet or Steal, 178
  Falsely Accuse, 178
  Freeload, 178
  Harm or Kill, 178
  Lie or Cheat, 178
  Neglect Children, 178
Prudence, 167–82
  Fitness, Courage, Knowledge,
    Discipline, 167
Prudent Regulation, 377–86
Prudent Taxation, 467–72, 485,
  See Taxation
Public Education, 338–39
Public Goods, 363
Public Infrastructure, 429–30
Punctuality, 203
Purpose, 133–34, 158–59
  Detecting, 158
Putnam, Robert, 30, 143, 259

Qualifications
  Citizenship, 437–38
  President and Executive
    Council, 426
  Voter, 438
Quiet, 149
Quotas, 383
Rand, Ayn, 251, 313-14, 364-65,
  431, 434
Reagan, Ronald, 2, 22, 143
Real Estate Investments, 566
Realism, 232–33, 535
Real-World Feedback, 326
Recycling, 543
Redistribution of Wealth, 492–96
Reeve, Christopher, 149
Reflection, 132–33
Rehearsal, 141
Reliability, 147
Rent Controls, 383
Republic, 413–14
Research, 139
Research and Development,
  249–50
Resource Use, 543
Respectfulness, 211
Responsibilities, 436–37
Responsibility, 160
Responsible Corporate
  Governance, 371–75
Responsible Parenting, 279–96
  Education, 287–89
Results-Oriented Education,
  347–56
Reverse Engineering, 139
Rewards, 298
Rights, 433–36

Right-to-Work Laws, 350, 380
Riley, Jason, 464-65, 516-17
Roberts, Brent, 354–55
Robustness, 174
Role Models, 293–94
Roosevelt, Franklin, 21, 22, 26, 34
Roosevelt, Theodore, 20–24
Routines, 298
Rule of 69, 190
Rule of Law, 441–52, See Laws
Ruvalcaba, Jaime, 517
Sagan, Carl, 3, 52, 53, 106, 112, 143, 309, 314, 405-06, 569
Savings Accounts, 491–504, 496–98, 510
Savings Accounts and Social Safety Nets, 491–504
Scale, 61–65
Scarcity and Ruthlessness, 208
Science-Based Curriculum, 328
Scientific Method, 310–14
Self-Control, 302–3
Self-Discipline, 302–3
Senate, 422–24
Separation from Nature, 45
Service, 559
Seven Levels of Human Fitness, 526
Seven Levels of Human Organization, 553–55
Seven Secondary Tracks, 331–33
Shakespeare, 79
Shared Experience, 220–21
Shaw, George Bernard, 232, 401
Short-Term Business Cycles, 479
Short-Term Thinking, 402

Singapore
  Carbon Emissions, 14
  Corruption, 11
  Crime, 11
  Cultures, 9
  Home Ownership, 14
  Homicide Rate, 11
  Incarceration Rate, 11
  Life-Expectancy, 13
  National Savings, 13
  Obesity, 13
  Per Capita Income, 13
  Population, 10
  Public Debt, 14
  Religions, 9
Skin in the Game, 177, 241
Sleep, 128
Slow to Make Important Decisions, 182
Smith, Adam, 143, 360, 367-68, 374, 401-02, 429, 481, 528, 554, 563
Social Interaction, 133–34
Social Justice Missteps, 33–34
Social Safety Nets, 385, 491–504, 498–502
Socialism, 492–96
  Redistribution of Grades, 493
Sound Lending Practices, 481–82
Sound Money, 477–81, See Money
Special Interests, 28–29, 399
Special Sources, 569–70
Specialization, 242, 272–73
Spending Restraints, 470–71
Spock, 436
Spouse Selection, 257–68
Stakeholder Directors, 373

Stakeholder Inclusion, 226, 371–72

Standards of Journalism, 318

State Goals and Exams, 344–45

State Social Safety Nets, 498–502

Strategy, 224–26

Stroup, Richard, 143, 489

Structure, 226

Student Accountability, 324–25

Sufficient Condition, 58

Sugarman, Joseph, 162

Sun Tzu, 529, 531

Supermajorities, 414–15

Superorganism, 91

Supreme Court, 428
  Constitutional Failings, 25–27
Sustainability, 539–47

Switzerland
  Carbon Emissions, 14
  Child Poverty, 11
  Corruption, 11
  Crime, 11
  Cultures, 9
  Home Ownership, 14
  Homicide Rate, 11
  Incarceration Rate, 11
  Life Expectancy, 13
  National Savings, 13
  Obesity, 13
  Per Capita Income, 13
  Population, 10
  Public Debt, 14
  Religions, 9
Symmetry, 168–69

Synergy, 242

Taleb, Nassim Nicholas, 143, 167, 173, 179

Tariffs, 384

Taxation, 467–72
  Disincentivize the
    Undesirables, 467–68
  Sales Taxes on
    Nonessentials, 468
  Spending Restraints, 470–71
  Uniform Application
    of Taxes, 469

Teacher Empowerment and
  Accountability, 351–52

Teamwork, 235–46

Tercek, Mark, 143, 546

Thales of Miletus, 310

Thatcher, Margaret, 2, 494, 495

The Butterfly, 291

Thought, 135–44

Thrift, 187–89

Thrift and Investment, 187–97
  Keys to Wealth, 196

Timeline, 65

Tocqueville, Alexis de, 144, 243-44, 294, 494

Tolstoy, Leo, 143, 165

Tononi, Giulio, 135

Total Quality Management, 249–50

Tough, Paul, 143, 354–56

Transparency, 378, 476

Treaty Powers, 534

Trials, 248

Triple Filter, 147

Truman, Harry, 21, 22, 24, 34

Trust, 217-18

Truth, 51–54, 549

Truth, Freedom, Fitness, and
  Decency, 549–61

Truthfulness, 145–46

Turkey
  Evolution, 77
  Turkey Problem, 173
Tutu, Desmond, 454
Unconditional Love, 282, 302–3
Underlying Aim of Life, 86
Understanding, 217–21
Unemployment, 502–3
Unions, 28, 32–33, 383, 391–93
United States
  Aggressive Driving, 29
  Carbon Emissions, 14
  Challenges, 15–17
  Child Poverty, 11
  Church Attendance, 29
  Corruption, 11
  Crime, 11, 29
  Ethnic Composition, 458
  Government Spending Percent
    GNP, 18–20
  Home Ownership, 14
  Homicide Rate, 11
  Household Income, 15–17
  Incarceration Rate, 11
  Life Expectancy, 13
  Living Standards, 15–17
  Marriage, 30
  National Savings, 13
  Obesity, 13
  Per Capita Income, 13
  Population, 10
  Promiscuity, 30
  Public Debt, 14
  Sexually Transmitted Disease, 29
United States v. Carolene
  Products, 27
United We Stand, 519
Universal Coverage, 511–12
Universal Education, 321–36
Vetted Love, 262–63
Vision, 224–26

Visualization, 137
Voice, 150–51
Volunteer Associations, 244–46
Wallerstein, Judith, 259
Wars, 106–7
Washington, George, 23, 33, 143,
  205, 236, 399, 406, 433, 469,
  484, 525
Waste Disposal, 543
Water, Air, and Land, 540–41
Wealth, 196–97
Webster, Daniel, 432
Weighting the Votes
  of Parents, 439
Welch, Jack, 49, 50, 143, 229,
  230, 236, 351
Well Kept Secret, 157
Whitman v. American Trucking
  Associations, 27
Wickard v. Filburn, 27
Wilson, E. O., 21, 22, 24, 76, 90,
  92, 110, 143, 525, 539
Wilson, Woodrow, 21–24
Winning, 555–57
Winning Culture, 374, 559
Winning Perspectives,
  49–50, 557
  Causality, 55–60
  Culture, 95–104
  Eco-Dependency, 109–12
  Evolution, 67–78
  Fitness, 79–86
  Human Nature, 87–94
  Periodic Disaster, 49–50
  Scale, 61–65
  Summary, 113–16
  Truth, 51–54

Winning Practices, 119–24, 253, 557

Overarching, 117

Criteria, 124

Best Practice, 123

Education Level, 120

Enterprise Level, 121

Family Level, 120

Government Level, 122

Group Level, 120

Individual Level, 119

Individuals and Groups, 303

Win-Win, 242, 272-73

Work, 162–63

Workforce, 390–93

Wright, Richard, 138

Wright, Robert, 143, 274

Yew, Lee Kuan, 10, 38, 39, 144, 305, 394, 398, 427, 461, 498, 520, 553-54

Zinsmeister, Karl, 341–42

About the Author

Mark Bitz is a successful entrepreneur, author, and community leader. He is a graduate of Purdue, Cornell, and Harvard Universities, and a lifelong student of evolution, history, culture, government, economics, business, investing, and leadership. Mark is well-read, educated, and traveled, close to nature, thoughtful, and practical. He was named among the "CNY 40 Under 40" and is the recipient of the Purdue University Alumni of Distinction Award.

Working his way up from farmhand to president, Mark owned and operated Plainville Turkey Farm, Inc. between 1991 and 2007. Under his leadership, the company grew sevenfold and pioneered an All-Natural-Ingredient deli line, Animal-Friendly Practices, and Turkeys Grown on a Vegetarian Diet and Without Antibiotics. The company was the first turkey company to receive the American Humane Association's "Free Farmed" certification, and the company also won the Onondaga County Conservation Farm of the Year Award, the American Culinary Institute Best Taste Award, and the New York State Agricultural Society Business of the Year. Mark founded a feed company that he currently owns in 1990 and co-founded a crop company in 2005 that became the largest organic crop operation in the Northeast.

Mark has coached youth soccer and basketball, was instrumental in building the Northwest YMCA in Baldwinsville, New York, and has served on numerous boards. He chaired the Empire State Young President's Organization, Northwest YMCA in Baldwinsville, and New York State 4-H Foundation. He was a director of the Greater Syracuse YMCA, Syracuse Metropolitan Development Association, New York State Business Council, National Turkey Federation, and International Chief Executives Organization. Mark served on the Cornell Agriculture and Life Science Dean's Advisory Board and the Cornell University Council. He is currently a trustee of the Florida Nature Conservancy and oversees the education of the Chief Executives Organization. Mark and his wife of 38 years, Leokadia, have two sons, two daughters-in-law, and two grand-daughters.

CPSIA information can be obtained
at www.ICGtesting.com
Printed in the USA
FSHW020724080619

9 780985 950477